*Special Edition*

# Using
# Perl for
# Web
# Programming

*Special Edition*

# USING
# PERL FOR
# WEB
# PROGRAMMING

*Written by David Harlan • Mícheál Ó Foghlú •*
*Paul Doyle • Shelley Powers • Matthew D. Healy*

# Special Edition Using Perl for Web Programming

Library of Congress Catalog No.: 96-69614

ISBN: 0-7897-0659-8

98 97 96    6 5 4 3 2 1

Interpretation of the printing code: the rightmost double-digit number is the year of the book's printing; the rightmost single-digit number, the number of the book's printing. For example, a printing code of 96-1 shows that the first printing of the book occurred in 1996.

All terms mentioned in this book that are known to be trademarks or service marks have been appropriately capitalized. Que cannot attest to the accuracy of this information. Use of a term in this book should not be regarded as affecting the validity of any trademark or service mark.

Screen reproductions in this book were created using Collage Plus from Inner Media, Inc., Hollis, NH.

# Credits

**PRESIDENT**
Roland Elgey

**PUBLISHER**
Joseph B. Wikert

**PUBLISHING MANAGER**
Fred Slone

**SENIOR TITLE MANAGER**
Bryan Gambrel

**EDITORIAL SERVICES DIRECTOR**
Elizabeth Keaffaber

**MANAGING EDITOR**
Sandy Doell

**STRATEGIC MARKETING MANAGER**
Barry Pruett

**ACQUISITIONS EDITOR**
Al Valvano

**PRODUCT MARKETING MANAGER**
Kim Margolius

**ASSISTANT PRODUCT MARKETING MANAGER**
Christy M. Miller

**TECHNICAL EDITORS**
Alden Hutchinson
Jim Jagelski
Sean Chisham

**TECHNICAL SUPPORT SPECIALIST**
Nadeem Muhammed

**ACQUISITIONS COORDINATOR**
Carmen L. Krikorian

**SOFTWARE RELATIONS COORDINATOR**
Patty Brooks

**EDITORIAL ASSISTANT**
Andrea Duvall

**BOOK DESIGNER**
Ruth Harvey

**COVER DESIGNER**
Dan Armstrong

**PRODUCTION TEAM**
Stephen Adams
Debra Bolhuis
Jason Carr
Erin M. Danielson
Daniel Harris
Jason Hand
Daryl Kessler
Casey Price
Kaylene Riemen
Bobbi Satterfield

**INDEXER**
Tim Tate

Composed in *Century Old Style* and *ITC Franklin Gothic* by Que Corporation.

# About the Authors

**David Harlan's** degree in American History and five years of experience in a security department at a small university may make him seem to be an unlikely author for a high-end programming book. But computers have always been a key part of his day-to-day activities. He learned programming (and was just short of a computer science degree) at the University of Puget Sound. After graduation, he stayed on at Puget Sound as assistant director of security for five years before joining Canyon Online Media in Seattle, where he helped develop the company's commercial Web site. Currently, he is a member of the Web development team at White Horse Studios in Portland, Oregon.

**Micheal O Foghlu** is now a lecturer in applied computing and information systems at Waterford Regional Technical College, Ireland (**http://www.rtc-waterford.ie**). Until September 1996, he worked in the computer services department of University College, Galway, Ireland (**http://www.ucg.ie**). His interests include Natural Language Processing, WWW programming and development, Linux, computing using the Irish language, and Z39.50. When not slaving over a hot computer, he is sometimes seen nursing a quiet pint while listening to loud Irish music and/or meandering through the hills in no particular direction. He can be contacted at the e-mail address **ofoghlu@indigo.ie**.

**Paul Doyle** has several years of experience in the planning, implementation, and management of networks in multiprotocol, multivendor environments. His specialist areas include client configuration and server management.

**Shelley Powers** is an incorporated independent contractor who has her own company, YASD. She works in and out of Portland, Oregon, and has worked with some of the leading companies in the Northwest. Shelley has worked with UNIX- and Windows-based client/server applications for several years; now she is working with Web application and development for both environments. She has written books on PowerBuilder 5.0 and on JavaScript. YASD's Web site is at **http://www.yasd.com**.

**Matthew D. Healy** performs a variety of tasks, ranging from UNIX system administration and database administration to building WWW front ends on top of Sybase, Msql, and Illustra relational databases at the Yale Center for Medical Informatics. He contributed to *Special Edition Using CGI*, also published by Que Corporation. Before joining YCMI, he was an engineer, a graduate student, a teaching assistant, and a LAN administrator—and always a rabid SF fan. Along the way, he earned a BS in engineering from Purdue and a PhD in zoology from Duke. He'd love to get e-mail at **Matthew.Healy@yale.edu**, and his home page (**http://ycmi. med.yale.edu/~healy**) always welcomes visitors. Scientific and technical prose constitutes something of a family affair for him—his wife edits medical journals, and his brother is a technical writer for a large software company.

# We'd Like to Hear from You!

As part of our continuing effort to produce books of the highest possible quality, Que would like to hear your comments. To stay competitive, we *really* want you, as a computer book reader and user, to let us know what you like or dislike most about this book or other Que products.

You can mail comments, ideas, or suggestions for improving future editions to the address below, or send us a fax at (317) 581-4663. For the online-inclined, Macmillan Computer Publishing has a forum on CompuServe (type **GO QUEBOOKS** at any prompt), through which our staff and authors are available for questions and comments. The address of our Internet site is **http://www.mcp.com** (World Wide Web).

In addition to exploring our forum, please feel free to contact me personally to discuss your opinions of this book: I'm **74671,3710** on CompuServe, and I'm **avalvano@que.mcp.com** on the Internet.

Thanks in advance—your comments will help us continue to publish the best books available on computer topics in today's market.

Al Valvano
Acquisitions Editor
Que Corporation
201 W. 103rd Street
Indianapolis, Indiana 46290
USA

**NOTE** Although we cannot provide general technical support, we're happy to help you resolve problems you encounter related to our books, disks, or other products. If you need such assistance, please contact our Tech Support department at 800-545-5914, ext. 3833.

To order other Que or Macmillan Computer Publishing books or products, please call our Customer Service department at 800-835-3202 ext. 666. ▦

# Contents at a Glance

# Table of Contents

## IV | Databases and Internal Web Sites

# V | Reference

## 13 Special Variables 373

## 14  Operators  391

## 16 Subroutine Definition 533

## Appendixes

## A Perl Acquisition and Installation 549

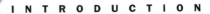

# Introduction

*by Paul Doyle*

This book is about a clever little programming language called Perl, and how you can use it to make the most of your World Wide Web server.

The book tells you what Perl is, how it works, and how to write Perl programs. Much of this material will be useful even if you never do any Web server work. The book also deals with some general Web server issues, such as security. But at heart, this book is about Perl programming applied to Web development. ■

# The Web

You've surely heard of the Internet and the World Wide Web by now. If you haven't, now may be a good time to put this book back on the shelf and check out one of the many introductory volumes about the Web instead. After you've used the Web for a while, you may find yourself producing Web pages for other people to use; then would be a good time to come back to this book.

The term *intranet*, which doesn't have the same currency as *Internet*, refers to a network along the lines of the Internet but internal to a corporation and usually protected from the Internet by a firewall. Web servers dominate on these so-called local Internets just as much as they do on the real thing, so this book is as relevant to them as it is to the global network.

### Terminology

If you're a Web user, terms such as *URL, httpd*, and *browser* are old hat to you. You're familiar with *Apache, CERN*, and *proxy*; and you're at least on nodding terms with the likes of *CGI, MIME*, and *socket*. (Don't worry if you've never heard of *Mozilla*.)

Still, just so that there's no confusion, review the following list:

- The *Internet* is the whole thing—the computers, the network infrastructure, the protocols, and the bizarre sense of community that arises spontaneously when 20 million people get together on a desktop.
- The *World Wide Web* is an interlinked collection of servers on the Internet that provide information. This information can consist of text, graphics, executable programs, or anything else that can be stored on disk.
- A *World Wide Web server* is one of the servers that form the World Wide Web. HTTP servers, FTP servers, and Gopher servers are all examples of Web servers.
- An *HTTP server* is a machine or a process (depending on the context) that serves up HTTP data. This data can include text, images, and binary data (if proper MIME encoding is used).

That list is a roundabout way of saying that a Web server and an HTTP server are not necessarily the same thing, and that this book is about Perl in the context of HTTP servers. We'll refer to Web servers frequently throughout the book, because the concept is often useful for dealing with the presentation of information on the Web. Also, *Web* is in the book's title because it reads better than *Using Perl for HTTP Server Programming*.

### Growth

**ON THE WEB**

The Internet is getting to be an awfully big place. According to Network Wizards (**http://www.nw.com**), there appeared to be more than 9 million Internet hosts at the time when this book was written.

Estimating the number of people who use the Internet is notoriously difficult, but it's generally recognized that more than 20 million people now use the Internet on a regular basis. This figure includes people who have electronic mail or FTP access, as well as those who are fortunate enough to have the type of connection and equipment that allow them to use the Web.

Not all of the 20 million Internet users have access to the Web, but the number who have Web access is growing faster than the overall number who have Internet access. Recently, publicity about the Web has become so overwhelming that many people think of the Internet purely as being the Web. Also, for the first time, many people are purchasing PCs for the primary purpose of Web access.

The Web, in short, is in an upward growth spiral that shows no sign of leveling out before the end of the century.

### Trends

Apart from the sheer scale of growth, some interesting facts about the development of the Web are beginning to emerge. All the facts presented in this section arise from a curious combination: the lack of rules about what you can do on the Web, and the very strict rules about how you do it.

One interesting fact is that people are astonishingly creative in thinking up uses for the system. Live share prices as a Web-based screen saver, political agitation and petition collection, merchandise sales via the Web, multimedia résumés…there's just no telling what people will get up to, given enough bandwidth.

Another interesting fact is that in spite of its scale (which suggests a homogenizing influence), the Web appears to act as an agent of diversity. Small companies, community groups, and schools are there along with the big corporations. The number of languages represented on the Web is growing, not declining. This broad spectrum of interests may be due, in part, to the increasing ease with which organizations can establish an effective Web presence.

### ON THE WEB

Perhaps the most important trend, from the point of view of this book, is that the Web is becoming a much more dynamic place. *Dynamic* doesn't just mean that pages are now being replaced on a regular basis (although they are, which is a welcome change from the time when Web pages tended to be less recent than printed matter). The word also doesn't just mean that the people who produce the Web every day have a dynamic, creative demeanor (although many of them do, which is why we have such wonders as Robotman, at **http://www.unitedmedia.com/comics/robotman**). *Dynamic* means that much more of the information available on the Web is generated live when a user requests it. Databases are searched, files are counted, text is translated, and so on.

This trend is part of the excitement of using the Web now. An interesting page is all very well, but if the page is static, you probably won't visit it again except to see whether it has been updated. If, however, the content of the page depends on the passage of time, on your input, or on the input of other users, you are much more likely to come back.

The trend is also a big part of the excitement of developing on the Web now. Web server management involves much more than writing pages of deathless HTML; a good deal of real-time programming goes on, too. This programming is real-time in the sense that the programs react to external events and produce output that is used there and then. You could also say that the programming is real-time because the pressure for rapid development and new features means that the code is often edited while it is in use.

# Perl and the Web

Which brings us to Perl.

Perl is the ideal development language for Web server work, for many reasons. Chapter 1, "Perl Overview," discusses the nature of Perl in much more detail; the following sections concentrate on the reasons why Perl suits Web server development.

## Rapid Development

Many Web server programming projects are high-level rather than low-level, which means that they tend not to involve bit-level manipulations, direct operating-system calls, or interaction with the server hardware. Instead, the projects focus on reading from files, reformatting the output, and writing to standard output—the browser, in other words. The programmer does not need (or want) to get involved in the details of how file handles and buffers are manipulated, how memory is allocated, and so on.

High-level tasks such as file manipulation and text formatting are exactly the kind of tasks at which Perl excels. You can tell Perl to slurp in the contents of a file and display it on the user's browser with all new lines replaced by tabs, as follows:

```
while ( <INFILE> )  {  s/\n/\t/;  print;  }
```

Don't worry about the details of that code example until you read Chapter 1, "Perl Overview." Just notice two things:

- The code is short.
- The code is almost legible even if you don't know any Perl, especially if you are familiar with C.

In a nutshell, the secret of rapid development is writing small amounts of powerful code without having to consider awkward issues of syntax at every step.

Perl is pithy; a little Perl code goes a long way. In terms of programming languages, that statement usually means that the code is difficult to read and painful to write. Although Larry Wall (the author of Perl) says that Perl is functional rather than elegant, most programmers quickly find that Perl code is very readable and that becoming fluent in writing it is not difficult. The fact that Perl is pithy rather than terse makes it especially appropriate for the high-level macro operations that are typically required in Web development.

As it happens, Perl is quite capable of handling some fairly low-level operations, too—handling operating-system signals and talking to network sockets, for example. But for most Web programming purposes, that level of detail is just not needed.

## Compiler and Interpreter

A program can't achieve anything by itself; to carry out its work, it needs to be fed to either a compiler or an interpreter. Each of these entities has its advantages, as follows:

- A *compiler* takes a program listing and generates an executable file. This executable file can then be executed as many times as necessary, copied to other computers, and so on without the need for the program source. Not distributing source code helps keep program details confidential.

    Because the compiler runs only one time, it can afford to take its time about generating the executable code. As a result, compilers tend to perform elaborate optimization on the program code, with the result that the executable code runs efficiently.

- An *interpreter* examines a program listing line by line, carrying out the tasks required by each line as it reads the listing. A separate compilation stage is unnecessary; when the program has been written, it can be executed without delay, making for a rapid development cycle.

Compilers and interpreters each have relative advantages and disadvantages. Compiled code takes longer to prepare, but it runs fast, and your source stays secret. Interpreted code gets up and running quickly, but it isn't as fast as interpreted code; in addition, you need to distribute the program source if you want to allow other people to run your programs.

Which of these categories describes Perl?

Perl is special in this regard: it's a compiler that thinks it's an interpreter. Perl compiles program code into executable code before running it, so an optimization stage occurs, and the executable code runs quickly. Perl doesn't write this code to a separate executable file, however; instead, it stores the code in memory and then executes it. Therefore, Perl combines the rapid development cycle of an interpreted language with the efficient execution of compiled code.

The corresponding disadvantages of compilers and interpreters also apply to Perl. The need to compile the program each time it is run makes for slower startup than a purely compiled language provides, and developers are required to distribute source code to users. In practice, however, these disadvantages are not too limiting, for the following reasons:

- The compilation phase is extremely fast, so you're unlikely to notice much lag between the invocation of a Perl script and the start of execution.
- Perl scripts on a Web server are executed by the server on behalf of the users, not by the users themselves. This arrangement means that the scripts can be hidden from prying eyes while they're being used by anyone on the Internet.

In summary, Perl is compiled behind the scenes for rapid execution, but you can treat it as though it were interpreted. Tweaking your HTML is easy; just edit the code, and allow the users to run it. But is that good programming practice? Hey, that's one for the philosophers.

**N O T E** Because Perl code is truly compiled, it has no such thing as a run-time syntax error (unless you get into the realm of generating Perl code on-the-fly and then executing it). This fact is important when you consider that your server is your interface to the outside world; sudden script crashes caused by minor typos are not what you want people to see. Quick execution of a Perl script tells you whether all the syntax in the script is valid.

Of course, that's no guarantee that your code won't disgrace you for some other reason. ■

### Flexibility

Perl was not designed in the abstract; it was written to solve a particular problem, and it evolved to serve an ever-widening set of real-world problems.

Perl's developer could have expanded the language to handle these tasks by adding more and more keywords and operators—by making the language bigger. Instead, the core of the Perl language started small and became more refined as time went on. In some ways, the language actually contracted. The number of reserved words in Perl 5.0 is actually less than half the number in Perl 4.0.

This situation reflects an awareness that Perl's power lies in its unique combination of efficiency and flexibility. Perl itself has grown slowly and thoughtfully, usually in ways that allow for enhancements and extensions to be added rather than hard-wired in. This approach has been critical in the development of Perl's extensibility over time, as the following section explains.

### Extensibility

Much of the growth in Perl as a platform has come by way of the increasing use of libraries (Perl 4.0) and modules (Perl 5.0). These add-on elements (discussed in more detail in Chapter 1, "Perl Overview," and in Chapter 16, "Subroutine Definition") essentially allow developers to write self-contained portions of Perl code that can be slotted into a Perl application. The add-ons range from fairly high-level utilities (such as a module that adds HTML tags to text) to low-level, down-and-dirty development tools (such as code profilers and debuggers).

The capability to use extensions such as these is a remarkable advance in the development of a fairly slick language, and it has helped to fuel the growth in Perl use. Perl developers can easily share their work with others, and the arrival of objects in Perl 5.0 makes structured design methodologies possible for Perl applications. The language has come of age without losing any of its flexibility or raw power.

**N O T E** Appendix B, "Perl Web Reference," describes several Perl libraries and modules. Browse through the appendix to get the flavor of the modules that are available. Also, the CD-ROM that comes with this book contains a collection of freely available modules, along with documentation that explains how to use them. For details, see Appendix C, "What's on the CD?" ■

### Web Server Work

Web servers generate huge amounts of HTML. The *M* stands for *markup*, and you need a great deal of it to make your Web pages more exciting than the average insurance contract. Using HTML is a fiddly business, though; problems can easily arise if tags are misplaced or misspelled. Perl is a good choice of language to look after the details for you while you get on with the big picture, especially if you call on the object-oriented capabilities of Perl 5.0.

Of particular interest to many Web server managers is the fact that Perl works well with standard UNIX DBM files. Also, support for proprietary databases is growing rapidly. These considerations are significant if you plan to allow users to query database material over the Web.

### Security

Security is a major issue on the Internet in general. If you use Perl for scripting on your Web server, you can easily prevent users from trying to sneak commands through for the server to execute on their behalf. Also, an excellent Perl 5.0 module called pgpperl (also known as Penguin) allows your server to use public-key cryptography techniques to protect sensitive data from eavesdroppers. For more information on pgpperl, see Appendix B, "Perl Web Reference."

### Ubiquity

Many people on the Web already use Perl. Going with the flow isn't always the best approach, but Perl has grown with the Web. A great deal of experience is available on the Web if you need advice. The Perl developers are keenly aware of Web issues as they add to Perl, and they have built many Perl modules with the Web in mind.

### Perl Summary

You want to use Perl for many reasons, including the fact that it is small, efficient, flexible, and robust. Perl is particularly well suited for Web development work, in which text output is a major preoccupation. And if these reasons aren't quite enough, consider this one: Perl is free.

# The Structure of This Book

By now, you should be sold on the idea of using Perl for Web development work. This book tells you how to do so, using the following structure:

- Part I, "Perl and CGI," starts with a crash course in Perl and an explanation of the Common Gateway Interface (CGI).

   Chapter 1, "Perl Overview," describes the Perl language, and introduces the syntax and constructs that will be used throughout the book.

   Chapter 2, "Introduction to CGI," explains how Perl programs on a Web server talk to the outside world and how data is sent from a browser to a Perl program running on a server.

■ Part II, "Form Processing, Data Storage, and Page Display," explains how to use Perl and CGI to interact with text files and UNIX databases on the server.

Chapter 3, "Advanced Form Processing and Data Storage," deals with the issues involved in accepting data from a user who is using HTML forms. The chapter also explains how to deal with the data when it arrives.

Chapter 4, "Advanced Page Output," is about using forms to manage server-based data.

Chapter 5, "Searching," explains how Perl can be used to facilitate database or flat-file searches on the server.

Chapter 6, "Using Dynamic Pages," describes some techniques that you can use to keep your pages current and make them respond to external events.

Chapter 7, "Dynamic and Interactive HTML Content in Perl and CGI," covers the issues involved in using Perl to translate documents to and from HTML on-the-fly.

■ Part III, "Authentication and Site Administration," deals with server management issues: protecting scripts that run on your server and coping with server log files.

Chapter 8, "Understanding Basic User Authentication," explains the security issues involved in allowing users to run programs on a Web server. In addition, the chapter describes how to manage server access rights.

Chapter 9, "Understanding CGI Security," shows how a CGI wrapper script can allow users on the server to make their own programs available on the server without compromising server security.

Chapter 10, "Site Administration," is about how Perl can be used both online and offline to help you with day-to-day server management tasks.

■ Part IV, "Databases and Internal Web Sites," explains how your Perl scripts can interact with commercial databases and how to use Perl to manipulate a database within your organization.

Chapter 11, "Database Interaction," is about the rapidly expanding field of Web-based databases and how Perl can be used to manage the interaction between the user and the database.

Chapter 12, "Database Application Using CGI," discusses the issues involved in running a database on a Web server inside your company but allowing external users to have limited access.

■ Part V, "Reference," has all the details on Perl syntax and functions.

Chapter 13, "Special Variables," describes all the tokens that have special meaning in Perl and give it its unique flavor.

Chapter 14, "Operators," lists the Perl operators and describes how they operate.

Chapter 15, "Function List," is a detailed reference to Perl's built-in functions.

Chapter 16, "Subroutine Definition," explains how to use subroutines, libraries, and modules to organize your programs and to produce reusable code.

■ The appendixes explain where to get Perl and associated resources, both on the Internet and on the CD-ROM that accompanies this book.

Appendix A, "Perl Acquisition and Installation," explains where to get Perl and how to install it on your UNIX or Windows NT machine.

Appendix B, "Perl Web Reference," describes many of the Perl modules, add-ons, and related tools that are available on the Internet and on the CD-ROM that comes with this book.

Appendix C, "What's on the CD?", provides some pointers to help you get off to a quick start with our Perl collection.

Throughout the book, we'll use snippets of Perl code and sometimes entire listings for illustration. All code listed in this manner is available on the CD-ROM.

**N O T E** This book (like life in general) is too short to describe how to do all the things in the list for all the HTTP servers and browsers that currently exist. For the sake of manageability, we'll concentrate on the Apache server and the Netscape browser, which were the most popular devices of their types at the time when this book was written. When significant differences exist between these products and other popular products, we'll draw your attention to that fact. ■

### The Conventions Used in This Book

There are many different ways to write a book, and even more ways to format one. The Que style is an excellent way of breaking information into a readable form that is easy to digest.

The majority of application programs written these days allow you to use either a mouse or a keyboard to operate the program. In steps that tell you how to perform a particular task, I always indicate the appropriate keystroke combinations that perform the action. Hot keys, or accelerators, are designated by an underline below the character that's the accelerator. If I were giving you instructions to open a file using Microsoft Word, for example, you would see:

From the File menu, choose Open.

To indicate a combination of keys to be pressed at the same time, the two keys are joined by a plus (+) character. If I were giving you instructions to paste a piece of text from the Clipboard into a Word document, you would see:

From the Edit menu, choose Paste, or press Ctrl+V.

The names of dialog boxes and windows, and the names of dialog-box and window options, are indicated by capitalizing the initial letters of the title. When you are saving a file in Microsoft Word, for example, the dialog box that you use to specify the file name is:

File Save

Any new terms and ideas are introduced in *italic* type, and messages that may appear on the screen are presented in a special font:

`All source code and examples of code listings are presented in a monospace font.`

**T I P** Tips are used to indicate some cool trick or a neat way to organize your code. Watch out for tips, and use them in your day-to-day work, because they'll generally save you time or offer you a unique solution to an existing problem.

**N O T E** Notes provide extra information related to the topic that is being discussed in the body of the text.

## CAUTION

Cautions are designed to alert you to dangerous actions or situations that could cause damage to your environment. You should pay particular attention to cautions so that you do not create a problem at your site.

If more information on a particular topic appears in another chapter, you see a cross-reference that indicates the chapter to look for. A right-facing triangle indicates that the reference is in a later chapter of the book. A left-facing triangle means that the reference is in an earlier chapter. Following is an example:

**See** Chapter 2, "Introducing Sybase System 11," **p. xx**

Enjoy the book!

# Perl and CGI

# Perl Overview

*by Paul Doyle*

**B**efore you get into the nitty-gritty of using Perl on World Wide Web servers, you need to take some time to look at Perl itself.

This chapter provides an overview of the Perl language. It is not a detailed course in Perl, but it should give you enough Perl to get by with; as you use the language; you'll probably want to delve into more deeply after you've been programming in it for a while. ■

### Syntax

Perl's syntax is more readable than C code and a good deal more concise than shell script.

### Data types

Perl data types are few in number but sensitive to the context in which they are evaluated.

### Flow control

Syntax and data types alone do not make a language; flow control provides a program's internal structure.

### Pattern matching

Perl's capability to match complex regular expressions is superb and has many applications.

### Structural issues

Most languages allow you to abstract program functionality into subroutines and modules; Perl goes one better, allowing you to extend the language itself.

---

### The "Camel Book"

When you're ready to learn more, you may want to purchase the excellent *Programming Perl*, by Larry Wall and Randal L. Schwartz (O'Reilly & Associates, Inc.). This book is the definitive work on Perl so far (as you might suspect with Wall's name on the cover). It's readable and humorous yet still sufficiently technical to be of genuine use in everyday Perl programming.

Incidentally, the book is called the "Camel book" after the dromedary that happens to adorn the cover. Because of the ubiquitous nature of the book in Perl-literate circles, this animal has become the emblem of the language.

---

We're not going to go into too much detail in this chapter; all the gory details are covered in Part V of this book. By the end of this chapter, you should know enough to find your way around the reference chapters for the answers to particular questions. If you already know Perl, you may want to just skim this chapter to refresh your memory of the language and how it works. If you don't already know how to program in at least one language, this book is not the place to start. ■

# Perl

The story of how Perl began is a simple tale of one man's frustration and (by his own account) inordinate laziness.

> **N O T E** This chapter is supposed to be a snappy introduction to the language, so why am I wasting your time with this stuff? The fact is, Perl is a unique language in ways that cannot be conveyed simply by describing the technical details of the language. Perl is a state of mind as much as it is a language grammar. So we'll take a few minutes to look at the external realities that provoked Perl into being; this information should give you some insight into the way that Perl was *meant* to be used. ■

## Origins

Back in 1986, a UNIX programmer by the name of Larry Wall found himself working on a task that involved generating reports from a great many text files, with cross-references. Because he was a UNIX programmer, and because the problem involved manipulating the contents of text files, he started to use awk for the task. But it soon became clear that awk wasn't up to the job, and with no other obvious candidate for the job, he'd just have to write some code.

Now, here's the interesting bit: Larry could have written a utility to manage the particular job at hand and gotten on with his life. He could see, though, that it wouldn't be long before he'd have to write another special utility to handle something else that the standard tools couldn't quite hack. (He may have realized that most programmers are *always* writing special utilities to handle things that the standard tools can't quite hack.)

So rather than waste any more of his time, he invented a new language and wrote an interpreter for it. That statement may seem to be a paradox, but it isn't. Setting yourself up with the right tools is always an effort, but if you do it right, the effort pays off.

The new language emphasized system management and text handling. After a few revisions, it could handle regular expressions, signals, and network sockets, too. The language became known as Perl and quickly became popular with frustrated, lazy UNIX programmers—and with the rest of us.

## Borrowings

Perl borrowed freely from many other tools, particularly sed and awk. That's *Perl*, the language, not *perl*, the interpreter. Perl does many of the things that sed, awk, and UNIX shell scripting languages do, but (arguably) better every time; the perl code is Larry's doing.

> **N O T E**   Is it *Perl* or *perl*? The definitive word from Larry Wall is that it doesn't matter. Many programmers like to refer to languages with capitalized names (Perl), but the program originated on a UNIX system, on which short lowercase names (awk, sed, and so on) are the norm. As is true of many things about the language, there's no single "right way" to use the term; just use it the way you want. Perl is a tool, after all, and not a dogma.
>
> If you're sufficiently pedantic, you may want to call it *[Pp]erl* after you read the "Regular Expressions" section later in this chapter.

Perl can handle low-level tasks quite well, particularly since Perl 5, when the whole messy business of references was put on a sound footing. In this sense, it has a great deal in common with C. But Perl handles the internals of data types, memory allocation, and so on automatically and seamlessly.

Perl code also bears a passing resemblance to C code, perhaps because Perl was written in C or perhaps because Larry found some of C's syntactic conventions to be handy. But Perl is less pedantic and much more concise than C is.

This magpie habit of picking up interesting features along the way—regular expressions here, database handling there—has been regularized in Perl 5. Now you can add your favorite bag of tricks to Perl fairly easily by using modules. Many of the added-on features of Perl, such as socket handling, are likely to be dropped from the core of Perl and moved out to modules in time.

## Cost and Licensing

Perl is free. The full source and documentation are free to copy, compile, print, and give away. Any programs that you write in Perl are yours to do with as you please; there are no royalties to pay and no restrictions on distribution, as far as Perl is concerned.

Perl is not completely a public domain product, though, and for very good reason. If the source were completely public domain, someone could make minor alterations in it, compile it, and then sell it—in other words, rip off its creator. On the other hand, without distributing the source code, it's hard to make sure that everyone who wants to can use Perl.

The GNU General Public License is one way to distribute free software without the danger of being taken advantage of. Under this type of license, source code may be distributed freely and used by anybody, but any programs derived from such code must be released under the same type of license. In other words, if you derive any of your source code from GNU-licensed source code, you have to release your source code to anyone who wants it.

This arrangement is often sufficient to protect the interests of the author, but it can lead to a plethora of derivative versions of the original package, which may deprive the original author of a say in the development of his or her own creation. The situation can also lead to confusion on the part of users—it becomes hard to establish which version of the package is the definitive version, whether a particular script will work with a given version, and so on.

That's why Perl is released under the terms of the Artistic License—a variation on the GNU General Public License that says that anyone who releases a package derived from Perl must make it clear that the package is not actually Perl. All modifications must be clearly flagged; executables must be renamed, if necessary; and the original modules must be distributed along with the modified version. The effect is that the original author is clearly recognized as the owner of the package. The general terms of the GNU General Public license also apply.

## Distribution

New versions of Perl are released on the Internet and distributed to Web sites and FTP archives across the world. The Perl source and documentation are distributed, as are executable files for many non-UNIX systems. UNIX binaries are generally not made available on the Internet, because it generally is better to build Perl on your system so you can be certain that it will work. All UNIX systems have a C compiler, after all.

See "Perl Acquisition and Installation," p. 549

The perl distribution comes with a nifty utility called Configure that tweaks the source files and the Makefile for your system. It probes your system software, shell, C compiler, and so on to determine the answers to various questions about how to build Perl—which compiler flags to use, the sizes of fundamental data types, and so on. You can override any of Configure's answers if you disagree with its findings, but it's generally very accurate indeed.

Running Configure before you make perl virtually guarantees you a perl installation that is not only successfully compiled and linked, but also well optimized for your particular system configuration—and with no tweaking or editing of source files on your part. You're more than welcome to tinker with obscure compiler flags if you want, however; that's why GNU C was invented.

# Perl Programs

After you install perl, how do you use it to do all those wonderful things to enrich the Web? What, in other words, is a Perl program, and how do you feed it to perl?

# Invocation

We're going to spend the rest of this chapter answering the first two questions, so we'll get the third question out of the way now. Invoking perl is quite simple, but the procedure varies a little from system to system.

Suppose that perl is correctly installed and working on your system. The simplest way to run perl on a Perl program is to invoke the perl interpreter with the name of the Perl program as an argument, as follows:

```
perl sample.pl
```

In this example, SAMPLE.PL is the name of a Perl file, and perl is the name of the perl interpreter. The example assumes that perl is in the execution path. If it isn't, you need to supply the full path to perl, too, as follows:

```
/usr/local/hin/perl sample.pl
```

This syntax is the preferred way of invoking perl, because it eliminates the possibility that you might invoke a copy of perl other than the one you intended to use. Because we'll be working with Web servers in this book—and, therefore, keenly aware of security issues—we'll use the full path from now on.

That much is the same on all systems that have a command-line interface. The following will do the trick in Windows NT, for example:

```
c:\NTperl\perl sample.pl
```

**Invoking Perl in UNIX**    UNIX systems have another way to invoke an interpreter in a script file. Place a line such as the following at the start of the Perl file:

```
#!/usr/local/bin/perl
```

This line tells UNIX that the rest of this script file is to be interpreted by /USR/LOCAL/BIN/PERL. Next, you make the script itself executable, as follows:

```
chmod +x sample.pl
```

Then you can execute the script file directly and have the script file tell the operating system what interpreter to use while running it.

**Invoking Perl in Windows NT**    The procedures in the preceding section are fine for UNIX, but Windows NT is quite different. You can use File Manager (Explorer, in Windows NT 4) to create an association between the file extension, .PL, and the perl executable. Then, whenever a file that ends in .PL is invoked, NT knows that perl should be used to interpret it.

> **N O T E**    Usually, a few more steps are required to get a Web server to execute Perl programs automatically. Refer to Appendix A, "Perl Acquisition and Installation," for platform-specific instructions on creating associations between scripts and interpreters. ■

# Command-Line Arguments

Perl takes several optional command-line arguments for various purposes (see Table 1.1). Most of these arguments are rarely used but are listed here for reference purposes. The -t switch in particular is *de rigueur* in Web-based Perl scripts.

**Table 1.1    Perl Command-Line Switches**

| Option | Arguments | Purpose | Notes |
|---|---|---|---|
| -0 | Octal character code | Specify record separator | Default is new line (\n) |
| -a | | Automatically split records | Used with -n or -p |
| -c | | Check syntax only do not execute | |
| -d | | Run script, using Perl debugger | If Perl debugger is installed |
| \-D | Flags | Specify debugging behavior | Refer to the PERLDEBUG man page on the CD-ROM that comes with this book |
| -e | Command | Pass a command to Perl from the command line | Useful for quick operations; see tip after this table for an example |
| -F | Regular expression | Expression to split by if -a is used | Default is white space |
| -i | Extension | Replace original file with result | Useful for modifying contents of files; see tip after this table for an example |
| -I | Directory | Specify location of include files | |
| -l | Octal character code | Drop new lines when used with -n and -p, and use designated character as line-termination character | |
| -n | | Process the script, using each specified file as an argument | Used for performing the same set of actions on a set of files |
| -p | | Same as -n, but each line is printed | |
| -P | | Run the script through the C preprocessor before Perl compiles it | |

| Option | Arguments | Purpose | Notes |
|--------|-----------|---------|-------|
| -s | | Enable passing of arbitrary switches to Perl | Use -s -*what* -*ever* to have the Perl variables $what and $ever defined within your script |
| -S | | Tell Perl to look along the path for the script | |
| -T | | Use taint checking; don't evaluate expressions supplied in the command line | Very important for Web use |
| -u | | Makes Perl dump core after compiling your script; intended to allow for generation of Perl executables | Very messy; wait for the Perl compiler |
| -U | | Unsafe mode; overrides Perl's natural caution. | Don't use this! |
| -v | | Print Perl version number | |
| -w | | Print warnings about script syntax | Extremely useful, especially during development; warning messages can confuse browsers if sent raw |

**T I P**   The -e option is handy for quick Perl operations from the command line. Want to change all the foos in WIFFLE.BAT to bars? Try this:

```
perl -i.old -p -e "s/foo/bar/g" wiffle.bat
```

This code says, "Take each line of WIFFLE.BAT (-p), store the original in WIFFLE.OLD (-i), replace all instances of foo with bar (-e), and write the result (-p) to the original file (-i)."

You can supply Perl command-line arguments in the interpreter-invocation line in UNIX scripts. Following is a good start for any Perl script:

```
#!/usr/local/bin/perl -w -T
```

**CAUTION**

The -w switch is best omitted in versions of Perl older than 5.002, because it may produce spurious warnings.

Also, take care when you use the -w switch in scripts that send data to Web browsers. Warning messages sent before the browser receives a content-type line may result in an error message.

# Program Layout

A Perl program consists of an ordinary text file that contains a series of Perl commands. Commands are written in what looks like a bastardized amalgam of C, shell script, and English. In fact, that's pretty much what it is.

Perl code can be quite free-flowing. The broad syntactic rules governing where a statement starts and ends are:

- Leading white space is ignored. You can start a Perl statement anywhere you want: at the beginning of the line; indented, for clarity (recommended); or even right-justified (definitely frowned on), if you like.
- Commands are terminated with a semicolon.
- White space outside string literals is irrelevant; one space is as good as a hundred, which means that you can split statements over several lines for clarity.
- Anything after a hash sign (#) is ignored. Use this fact to pepper your code with useful comments.

Here's a Perl statement inspired by Kurt Vonnegut:

```
print "My name is Yon Yonson\n";
```

No prizes for guessing what happens when Perl runs this code—it prints My name is Yon Yonson. If the \n doesn't look familiar, don't worry; it simply means that Perl should print a new-line character after the text (or, in other words, go to the start of the next line).

Printing more text is a matter of either stringing together statements like the following or giving multiple arguments to the print function:

```
print "My name is Yon Yonson,\n";
print "I live in Wisconsin,\n",
      "I work in a lumbermill there.\n";
```

That's right—print is a function. It may not look like one in any of the earlier examples in this chapter, which have no parentheses to delimit the function arguments, but it *is* a function, and it takes arguments. More accurately, in this example print takes a single argument that consists of an arbitrarily long list.

We'll have much more to say about lists and arrays in "Data Types" later in this chapter. You'll find a few more examples of the more common functions in the remainder of this chapter, but refer to Chapter 15, "Function List," for a complete rundown on Perl's built-in functions.

For now, if you're uncomfortable with functions that take arbitrary numbers of arguments with no parentheses to corral them, pretend that you see parentheses. You can use them in Perl programs, if you like, but it would be better to get used to the idea that Perl syntax is loose and groovy in a way that C, for example, is not.

What does a complete Perl program look like? Here's a trivial UNIX example, complete with the invocation line at the top and a few comments:

```
#!/usr/local/bin/perl -w                    # Show warnings

print "My name is Yon Yonson,\n";           # Let's introduce ourselves
print "I live in Wisconsin,\n",
      "I work in a lumbermill there.\n";    # Remember the line breaks
```

This example is not at all typical of a Perl program, though; it's just a linear sequence of commands with no structural complexity. The "Flow Control" section later in this chapter introduces some of the constructs that make Perl what it is and provides a more authentic flavor of what is normal in a Perl program. For now, we'll stick to simple examples like this one for the sake of clarity.

# Data Types

Perl has a small number of data types. If you're used to working with C, in which even characters can be either signed or unsigned, this fact makes for a pleasant change. In essence, Perl has only two data types: *scalars* and *arrays*. Perl also has *associative arrays*, which are a very special type of array and which merit a section of their own.

## Scalars

All numbers and strings are *scalars*. Scalar-variable names start with a dollar sign ($).

**N O T E** All Perl variable names, including scalars, are case-sensitive. $Name and $name, for example, are completely different quantities. ▪

Perl converts automatically between numbers and strings as required, so that

```
$a = 2;
$b = 6;
$c = $a . $b;   # The "." operator concatenates two strings
$d = $c / 2;
print $d;
```

yields the result

13

This example involves converting two integers to strings; concatenating the strings into a new string variable; converting this new string to an integer; dividing it by 2; converting the result to a string; and printing it. All these conversions are handled implicitly, leaving the programmer free to concentrate on what needs to be done rather than on the low-level details of how it is to be done.

This situation might be a problem if Perl were regularly used for tasks in which explicit memory offsets were used, for example, and data types were critical. But for the type of task for which Perl is normally used—and certainly for the types of tasks that we'll be using it for in this book—these automatic conversions are smooth, intuitive, and generally a Good Thing.

We can develop the earlier example script with some string variables, as follows:

```
#!/usr/local/bin/perl -w                        # Show warnings

$who = 'Yon Yonson';
$where = 'Wisconsin';
$what = 'in a lumbermill';

print "My name is $who,\n";                      # Let's introduce ourselves
print "I live in $where,\n",
      "I work $what there.\n";                               # Remember the line breaks

print "\nSigned: \t$who,\n\t\t$where.\n";
```

This script yields the following:

```
My name is Yon Yonson,
I work in Wisconsin,
I work in a lumbermill there.

Signed: Yon Yonson,
        Wisconsin.
```

Don't worry—it gets better.

## Arrays

A collection of scalars is an *array*. An array-variable name starts with an at symbol (@), whereas an explicit array of scalars is written as a comma-separated list within parentheses, as follows:

```
@trees = ("Larch", "Hazel", "Oak");
```

Array subscripts are denoted by brackets. $trees[0], for example, is the first element of the @trees array. Notice that it's @trees but $trees[0]; individual array elements are scalars, so they start with $.

Mixing scalar types in an array is not a problem. The code

```
@items = (15, '45.67', "case");
print "Take $items[0] $items[2]s at \$$items[1] each.\n";
```

results in the following:

```
Take 15 cases at $45.67 each.
```

All arrays in Perl are dynamic. You never have to worry about memory allocation and management; Perl does all that stuff for you. Combine that with the fact that arrays can contain arrays as subarrays, and you're free to say things like the following:

```
@A = (1, 2, 3);
@B = (4, 5, 6);
@C = (7, 8, 9);
@D = (@A, @B, @C);
```

As a result of this code, the array @D contains the numbers 1 through 9. The power of constructs such as the following takes getting used to:

```
@Annual = (@Spring, @Summer, @Fall, @Winter);
```

This code example combines arrays that represent some aspect of each of the seasons in a concise and intuitive way. The arrays for the seasons might in turn consist of arrays of months, each of which might consist of an array of daily values. The @Annual array then would consist of a value for each day of the year. By defining your data in chunks such as this, you give yourself the option of handling it on a daily, monthly, or annual basis.

**N O T E**    An aspect of Perl that often confuses newcomers (and occasionally old hands, too) is the context-sensitive nature of evaluations. Perl keeps track of the context in which an expression is being evaluated and can return a different value in an array context than in a scalar context. In this example, the array @B contains 1–4, whereas $C contains 4 (the number of values in the array):

```
@A = (1, 2, 3, 4);
@B = @A;
$C = @A;
```

This context sensitivity becomes more of an issue when you use functions and operators that can take either a single argument or multiple arguments. The function or argument behaves one way when it is passed a single *scalar* argument and another when it is passed multiple arguments, which it may interpret as a single *array* argument. ▪

Many of Perl's built-in functions take arrays as arguments. One example is sort, which takes an array as an argument and returns the same array, sorted alphabetically. The code

```
print sort ( 'Beta', 'Gamma', 'Alpha' );
```

prints AlphaBetaGamma.

You can make this code neater by using another built-in function, called join. This function takes two arguments: a string to connect with, and an array of strings to connect. join returns a single string that consists of all elements in the array joined with the connecting string. The code

```
print join ( ' : ', 'Name', 'Address', 'Phone' );
```

returns the string Name : Address : Phone.

Because sort returns an array, you can feed its output straight into join. The code

```
print join( ', ', sort ( 'Beta', 'Gamma', 'Alpha' ) );
```

prints Alpha, Beta, Gamma.

Notice that this code doesn't separate the initial scalar argument of join from the array that follows it. The first argument is the string to join things with. The rest of the arguments are treated as a single argument: the array to be joined. This is true even if you use parentheses to separate groups of arguments. The code

```
print join( ': ', ('A', 'B', 'C'), ('D', 'E'), ('F', 'G', 'H', 'I'));
```

returns A: B: C: D: E: F: G: H: I.

You can use one array or multiple arrays in a context such as this because of the way that Perl treats arrays; adding an array to an array gives you one larger array, not two arrays. In this case, all three arrays are bundled into one.

 **TIP** For even more powerful string-manipulation capabilities, refer to the `splice` function in Chapter 15, "Function List."

## Associative Arrays

Associative arrays have a certain elegance that makes experienced Perl programmers a little snobbish about their language of choice. Rightly so! Associative arrays give Perl a degree of database functionality at a very low, yet useful, level. Many tasks that would otherwise involve complex programming can be reduced to a handful of Perl statements by means of associative arrays.

Arrays of the type that you've already seen are *lists of values indexed by subscripts*. In other words, to get an individual element of an array, you supply a subscript as a reference, as follows:

```
@fruit = ( "Apple", "Orange", "Banana" );
print $fruit[2];
```

This example yields `Banana`, because subscripts start at zero, so 2 is the subscript for the third element of the `@fruit` array. A reference to `$fruit[7]` here returns the null value, because no array element with that subscript has been defined.

Now, here's the point of all this: *Associative arrays are lists of values indexed by strings.* Conceptually, that's all there is to them. The implementation of associative arrays is more complex, because all the strings (*keys*) need to be stored in addition to the values to which they refer.

When you want to refer to an element of an associative array, you supply a string (the key) instead of an integer (the subscript). Perl returns the corresponding value. Consider the following example:

```
%fruit = ("Green", "Apple", "Orange", "Orange", "Yellow", "Banana" );
print $fruit{"Yellow"};
```

This code prints `Banana`, as before. The first line defines the associative array in much the same way that you have already defined ordinary arrays; the difference is that instead of listing values, you list key/value pairs. The first value is `Apple`, and its key is `Green`. The second value is `Orange`, which happens to have the same string for both value and key. Finally, the value `Banana` has the key `Yellow`.

On a superficial level, you can use string subscripts to provide mnemonics for array references, allowing you to refer to `$Total{'June'}` instead of `$Total[5]`. But you wouldn't even be beginning to use the power of associative arrays. Think of the keys of an associative arrays as you might think of a key that links tables in a relational database, and you're closer to the idea. Consider this example:

```
%Folk =    ( 'YY', 'Yon Yonson',
             'TC', 'Terra Cotta',
             'RE', 'Ron Everly' );

%State = ( 'YY', 'Wisconsin',
           'TC', 'Minnesota',
           'RE', 'Bliss' );

%Job = ( 'YY', 'work in a lumbermill',
         'TC', 'teach nuclear physics',
         'RE', 'watch football');

foreach $person ( 'TC', 'YY', 'RE' )  {
        print "My name is $Folk{$person},\n",
              "I live in $State{$person},\n",
              "I $Job{$person} there.\n\n";
        }
```

We had to sneak the foreach construct in there for that example to work. That construct is explained in full in "Flow Control" later in this chapter. For now, you'll just have to take it on trust that foreach makes Perl execute the three print statements for each of the people in the list after the foreach keyword. Otherwise, you could try executing the code in the sample and see what happens.

You also can treat the keys and values of an associative array as separate (ordinary) arrays by using the keys and values keywords, respectively. The code

```
print keys %Folk;
print values %State;
```

prints the string YYRETCWisconsinBlissMinnesota.

Looks as though we need to do some more work on string handling. That task is best left until after we cover some flow-control mechanisms, however.

> **N O T E** A special associative array called %ENV stores the contents of all environment variables, indexed by variable name. $ENV{'PATH'}, for example, returns the current search path.
> Following is a way to print the current values of all environment variables, sorted by variable name for good measure:
>
> ```
> foreach $var (sort keys %ENV ) {
>     print "$var: \"$ENV{$var}\".\n";
>     }
> ```
>
> The foreach clause sets $var to each of the environment-variable names in turn (in alphabetical order), and the print statement prints each name and value. The backslash-quote (\") in there produces quotation marks around the values. ■

# File Handles

This chapter finishes discussing Perl data types by discussing file handles. A *file handle* is not really a data type at all, but a special kind of literal string. A file handle behaves like a variable in many ways, however, so this section is a good place to cover them. (Besides, you won't get very far in Perl without them.)

You can regard a file handle as being a pointer to a file from which Perl is to read or to which it will write. (C programmers are familiar with the concept.) The basic idea is that you associate a handle with a file or device, and then refer to the handle in the code whenever you need to perform a read or write operation.

File handles generally are written in uppercase. Perl has some useful predefined file handles, as Table 1.2 shows.

**Table 1.2   Perl's Predefined File Handles**

| File Handle | Points to... |
| --- | --- |
| STDIN | Standard input (normally, the keyboard) |
| STDOUT | Standard output (normally, the console; in many Web applications, the browser) |
| STDERR | Device where error messages should be written (normally, the console; in a Web server environment, normally, the server-error log file) |

The print statement can take a file handle as its first argument, as follows:

```
print STDERR "Oops, something broke.\n";
```

Notice that no comma appears after the file handle in this example. That helps Perl figure out that the STDERR is not something to be printed. If you're uneasy with this implicit list syntax, you can put parentheses around all the print arguments, as follows:

```
print (STDERR "Oops, something broke.\n");
```

You still have no comma after the file handle, however.

**TIP**    Use the standard file handles explicitly, especially in complex programs. Redefining the standard input or output device for a while is convenient sometimes; make sure that you don't accidentally wind up writing to a file what should have gone to the screen.

You can use the open function to associate a new file handle with a file, as follows:

```
open (INDATA, "/etc/stuff/Friday.dat");
open (LOGFILE, ">/etc/logs/reclaim.log");
print LOGFILE "Log of reclaim procedure\n";
```

By default, open opens files for reading only. If you want to override this default behavior, add to the file name one of the special direction symbols listed in Table 1.3. (The > at the start of the file name in the second output statement of the preceding example, for example, tells Perl that you intend to write to the named file.)

### Table 1.3  Perl File-Access Symbols

| Symbol | Meaning |
| --- | --- |
| < | Open the file for reading (the default action) |
| > | Open the file for writing |
| >> | Open the file for appending |
| +< | Open the file for both reading and writing |
| +> | Open the file for both reading and writing |
| ¦ (before file name) | Treat file as command into which Perl is to pipe text |
| ¦ (after file name) | Treat file as command from which input is to be piped to Perl |

To take a more complex example, here's one way to feed output to the mypr printer on a UNIX system:

```
open (MYLPR, "¦lpr -Pmypr");
print MYLPR "A line of output\n";
close MYLPR;
```

A special Perl operator for reading from files consists of two angle brackets—<>—around the file handle of the file from which you want to read. This operator returns the next line or lines of input from the file or device, depending on whether the operator is used in a scalar or an array context. When no more input remains, the operator returns false.

A construct such as

```
while (<STDIN>) {
        print;
        }
```

simply echoes each line of input back to the console until Ctrl+D (Ctrl+Z in Windows NT) is pressed, because the print function takes the current default argument here: the most recent line of input. For an explanation, see "Special Variables" later in this chapter.

If the user types

```
A
Bb
Ccc
^D
```

the screen looks like this:

```
A
A
Bb
Bb
```

```
Ccc
Ccc
^D
```

Notice that in this case, `<STDIN>` is in a scalar context, so one line of standard input is returned at a time. Compare that example with the following example:

```
print <STDIN>;
```

In this case, because `print` expects an array of arguments (it can be a single-element array, but it's an array as far as `print` is concerned), the `<>` operator obligingly returns all the contents of `STDIN` as an array, and then `print` prints it. Because the array is fully built before it is printed, nothing is written to the console until the user presses Ctrl+D:

```
A
Bb
Ccc
^D
A
Bb
Ccc
```

This script prints out the contents of the file .SIGNATURE, double-spaced:

```
open (SIGFILE, ".signature");
while ( <SIGFILE> )  {
        print; print "\n";
        }
```

The first `print` here has no arguments, so it takes the current default argument and prints it. The second `print` has an argument, so it prints that instead. Perl's habit of using default arguments extends to the `<>` operator; if that operator is used with no file handle, Perl assumes that `<ARGV>` is intended. `<ARGV>` expands to each line in turn of each file listed in the command line.

If no files are listed in the command line, Perl instead assumes that `STDIN` is intended. The following code, therefore, keeps printing *more...* as long as something other than Ctrl+D appears in standard input:

```
while (<>) {
print "more.... ";
}
```

**N O T E**   Perl 5 allows array elements to be references to any data type. As a result, you can build arbitrary data structures of the kind used in C and other high-level languages, but with all the power of Perl. You can have an array of associative arrays, for example.  ■

# Special Variables

Like all languages, Perl has its special hieroglyphs, which are laden with meaning. This section briefly examines some of the most common and useful variables, and provides some examples of typical Perl idioms in which you might find them.

**See** "Special Variables," **p. 373**

# Environment Variables

You have already seen one special variable: the environment-variable associative array %ENV. This special associative array allows you to easily use the value of any environment variable within your Perl scripts:

```
print "Looking for files along the path ($ENV{'PATH'})…\n";
```

The %ENV array is quite useful in CGI programming, in which parameters are passed from the browser to CGI programs as environment settings.

# Program Arguments

Any arguments specified in the Perl command line are passed to the Perl script in another special array: @ARGV.

> **CAUTION**
>
> C programmers, beware: The first element of this array is the first actual argument, not the name of the program. The special variable $0 contains the name of the Perl script that is being executed.

The following code prints the command-line arguments one per line, sorted alphabetically:

```
print join("\n", sort @ARGV);
```

The command-line arguments are of limited use in CGI scripts, in which arguments are passed via the environment rather than the command line. These arguments are quite useful in normal Perl work, of course.

# Current Line

The special variable $_ is often used to store the current line of input. This situation is true when the <> input operator is used. The following code, for example, prints a numbered listing of the file pointed to by SOMEFILE:

```
$line=0;
while ( <SOMEFILE> )  {
        ++$line;
        print "Line $line : ", $_;
        }
```

You occasionally need to store the contents of $_ somewhere, as in the following example:

```
$oldvalue = $_;
```

But the opposite operation—setting the value of $_ manually—is rarely appropriate, as in this example:

```
$_ = $oldvalue;
```

Pattern matching and substitution take place on the contents of this variable unless you specify otherwise. These topics are covered in "Regular Expressions" later in this chapter.

## System Error Messages

The special variable $! contains the current system-error number (errno, on UNIX systems) or system-error string, depending on whether it is evaluated in a numeric or string context. This variable may not contain anything meaningful; it should be used only if an error occurred.

This example reports failure if the open call failed:

```
open ( INFILE, "./missing.txt") || die "Couldn't open \"./missing.txt\" ($!).\n";
```

The || here is the Boolean or operator, which is covered in "Flow Control" later in this chapter. die causes Perl to terminate after printing the string given to die as an argument.

If the file does not exist, Perl terminates after displaying something like this:

```
Couldn't open "./missing.txt" (No such file or directory).
```

The form and content of error messages vary from one system to the next.

# Flow Control

The examples that you have seen so far have been quite simple, with little or no logical structure beyond a linear sequence of steps. We managed to sneak in the occasional while and foreach; think of those as being sneak previews. Perl has all the flow-control mechanisms that you'd expect to find in a high-level language, and this section takes you through the basics of each mechanism.

## Logical Operators

Two operators—|| (or) and && (and)—are used like glue to hold Perl programs together. They take two operands and return either true or false, depending on the operands. In the following example, if either $Saturday or $Sunday is true, $Weekend will be true, too:

```
$Weekend = $Saturday || $Sunday;
```

In the next example, $Solvent is true only if $income is greater than 3 and $debts is less than 10:

```
$Solvent = ($income > 3) && ($debts < 10);
```

Now consider the logic of evaluating one of these expressions. It isn't always necessary to evaluate both operands of either an && or a || operator. In the first example earlier in this section, if $Saturday is true, you know that $Weekend will be true, regardless of whether $Sunday is also true (the midnight condition, perhaps?).

This means that when the left side of an or expression is evaluated as true, the right side is not evaluated. Combine this with Perl's easy way with data types, and you can say things like the following:

```
$value > 10 || print "Oops, low value…\n";
```

If $value *is* greater than 10, the right side of the expression is never evaluated, so nothing is printed. If $value *is not* greater than 10, Perl needs to evaluate the right side, too, so as to decide whether the expression as a whole is true or false. That means that Perl evaluates the print statement, printing out the message.

OK, it's a trick, but it's a very useful one.

Something analogous applies to the && operator. In this case, if the left side of an expression is false, the expression as a whole is false, so Perl does not evaluate the right side. The && operator can, therefore, be used to produce the same kind of effect as the || trick, but with the opposite sense, as in the following example:

```
$value > 10 && print "OK, value is high enough…\n";
```

As is true of most Perl constructs, the real power of these tricks comes when you apply a little creative thinking. Remember that the left and right sides of these expressions can be any Perl expressions; think of them as being conjunctions in a sentence rather than logical operators, and you'll get a better feel for how to use them. Expressions such as the following give you a little of the flavor of creative Perl:

```
$length <= 80 || die "Line too long.\n";
$errorlevel > 3 && warn "Hmmm, strange error level ($errorlevel)…\n";
open ( LOGFILE, ">install.log") || &bust("Log file");
```

The &bust in this example is a subroutine call, by the way. Refer to "Subroutines" later in this chapter for more information.

## Conditional Expressions

The most basic kind of flow control is a simple branch. A statement is either executed or not, depending on whether a logical expression is true or false. You can do this by following the statement with a modifier and a logical expression, as follows:

```
open ( INFILE, "./missing.txt") if $missing;
```

The execution of the statement is contingent upon *both* the evaluation of the expression and the sense of the operator.

The expression is evaluated as either true or false and can contain any of the relational operators listed in Table 1.4 (although it need not). Following are a few examples of valid expressions:

```
$full
$a == $b
<STDIN>
```

**Table 1.4   Perl's Relational Operators**

| Operator | Numeric Context | String Context |
|---|---|---|
| Equality | == | eq |
| Inequality | != | ne |
| Inequality with signed result | <=> | cmp |
| Greater than | > | gt |
| Greater than or equal to | >= | ge |
| Less than | < | lt |
| Less than or equal to | <= | le |

**N O T E**   When we're comparing strings, *less than* means *lexically less than*. If $left comes before $right when the two are sorted alphabetically, $left is less than $right. ▩

Perl has four modifiers, each of which behaves the way that you might expect from the corresponding English word:

■ **if**. The statement is executed if the logical expression is true and is not executed otherwise. Examples:

```
$max = 100 if $min < 100;
print "Empty!\n" if !$full;
```

■ **unless**. The statement is not executed if the logical expression is true and is executed otherwise. Examples:

```
open (ERRLOG, "test.log") unless $NoLog;
print "Success" unless $error>2;
```

■ **while**. The statement is executed repeatedly until the logical expression is false. Examples:

```
$total -= $decrement while $total > $decrement;
$n=1000;  "print $n\n" while $n— > 0;
```

■ **until**. The statement is executed repeatedly until the logical expression is true. Examples:

```
$total += $value[$count++] until $total > $limit;
print RESULTS "Next value: $value[$n++]" until $value[$n] = -1;
```

Notice that the logical expression is evaluated only one time in the case of if and unless, but multiple times in the case of while and until. In other words, the first two are simple conditionals, and the last two are loop constructs.

# Compound Statements

The syntax changes when you want to make the execution of multiple statements contingent on the evaluation of a logical expression. The modifier comes at the start of a line, followed by the logical expression in parentheses, followed by the conditional statements in braces. Notice that the parentheses around the logical expression are required, although they are not required in the single statement branching described in the preceding section.

The following example is somewhat similar to C's if syntax:

```
if ( ( $total += $value ) > $limit )  {
   print LOGFILE "Maximum limit $limit exceeded. Offending value was $value.\n";
   close (LOGFILE);
   die "Too many! Check the log file for details.\n";
   }
```

The if statement is capable of a little more complexity, with else and elsif operators, as in the following example:

```
if ( !open( LOGFILE, "install.log") )   {
   close ( INFILE );
   die "Unable to open log file!\n";
   }
elsif ( !open( CFGFILE, ">system.cfg") ) {
   print LOGFILE "Error during install: Unable to open config file for
writing.\n";
   close ( LOGFILE );
   die "Unable to open config file for writing!\n";
   }
else  {
   print CFGFILE "Your settings go here!\n";
   }
```

# Loops

The loop modifiers (while, until, for, and foreach) are used with compound statements in much the same way, as the following example shows:

```
until ( $total >= 50 )  {
   print "Enter a value: ";
   $value = scalar (<STDIN>);
   $total += $value;
   print "Current total is $total\n";
   }
print "Enough!\n";
```

The while and until statements are described in "Conditional Expressions" earlier in this chapter. The for statement resembles the one in C. for is followed by an initial value, a termination condition, and an iteration expression, all enclosed in parentheses and separated by semicolons, as follows:

```
for ( $count = 0; $count < 100; $count++ )  {
   print "Something";
   }
```

The `foreach` operator is special; it iterates over the contents of an array and executes the statements in a statement block for each element of the array. Following is a simple example:

```perl
@numbers = ("one", "two", "three", "four");
foreach $num ( @numbers )    {
   print "Number $num...\n";
   }
```

The variable `$num` first takes on the value one, then two, and so on. That example looks fairly trivial, but the real power of this operator lies in the fact that it can operate on any array, as follows:

```perl
foreach $arg ( @ARGV )    {
   print "Argument: \"$arg\".\n";
   }

foreach $namekey ( sort keys %surnames )   {
   print REPORT "Surname: $value{$namekey}.\n",
                "Address: $address{$namekey}.\n";
   }
```

# Labels

You can use labels with the `next`, `last`, and `redo` statements to provide more control of program flow through loops. A label consists of any word, usually in uppercase, followed by a colon. The label appears just before the loop operator (`while`, `for`, or `foreach`) and can be used as an anchor for jumping to from within the block. The following code snippet prints all the odd-numbered records in INFILE:

```perl
RECORD:  while ( <INFILE> )  {
   $even = !$even;
   next RECORD if $even;
   print;
   }
```

The three label-control statements are:

- **next.** Jumps to the next iteration of the loop marked by the label or to the innermost enclosing loop, if no label is specified.
- **last.** Immediately breaks out of the loop marked by the label or out of the innermost enclosing loop, if no label is specified.
- **redo.** Jumps back to the loop marked by the specified label or to the innermost enclosing loop, if no label is specified. `redo` causes the loop to execute again with the same iterator value.

# Subroutines

Subroutines in Perl are defined with the `sub` keyword, as follows:

```perl
sub Usage {
   print "Usage: \n",
         "twiddle [-args] infile outfile\n";
```

```
   print "Copyleft 1996, Jonathan F. Squirmsby.";
}
```

Subroutines are called with &, as follows:

```
sub bust  {
   print "Oops, some kind of error seems to have occurred.\n";
   die "Fatal error, terminating.\n";
   }
open ( LOGFILE, ">install.log") ¦¦ &bust;
```

In this example, the subroutine was defined before it was called. You can define and call subroutines in any order in Perl; the convention is to define them after the main routine.

**Passing Arguments**    You can pass arguments to a subroutine in the usual way, as follows:

```
open ( LOGFILE, ">install.log") ¦¦ &bust("Failed to open log file
\"install.log\".");
```

But here is where Perl's subroutine syntax starts to get a little strange; C programmers may want to take a seat before reading on.

All Perl subroutines receive their arguments as an arbitrarily long array of scalars with the special name of @_. There is no mechanism for declaring the arguments when the subroutine is declared. There is no fixed number of arguments. Also, the calling function can pass any mixture of scalars and arrays; they are all treated as one big @_ array when they get to the subroutine.

In the example earlier in this section, in which bust is called with a single argument, you can pick it up in the subroutine and use it to provide a more sensible error message, as in the following example:

```
sub bust  {
   ($errortext) = @_;
   print "Oops, an error occurred ($errortext).\n";
   die "Fatal error, terminating.\n";
   }
```

Notice that we went to the trouble of assigning the scalar $errortext to the argument array @_. This assignment may seem to be unnecessary; in fact, we could have simply used @_ instead of $errortext in the print statement. Explicitly assigning variables to the contents of the @_ array is much clearer, though, especially when the subroutine takes multiple arguments. Compare the example

```
print "Error $_[0] opening file $_[1].\n";
```

with this one:

```
($errfile, $errtext) = @_;
print "Error $errtext opening file $errfile.\n";
```

Notice, too, that when we assigned the single value $errortext to the @_ array in the bust example, we placed it in parentheses. We did so to force an array context, so that what gets assigned to $errortext is the first (and only) value of the @_ array, not the number of values in

@_. In effect, we're telling Perl to treat $errortext as a single-element array. The earlier example that uses $errfile and $errtext is a clearer example of an array-to-array assignment.

In "Variable Scope" later in this chapter, you learn how to protect local variables such as $errortext in subroutines by using the local and my keywords.

**Passing Arrays**     Perl's grouping of all subroutine arguments makes it impossible to pass more than one array to a Perl subroutine. Suppose that you have a subroutine call of the following form:

```
&PrintRes( "alpha", (1, 3, 5, 7), "beta", (2, 4, 6, 8) );
```

Try to unpack these arguments into the following values as they come into the subroutine:

```
$p1 = "alpha";
@p2 = (1, 3, 5, 7);
$p3 = "beta";
@p4 = (2, 4, 6, 8);
```

A statement like

```
( $p1, @p2, $p3, @p4 ) = @_;
```

won't get beyond the second parameter. The following list explains what happens:

1. The first variable in the list, $p1, is assigned the value of the first scalar in the @_ argument array, which is alpha.

2. Then the next variable in the list, @p2, is assigned the value of the next argument in the @_ argument array. This is an array assignment because @p2 is an array, so the entire @_ array, from its second element on, is assigned to @p2—(1, 3, 5, 7, "beta", 2, 4, 6, 8), in other words.

3. The next variable to be assigned is $p3. This variable is assigned the value of the next element in the @_ argument array—but there aren't any left, because they've all been slurped by @p2. $p3, therefore, is null.

4. The final variable, @p4, suffers the same fate and is also null.

There's no point in trying to specify subarrays, as in the following example, because Perl expands the array on the left to the same thing as before:

```
( $p1, (@p2), $p3, (@p4) ) = @_;
```

The moral of the story is: Don't pass more than one array into a subroutine. And if you do pass an array, make sure that it's the last argument.

**Returning Values**     Perl is just as casual about returning values from subroutines as it is about passing arguments to them. A subroutine returns a single value: the value of the last assignment made in the subroutine. If you pass (4, 3) to this subroutine, the value 7 is returned:

```
sub AddIt  {
   ( $a, $b ) = @_;
   $a + $b;
   }
```

That means that the value 7 is substituted for the subroutine call after evaluation. The code

```perl
print "Summing 4 and 3 yields ", &AddIt(4, 3), ".\n";
```

prints the following:

```
Summing 4 and 3 yields 7.
```

Notice that we had to keep the subroutine call outside the quotes to allow Perl to recognize &
as a subroutine invocation.

It isn't always clear which statement is the last to be executed in a subroutine, particularly if it
contains loops or conditional statements. One way to ensure that the correct value is returned
is to place a reference to the variable on a line by itself at the end of the subroutine, as follows:

```perl
sub Maybe  {
    # Various loops and conditionals here which set the value of "$result"…
    $result;
    }
```

> **CAUTION**
>
> Take care not to add seemingly innocuous statements near the end of a subroutine. A `print` statement
> returns a value of 1 (if successful) for example, so a subroutine that prints something just before it returns
> always returns 1.

The return value can be a scalar, an array, or an associative array. Listing 1.1 shows a complete
example in which a subroutine builds an associative array of names keyed by initials and then
returns the associative array. The keys of this array—the initials—are then printed in sorted
order. Take your time reading through this example; a lot is going on in there, but it's compre-
hensively commented.

---

**Listing 1.1   INITIALS.PL: Returning an Associative Array from a Subroutine**

```perl
#!/usr/local/bin/perl -w

# Pass the names into the subroutine.
# Store the results in an associative array called "keyedNames".
%keyedNames = &GetInitials("Jane Austen", "Emily Bronte", "Mary Shelley" );

# Print out the initials, sorted:
print "Initials are ", join(', ', sort keys %keyedNames), ".\n";

# The GetInitials subroutine.
sub GetInitials  {

    # Let's store the arguments in a "names" array for clarity.
    @names = @_;

    # Process each name in turn:
    foreach $name ( @names )  {
```

*continues*

**Listing 1.1   Continued**

```
        # The "split" function is explained in Chapter 15, "Function List".
        # In this statement, we're getting split to look for the ' ' in the name;
        # It returns an array of chunks of the original string (i.e. $name) which
were
        # separated by spaces, i.e. the forename and surname respectively in our
case.
        # The variables "$forename" and "$surname" are then assigned to this array
        # using parentheses to force an array assignment.
        ( $forename, $surname ) = split( ' ', $name );

        # OK, now we have the forename and surname. We use the "substr" function,
        # also explained in chapter 15, to extract the first character from each
of these.
        # The "." operator concatenates two strings (for example, "aa"."bb" is
"aabb")
        # so the variable "$inits" takes on the value of the initials of the name:
        $inits = substr( $forename, 0, 1 ) . substr( $surname, 0, 1 );

        # Now we store the name in an associative array using the initials as the
key:
        $NamesByInitials{$inits} = $name;
        }

    # Having built the associative array, we simply refer to it at the end of the
    # subroutine so that it's value is the last thing evaluated here. It will then
    # be passed back to the calling function.
    %NamesByInitials;
    }
```

# Variable Scope

Perl uses separate name spaces to store scalars, arrays, associative arrays, and so on. As a result, you can use the same name for variables of different types without fear of confusion (at least on Perl's part; for your own sake, use unique names). This example uses three different kinds of variables, each called name:

```
$name = "Dana";
@name = ("Donna", "Dana", "Diana");
%name = ("Donna", "Elephants", "Dana", "Finches", "Diana", "Parakeets");
print "I said $name{$name}, not $name{$name[0]}!\n";
```

The bad news is that by default, Perl uses just one name space for each data type, for all functions. So if you have a variable called $temp in the main function, and you call a routine that uses another variable called $temp, the value of $temp in the main function gets clobbered. The references to the two variables are in fact two references to the same variable, as far as Perl is concerned.

That's where the local (Perl 4 and 5) and my (Perl 5 only) functions come in. These functions force Perl to treat variables as though they are local to the current code block, whether that block is a loop, an if-block, or a subroutine.

The following example uses two variables called `$temp` (one outside and one inside a `while` loop):

```
$temp = "Still here!\n";
print "Enter a few words at a time, Ctrl+D to terminate:\n";
while (<>)  {
   local( $temp, @etc ) = split(' ', $_ );
   print "You said $temp";
   @etc && print " and then you said @etc";
   print ".  Enter some more, or press Ctrl+D to end:\n";
   }
print $temp;
```

The difference between Perl 4's `local()` and Perl 5's `my()` is that `local` variables are local to the current package, whereas `my` variables are *really* local.

**See** "Subroutine Definition," **p. 533**

# Patterns

We'll finish this overview of Perl by discussing its pattern-matching capabilities. The capability to match and replace patterns is vital to any scripting language that claims to be capable of useful text manipulation. By this stage, you probably won't be surprised to read that Perl matches patterns better than any other general-purpose language does. Perl 4's pattern matching is excellent, but Perl 5 introduces some significant improvements, including the capability to match on even more arbitrary strings than before.

The basic pattern-matching operations discussed in this section are:

- *Matching*, in which we want to know whether a particular string matches a pattern
- *Substitution*, in which we want to replace portions of a string based on a pattern

The patterns referred to here are more properly known as regular expressions, and we'll start by looking at them.

## Regular Expressions

A *regular expression* is a set of rules that describes a generalized string. If the characters that make up a particular string conform to the rules of a particular regular expression, the regular expression is said to *match* that string.

A few concrete examples usually help after an overblown definition like that one. The regular expression `b.` matches the strings `bovine`, `above`, `Bobby`, and `Bob Jones`, but not the strings `Bell`, `b`, or `Bob`. That's because the expression insists that the letter *b* (lowercase) must be in the string and must be followed immediately by another character.

The regular expression `b+`, on the other hand, requires the lowercase letter *b* at least once. This expression matches `b` and `Bob` in addition to the example matches for `b.` in the preceding paragraph. The regular expression b* requires zero or more *b*s, so it matches any string. That seems to be fairly useless, but it makes more sense as part of a larger regular expression. Bob*y, for example, matches all of Boy, Boby, and Bobby but not Boboby.

**Assertions**    Several so-called *assertions* are used to anchor parts of the pattern to word or string boundaries. The ^ assertion matches the start of a string, so the regular expression ^fool matches fool and foolhardy but not tomfoolery or April fool. Table 1.5 lists the assertions.

| Table 1.5 | Perl's Regular-Expression Assertions | | | |
|---|---|---|---|---|
| **Assertion** | **Matches** | **Example** | **Matches** | **Doesn't Match** |
| ^ | Start of string | ^fool | foolish | tomfoolery |
| $ | End of string | fool$ | April fool | foolish |
| \b | Word boundary | be\bside | be side | beside |
| \B | Nonword boundary | be\Bside | beside | be side |

**Atoms**    The . (period) that you saw in b. earlier in this chapter is an example of a regular-expression atom. *Atoms* are, as the name suggests, the fundamental building blocks of a regular expression. A full list of atoms appears in Table 1.6.

| Table 1.6 | Perl's Regular-Expression Atoms | | | |
|---|---|---|---|---|
| **Atom** | **Matches** | **Example** | **Matches** | **Doesn't Match** |
| period (.) | Any character except new line | b.b | bob | bb |
| List of characters in brackets | Any one of those characters | ^[Bb] | Bob, bob | Rbob |
| Regular expression in parentheses | Anything that regular expression matches | ^a(b.b)c$ | abobc | abbc |

**Quantifiers**    A *quantifier* is a modifier for an atom. It can be used to specify that a particular atom must appear at least once, as in b+. The atom quantifiers are listed in Table 1.7.

**Table 1.7   Perl's Regular-Expression Atom Quantifiers**

| Quantifier | Matches | Example | Matches | Doesn't Match |
|---|---|---|---|---|
| * | Zero or more instances of the atom | ab*c | ac, abc | abb |
| + | One or more instances of the atom | ab+c | abc | ac |
| ? | Zero or one instances of the atom | ab?c | ac, abc | abbc |
| {n} | n instances of the atom | ab{2}c | abbc | abbbc |
| {n,} | At least n instances of the atom | ab{2,}c | abbc, abbbc | abc |
| {nm} | At least n, at most m instances of the atom | ab{2,3}c | abbc | abbbbc |

**Special Characters**   Several special characters are denoted by backslashed letters, with \n being especially familiar to C programmers, perhaps. Table 1.8 lists the special characters.

**Table 1.8   Perl's Regular-Expression Special Characters**

| Symbol | Matches | Example | Matches | Doesn't Match |
|---|---|---|---|---|
| \d | Any digit | b\dd | b4d | bad |
| \D | Nondigit | b\Dd | bdd | b4d |
| \n | New line | | | |
| \r | Carriage return | | | |
| \t | Tab | | | |
| \f | Form feed | | | |
| \s | White-space character | | | |
| \S | Non-white-space character | | | |
| \w | Alphanumeric character | a\wb | a2b | a^b |
| \W | Nonalphanumeric character | a\Wb | aa^b | aabb |

**Backslashed Tokens**    It is essential that regular expressions be capable of using all characters, so that all possible strings that occur in the real word can be matched. With so many characters having special meanings, a mechanism is required that allows you to represent any arbitrary character in a regular expression.

This mechanism is a backslash (\), followed by a numeric quantity. This quantity can take any of the following formats:

- **Single or double digit:** matched quantities after a match. These matched quantities are called *backreferences* and are explained in the following section.

- **Two-or three-digit octal number:** the character with that number as character code, unless it's possible to interpret it as a backreference.

- **x, followed by two hexadecimal digits:** the character with that number as its character code. \x3e, for example, is >.

- **c, followed by a single character:** the control character. \cG, for example, matches Ctrl+G.

- **Any other character:** the character itself. \&, for example, matches the & character.

# Matching

Now you're ready to start putting all that information together with some real pattern matching. The match operator normally consists of two forward slashes with a regular expression in between, and it normally operates on the contents of the $_ variable. So if $_ is serendipity, / ^ser/, /end/, and /^s.*y$/ are all true.

**Matching on $_**    The $_ operator is special; see Chapter 13, "Special Variables," for full details. In many ways, $_ is the default container for data that is being read in by Perl. The <> operator, for example, gets the next line from STDIN and stores it in $_. So the following code snippet allows you to type lines of text and tells you when your line matches one of the regular expressions:

```
$prompt = "Enter some text or press Ctrl+D to stop: ";
print $prompt;
while (<>)  {
   /^[aA]/ && print "Starts with a or A.  ";
   /[0-9]$/ && print "Ends with a digit.  ";
   /perl/ && print "You said it!    ";
   print $prompt;
   }
```

**Bound Matches**    Matching doesn't always have to operate on $_, although this default behavior is quite convenient. A special operator, =~, evaluates to either true or false, depending on whether its first operand matches on its second operand. So $filename =~ /dat$/ is true if $filename matches on /dat$/. You can use =~ in conditionals in the usual way, as follows:

```
?$filename =~ /dat$/ && die "Can't use .dat files.\n";
```

A corresponding operator, !~, has the opposite sense. !~ is true if the first operator does not match on the second, as follows:

```
$ENV{'PATH'} !~ /perl/ && warn "Not sure if perl is in your path…";
```

**Alternative Delimiters**   The match operator can use characters other than //—a useful point if you're trying to match a complex expression that involves forward slashes. A more general form of the match operator than // is m//. If you use the leading m, you can use any character to delimit the regular expression. For example,

```
$installpath =~ m!^/usr/local! ¦¦ warn "The path you have chosen is odd.\n";
```

warns that "The path you have chosen is odd.\n" if the variable $installpath starts with /usr/local.

**Match Options**   You can apply several optional switches to the match operator (either // or m//) to alter its behavior. These options are listed in Table 1.9.

### Table 1.9   Perl's Match-Operator Optional Switches

| Switch | Meaning |
| --- | --- |
| g | Perform global matching |
| i | Perform case-insensitive matching |
| o | Evaluate the regular expression one time only |

The g switch continues matching even after the first match has been found. This switch is useful when you are using backreferences to examine the matched portions of a string, as described in the "Backreferences" section later in this chapter.

The i switch forces a case-insensitive match.

Finally, the o switch is used inside loops in which a great deal of pattern matching is taking place. This switch tells Perl that the regular expression (the match operator's operand) is to be evaluated one time only. The switch can improve efficiency when the regular expression is fixed for all iterations of the loop that contains it.

**Backreferences**   As we mentioned in the "Backslashed Tokens" section earlier in this chapter, pattern matching produces quantities that are known as *backreferences*. These quantities are the parts of your string in which the match succeeded. You need to tell Perl to store them by surrounding the relevant parts of your regular expression with parentheses, and you can refer to them after the match as \1, \2, and so on. The following example determines whether the user typed three consecutive four-letter words:

```
while (<>)  {
   /\b(\S{4})\s(\S{4})\s(\S{4})\b/ && print "Gosh, you said $1 $2 $3!\n";
   }
```

The first four-letter word lies between a word boundary (\b) and some white space (\s), and consists of four non-white-space characters (\S). If there is a match on the expression \b(\S{4})\s—if a four-letter word is found—the matching substring is stored in the special variable \1, and the search continues. When the search is complete, you can refer to the backreferences as $1, $2, and so on.

What if you don't know in advance how many matches to expect? Perform the match in an array context; Perl returns the matches in an array. Consider this example:

```
@hits = ("Yon Yonson, Wisconsin" =~ /(\won)/g);
print "Matched on ", join(', ', @hits), ".\n";
```

We'll start at the right side and work backward. The regular expression (\won) means that we match any alphanumeric character followed by on and store all three characters. The g option after the // operator means that we want to do this for the entire string, even after we find a match. The =~ operator means that we carry out this operation on a given string (Yon Yonson, Wisconsin). Finally, the whole thing is evaluated in an array context, so Perl returns the array of matches, and we store it in the @hits array. Following is the output from this example:

```
Matched on Yon, Yon, son, con.
```

## Substitution

When you get the hang of pattern matching, you'll find that substitutions are quite straightforward and very powerful. The substitution operator is s///, which resembles the match operator but has three rather than two slashes. Just as you can do with the match operator, you can substitute any other character for the forward slashes, and you can use the optional i, g, and o switches.

The pattern to be replaced goes between the first and second delimiters, and the replacement pattern goes between the second and third delimiters. This simple example changes $house from henhouse to doghouse:

```
$house = "henhouse";
$house  =~ s/hen/dog/;
```

Notice that it isn't possible to use the =~ operator with a literal string as you can when matching, because you can't modify a literal constant. Instead, store the string in a variable and modify that variable.

# From Here...

You have reached the end of your whirlwind tour of Perl. You saw how Perl's deceptively simple constructs can be used to write deceptively simple programs, and you got a brief look at the basic elements of the language. At minimum, you should have a clear idea of how the language works, and you should know where to go for more information on Perl as the need arises throughout the rest of this book.

This book now moves on to Web matters, but look in the following places for more information about Perl:

- Refer to Part V of this book for comprehensive information on Perl special variables, operators, and built-in functions.
- Also refer to Part V to learn how to use modules and libraries to compartmentalize your code for greater robustness and extensibility.
- Consider buying a book that deals in detail with the Perl language. The definitive work is the "Camel book," cited at the beginning of this chapter.

# Introduction to CGI

*by David Harlan*

**P**erl and the World Wide Web are a natural team. A good Web site is, by definition, in constant flux. Users will not want to come back to a boring site too often, so all Webmasters are looking for any possible means to liven up their sites. The liveliest sites are *dynamic sites*—sites that show users different content from visit to visit. These types of sites also enable users to interact or create content on-the-fly.

Because you're reading this book, you're probably wondering just how to create a dynamic Web site. You're in the right place. Basically, the Webmaster has to become a programmer and use some of the great built-in features of the Web protocol to their fullest. To this end, a programmer has to have a language that facilitates quick programming, easy debugging, and fast revision. Perl fits this role perfectly. ■

### What CGI is

CGI is the programming interface that is built into the World Wide Web communications protocol.

### The advantages of Perl

Perl is the de facto standard for Web programming; its power and ease of use are its most striking advantages.

### The different methods of using a Perl script with CGI

Form processing is the most obvious use of CGI. You can also call CGI scripts directly or through server-side includes.

### How information is passed through CGI to Perl

The CGI standard provides a list of standard variables that your Perl scripts use to access user data.

### How to return the proper information from the script

A programmer must format the output of a script according to the CGI standard.

# Justifying the Use of CGI

When you started looking at Web sites, one of the first items that you probably were curious about was the .HTML extension on the files. Soon, you found out that *HTML* stands for *Hypertext Markup Language,* and you discovered that HTML is the foundation on which the Web is built. If you were interested in building your own Web site, you probably looked next at the source of a few Web sites to see how they were built. At that point, you may have exhausted your resources. But that's OK, because you discovered that HTML is not difficult to use. Strangely, this fact may be the Web's greatest advantage, as well as its major shortcoming.

Almost anyone can throw together some HTML and hang a home page out on the Web. But most sites are, quite frankly, boring. Why? Most sites are built as a simple series of HTML documents that never change; the sites are completely static. No one is likely to visit a static page more than once or twice. Think about the sites that you visit most often. Those sites have interesting content, certainly, but more important, they also have dynamic and interactive content.

What's a Webmaster to do? None of us has the time to update a Web site by hand every day. Fortunately, the people who developed the Web protocol thought of this problem and gave us the *Common Gateway Interface,* or *CGI.* CGI, which is the standard programming interface to Web servers, gives us a way to make our sites dynamic and interactive. To be specific, CGI is a set of standards (in Internet lingo, a set of protocols) that allows Web servers to communicate with external programs.

## Reasons for Using Perl

The reason why I use Perl for my CGI programming is simple: it is the best tool for the job.

Perl is the de facto standard for CGI programming for several reasons, but perhaps the most important are the language's flexibility and ease of use. The primary reason why Perl is so easy to use is that it is an interpreted language—which means that every time you run a Perl program, a separate program called (appropriately enough) an *interpreter* starts and processes the code in your Perl script. An interpreted language differs from a compiled language, such as C, in which you have to (not surprisingly) compile your code into an executable file before you can run it.

Why is the Perl way better? In some cases, C may be preferable to Perl. At times, you may not want the overhead of the interpreter and prefer a stand-alone executable. (I haven't run into those situations yet, but I'm sure that they exist.) The advantage of using an interpreted language in CGI applications is the language's simplicity in development, debugging, and revision. With the compilation step removed, you and I can move more quickly from task to task without the frustration that sometimes arises from debugging compiled programs.

Not just any interpreted language will do, of course. Perl has the distinct advantage of having an extremely rich and capable functionality.

## How to Make Perl Do CGI

When I started programming CGI scripts, few resources were available to help me. Unlike viewing the HTML source of a document, you cannot get a browser to show you the script that produced any given result on your browser. (For security reasons, this situation is good; it just makes learning a little more difficult.) So, like many CGI programmers, I learned by trial and error. The next few pages should help you avoid this frustrating process and move quickly to more advanced topics.

You need a few basic pieces of information before you successfully program a CGI script:

- How the script gets information from the user
- How Perl can process that information
- How the script returns information to the user

## Understanding CGI

Unlike normal HTML files that are simply called up by a browser, a CGI script can be used in several ways. The most common use of CGI is for processing user input. (You probably have seen other uses of CGI without even knowing it.) This section takes a detailed look at that most common use of CGI: the fill-out form. In the next few pages, you'll see a form application being built from the ground up.

## Calling a Script from a Form

Undoubtedly, one of the first uses of CGI that you experienced was filling out and submitting a form. Perhaps that form looked something like the Guestbook sign-in form shown in figure 2.1.

**FIG. 2.1**
This form allows a user to sign a Guestbook on a Web site.

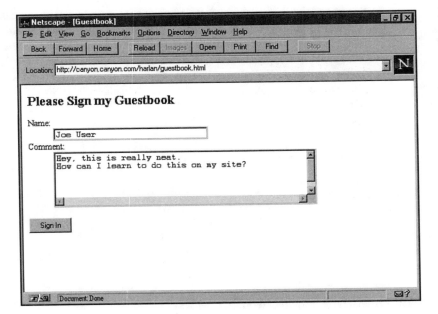

When the proper script support this simple form, it performs its function easily. You may be wondering how to call a script from this form. Listing 2.1 contains the source for this form and shows you where the script is referenced.

---

**Listing 2.1   Calling a CGI Script (GUESTBOOK.HTML)**

```
<html>
<body bgcolor="#FFFFFF">
<title>Guestbook</title>
<h2>Please Sign My Guestbook</h2>
<form method=get action="/cgi-bin/harlan/guestbook">
<dt>Name:<br>
<dd><input type=text name=name size=30>
<dt>Comment:<br>
<dd><textarea name=comment rows=5 cols=50></textarea><p>
<input type=submit value="Sign In">
</form>
</html>
```

---

In line 4 of the HTML code in Listing 2.1, you see the following:

```
...action="/cgi-bin/harlan/guestbook"...
```

This line tells the form what script to call to process the entered information.

The location /CGI-BIN/HARLAN/GUESTBOOK is what's called a *virtual path*. The actual location of the script on the Web server computer depends on the configuration of the server software and the type of computer that is being used. In this case, the computer uses the Linux operating system and is running the NCSA Web server in a standard configuration. The physical path to the script in this case is /USR/LOCAL/ETC/HTTPD/CGI-BIN/HARLAN. Although a nearly infinite number of combinations of operating systems and Web servers is possible, the Linux/NCSA combination is relatively common. If you install and administer the Web server yourself, you know exactly where to place your scripts. If you are using a service provider's Web server, you may have to ask the server's administrator where to put your scripts and how to reference them from your documents.

What happens if you sign this Guestbook? In its simplest form, the result of signing the book looks like figure 2.2.

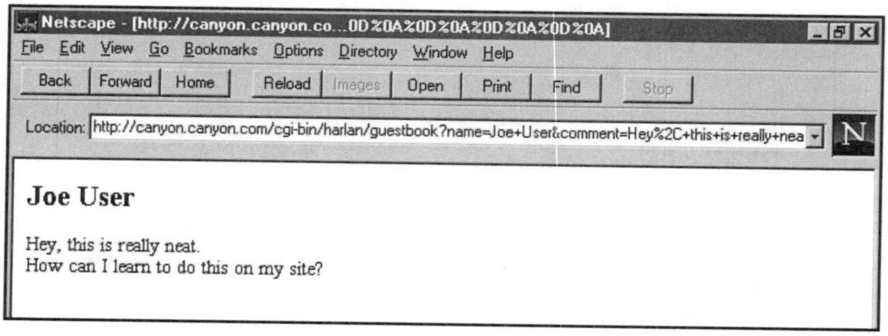

**FIG. 2.2**
This screen shows the result of the Guestbook form submission.

# Getting Information to the Script

To understand how submitting the form in figure 2.1 produces the result shown in figure 2.2, you first need to know how information is passed from the form to your Perl script.

Perl provides a special variable called %ENV. This variable is an *associative array*, or *hash*—essentially, a list of identifiers or keys and their associated values. I'll explain the syntax of a Perl hash later in this chapter. For now, look at the contents of %ENV. This particular hash contains information about the script's environment. If you have UNIX experience, you may have heard of environment variables. A UNIX user can set certain options, such as a default editor or default shell, by using environment variables.

A Perl script also has an environment. Much of the environment is inherited from the server that's running the script, but a CGI script gets some additional goodies. The CGI specification tells Web server software to provide a wealth of useful information to CGI scripts.

**Using QUERY_STRING**   Perhaps the most-used CGI environment variable is QUERY_STRING. When a form is submitted, the Web server software processes the information that the user provided in the form and passes that information to the script specified in the form. The processing isn't too complex. Spaces in the data are replaced by plus signs, and special characters are translated into a code that is related to their ASCII value; then all the data is put together in one long string.

When the script is called with the GET method (as the Guestbook script is; see line 5 of Listing 2.1), the server places the string described earlier in the QUERY_STRING variable. Because this variable becomes part of the script's environment, you can access it through %ENV, as you'll see later in this chapter.

**Using Other CGI Variables**   Several variables in addition to QUERY_STRING are provided in the CGI specification. Some of the descriptions may not make much sense to you right now. But if you refer to Table 2.1 periodically as you continue to read this book, you'll discover just how useful some of this information is.

**Table 2.1   CGI Environment Variables**

| Variable Name | Description |
|---|---|
| AUTH_TYPE | The authentication protocol that is currently being used. This variable is defined only if the server supports authentication and if authentication is required for access to the script. |
| CONTENT_LENGTH | The length, in bytes, of the content provided to the script in STDIN. This variable is used particularly in POST-method form processing. |
| CONTENT_TYPE | The type of content contained in STDIN. This variable is used for POST-method form processing. |
| GATEWAY_INTERFACE | The version of CGI supported by the Web server. |

*continues*

**Table 2.1 Continued**

| Variable Name | Description |
| --- | --- |
| HTTP_ACCEPT | A comma-separated list of MIME types that the browser software accepts. You might check this variable to see whether the client will accept a certain kind of graphic file. |
| HTTP_USER_AGENT | The browser software and version number. |
| PATH_INFO | Extra path information from the request. |
| PATH_TRANSLATED | Maps the script's virtual path (from the root of the server directory, for example) to a physical path that could be used to call the script. |
| QUERY_STRING | A string containing the data from a form submission. |
| REMOTE_ADDR | The IP address of the client machine. |
| REMOTE_HOST | The host name of the client machine. |
| REMOTE_USER | The authenticated user ID of the user who is requesting the script. This variable is defined only if the server supports authentication and if authentication is required for access to the script. |
| REQUEST_METHOD | The method by which the script was called (most often, GET or POST). |
| SCRIPT_NAME | The virtual path to the script. |
| SERVER_NAME | The configured host name for the server (usually, **www.something.com**). |
| SERVER_PORT | The number of the port on which the server software is "listening" (usually, 80, the default Web port). |
| SERVER_PROTOCOL | The version of the Web protocol that this server uses. |
| SERVER_SOFTWARE | The name and version of the Web server software. |

# Processing *QUERY_STRING* into Useful Chunks

Now that you know where the information comes from, you're ready to learn how you might use Perl to process this information. The script that performs the transformation from figure 2.1 to figure 2.2 actually is quite simple and is shown in Listing 2.2.

**Listing 2.2 The First Guestbook Script (GUESTBOOK1.PL)**

```
#!/usr/bin/perl
$temp=$ENV{'QUERY_STRING'};
@pairs=split(/&/,$temp);
foreach $item(@pairs) {
```

```
5   ($key,$content)=split (/=/,$item,2);
6   $content=~tr/+/ /;
7   $content=~ s/%(..)/pack("c",hex($1))/ge;
8   $fields{$key}=$content;
}
print "Content-type: text/html\n\n";
print "<body bgcolor=\"#FFFFFF\">\n";
print "<h2>$fields{'name'}</h2>\n";
print "<pre>$fields{'comment'}</pre>\n";
```

The next few pages examine this script line by line.

Line 1 is a line that you need to use in every Perl script that you write for your Web site. This line tells the operating system that the script must be processed by the program listed after the exclamation point. In this example, /USR/BIN/PERL is the location of the Perl interpreter on my Web server computer.

**NOTE** The #!/usr/bin/perl line in Listing 2.2 is needed only for UNIX and UNIX-variant versions of Perl. If your Web server is running another operating system (such as Windows NT or Macintosh System software), you need to check your Web server documentation for information on how to invoke CGI scripts. ∎

When the user submits the form, the Web server software passes the information to the script in the $ENV{'QUERY_STRING'} variable. Line 2 of the script copies this information to the variable $temp. The Perl syntax is straightforward; this line is a simple assignment of one variable to another. $temp is a *scalar variable*—the most common Perl variable. A scalar variable can contain almost any kind of data you can imagine. $ENV{'QUERY_STRING'} refers to an element in the associative array %ENV, which is described in "Getting Information to the Script" earlier in this chapter.

An associative array (designated in Perl with a leading %) contains a series of scalar values. Each value is associated with a key. In this example, the key is QUERY_STRING, and the value is the encoded data from the form. (I performed this assignment for purposes of readability; the step is not strictly necessary.)

Line 3 of the script splits the data from the script into an array of strings: @pairs. Notice that this kind of array is different from %ENV. The @pairs array is a standard array that uses integers (starting at 0) to designate each separate element. Each element is a string that contains the variable name from the form, followed by an equal sign, followed by the text that the user entered at that spot in the form.

split() is a standard Perl function that takes two required parameters and one optional one. The first parameter is the string that separates the values that are to be split. The CGI protocol specification states that key/value pairs are separated by an ampersand (&), so in this example, the ampersand character is the first parameter. The second parameter is the string that you want to split ($temp). The optional third parameter (not present in this example) is a number that indicates the maximum number of times that the string should be split.

Lines 4 through 9 of the script run through the newly created @pairs array, processing the information from the form into a new associative array to be used in the following lines.

Line 4 starts a loop structure. This particular loop—a foreach loop—iterates through the @pairs array, placing each value in turn in the $item scalar variable. The commands between the brace on line 4 and the one on line 8 are executed one time for each item in the array.

---

### Using Shortcuts and Writing Readable Perl Code

When reading another programmer's code, an inexperienced programmer sometimes finds various incarnations of foreach loops to be confusing. Many Perl programmers pride themselves on writing the shortest code possible. Perl provides numerous shortcuts and options that cut the length of a script—but that have the unfortunate side effect of making the script much more difficult to read and understand.

The foreach structure requires a list between the parentheses. Most commonly, this list is simply an array. Sometimes, however, you see something like foreach(1..10), foreach (1,2,3,4,5,6,'blah'), or foreach (keys(%foobar)). Each of the expressions inside the parentheses represents a list. The first expression is a range of integers ranging from 1 to 10. The second should be obvious. The third uses the keys() function to get the list of keys for the %foobar hash. If you remember that foreach always requires a list between the parentheses, you will always have a basis from which you can figure out exactly what the loop does.

More obscure, however, is the fact that the loop doesn't actually require you to provide a variable to contain each successive list item. If a variable isn't provided, the list item is assigned to the special variable $_. Therefore, I could have written lines 4 and 5 this way:

```
foreach (@pairs) {
($key,$content)=split (/=/,$_,2);
```

This syntax would have done nothing to the functionality of the script but certainly would have obscured the meaning of the code.

---

In line 5, split() is used again, this time to separate the key and value. Notice that the left side of the assignment in this line is not an array, as it was in line 3, but two scalars enclosed in parentheses. This syntax tells Perl that you want the enclosed list of scalars to be treated as an array for assignment purposes.

Lines 6 and 7 decode the information in the value portion of the key/value pair. This decoding is necessary, because the Web server software encodes the data (according to a standard scheme that is part of the CGI protocol specification) before placing the information in the $ENV{'QUERY_STRING'} variable. Therefore, you have to decode the information before you can present it to the user.

# Using Regular Expressions *tr///* and *s///*

If you have no experience in Perl or UNIX, lines 6 and 7 of Listing 2.2 are likely to be the least understandable in the entire script. This section examines those lines one at a time to help you figure them out.

Line 6 uses the `tr///` operator. This command takes two lists of characters as arguments. The first list (between the first two slashes) contains a list of characters to search for. The second list (between the second and third slashes) contains a list of replacement characters. The first character in the search list is replaced by the first character in the replacement list. The second character in the search list is replaced by the second character in the replacement list, and so on through the two lists. Thus, this syntax tells `tr///` to perform this translation on `$content`, using the binding operator `=~`. So if you look at line 6 again, you see that the plus signs in `$content` are being translated into spaces.

**See** "Operators," **p. 391**

Line 7 looks similar to its predecessor but is a little more complex. This line uses the `s///` operator to perform further translation on `$content` (as designated by the `=~` binding operator). This command takes a text pattern or regular expression between the first two slashes. Text that matches the first pattern is replaced by text designated by the replacement text between the second and third slashes. Some options for this command are designated by letters that follow the third slash.

What text pattern is the command searching for? This functionality looks benign and simple enough in this example, but Perl's pattern matching is so rich and useful that I'm going to explain the syntax briefly.

Regular expressions are familiar to veteran UNIX users, but they are likely to be Greek to everyone else. In its simplest form, a *regular expression* is a group of letters between two slashes, as in `/word/`. You might use a regular expression as follows:

```
if ($var=~/word/) { #do something here }
```

The conditional in this statement evaluates to `true` if `$var` contains the string `word`. This use of regular expressions is useful but very simple; Perl offers so much more.

First, Perl regular expressions, like normal UNIX regular expressions, provide a set of characters called *metacharacters*, which have special meaning within a search pattern. These characters are listed in Table 2.2.

**Table 2.2  Perl Regular-Expression Metacharacters**

| Character | Meaning |
|---|---|
| ^ | Matches the start of the line or variable that is being searched. |
| $ | Matches the end of the line. |
| . (period) | Matches any character except a new-line character. |
| \ | When followed by another metacharacter, the two metacharacters combined match the second character. |
| () | Groups the enclosed pattern for later reference. The first such grouping is saved in $1; the second, in $2; and so on. |

*continues*

**Table 2.2 Continued**

| Character | Meaning |
| --- | --- |
| [ ] | Encloses a list of characters, any one of which you want to match. |
| \| | Provides or functionality. |

In addition to metacharacters, Perl provides a set of predefined character classes, which are very useful; they are shown in Table 2.3. Each class is designated by a string containing a backslash followed by a single character.

**Table 2.3 Predefined Character Classes**

| String | Meaning |
| --- | --- |
| \d | Matches any digit; same as [0..9] or [0123456789] |
| \D | Matches any nondigit character |
| \s | Matches any white-space character (for example, space and tab) |
| \S | Matches any non-white-space character |
| \w | Matches a word character: letters, digits, and underscore characters (_) |
| \W | Matches a nonword character |

Finally, Perl defines a set of quantifiers (shown in Table 2.4) that you can use to modify your pattern.

**Table 2.4 Regular-Expression Character Quantifiers**

| String | Meaning |
| --- | --- |
| * | Matches the preceding character zero or more times |
| + | Matches the preceding character one or more times |
| ? | Matches the preceding character zero times or one time |
| {x} | Matches the preceding character exactly x times |
| {x,y} | Matches the preceding character at least x times and at most y times |

A couple of examples may help make all this information a little clearer. The pattern /w..d/, for example, would match *word* and *wand*; it would also match *forwarding* and even *how odd*. So in the end, this pattern wouldn't be very useful. If you want to look in a string for four-letter words that start with *w* and end with *d*, you might use something like /\sw\w\wd\s/. If you want to find these occurrences and also save only the word (without the surrounding white space), you would modify this pattern to /\s(w\w\wd)\s/. So whenever this pattern matched, you would be able to find the word in $1.

You can also search for more complex patterns. Consider this pattern: /[ ^]\w(\w{2}) \w$1 \w$1[ $]/. You might use this pattern to find the name of a certain canine cop and similar three-word phrases. This pattern would match *rin tin tin*, *fun gun run*, or even *six six six*; I think you get the idea.

In the Guestbook script, the search text is %(..). The percentage sign is a normal character. You're looking for a percentage sign, which is why % is in the pattern. All of the following four characters are metacharacters. You're not actually looking for two periods enclosed in parentheses; the period stands for any character. Therefore, you're looking for any two characters. The parentheses mean that you want to save the text that matches the enclosed portion of the pattern for later use.

This pattern will match something like %0D, placing 0D in the variable $1. The entire matched string then is replaced by the replacement text. Because the e option is specified after the last slash, the replacement text is evaluated as an expression before replacement.

The replacement expression contains two functions. The innermost function hex($1) is evaluated first. This function takes the two characters following any percentage sign and converts them from a hexadecimal number to a decimal number. That decimal number then acts as the second argument of the pack() function. pack() is used to pack the second argument into a binary value, as in the method designated by the first value. In this case, the c in the first argument tells pack to transform the number in the second argument into a character. Basically, this method is a fancy way of translating an integer into its corresponding ASCII character.

**See** "Operators," **p. 391**

In the Location box in figure 2.2, the comma after Hey is translated into %2C by the Web server. The hexadecimal number 2C is the decimal number 44; the comma is ASCII character number 44.

The final piece of information that you should know about line 7 in Listing 2.2 is that in addition to the e option, the g option is specified. This option indicates that the specified pattern should be replaced every time it occurs in the $content variable. Without the g option, the command would end immediately after the first time that the pattern matched and the text was replaced.

**TIP**
A common mistake that beginners make with tr/// or s/// is to accidentally use the plain = operator instead of the binding =~ operator. If you run into a strange problem with a script and think that the problem is related to s/// or tr///, but can't figure it out, check to see whether you're using the proper operator between the sides of the expression. The mistake is an easy one to make—and an easy one to miss when you're looking for problems.

Line 8 simply associates each key and freshly translated value in the %fields hash.

Now look at a short example to make sure that all the preceding information makes some sense. The name in figure 2.1 is entered in the text-entry field created with this code:

```
<dd><input type=text name=name size=30>
```

Because this field is the first field in the form, the first element in @pairs contains
name=Joe+User after the information in figure 2.1 is submitted. So you can see that the names
of the fields in the form are passed directly to the script. If you process the provided data properly, you end up with an associative array with keys that correspond to the names of the fields
in the form. Thus, in this example $fields{'name'} equals Joe User.

# Printing the Page

Now that the form data is properly translated, you want to output data to the user. Line 10
prints a header. Whenever you print information from your script back to the user, you have to
print this line (or a similar one). The header tells the browser the type of information contained
in the document that the script is about to produce (thus, "Content-type"). Notice the \n\n at
the end of the quoted string. The backslash is an escape sequence. In a string enclosed in
double quotes in a Perl script, escape sequences are translated into special characters that you
would not otherwise be able to include in a string (see Table 2.5). In this case, \n translates
into a new line. The two new lines after the header are required, according to the HTTP
specification.

In addition to \n, several escape sequences in Perl allow programmers to output special characters. Table 2.5 describes the escape sequences.

**Table 2.5   Escape Sequences for Special Characters in Interpolated (Double-Quoted) Strings**

| String | Translation |
| --- | --- |
| \a | Produces a bell character. |
| \cX | Produces a control character. \cM, for example, translates into Ctrl+M or a carriage return. |
| \e | Produces an escape character. |
| \E | Ends a case modification started with \L or \U. |
| \f | Produces a form feed. |
| \l | Makes the next character lowercase. |
| \L | Makes all succeeding characters until the next \E lowercase. |
| \n | Produces a new line. |
| \Onn | Produces the character with the octal ASCII character code nn. |
| \Q | Puts backslashes before any regular-expression metacharacters until the next \E. |
| \r | Produces a return. |
| \t | Produces a tab. |
| \u | Makes the next character uppercase. |

| String | Translation |
|--------|-------------|
| \U | Makes all succeeding characters uppercase until the next \E. |
| \v | Produces a vertical tab. |

The final three lines of the script print the necessary HTML to make a simple page for the user to view. Notice that the script is still printing double-quoted strings. The double quotes tell Perl not only to translate the escape sequences, but also to print the contents of any variable referenced in the string. If you mistakenly enclosed this string in single quotes, instead of the value of `$fields{'name'}`, enclosed in some HTML tags and followed by a new line, the script would have printed the string literally—`"<h2>$fields{'name'}</h2>\n."` Clearly, that result is not what you want.

Always remember that double-quoted strings are parsed and that variables and escape sequences are translated appropriately. Single-quoted strings are not parsed and are interpreted literally.

**T I P**  When you're creating HTML forms, remember that you will be using the names of your various input fields as keys for associative arrays. For ease of programming, you'll want to keep the names as short as possible.

## Creating a Script on Your Web Server

Now that you know some basic Perl, you'll want to know how you create a Perl script on your computer. The procedure isn't difficult. Perl scripts are just simple text files. If you have a favorite way of creating HTML files on your server, you can use the same method to program in Perl.

Some people edit their scripts on their desktop computers (using something like Wordpad in Windows 95 or SimpleText on a Macintosh), save the scripts as text files, and then transfer them to the server with FTP. Using this method to write a large number of scripts, however, would be tedious, so most people find a file-editor program to use on the Web server computer.

Many UNIX veterans swear by an editor called vi. In fact, many of these people say that if you don't use vi as your only editor, you must be a UNIX dabbler. Don't listen to them. I'm sure that vi is a wonderful text editor, but I discovered early in my experience with UNIX that its command structure was so counterintuitive that it was useless for me. So I looked around until I found an editor called joe, which is the only text editor that I use now. joe's commands are based on the commands in an early DOS-based word processor called Wordstar, which I used to use, so joe's commands were a snap for me to pick up. (Don't tell anyone; they might not respect me as a programmer.) You also have other options. If you have experience with the UNIX mail program pine, you may want to try pico, an editor that uses the same commands as the message editor in pine.

My point in this little digression is that you should find and editor that is quick and easy for you to use. Most CGI scripts are short and simple, so you don't need many advanced features.

One final note about script-file creation: when you first make a file on a UNIX computer, the file has a default set of file permissions. A file's *permissions* tell the operating system what a user can do with that file. Usually, default permissions do not allow that file to be executed as a program, so you'll have to change them. The command that you use for this purpose is chmod. In most cases, you want to issue the command chmod 755 scriptname after you create your Perl scripts; this command gives the file proper permissions for execution by the Web server. For more information about the chmod command, type **man chmod** at the command prompt on your UNIX server.

# Calling a CGI Script Directly

With the information provided in the preceding few pages, and with a little knowledge of your Web server and operating system, you should now be able to use a Perl CGI script to process information from a form and print a simple page. This knowledge is a good start; now you learn how to build on it.

In addition to processing form input, CGI can be used to create and display documents on-the-fly. To start this example, I modified Listing 2.2 slightly to come up with the script shown in Listing 2.3.

**Listing 2.3   Revised Guestbook Script (GUESTBOOK2.PL)**

```perl
#!/usr/bin/perl
$temp=$ENV{'QUERY_STRING'};
@pairs=split(/&/,$temp);
foreach $item(@pairs) {
($key,$content)=split (/=/,$item,2);
$content=~tr/+/ /;
$content=~ s/%(..)/pack("c",hex($1))/ge;
$fields{$key}=$content;
}
$fields{'comment'}=~s/\cM//g;
$fields{'comment'}=~s/\n\n/<p>/g;
$fields{'comment'}=~s/\n/<br>/g;

($sec,$min,$hour,$mday,$mon,$year,$wday,$yday,$isdst)=localtime(time);
if (length ($min) == 1) {$min = '0'.$min;}
$date="$mon/$mday/$year, $hour:$min";

open (gbfile, ">> guestbook.txt");
print gbfile $date,"::$fields{'name'}::$fields{'comment'}\n";
close (gbfile);
print "Content-type: text/html\n\n";
print "<body bgcolor=\"#FFFFFF\">\n";
print "<h2>$fields{'name'}</h2>\n";
print "$fields{'comment'}\n";
```

This script functions exactly like the original from the user's standpoint. A couple of key differences exist, however.

First, immediately after processing the data as in the original version of the script, the script performs three additional substitutions on the $fields{'comment'} variable. The first of these three lines removes any carriage returns that the browser inserts into the comment field. The escape character \c tells Perl that the next character in the pattern should be taken as a control character. Thus, \cM matches Ctrl+M, which is a carriage return.

The next two lines substitute a <p> HTML tag wherever two new lines appear in a row. The second line substitutes a <br> tag for a single new line. These new tags replace the <pre> tags that were used in Listing 2.2, making the output prettier.

Next, you see a call to the localtime() function. This function returns a nine-element array that contains various portions of the current time. I used fairly standard descriptive variables on the left side of the equation; these variables do a good job of showing what each element of the returned array is.

After getting the time information, the script uses the length() function to determine whether $min is a single digit. If so, the script adds 0 on the left, using the dot operator; otherwise, $min is used as is. The script creates a date/time string from the data returned from localtime().

This string is used in the final new section of the script. The first line opens a file handle (gbfile) that points to a file called guestbook.txt. The >> characters before the file name indicate that I want to append to the file. The following print command writes the data from the form into a single line in the Guestbook file. Notice that this print statement has two arguments. The first argument is the handle of the file that you're writing to; the second is the expression to be printed. In all the other print statements used so far, no file handle is specified. In these cases, the output defaults to STDOUT, which is the standard output on UNIX systems. In CGI scripts, STDOUT is ultimately redirected back to the browser.

All these changes to the form-processing script are carried out in such a way that you can save and, later, access all Guestbook entries. You'll use a CGI script to access the entries. Figure 2.3 shows what simple output might look like.

Listing 2.4 shows the Perl script that created the output shown in figure 2.3.

**Listing 2.4   Guestbook Display Script (SHOWGUESTBOOK1.PL)**

```perl
#!/usr/bin/perl
print "Content-type: text/html\n\n";
print "<body bgcolor=\"#FFFFFF\">\n";
print "<title>Guestbook</title>\n";
open (gbfile, "guestbook.txt");
while (defined($line=<gbfile>)) {
    ($date,$name,$comment)=split(/:::/,$line);
    print "<b>$name</b>, $date<p>\n";
    print "$comment<hr>";
}
close (gbfile);
```

**FIG. 2.3**

This screen shows a display of multiple Guestbook entries.

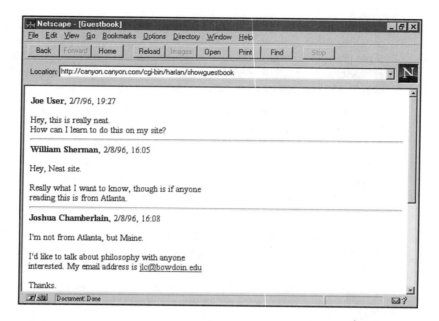

This script contains only one new concept: the `while` loop. This loop simply runs through each line of the file referenced by the `gbfile` file handle. First, the script opens the file. The `open` command is the same as in the Guestbook script, with one key difference: the `>>` characters are missing. When a file is opened with no symbol before the file name, the file is opened for reading. Then the script in Listing 2.4 starts the `while` loop.

The conditional for the `while` loop works as follows. When a file handle is enclosed in angle brackets and evaluated in a scalar context, it returns the next line of the file. Perl's `defined()` function evaluates as `true` if the expression is defined. The expression `$line=<gbfile>` is undefined (and the loop exits) when all the lines in the file have been processed. The statements in the loop are fairly simple. The first line splits the data into three separate variables; the next two lines print the data.

> **N O T E**   Looping through and processing each line in a file is one of the most common operations in Perl. For that reason, a common shortcut is used for that operation. That shortcut looks like this:
>
> ```
> while (<gbfile>) {
> #process gbfile info here
> }
> ```
>
> In a `while` loop, if a file handle enclosed in angle brackets is the only conditional in the loop, the current line from the file is assigned to `$_` each time through the loop. The expression `<gbfile>` is `true` until all lines in the file have been read. ■

At this point, you may be curious about why I didn't just write the Guestbook information to a straight HTML file in the first place, so that the user could just call up that file to look at the

Guestbook list. Certainly, that method is an option, and many guestbook programs do just that. But this method provides some additional flexibility that straight HTML can't offer.

If, for example, you want to display only x number of lines on any given page and limit the total number of entries in the file, the result would look like figures 2.4, 2.5, and 2.6. Figure 2.4 shows the result of the initial call to this new script. Figure 2.5 shows the page that is returned after the user selects the Show next two entries link in figure 2.4. The URL in the Location box in figure 2.6 also has a number, but the text does not include a Show next... link.

Part
I
Ch
2

**FIG. 2.4**
The screen in this figure shows a new way of displaying the entries.

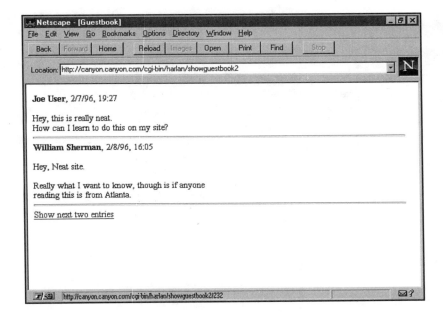

To figure out how this output is produced, examine Listing 2.5, which contains the SHOWGUESTBOOK2 script.

**Listing 2.5  Revision of the Guestbook Display Script (SHOWGUESTBOOK2.PL)**

```perl
#!/usr/bin/perl
$filepos=$ENV{'PATH_INFO'};
$filepos=~s/^\///;
$filepos=0 if $filepos eq '';
print "Content-type: text/html\n\n";
print "<body bgcolor=\"#FFFFFF\">\n";
print "<title>Guestbook</title>\n";
open (gbfile, "guestbook.txt");
seek (gbfile,$filepos,0);
$i=1;
```

*continues*

**Listing 2.5 Continued**

```
while (<gbfile>) {
    ($date,$name,$comment)=split(/::/,$_);
    print "<b>$name</b>, $date<p>\n";
    print "$comment<hr>";
    $i++;
    last if $i==3;
}
$newfilepos=tell(gbfile);
if (<gbfile>) {
    print "<a href=/cgi-bin/harlan/showguestbook2/$newfilepos>Show next two
    ➥entries</a>\n";}
close (gbfile);
```

**FIG. 2.5**

Two more entries are displayed after the user selects the link in figure 2.4.

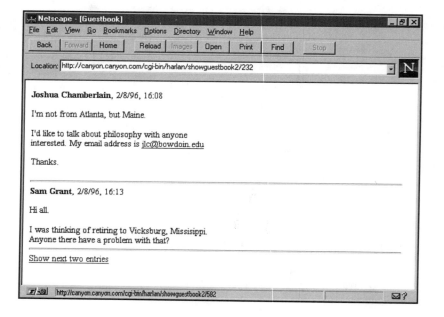

The changes in this script introduce one new CGI concept and a couple of new Perl commands. As pointed out earlier in this section, the URL in the Location box shown in figures 2.5 and 2.6 has additional information tacked on at the end. At first glance, this information might seem to be a bit odd. In figure 2.5, it appears that you're calling a script called 232 in the /CGI-BIN/HARLAN/SHOWGUESTBOOK2 directory. Clearly, that's not what's happening, though.

The CGI specification includes an environment variable called PATH_INFO. All CGI-compliant Web servers can translate any URL appropriately. If the URL that points to a script includes any information after the script name, all that information is passed to the script in the PATH_INFO environment variable.

**FIG. 2.6**
The final entry is
displayed after the user
selects the link in figure
2.5. Notice the absence
of the final link.

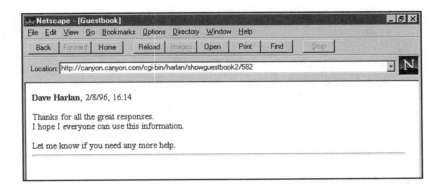

When you click the link at the bottom of figure 2.4, `/232` is passed to `showguestbook2`. Line 1 of the script assigns this value to `$filepos`; line 2 removes the leading slash. To make the script work the first time through (that is, when `PATH_INFO` contains no information), line 3 makes `$filepos` zero when it contains the null string. After printing the top of the document to be sent back to the user and opening the GUESTBOOK.TXT data file, line 9 performs the key action in the new script.

Perl's `seek()` function takes three arguments: a file handle, a position, and a number that indicates what this position is relative to. In this script, the third argument is zero. This argument indicates that you want the change in position to be relative to the top of the file. Because `$filepos` is 232, the `seek()` command in line 9 moves the position pointer to 232 bytes from the top of the file. This position is where the script will start reading lines from GUESTBOOK.TXT after the user clicks the link in figure 2.4, producing the result shown in figure 2.5. When the user selects the link in figure 2.5, the script starts reading 582 bytes into the file, producing the output shown in figure 2.6.

 `$ENV{'PATH_INFO'}` is an extremely effective means of passing information to scripts. Many times, you can avoid using a trivial form by using `PATH_INFO` instead of the form to pass information.

All this should make sense now, although you might be curious about where the numbers that end up in the `PATH_INFO` variable come from. Look at line 16:

```
last if $i==3;
```

The `last` command is something that you haven't seen before. The command breaks the script out of a loop when the condition of the loop otherwise would tell the script to continue. In this case, you want the loop to end if the counter variable `$i` equals 3, because if it has reached 3, the script has printed two Guestbook entries, and you don't want to print any more.

So you exit the loop and end up at line 18, where you get the magic number that tells the script where in the file to start the next time around. The `tell()` command returns the current file position of the provided file handle. By saving this value at this point in the script, you know exactly where the last Guestbook entry that you printed ends and where the next one begins.

All you have to do now is print the link at the bottom of the page. The `if` statement in line 19 makes sure that the script prints the link only if some entries in the GUESTBOOK.TXT file haven't been printed.

## Limiting Data-File Size

Now that you have an effective means of printing the Guestbook entries, you want to make more changes to the Guestbook entry script, as shown in Listing 2.6.

**Listing 2.6   The Further-Revised Guestbook Script (GUESTBOOK3.PL)**

```
$date="$mon/$mday/$year, $hour:$min";
#revisions start here...
open (gbfile, "guestbook.txt");
@gbfile=<gbfile>;
close (gbfile);
open (gbfile, "> guestbook.txt");
print gbfile $date,"::$fields{'name'}::$fields{'comment'}\n";
$i=1;
foreach (@gbfile) {
    print gbfile $_;
    last if $i==9;
    $i++;
}
close (gbfile);
print "Location: http://192.0.0.1/cgi-bin/harlan/showguestbook2\n\n";
```

Listing 2.6 makes two major changes in the Guestbook entry script. In line 3, the script opens the GUESTBOOK.TXT file. The script reads the entire file into an array in line 4 and closes the file in line 5.

To reopen the file in line 6, I used the > character to tell Perl that I want to overwrite the file. (Recall that in the preceding version of this script, I used the >> symbol because I wanted to append to the file.) Why would I want to overwrite the file? Displaying the entries in reverse chronological order makes more sense, so I overwrite the file each time to accomplish this task.

In line 7, the script writes the new entry to the file. In line 9, the script starts a loop that writes the rest of the old entries back into the file. Line 11 terminates the loop after 9 entries have been written to the file, discarding the last entry. This line limits the file to the 10 most recent entries.

## Using the Location Header

Now that the output has been refined, you want to send the user straight to the Guestbook display script after he signs in. That task is exactly what the last line of Listing 2.6 accomplishes.

When a browser receives a properly formatted Location header, it knows to retrieve the document specified after the colon. This feature can save a programmer a great deal of time. Instead of reinventing the wheel that displays the data by churning out HTML in the form-processing script, the programmer can write output code only once, in some cases. This function isn't a cure-all, but you should keep it in mind.

## Using CGI in Server-Side Includes

If you have done extensive HTML development, you may know about *server-side includes,* or *SSI*—a set of functions built into some Web servers that allow a developer to use special HTML directives to insert some data into documents on the fly.

The information that you can insert can take the form of a local file or a file referenced by a URL. You can also include information from a limited set of variables. Finally, you can execute scripts to output the data that will be inserted into the document; for details, see the sidebar titled "What Else Can You Do with SSI?"

One thing that you may notice about the page shown in figure 2.7 is the fact that the file name has changed to GUESTBOOK.SHTML. The change in the file extension tells the server that it should check the file for SSI commands. The file extension depends on server configuration, but .SHTML is a common choice.

Part
I
Ch
2

**FIG. 2.7**
This new Guestbook form includes a quote to spice up the page a little.

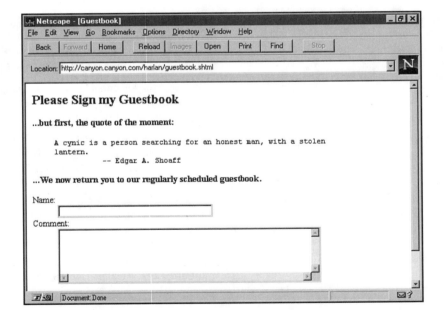

---

### What Else Can You Do with SSI?

When they're available, server-side includes are a good way to make simple pages more interesting. In this chapter, you see an example of executing CGI to create dynamic sections in otherwise-static documents. This sidebar describes what else SSI can do.

*continues*

*continued*

The format for any SSI command is as follows:

`<! —#command option=value —>`

Table 2.6 lists the SSI commands and their options.

**Table 2.6   SSI Commands and Options**

| Command | Options | Explanation |
| --- | --- | --- |
| config | errmsg | Sets the value that will be sent if an error occurs when future SSI commands are parsed in a document. |
| | timefmt | Sets the format for outputting dates from SSI commands. See the `strftime()` UNIX manual page for details on how to format dates with this command. |
| | sizefmt | Sets the manner in which file sizes are displayed. Set this option to `bytes` (to display SSI file-size command results in bytes) or `abbrev` (to display sizes in kilobytes or mega-bytes, as appropriate). |
| echo | var | Prints the specified variable. All CGI environment variables and the following SSI variables can be echoed: `DATE_GMT`, `DATE_LOCAL`, `DOCUMENT_NAME`, `DOCUMENT_URI`, `LAST_MODIFIED`, and `QUERY_STRING_UNESCAPED`. |
| exec | cmd | Executes the specified command, using /BIN/SH, and includes the resulting output on the page. Requires a physical path to the command. |
| | cgi | Executes the specified CGI script. Takes a virtual path to the script (for example, /CGI-BIN/HARLAN/FORTUNE rather than /USR/LOCAL/ETC/HTTPD/CGI-BIN/ HARLAN/FORTUNE). |
| flastmod | file | Includes the last modification date of the indicated file in the document. Requires a physical path to the document. |
| | virtual | Same as `file`, except that it takes a virtual path. |
| fsize | file | Includes the size of the indicated file in the document. Requires a physical path to the document. |
| | virtual | Same as `file`, except that it takes a virtual path. |
| include | file | Includes the text of the indicated file in the document. Requires a physical path to the document. |
| | virtual | Same as `file`, except that it takes a virtual path. |

As you can see, SSI provides a fairly rich set of features to the programmer. You might use SSI if you have an existing set of documents to which you want to add modification dates. You also could have a file that you want to appear on several of your pages. You could use the SSI include command on each of those pages instead of copying the document into each page individually.

One problem is the fact that SSI may not be available on all Web servers; it opens some security holes that some site administrators are not willing to risk. If you administer your own site and trust all the page designers on your site, however, SSI is a useful tool in your Web development arsenal.

The following paragraphs focus on the exec command. Refer to figure 2.7, which appears earlier in this section. This figure shows the familiar Guestbook entry form, with a twist: a "quote of the moment" appears at the top of the form. Knowing what you do from having read this far, you probably could write a CGI script that would read a quote from a file, print that quote, and then print the HTML for the form.

But that's not how I created this page. Listing 2.7 shows the source for the page in figure 2.7.

### Listing 2.7 Source for GUESTBOOK.SHTML

```
<HTML>
<body bgcolor="#FFFFFF">
<title>Guestbook</title>
<h2>Please Sign My Guestbook</h2>
<b>...but first, the quote of the moment:</b><p>
<!--#exec cgi="/cgi-bin/harlan/fortune"-->
<b>...We now return you to our regularly scheduled guestbook.</b><p>
<form method=get action="/cgi-bin/harlan/guestbook">
<dt>Name:<br>
<dd><input type=text name=name size=30>
<dt>Comment:<br>
<dd><textarea name=comment rows=5 cols=50></textarea><p>
<input type=submit value="Sign In">
</form>
</html>
```

You can see that I added three lines to the document. Two lines are straight HTML. The third line—the one that you may not recognize—is an SSI command. The syntax is straightforward; it says, "Execute the CGI script /CGI-BIN/HARLAN/FORTUNE." Easy, right?

**N O T E** If you point your browser at GUESTBOOK.SHTML and then use your browser's View Source command, you do not see the code in Listing 2.7. When you use SSI, the commands inside the `<!-- ... -->` tags are translated into straight HTML before they get to the browser. ■

The fortune CGI script isn't difficult, either. Listing 2.8 shows the code.

**Listing 2.8   Code Listing for *fortune* (FORTUNE.PL)**

```perl
#!/usr/bin/perl
open (fortune,"/usr/games/fortune |");
print "Content-type: text/html\n\n";
print "<pre>\n";
while (<fortune>){
    print "     $_";
}
print "</pre>";
```

This script presents only one new concept. Look at line 2. You saw the `open()` command earlier in this chapter, but this time, it uses a new option. The pipe (|) at the end of `/usr/games/fortune |` tells Perl to run the operating-system command /USR/GAMES/FORTUNE (on the server machine) and to provide (or pipe) the information in the given file handle as though the result of the command was being read from a file.

`fortune` is a common UNIX command that spits out a random quote, so if you look at the rest of the script, you can see what happens. First, the script prints the standard HTML header; then it outputs the opening `<pre>` tag. Next, the script simply loops through the lines of output from the command. Then the script prints each line of output back to the browser with five leading spaces, indenting the output on the resulting page. Finally, the script prints the closing `</pre>` tag.

The result is the page shown in figure 2.7. Of course, the next user (or you, if you reload) will see a different quote at the top of the page.

# From Here...

You now have basic knowledge of CGI and Perl. In this chapter, you learned how to process data from a form and print a properly formatted page. You also learned how to call Perl scripts directly and how to use Perl in server-side includes. Finally, you were exposed to a useful subset of Perl. Regular expressions, saving and retrieving data in text files, printing, and looping should all be within your grasp now.

For further information, read the following chapters:

- Chapter 3, "Advanced Form Processing and Data Storage." Look in this chapter for more advanced information on form processing.

- Chapter 6, "Using Dynamic Pages." Head to this chapter for more examples of SSI and on-the-fly pages.

- Chapter 15, "Function List." If you want to strike out on your own, you'll find extensive Perl syntax information in this chapter.

# Form Processing, Data Storage, and Page Display

# Advanced Form Processing and Data Storage

*by David Harlan*

In Chapter 2, "Introduction to CGI," you created a fairly simple (but usefully extensible) Guestbook application for your Web site. This chapter discusses a more advanced user-input example: an online Internet-use survey. You probably have seen similar surveys, but this chapter takes the concept a step further. In your survey, the data will be saved so that you can refer to it later, online. You also add to the user data from another form. ■

### Using the POST method

CGI provides two methods for gathering data from a form. You saw the GET method in the preceding chapter. This chapter discusses the POST method, examining the differences, advantages, and disadvantages.

### Making your code modular

Not surprisingly, CGI programming involves several repetitive tasks. This chapter illustrates some methods of reusing certain pieces of code.

### Storing data in DBM files

The text file was adequate to store the information for your Guestbook program. But as you put more and more data into your program, you need a faster, more flexible way to access the data. The DBM file provides this method.

# Using the *POST* Method

The CGI specification provides two methods of calling a script: the GET method, which you used in Chapter 2; and the POST method, which is discussed in this section. Look at the form shown in figure 3.1.

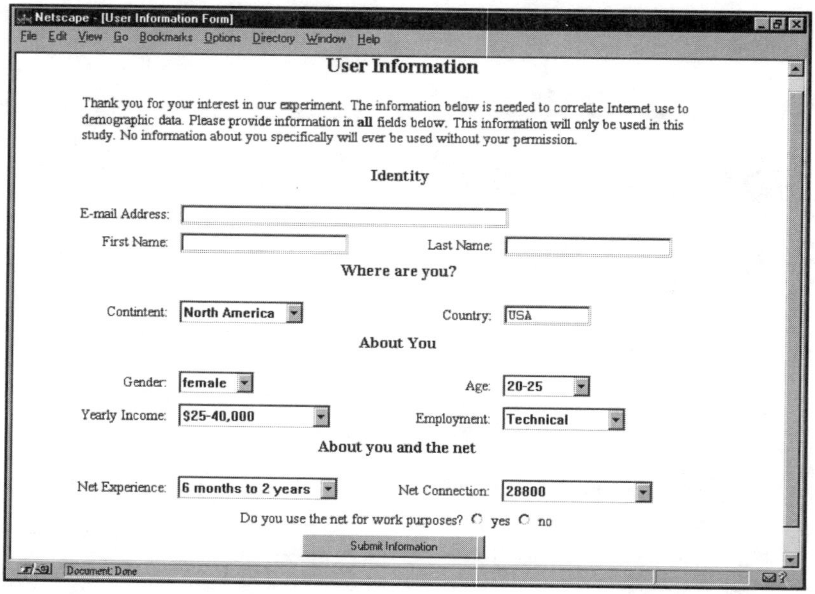

**FIG. 3.1**
This figure shows the first form from the online experiment.

The first thing that you should notice about this form is that it's much bigger and more complex than the Guestbook form in Chapter 2. You're asking for significantly more data this time. Why is this fact significant? Recall that when you posted the form in Chapter 2, the data from the form appeared in the Location box, as part of the URL of the resulting screen (refer to fig. 2.2 in the preceding chapter).

Some people may complain that this huge URL clutters the screen and makes things too messy for their taste. This may be true, but as you'll soon see, aesthetics are not the only reasons why you won't always use this method of forms processing.

## Comparing *GET* and *POST*

What can you do about this ugly URL? Fortunately, you can use either of two methods for submitting HTML forms. If you look at line 2 of Listing 2.1 (refer to Chapter 2), you notice that the form element of this page is opened with the following tag:

```
<form method=get action="/cgi-bin/harlan/guestbook">
```

The key portion of this tag in the current discussion is method=get, which tells the browser that the /CGI-BIN/HARLAN/GUESTBOOK script is expecting an HTTP request of type get from this form. The browser must know the request method so that it can send the information back to the server properly. The most important thing that this syntax change affects is where the user-submitted data appears when it gets to the CGI script.

The GET method places all the data in the URL portion of the request. Specifically, everything after the question mark in the URL portion of a GET request is user-submitted data. The server software puts this information in the QUERY_STRING environment variable for use in the script that will process the form. Aside from the obvious aesthetic difficulties, this method also creates a significant functional roadblock.

Some Web servers limit the length of the URL portion of a request (check the documentation for your server). So you might not be able to submit larger forms by using the GET method on some servers. Fortunately, you have the POST method to handle larger forms. Listing 3.1 shows the HTML code for the form shown in figure 3.1.

### Listing 3.1   The First Part of the Experiment Registration Form (USERFORM.HTML)

```
<body bgcolor="#FFFFFF">
<title>User Information Form</title>
<center>
<h2>User Information</h2>
<table width=650>
<tr><td colspan=4>
Thank you for your interest in our experiment. The information below is needed
to correlate Internet use to demographic data. Please provide information in
<b>all</b> fields below. This information will only be used in this study. No
information about you specifically will ever be used without your permission.
<form method=post action=/cgi-bin/harlan/postuser>
<tr><td colspan=4 align=center>
<h3>Identity</h3>
<tr><td align=right>E-mail Address:
<td colspan=3><input type=text size=40 name=email>
<tr><td align=right>First Name:
<td><input type=text size=20 name=firstname>
<td align=right>Last Name:
<td><input type=text size=20 name=lastname>
<tr><td colspan=4 align=center>
```

The most obvious difference is in line 11, in which the script opens the form definition with the POST method specified.

## Processing the Information from a *POST*-Method Form

How do you get the information from this form? See Listing 3.2. This script processes and saves the information, and prints a simple thank-you page in response.

**Listing 3.2   The *postuser* Script (POSTUSER1.PL)**

```perl
#!/usr/bin/perl

read(STDIN,$temp,$ENV{'CONTENT_LENGTH'});
@pairs=split(/&/,$temp);
foreach $item(@pairs) {
   ($key,$content)=split (/=/,$item,2);
   $content=~tr/+/ /;
   $content=~ s/%(..)/pack("c",hex($1))/ge;
   $fields{$key}=$content;
}
dbmopen(%users,"users",0666);
print "Content-type: text/html\n\n";
if (!defined($users{$fields{'email'}})) {
  $users{$fields{'email'}}="$fields{'firstname'}::$fields{'lastname'}::$fields{'cont'}
::$fields{'country'}::$fields{'gender'}::$fields{'age'}::$fields{'income'}::$fields{'employment'}
::$fields{'netexp'}::$fields{'netconn'}::$fields{'workuse'}";
   print "Thanks for registering for our survey. Please remember to come back
weekly to record your net use.";
}
else {
   print "Someone has already registered from that e-mail address. Sorry.";
}
```

Except for line 3, much of the beginning of this script should look familiar. If you look at Listing 2.2 in Chapter 2, you see that the text-processing lines are almost identical to those in Listing 3.2. Both lines take the text in the `$temp` variable; split it into an array of key/value pairs; and then place each pair in an associative array, associating each key with its value.

The unfamiliar line is fairly simple. The `read()` function takes a file handle, a variable, and an integer for arguments. So the script in Listing 3.2 is reading `$ENV{'CONTENT_LENGTH'}` bytes from the file handle `STDIN` and putting the information that it finds in the variable `$temp`. Recall that in the `guestbook` script, you copied `$temp` from `$ENV{'QUERY_STRING'}`. So you see the major difference between processing `GET`-method forms and `POST`-method forms.

---

### Built-in File Handles

Perl uses normal UNIX names for its built-in file handles. `STDOUT`, which is the standard file handle for output, is where you normally print from a Perl script. If you are running a script from the command line, output directed to `STDOUT` appears on the console. In CGI applications, `STDOUT` goes back to the Web server to be sent to the browser.

`STDERR` is a file handle that is used for error messages. Operating systems do different things with `STDERR`, but text printed to this special file handle generally ends up in some sort of log. In CGI applications, most Web servers print messages that are directed to `STDERR` to the server's error log— a useful fact that you can use to debug your CGI scripts.

`STDIN` is a file handle in which you can often find input for your Perl script. Running scripts from the command line, you would read from `STDIN` if input were piped to your script from another command. (This syntax might look something like `cat filename ¦ myperlscript`.) In CGI, the Web server puts `POST`-method form input in `STDIN`.

As I said earlier, the rest of the processing is exactly the same. So, you might now be asking yourself, if you're going to do a great deal of form processing, wouldn't it be much easier to write some of this code once and reuse it? The answer, of course, is yes.

# Making Your Perl Code Modular

One thing that almost all good programmers have in common is an abhorrence for redoing work. We all want to do things as efficiently as possible. One of the best ways to make programming more efficient is to put code for common tasks in a place where other programs can easily use it.

Perl provides an effective feature for this purpose. The simplest method, which works for both versions 4 and 5 of Perl, is to create a Perl library. Perl 5 adds a new entity called a *module* to the mix. Modules are similar to libraries, but they allow the advanced Perl programmer to use object-oriented programming syntax.

 To find out what version of Perl you are using, type **perl -v** at your command line. My machine shows the following display when I type this command:

```
portland:~/# perl -v

This is perl, version 5.002

Copyright 1987-1996, Larry Wall

Perl may be copied only under the terms of either the Artistic License or
the GNU General Public License, which may be found in the Perl 5.0 source
kit.
```

 You can see that I'm using Perl 5.002. If you're using Perl 4, this command tells you that you're using Perl 4 and then gives you a patch level. If the display shows anything other than patch level 036, you'll want to upgrade. You probably should upgrade to version 5 anyway; it's available for most platforms on the CD-ROM that accompanies this book.

Listing 3.3 shows what the postuser script might look like with a more modular approach. You can see that the code is much shorter and easier to read.

**Listing 3.3   The Modular *postuser* Script (POSTUSER2.PL)**

```perl
#!/usr/bin/perl
require ("process_cgi.pl");

&parse_input(*fields);
&print_header;
dbmopen(%users,"users",0666) || die "Can't open users DBM file\n";
if (!defined($users{$fields{'email'}})) {
    $users{$fields{'email'}}="$fields{'firstname'}::$fields{'lastname'}::
$fields{'cont'}::$fields{'country'}::$fields{'gender'}::$fields{'age'}::
```

*continues*

**Listing 3.3   Continued**

```
$fields{'income'}::$fields{'employment'}::$fields{'netexp'}::
$fields{'netconn'}::$fields{'workuse'}";
    print "Thanks for registering for our survey. Please remember to come back
weekly to record your net use.";
}
else {
  print "Someone has already registered from that e-mail address. Sorry.";
}
```

What's going on in this new script? The first new command that you see is require(). This command tells the Perl interpreter to find the file specified in the argument (PROCESS_CGI.PL, in this case) and use it as though it were part of the script. You then see the two lines &parse_input(*fields) and &print_header. The first line parses the form input; the second line prints the page header.

These two lines demonstrate one of the major advantages of modular programming: it makes code much more readable. You may not know exactly how these lines do their thing, but you can read this program and understand it. In this case, however, you really *do* want to know what's happening. The following sections look at these lines a little more closely.

# Defining and Calling Subroutines

The ampersand tells the interpreter that each line is a call to a subroutine. Because no subroutines are defined in this script, they must be defined by the code in the require("process_cgi.pl") statement near the top of Listing 3.3. Listing 3.4 shows process_cgi.pl.

**Listing 3.4   The First Incarnation of *process_cgi.pl* (PROCESS_CGI1.PL)**

```perl
#process_cgi.pl. A Perl library for CGI processing.

sub form_method {
   $method=$ENV{'REQUEST_METHOD'};
}

sub print_header {
   if (!defined(@_)) {
     print "Content-type: text/html\n\n";
   }
   else {
     print "Location: @_\n\n";
   }
}

sub parse_input {
   if (defined(@_)) {
     local(*input)=@_;
   }
```

```
     else {
       local(*input)="*cgiinput";
     }
     local ($temp,@pairs);
     if (&form_method eq 'POST') {
       read(STDIN,$temp,$ENV{'CONTENT_LENGTH'});
     }
     else {
       $temp=$ENV{'QUERY_STRING'};
     }
     @pairs=split(/&/,$temp);
     foreach $item(@pairs) {
       ($key,$content)=split (/=/,$item,2);
       $content=~tr/+/ /;
       $content=~ s/%(..)/pack("c",hex($1))/ge;
       $input{$key}=$content;
     }
   return 1;
   }
   return 1;
```

This code introduces several concepts. First, this file defines three subroutines. The syntax for subroutine definition is simple; the keyword sub is followed by a word that becomes the subroutine name. The final portion of the subroutine definition is a block of statements enclosed in braces ({}). Unfortunately, the way in which these subroutines do their jobs is not immediately clear. The following paragraphs examine each subroutine.

Subroutines are not used only in Perl libraries; you can define a subroutine in any Perl script to reuse code within that script. Suppose that you have a script that reads a given file into a given array a certain number of times. Instead of reproducing that code each time, you could (and perhaps should) create a subroutine and then call that subroutine each time you want to read a file.

The form_method subroutine has a very simple function—it returns the contents of the REQUEST_METHOD environment variable. But how does the subroutine work? Notice that line 9 of the parse_input subroutine checks the value of the &form_method subroutine call. If you have ever done any Pascal programming, you would expect $ENV{'REQUEST_METHOD'} to be assigned to the subroutine name somewhere in the form_method sub. This script clearly doesn't do that, however; Perl takes a different, behind-the-scenes approach. In any subroutine, the last assignment performed in the block is returned as the value of the subroutine. (The only exception to this rule arises when you use the return function, which returns the specified value.)

By assigning $ENV{'REQUEST_METHOD'} to $method in the form_method sub, then, you can check the value of &form_method, as in parse_input.

The second subroutine in Listing 3.4 prints the proper header for an HTML page. The first line of the procedure checks to see whether the Perl special variable @_ is *not* defined. The exclamation point before the defined() function tells Perl to negate the result. So if the function tells you that @_ is not defined (that is, if it returns false), the conditional returns true and executes the first statement block. The @_ variable contains any arguments of the subroutine.

So if you call this subroutine with `&print_header;`, `@_` is not defined, and the script prints the `Content-type: text/html\n\n` header.

If you call the subroutine with `&print_header("http://192.0.0.1/cgi-bin/harlan/showguestbook2");`, `@_` is defined, and the script prints `Location: http://192.0.0.1/cgi-bin/harlan/showguestbook2\n\n`. This code should look familiar. Refer to Listing 2.6 in Chapter 2, where this precise string was used at the end of the `guestbook` script to send the browser to the `guestbook` display script.

You have created a very useful subroutine that not only prints the standard HTML page header but also prints the Location header when you want to redirect the browser to an existing page, rather than print HTML from the script.

## Using Variable Aliases

The final subroutine in Listing 3.4 performs the all-important input processing. The first part of the sub is an if/else construct, similar to the one in the preceding subroutine. Here, the script checks to see whether there were any arguments when the sub was called; if so, it performs a little Perl magic on that argument.

The line `local(*input)=@_;` is not an easy one to understand. The `local()` function makes the variables listed as arguments local to the program block from which `local()` was called. Look at line 8, which makes `$temp` and `@pairs` local variables. This syntax ensures that the script won't change the values of any other variables with the same names in the program that's calling this subroutine.

But what's happening in the first two calls to `local()`? You're not seeing a new variable type. These lines perform *type-globbing*; a simpler name is *aliasing*. What you want to do in this subroutine is assign the form data to a user-specified associative array. To do so, you have to work with a global copy of that array. You may think that you should just pass the `%fields` array as the argument to this subroutine call. That procedure wouldn't work, though, because Perl would assume that you want to work with the values in `%fields` and not with the array itself.

So the Perl developers came up with a method. If you assign one variable name, preceded by an asterisk (`*`), to a localized variable name, also preceded by an asterisk, Perl works with the local variable as an alias to the other. An important point is that all variables with that name are aliased. Although you only work with the associative array in this example, you could also play with the global copies of similarly named scalar variables and standard arrays in this routine, modifying their global values accordingly.

Now, as you recall, the location of the input data depends on the method that the form uses to call the script. Because you really want to make `parse_input` universal, you want to be able to use it for either method; the second if/else construct in Listing 3.4 does just this. If the form method (as determined by a call to the `form_method` subroutine described in "Defining and Calling Subroutines" earlier in this chapter) is POST, the script gets the data from STDIN and places it in `$temp`; otherwise, the value of `$temp` comes from `$ENV{'QUERY_STRING'}`.

The final portion of the routine does the input processing exactly as described in Chapter 2.

Thus, in your `parse_input` routine, you're telling Perl to use `input` as an alias to the variable specified in `@_`. The script then parses the form input into that alias. When the script makes the call in line 3 of Listing 3.3, `parse_input` works on `%input` as an alias to `%fields`. The result is that the data is placed in the `%fields` array *exactly* as it was in Listing 3.2.

One final note about `parse_input`: notice the first conditional. This conditional allows a user to call `parse_input` without arguments and have the routine assign the form input to a default variable—in this case, `%cgiinput`.

# Using DBM Files for Data Storage

Now you see how you get the information from the form into the `%fields` array in Listing 3.3. But when you look farther down in the script (and also in Listing 3.2, the last few lines of which are identical to those in Listing 3.3), you see some new commands that I need to explain.

In the Guestbook program in Chapter 2, you stored the data in a text file. This method was acceptable because you didn't need to access the data in any way except to print it. Suppose, however, that you don't want any given person to sign in more than once. You would have to scan the file each time to see whether the name existed in the file. The necessary code would look something like Listing 3.5.

**Listing 3.5   Example Code for Scanning the GUESTBOOK.TXT File**

```
open (gbfile, "guestbook.txt");
while (<gbfile>) {
   ($date,$name,$comment)=split(/::/,$_);
   if ($name eq $fields{'name'}) {
     $nameused='y';
     last;
   }
}
close (gbfile);
if ($nameused eq 'y') {
   #Do stuff here to tell the user that she can't sign in more than once
}
else {
   #go on with the rest of the guestbook script as normal
```

Aside from the fact that you wouldn't want to depend on this method for preventing multiple sign-ins, it should be fairly obvious that scanning the entire text file for a name each time a user signs the guestbook could become time-consuming as the file got larger. So there must be a better way, right? The answer, of course, is yes (I wouldn't have posed the question otherwise). Perl provides the DBM file for just this situation.

A DBM file (*DBM* stands for *database management*) is a special type of file that is inherited from Perl's UNIX roots. DBM files perform very simple database functions. The following sections examine how DBM files work.

# Opening a DBM File

Line 5 of POSTUSER2.PL reads as follows:

```
dbmopen(%users,"users",0666) || die "Can't open users DBM file\n";
```

As you might expect from its name, this line opens a DBM file. To be precise, the line opens the DBM file called USERS and links it to the associative array %users. 0666 stands for a file mode that tells Perl to provide read and write access for this file for everyone. (See "Initializing a DBM File" later in this chapter for details on file modes.) If the file does not exist, Perl attempts to create it with the specified file mode. If the file can't be opened or created, the || die... construct tells Perl to exit the program.

Take a closer look at the || die... syntax. The || symbol is a standard Perl operator—basically, a logical or. If the code before || does not return a value of true, the script performs the action specified after ||. In this case, you want to perform the die function, which tells Perl to exit the program immediately and print die's arguments to STDERR. (Remember that in CGI programming output, STDERR usually ends up in the server's error log.)

This piece of code is a very useful part of your CGI programming arsenal. If you did not have die at the end of this line, Perl would go on with the program blithely, even if it couldn't open your DBM file. Because the user wouldn't be alerted to the problem, he wouldn't know that anything was amiss. You wouldn't be aware of the problem, either, until you started wondering why no data was showing up anywhere. By then, you would have lost the registration data of who knows how many users. With die (in this case, anyway), the user would get a malformed header from script error, and you would be alerted to the problem. Then you could go back to the error logs and track down the problem with little difficulty.

I use die liberally in my CGI programs. die is particularly valuable for dealing with external files, but you'll find many other uses for it as you get deeper into CGI programming.

# Assigning Values to a DBM File

Now that you have the DBM file open, you need to assign values to it. The first thing that you need to decide is what value in your data set will serve as your key. Each key must be unique within any DBM file. In the postuser script, I chose an e-mail address as the key for this DBM file. This key makes sense, because an e-mail address should be a unique identifier for a user. (Sorry—those who share e-mail boxes need not apply here.)

After you decide on a key, you can assign your values to the file. To be safe, before you make any assignments to this file, check to make sure that the key doesn't exist in the file, using the following code:

```
if (!defined($users{$fields{'email'}})) {
```

This statement says, "If the address in $fields{'email'} does not already exist in the user's DBM file, execute the lines that follow." Those lines simply assign the data from the form to a long string associated with the e-mail address in the user's DBM file. The script then prints a one-line HTML page that thanks the user for registering.

If the e-mail address already exists in the database file, the script prints a one-line HTML page, telling the user that the address is already in use.

Essentially, when the DBM file is open, working with it is just like working with a standard associative array. You can assign to it, read from it, and iterate over it exactly the same way that you would a normal hash. Some things are different, however; you learn about them later in the following section and in Chapter 4, "Advanced Page Output."

## Initializing a DBM File

If you take USERFORM.HTML and the postuser script off the CD-ROM and put them on your Web server, changing the directory references as necessary, you may be able to start collecting data right away—but probably not.

Most Web servers run CGI scripts under a nonprivileged user name (frequently, the user nobody) to avert security problems. This arrangement is a good thing, in general; keeping your computer safe from intruders is important. But when you want to write to files on the computer, this situation can become bothersome. You need some knowledge of UNIX file permissions to get around the problem. To explain this concept thoroughly, I have to digress a bit. (If you already know about UNIX file permissions, feel free to skip ahead.)

UNIX and its many cousins use a very flexible—and sometimes confusing—system for file permissions. To look at the files in your directory, use the ls command. Figure 3.2 shows a full listing of the directory that I've been working in.

**FIG. 3.2**
This screen shows a listing of files on the author's server.

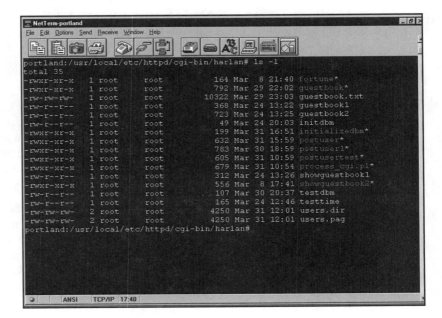

Consider an example file from this listing. The third file listed is the GUESTBOOK.TXT file, which was used to store the data for the Guestbook example in Chapter 2. Starting from the left, the first string of characters defines who can do what to this file (I'll get back to that topic soon). The next two items define the user who owns the file and the group to which that file belongs. In this case, the file belongs to the user root and the group root. root is the most privileged user on a UNIX system. In this example, I own and administer the server that I'm working on, so I'm root. A more typical listing would show user harlan and group users, or something similar. The next entry in this line is the size of the file, in bytes, followed by the date and time of the last modification, and ending with the file name.

Now all that's left to explain is that first string of characters. The first character in this string is a dash except under very special circumstances that don't apply here. (This character tells you whether the listing is a directory, among other things.) The next nine characters indicate the permissions for this file. The first three characters refer to the owner of the file; the second three, to the group; and the final three, to everyone else. Each trio of characters indicates read, write, and execute permissions, in that order. If the group portion of the permissions reads rwx, any member of the group indicated on the line can read from, write to, and execute that file.

Sometimes, these permissions are designated numerically, as in the dbmopen command. For the GUESTBOOK.TXT file, for example, the permissions equal 0666. The first zero sets the initial character to a dash. Each successive digit sets the values of the rwx characters for the user, then for the group, and then for everyone else. The digits are calculated as follows:

- Read permission equals 4, write permission is 2, and execute permission is 1. Thus, the permissions for GUESTBOOK.TXT (-rw-rw-rw-) come out to 0666.

- If you want the user to have all permissions and everyone else to have no permissions, set the mode to 0700.

- As indicated in Chapter 2, you generally set the mode for scripts to 0755. This mode means that the user can read, write, and execute the file (4+2+1=7). Group members and others can read and execute the file (4+1=5).

In the case of the GUESTBOOK.TXT file, the permissions for the user, group, and others are all the same: rw-, which means that anyone on the server can read from and write to this file. The permissions must be set this way, because the CGI scripts that use this file are run by the user nobody (not root). The user nobody does not belong to the group root, either. So the scripts must abide by the permissions for the "everybody else" category.

Where does that leave you with the DBM file? As I said earlier in this section, the dbmopen() command tries to create the file if it does not already exist. If directory permissions are set to allow writing by the script, this will work. But the permissions are not likely to be set this way by default. Figure 3.3 shows the full directory listing one level up from the listing in figure 3.2. As you can see, in the "everybody else" category for the directory HARLAN, the permissions don't allow writing—which makes sense, because you don't want just anyone on the server to write to the directory.

**FIG. 3.3**

Here, you see a listing of files one level up from figure 3.2.

What can you do? The solution is to create your data files beforehand and set the permissions on those files to allow the CGI scripts to write to them. I wrote a simple script that does all these things for me whenever I want to use a new DBM file. Listing 3.6 shows the code.

---

**Listing 3.6   A Script to Initialize DBM Files for CGI Use (INITIALIZEDBM.PL)**

```perl
#!/usr/bin/perl
($filename,$mode)=@ARGV;
$mode="0666" if !defined($mode);
dbmopen (%temp, $filename, oct($mode))
    || die "Couldn't open $filename\n";
dbmclose (%temp);
system "chmod $mode $filename.*";
```

---

To make this code do its job, you run this script from the command line, with the name of the DBM file that you want to initialize as an argument. Before you run the postuser script for the first time, for example, you would issue the command initializedbm users from the command line in your CGI directory. This command creates the DBM file (on some systems, it creates two files) and sets the proper file permissions.

This code presents several new Perl concepts. Line 2 assigns the contents of the array @ARGV to $filename and $mode. (Remember that if you enclose a list of scalars in parentheses, they act like an array.) @ARGV is a special Perl variable that contains the command-line arguments for this script. The arguments are everything that follows the script when it is called. The arguments are separated by spaces on the command line, and each argument becomes an element of @ARGV.

Part

II

Ch

3

Line 3 checks to see whether a mode was specified on the command line; if not, a default mode of 0666 is assigned. This line may seem to be strange at first. It is functionally identical to the following:

```
if (!defined($mode)) {$mode="0666"}
```

The syntax in the script is a shortcut. The `if` portion of the statement is a *statement modifier*, which does exactly what it sounds like in English ("Set $mode to 0666 if $mode is not yet defined"). When I first saw this syntax, I assumed that the first part of the statement was always executed; then I couldn't figure out what the `if` was doing. When I got it through my thick skull that the right portion of the line was checked before the action on the left was performed, everything became clear. I hope that this explanation gets you past that confusion.

Line 4 opens the DBM file just as it does in Listing 3.3. The only difference is that because I was not using a literal value for the file mode, I had to convert the number from the octal string that we start with to a decimal value. To do so, I used the Perl function `oct()`. Line 5 is just a continuation of the `dbmopen` line, which tells Perl that I want to `die` if the script can't open the specified DBM file for some reason.

Line 6 closes the DBM file. Finally, you come to line 7, which illustrates one of the nicest features of Perl—and also one of its most dangerous features. The `system` function tells Perl that I want to execute the text enclosed in quotes as an operating-system command on the server.

This specific line executes the system `chmod` command on the newly created DBM files to make sure that they are world-readable and -writable. This line is functionally identical to typing the command `chmod 0666 users.*` at the UNIX command line. Depending on your system setup, this command may not always be necessary. Sometimes, however, Perl won't be able to set the permissions properly in the `dbmopen` command (or even in its own `chmod` command), so you have to set them from the system level. Including this command ensures that this script will initialize the DBM files correctly for almost any UNIX system.

What's so powerful and dangerous about the `system` function? It allows you to automate some repetitive tasks, as well as to perform some functions with your data that you might not be able to perform with Perl alone.

**See** "Advanced Page Output," **p. 97**

But this power also means that you can easily cripple your system or compromise its security if you're not careful. A simple example of something that you don't want to do is `system 'rm *';`. This command removes all files in the current directory. You could do the same thing at the command line, but some systems would warn you about what you were doing. The Perl `system` function bypasses these warnings.

In CGI applications, use of the `system` function with user-entered data must be closely monitored. If you don't carefully check the data that users are passing to the system, an expert UNIX user can easily compromise the security of your system.

## Adding Data to the DBM File

After that extensive digression from the task at hand (the online experiment), consider one other major advantage that DBM files have over text files for data storage: appending data to a record. If you wanted to change one of the records in the GUESTBOOK.TXT file, you would have to scan the entire file to find the correct record; save all the data (except the record to be changed) to memory; and then write the data back to the file, with the new data appended to the appropriate record. This process is much easier with DBM files.

You can change your current application to ask your users to give you a password for their data immediately after they register. First, you need to change the postuser script as shown in Listing 3.7. This change sends the user to the password-entry form after the user has been added to the database.

Part

II

Ch

3

**Listing 3.7   A New Version of _postuser_ (POSTUSER.PL)**

```perl
#!/usr/bin/perl
require ("process_cgi.pl");

&parse_input(*fields);

dbmopen(%users,"users",0666) || die "Can't open users DBM file\n";
if (!defined($users{$fields{'email'}})) {
  $users{$fields{'email'}}="$fields{'firstname'}::$fields{'lastname'}::$fields{'cont'}::
$fields{'country'}::$fields{'gender'}::$fields{'age'}::$fields{'income'}::
$fields{'employment'}::$fields{'netexp'}::$fields{'netconn'}::$fields{'workuse'}";
    &print_header("http://192.0.0.1/userpassword.html");
}
else {
    &print_header;
    print "Someone has already registered from that e-mail address. Sorry.";
}
```

The form in figure 3.4 asks the user for his password. I use password-type input boxes in this example, so that the password doesn't appear on-screen as the user types it in the form. For this reason, I ask the user to type it twice, so that I can confirm that he knows what password he typed.

**FIG. 3.4**
This form requests a
new password from
the user.

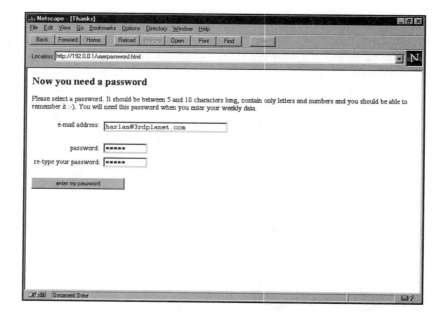

When the user submits this form, the password is checked and then the data is added to the
appropriate record of the DBM file. This task is accomplished with the addpassword script,
shown in Listing 3.8.

**Listing 3.8   Script for Adding a Password to the DBM File Data
(ADDPASSWORD.PL)**

```perl
#!/usr/bin/perl
require("process_cgi.pl");
&parse_input(*fields);
dbmopen (%users, "users", 0666);
&print_header;
if (!defined($users{$fields{'email'}})) {
   print "The email address you entered does not exist in our
      database. Please hit the back button on your browser,
      correct your entry and re-submit the form.";
}
elsif (!($users{$fields{'email'}} =~ /::yes$|::no$/)) {
   print "There is already a password registered for the provided
      email address. Please contact the survey administrator
      if you have forgotten you password.\n";
}
elsif (!($fields{'pass1'} =~ /^[a-zA-Z0-9]{5,10}$/)) {
   print "You entered an illegal password. Please try again.";
}
elsif ($fields{'pass1'} ne $fields {'pass2'}) {
   print "The passwords you typed did not match. Please
      return to the previous screen and try again.";
```

```
    }
    else {
        $users{$fields{'email'}} .= "::$fields{'pass1'}";
        print "Your password has been registered. Thank you.";
    }
```

The addpassword script brings together most of the concepts that this chapter has discussed. First, you see that I'm using the PROCESS_CGI.PL library. I parse the input into the hash %fields, open the DBM file USERS, and then print the HTML header. The next line checks to see whether the e-mail address entered by the user exists in the database; if not, the script prints a brief error page and asks the user to check his work.

If the e-mail address does exist, the script moves on to ensure that a password hasn't already been entered for this user. If this test fails, the script again prints a brief error page.

Next, the script checks the password to see whether it is the right length and contains only alphanumeric characters. This line uses a regular expression, as discussed in Chapter 2. The pattern /^[a-zA-Z0-9]{5,10}$/ translates as follows:

- The caret (^) indicates that you want to match the beginning of the string.
- The characters in brackets define a range of characters, any one of which should match. Because this range is followed by {5,10}, Perl looks for no fewer than 5 and no more than 10 characters that match the given range.
- Finally, the dollar sign ($) indicates that you want to match the end of the string.

What you want to match with this pattern is a string that contains only 5 to 10 alphanumeric characters. Because the entire expression is negated (with the leading exclamation point), the error text that follows prints whenever the pattern is *not* matched.

Next, the script checks to see whether both copies of the password are identical; if not, it again prints a brief error page, asking the user to check the information that he entered and try again.

Finally, if the address checks out, the password is legal, and the two versions of the password match, the script appends the password to the end of the data already entered for the given e-mail address.

The line that does the appending presents a new piece of Perl; it uses .=, which is Perl's append assignment operator. This little gem shortens the line that might have otherwise been written like this:

```
$users{$fields{'email'}} = $users{$fields{'email'}} . "::$fields{'pass1'}";
```

The functionality of this line is slightly more obvious. The dot (.) is the string-append operator. So this line connects the two strings and assigns them to $users{$fields{'email'}}. The line as I wrote it in Listing 3.8 functions identically. This is one more Perl shortcut. If you have, in a scalar variable, a string to which you want to append text to, the append assignment operator performs that task without requiring the repetitious typing of the longer (if equally correct) version of the command.

Now you see how much simpler it can be to work with data in DBM files. The following section takes all the Perl and CGI that you've learned so far and puts it to the test.

# Using Complex Forms and Storing Related Data

The data that you processed in the first part of this chapter is intended to be the first part of an online survey of Internet use. You know how to register your users. Now you can take a crack at collecting some data.

First, consider some general assumptions. You are asking users to carefully track their Internet use on a weekly basis. You want to keep each week separate, so that you can chart any changes over time. You won't try to be comprehensive in your survey questions, but you'll try to hit some key areas.

Where do you start? Begin with the form that users will fill out when they enter their weekly data (see fig. 3.5). The form itself seems to be fairly simple, but it presents some interesting programming problems.

**FIG. 3.5**
This form is the main data-entry point for the survey.

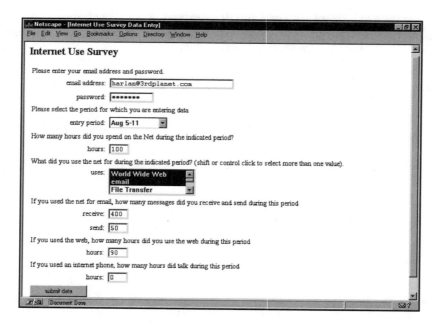

## Processing the Form Data and Checking the Password

The first order of business is to grab the data from the form and put it in your associative array. You should be able to do that just as you did before, right? Well, almost. This form contains an input method that you haven't seen before. Notice that the uses list shown in figure 3.5 has two items selected. The list has only one name, so if you leave PROCESS_CGI.PL as it is, each time a new uses entry is processed into the array, the old one is erased. So you need to change the `parse_input` routine in PROCESS_CGI.PL, as shown in Listing 3.9.

**Listing 3.9   A New Parse_Input Routine for PROCESS_CGI.PL**

```
sub parse_input {
   if (defined(@_)) {
      local(*input)=@_;
   }
   else {
      local(*input)="*cgiinput";
   }
   local ($temp,@pairs);
   if (&form_method eq 'POST') {
      read(STDIN,$temp,$ENV{'CONTENT_LENGTH'});
   }
   else {
      $temp=$ENV{'QUERY_STRING'};
   }
   @pairs=split(/&/,$temp);
   foreach $item(@pairs) {
      ($key,$content)=split (/=/,$item,2);
      $content=~tr/+/ /;
      $content=~ s/%(..)/pack("c",hex($1))/ge;
      if (!defined($input{$key})) {
          $input{$key}=$content;
      }
      else {
          $input{$key} .= "\0$content";
      }
   }
 return 1;
}
```

The new code in this subroutine is the `if`/`else` construct at the end of the last `foreach` loop. This code looks to see whether the key in the key/value pair that is being processed already exists in the %input hash; if not, the key is associated with the current value, just as in the first incarnation of this routine. If the key does exist, you don't want to erase the current value, but we want to save this one. You might tack the new value to the end of the old value (which actually may be old *values*), separating the two with the null character (\0). You use the null character because it never will exist in the user data; other characters might.

After getting the data, you want to make sure that the user exists in the database, that the user has a password, and that the password provided matches the one you have on file. If all these conditions are met, you want to add the data to your database. The code in Listing 3.10 accomplishes these tasks.

**Listing 3.10   Script to Post Periodic Data to the Database
(POSTPERIODDATA.PL)**

```perl
#!/usr/bin/perl
require "process_cgi.pl";
&parse_input(*fields);
&print_header;
dbmopen (%users,"users",0666);
if (!defined($users{$fields{'email'}})) {
    print "The email address you entered does not exist in our
       database. Please hit the back button on your browser,
       correct your entry and re-submit the form.";
}
else {
    $temp=$users{$fields{'email'}};
    dbmclose(%users);
    $temp=~/([a-zA-Z0-9]{5,10})$/;
    $actualpass=$1;
    if ($actualpass eq '') {
      print "There is no password entered for this e-mail
          address. Please enter one
          <a href=/userpassword.html>here</a>
          before you enter your data.";
    }
    elsif ($fields{'pass'} ne $actualpass) {
      print "The password you entered is incorrect. Please
          return to the previous screen and try again.";
    }
    else {
      &post_data;
    }
}
```

The first `if` should look familiar; it's the same code that you used in listings 3.7 and 3.8 to see whether the user exists in the database. If the user does exist, the script ends up in the `else` portion of the construct. Here, you want to get the password from the user data, and you do so with another regular expression. Because you set up the data so that the password (if it exists) is always be the last piece of data, all you need to do is check for 5 to 10 alphanumeric characters at the end of the string. Because this pattern is enclosed in parentheses, Perl saves any match in the special variable $1. So assign $1 to $actualpass and then test to make sure that $actualpass is not null.

This test tells you whether the user has entered a password, because if the user hasn't entered a password, the data string ends with yes or no. Because neither of these elements matches your password pattern, $1—thus, $actualpass—will be blank if no password exists in the USERS DBM file for this e-mail address.

Last, the script checks to see whether the password entered with the data actually matches the one that you have on file; if it does, you can finally enter the data in your database.

## Working Around the Limitations of DBM Files

As powerful as DBM files are, in many implementations of Perl they suffer from one severe limitation: you can make only one call to dbmopen() per program. For the application that you're working on now, this limitation causes a problem, because you prefer to store the survey data in a DBM file.

Your implementation of Perl *may* allow multiple dbmopens per program. The limitation depends on the version of the DBM libraries that your system uses. If your system has the NDBM libraries (instead of GDBM), you're in luck. If your Perl interpreter was compiled with those libraries, you can have multiple dbmopen commands; otherwise, you're stuck.

To figure out what version of DBM your system uses, you'll have to find the computer's libraries and look for a file such as LIBNDBM.A or LIBGDBM.A.

Fortunately, a way around this limitation exists: you can use the system command to tell a separate Perl program to deal with this data. First, save the data from the form in a temporary text file, as shown in Listing 3.11.

### Listing 3.11    The *postdata* Subroutine from POSTPERIODDATA.PL

```
sub post_data {
   $filename=$$.time.".txt";
   open (f, ">scratch/$filename") || die "couldn't open file $!";
   print f "email:$fields{'email'}\n";
   print f "period:$fields{'period'}\n";
   print f "hours:$fields{'hours'}\n";
   print f "webhours:$fields{'webhours'}\n";
   print f "phonehours:$fields{'phonehours'}\n";
   print f "send:$fields{'send'}\n";
   print f "receive:$fields{'receive'}\n";
   print f "uses";
   foreach $use(split(/\0/,$fields{'uses'})) {
     print f ":$use";
   }
   print f "\n";
   close f;
   system "postdatasup scratch/$filename >> /dev/null";
   system "rm scratch/$filename";
   print "Thanks for sending in your data.";

}
```

The first line of this subroutine creates a string that will serve as the file name. This string looks odd but serves an important purpose. $$ is a special Perl variable that stands for the *process ID*—a number that identifies this script when it's running. Every process that is running has a process ID, and process IDs are unique *at any given moment*. After a process ends, the IDs can be reused. This last fact means that to ensure the uniqueness of the temporary file that you're creating, you need to put a time stamp on it. To do so, use the time function, which returns the number of seconds since January 1, 1970.

With a unique file name ensured, you next need to open the file. Line 3 of Listing 3.11 performs this task, opening a new file with the name designated in the directory SCRATCH. I created this directory to be world-writable for just such a purpose: to write temporary files for immediate use. Having a SCRATCH directory around can be quite handy.

With the file open, the script prints the data to the file, one item per line. Because the uses item can have multiple values, it takes a little more processing, as shown in lines 11 and 12. This loop iterates over the array that results from the split(/\0/,$fields{'uses'}) command, printing each item from the null-character-separated list.

When all the data is printed to the temporary file, the file is closed, and the system function calls the program that will place the data in the DBM file. When that task is finished, the script deletes the temporary file and prints the "thank you" line back to the browser.

The final piece of this puzzle is the postdatasup script, shown in Listing 3.12. The script reads the appropriate file name from the command line. Notice that in Listing 3.11, I called this script (using the system function) with the temporary file name immediately following it. postdatasup opens that file and reads the data into an array.

### Listing 3.12    The Support Script for Periodic Data Entry

```perl
#!/usr/bin/perl
open (f, $ARGV[0]) || die "Couldn't open file $ARGV[0]";
$i=0;
while (<f>) {
    chop;
    $file[$i]=$_;
    $i++;
}
close f;
($trash,$email)=split(/:/,$file[0]);
($trash,$period)=split(/:/,$file[1]);
($trash,$hours)=split(/:/,$file[2]);
($trash,$webhours)=split(/:/,$file[3]);
($trash,$phonehours)=split(/:/,$file[4]);
($trash,$send)=split(/:/,$file[5]);
($trash,$receive)=split(/:/,$file[6]);
($trash,@uses)=split(/:/,$file[7]);
$dbfile="period".$period;
dbmopen (%data, $dbfile, 0666);
$data{$email}=join ('::',$hours,$webhours,$phonehours,$send,$receive);
$data{$email}.= "::".join (',', @uses);
```

Notice that line 5 issues the command chop—a standard Perl function that chops one character off the end of a string. If it is called without any arguments, chop works on the Perl special variable $_. Recall that in a loop such as this that reads in a file, $_ is set to equal each successive line in the file.

Lines 10 through 17 put the appropriate data in named variables. Notice that when the script processes the uses data, the data is put into an array rather than a scalar variable, because uses can have multiple entries.

Finally, the script opens the appropriate DBM file. You can see from the code that the files are named PERIOD1, PERIOD2, and so on. You have to initialize these files, using the `initializedbm` script (shown in "Initializing a DBM File" earlier in this chapter), before they can be used. The script then associates the e-mail address with the rest of the data as a delimited string.

# From Here...

With the examples in this chapter, you should now have a solid knowledge of form processing and data storage in DBM files. You should be able to take any form and know what you need to do to save submitted data. You know how to write to text files and to DBM files. You also know how to append data to DBM records and how to check the data in those records.

You may want to branch out to the following areas:

- Chapter 4, "Advanced Page Output." This chapter concentrates on processing existing data and page output.
- Chapter 11, "Database Interaction." If you're interested in high-end data storage, head to this chapter for information about interacting with SQL databases.
- Chapter 16, "Subroutine Definition." This chapter provides extensive information on creating subroutines, libraries and modules.

# Advanced Page Output

*by David Harlan*

**Y**ou may have sensed that something important was missing from the preceding chapter, which explained in detail how to get and save data but did not explain how to get that information from your data files back to an HTML page. This chapter fills in those gaps. ■

**Retrieving and parsing data from DBM files**

In Chapter 3, "Advanced Form Processing and Data Storage," you put data into DBM files. This chapter builds on that foundation, showing you ways to scan, manipulate, and output that data back to the user.

**Restoring information to forms**

Among the most important skills that an accomplished CGI programmer will want in his or her arsenal is the ability to restore information to forms so that users can edit and resubmit them. This chapter demonstrates several techniques in this area.

**Creating custom pages**

As you go about collecting data, you're always looking for new and better ways to display it. Although you may have good ideas, the users may have some, too. This chapter discusses a couple of ways to give users control of the information that they receive from your CGI programs.

# Parsing the DBM File and Printing Pages

Saving your experiment data as you did in Chapter 3 is all well and good, but without a suitable output method, all that data is useless. You certainly don't want to waste all the work that you just finished. This section discusses some good ways to use the data that you're gathering from those scripts and forms.

## Printing a Standard Page

The most obvious thing that you can to do with the experiment data is print an up-to-date summary of a user's data after that user enters a new weekly data set. The result might look something like figure 4.1.

**FIG. 4.1**

The user can view a summary of his or her survey data in this format.

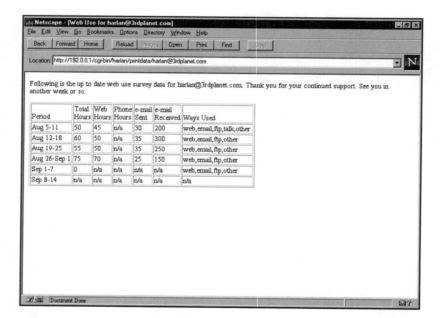

This page is fairly simple. The first thing that you see is a simple thank-you/introduction line; then you see a table that shows all the data to date for the user. The script that creates this page, shown in Listing 4.1, is correspondingly simple.

**Listing 4.1 Script to Print a Summary of User-Survey Data (PRINTDATA1.PL)**

```perl
#!/usr/bin/perl
require "process_cgi.pl";

$period[1]="Aug 5-11";
$period[2]="Aug 12-18";
$period[3]="Aug 19-25";
$period[4]="Aug 26-Sep 1";
```

```
$period[5]="Sep  1-7";
$period[6]="Sep  8-14";
$period[7]="Sep 15-21";
$period[8]="Sep 22-28";

$email=&path_info;

&print_header;
print "<title>Web Use for $email</title>\n";
print '<body bgcolor="#FFFFFF">';
print "Following is the up-to-date web use survey data for $email. Thank you for
    your continued support. See you in another week or so.<p>\n";
print "<table border=1><tr><td valign=bottom>Period<td>Total<br>Hours<td>Web<br>
    Hours<td>Phone
    <br>Hours<td>e-mail<br>Sent<td>e-mail<br>Received<td valign=bottom>Ways
Used\n\n";

for ($i=1; $i<9; $i++) {
    open (data, "printdatasup period$i $email ¦");
    $data=<data>;
    $data=~s/:::::/::n\/a::/g;
    $data=~s/:::::/::n\/a::/g;
    $data=~s/::$/::n\/a/;
    $data=~s/^::/n\/a::/;
    $data=~s/::/<td>/g;
    print "<tr><td>$period[$i]<td>",$data,"\n" if $data ne '';
}
print "</table>";
```

The following paragraphs examine how `printdata` works. The first two lines constitute the familiar header, common to most of the scripts in this book, that tells the operating system where to find the interpreter and that tells the interpreter that you want to include some code from an outside file. The next section of code defines an array of strings that you'll use to put labels on the period data later in the script.

Next comes the line `$email=&path_info`. If you read chapters 2 and 3, you know that this statement is calling the subroutine `&path_info` and placing the result in the variable `$email`. As you see in Listing 4.1, this program has no `path_info` subroutine. I added another useful function to PROCESS_CGI.PL. As you learned in Chapter 2, "Introduction to CGI" (specifically, in Listing 2.5), the PATH_INFO environment variable is a useful way to pass information to a CGI script. I use this method with some frequency, so I decided that the code that gets this variable was a good candidate to reside in PROCESS_CGI.PL. As Listing 4.2 shows, the subroutine is as simple as subroutines come. This code contains no new Perl.

## Listing 4.2  Subroutine to Return the *PATH_INFO* Environment Variable

```
sub path_info {
    $path=$ENV{'PATH_INFO'};
    $path= s/\////;
    $return=$path;
}
```

After assigning $ENV{'PATH_INFO'} to $path, the script removes the leading slash. The final assignment ensures that the appropriate information is returned to the script. This is easy enough that you could put this code into each script that required it, but why bother if you're going to be using the library anyway? Write the code once, and get the information that you need with one line of code instead of three.

In Listing 4.1, after getting the e-mail address from the &path_info subroutine, the script prints the HTTP header and the beginning of the page, setting the page background color to white, printing the introductory text, starting a table, and printing the first row of the table.

The next (and most important) section of code is a loop that prints the data that the user entered into the survey database. You may recall from the preceding chapter that some versions of Perl are limited to one dbmopen statement per script. Therefore, you have to call an outside program each time you want to access the DBM file for a new time period. Chapter 3 used the system function for that purpose. Listing 4.1 uses a version of the open command that you saw in Chapter 2 (refer to Listing 2.8). This syntax calls the listed program—in this case, printdatasup—and puts the resulting output in the file handle listed in the first argument (data).

printdatasup is not a built-in function; you probably have guessed that it's a Perl program that I wrote for this specific purpose. Listing 4.3 shows the code.

**Listing 4.3  Listing of *printdatasup* (PRINTDATASUP.PL)**

```perl
#!/usr/bin/perl
dbmopen (%data, $ARGV[0], 0666);
print $data{$ARGV[1]};
```

This program is as straightforward as it looks; all it does is open the DBM file provided in the first argument and then print the data from that file that corresponds to the key provided in the second argument. The first time through the loop, printdata calls this command with the arguments period1 and harlan@3rdplanet.com, so printdatasup simply prints the appropriate data from the period1 DBM file. printdata then saves this data in the variable $data (appropriately enough) for processing later in the script. Each time through the loop, $i is incremented, so each time through the loop, the next period's DBM file is queried for data for the given e-mail address.

The rest of the loop processes the information in $data before printing it. For the sake of clarity in output, I made sure that any empty fields were replaced by n/a. The successive s/::::/ ::n\/a::/g commands ensure that any lines of data that contain several null fields in succession (such as the last line of fig. 4.1) print with the appropriate number of n/a fields. With only one of these substitutions, alternating fields would be blank.

The following two lines make sure that blank fields at the beginning or the end of the data also contain n/a. Finally, the script substitutes <td> tags for the :: field delimiters in $data.

**TIP** Tables and other complex HTML structures sometimes cause problems when you're trying to debug a CGI program. To make this process easier, I sometimes print an <xmp> tag after the HTML header during the debugging phase.

When you run a script such as this, the HTML tags after the <xmp> tag are printed rather than interpreted, so you can quickly see what's going on. You can forgo this method and view the source every time, but this method is more convenient if you are doing extensive debugging. (Don't forget to remove the <xmp> tag before you put the script online.)

With all the processing done, the script then prints the row in the table, beginning with the appropriate data from the @period array, followed by the fully processed information in $data. The conditional at the end of the line ensures that nothing will print if $data is empty. This variable is blank for any periods that the user did not supply data for. You can see that even though the script checked periods one through eight, only the first six periods have rows in the table. Data was not entered for the final two periods of the survey, so those rows don't appear in the table. When the loop is finished, the script simply prints the closing table tag and exits.

## Printing User-Designed Pages

The preceding example is a good starting point for presenting the survey data, but it's really only the beginning of what you can do with it. You can imagine any number of ways that you may want to view this kind of data, and perhaps your users can, too, so give them an opportunity to see the data exactly as they want to. Consider the form shown in figure 4.2.

Part
II

Ch
4

**FIG. 4.2**
The user uses this form to choose the data to be displayed.

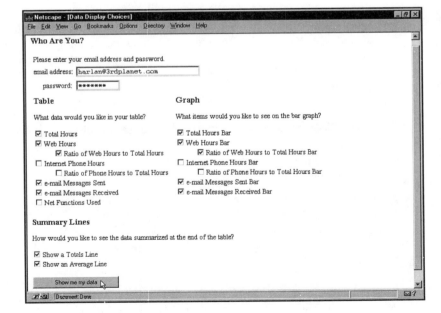

As you can see, the form in figure 4.2 presents a multitude of choices. Figure 4.3 shows the page that was produced when I submitted the form as shown. The script that processed this form and created the page is by far the most complex that you've seen so far in this book.

**FIG. 4.3**

The page results from the submission of the form in figure 4.2.

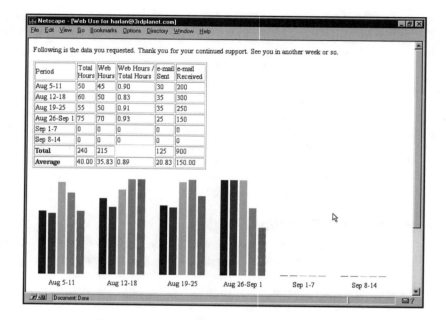

You must deal with many issues when you design a script such as this to create a user-designed page. You might be tempted to use conditionals, hard-coding the form fields into the script. This method would work, but it would make the script large and difficult to adapt to changes in the data. Instead, through careful form design and the use of some interesting Perl, you can make this script relatively short and fairly adaptable. Listing 4.4 shows the code.

**Listing 4.4   Part 1 of the *printcustomdata* Script (PRINTCUSTOMDATA.PL)**

```perl
#!/usr/bin/perl
require "process_cgi.pl";
require "check_pass.pl";

@fieldorder=('hours','webhours','webhourratio','phonehours',
    'phonehourratio','sentmail','receivedmail','waysused');

@fieldtitles=('Total<br>Hours','Web<br>Hours',
    'Web Hours /<br>Total Hours','Phone<br>Hours',
    'Phone Hours /<br>Total Hours','E-mail<br>Sent',
    'E-mail<br>Received','Ways Used');

@graphgifs=('hoursbar.gif','webhoursbar.gif','webhourratiobar.gif',
    'phonehoursbar.gif','phonehourratiobar.gif','sentmailbar.gif',
    'receivedmailbar.gif');
```

```
@period=('',"Aug 5-11","Aug 12-18","Aug 19-25",
    "Aug 26-Sep 1","Sep 1-7","Sep 8-14","Sep 15-21",
    "Sep 22-28");

&parse_input(*fields);
&print_header;
```

The code shown in Listing 4.4 presents nothing new but is important nonetheless. After requiring two outside files (you should recognize one and should be able to guess the function of the other), the script defines some arrays. The @fieldorder array does exactly what its name suggests; it establishes a field order for the data from the form. Each of the strings in the array is the name of one of the fields in the table section of the form. Recall that a comma-separated list of scalar data enclosed in parentheses is the equivalent of an array. This syntax is similar to the shorthand used in previous examples to extract array-type data from functions; it just goes in the other direction. (The importance of the @fieldorder array will become clear soon.)

The next two arrays establish two additional sets of string data. Notice that the data in these arrays follows the same order as the data in @fieldorder. Again, this is quite important, as you soon will see. The definition of the @period array is functionally identical to the way that this array is defined in Listing 4.1; this method simply requires less typing. Notice that a null string is the first element of this array. This is necessary because Perl arrays begin at index 0, and you want your data to start at 1.

Finally, the script parses the form input into the %fields array and prints the page header. This section of code sets the stage for a little fancy footwork, as you see in the following sections.

**Creating Code On-the-Fly**   The short section of code shown in Listing 4.5 begins the actual processing of the form. After setting $j (which will keep track of the script's progress through the loop in the following listing), the script defines a series of strings. You should notice that each string (up to $graphkey) is the beginning of a Perl statement.

> **Listing 4.5   Part 2 of the *printcustomdata* Script (PRINTCUSTOMDATA.PL)**

```
$j=0;
if (&check_pass($fields{'email'},$fields{'pass'})) {

    #Begin writing our 'mini-programs'

    $printtop='print "<tr><td>Period';
    $printrow='print "<tr><td>$period[$i]';
    $printtot='print "<tr><td><b>Total</b>';
    $printavg='print "<tr><td><b>Average</b>';
    $graph='$return=\'';
    $calchght='$return="';
    $printgraph = 'print "<table border=0><tr>';
    $graphkey='print "';

    $tableit='n';
    $graphit='n';
```

Part
II

Ch
4

The comment near the top of this block in Listing 4.5 says, "Begin writing our 'mini-programs,'" which is exactly what the code in Listings 4.6, 4.7, 4.8, and 4.9 does. By the end of these sections, the script will have created several strings that contain Perl statements for use later in the program. Why you're doing this will become clear soon.

Also notice that the first line of Listing 4.5 checks the subroutine &check_pass before moving on. This routine, which resides in the file CHECK_PASS.PL, checks that the user information submitted with the form is correct. Listing 4.6 shows the code.

**Listing 4.6   A Subroutine to Check User and Password Information (CHECK_PASS.PL)**

```perl
#!/usr/bin/perl

sub check_pass {
    $email=$_[0];
    $pass=$_[1];
    dbmopen (%users,"users",0666);
    if (!defined($users{$email})) {
      print "The email address you entered does not exist in our
          database. Please hit the back button on your browser,
          correct your entry and re-submit the form.";
      return 0;
    }
    else {
      $temp=$users{$email};
      dbmclose(%users);
      $temp=~/([a-zA-Z0-9]{5,10})$/;
      $actualpass=$1;
      if ($actualpass eq '') {
         print "There is no password entered for this e-mail
            address. Please enter one
            <a href=/userpassword.html>here</a>
            before you view your data.";
         return 0;
        }
      elsif ($pass ne $actualpass) {
         print "The password you entered is incorrect. Please
            return to the previous screen and try again.";
         return 0;
      }
      else {
         return 1;
      }
    }
}
return 1;
```

CHECK_PASS.PL should look familiar; the code is nearly identical to the section of code that performs the same function in Listing 3.8 (refer to Chapter 3, "Advanced Form Processing and Data Storage"). The first difference that you should notice is that whenever the test fails—that is, when the address does not exist in the database, or when the password doesn't exist or doesn't match—the subroutine returns a value of 0. When the password test passes, the subroutine returns a value of 1. This allows you to use the syntax `if (&check_pass()) {` to make sure that the user is authorized to execute the rest of the script.

You should also notice that because `&check_pass` prints the appropriate error message, the script doesn't need to do anything if this test fails. In fact, the last line of `printcustomdata` is the bracket that closes the block that starts at the top of Listing 4.5. Other than initialization, nothing happens if the `&check_pass` test fails.

Now that the password checking is finished and the various strings are initialized, you can move on to the meat of the program, shown in Listing 4.7. This section of the script is the first section of a loop over the `@fieldorder` array. You'll recall that a `foreach` loop starts processing at the first item of the given list or array. Because this particular loop has no scalar variable before the array, the loop places each successive item in the Perl special variable `$_`.

**Listing 4.7  Part 3 of the *printcustomdata* Script**

```
foreach (@fieldorder) {
    $findmax .= "\$max$_=\$$_ if \$$_ > \$max$_;\n";
    $calctotal .= "\$tot$_ += \$$_;\n";
    if (/ratio/) {
        $calcavg .= "\$avg$_ = sprintf ('%.2f', \$tot$_ / \$rationum) if
            \$rationum != 0;\n";
    }
    else {
        $calcavg .= "\$avg$_ = sprintf ('%.2f', \$tot$_ / \$num) if \$num !=
0;\n";
    }
```

The remainder of the loop occupies itself with appending appropriate text to the various strings that were initialized in Listing 4.5. Take a closer look at the first of those lines:

```
$findmax .= "\$max$_=\$$_ if \$$_ > \$max$_;\n";
```

What does this line do? You saw the `.=` assignment operator previously; it simply appends the string on the right to the variable on the left. What the string on the right will turn out to be may not be entirely clear at first; I'll explain.

Because the string is enclosed in double quotes, you are asking Perl to interpolate any variables or special escape sequences in the string. Right off the bat, though, you want the string to include a dollar sign before `max`. Putting a backslash before the dollar sign tells Perl that you want the actual dollar sign to be included in the string. Without the backslash, Perl would have looked for the variable `$max` and, finding nothing, replaced it with the null string.

Next comes the variable `$_`. Remember that this string is interpolated, so this variable is replaced by whatever `$_` contains at that point in the execution of the script.

Following the equal sign, another `\$` sequence tells the interpreter that you want another dollar sign. That sequence is followed by `$_` (no backslash).

You should have the idea by now. Each time through the loop, another line is added to $findmax. At the end, the contents of the string would look something like this:

```
$maxhours=$hours if $hours > $maxhours;
$maxwebhours=$webhours if $webhours > $maxwebhours;
$maxwebhourratio=$webhourratio if $webhourratio > $maxwebhourratio;
$maxphonehours=$phonehours if $phonehours > $maxphonehours;
$maxphonehourratio=$phonehourratio if $phonehourratio > $maxphonehourratio;
$maxsentmail=$sentmail if $sentmail > $maxsentmail;
$maxreceivedmail=$receivedmail if $receivedmail > $maxreceivedmail;
$maxwaysused=$waysused if $waysused > $maxwaysused;
```

You should be able to figure out what the next line does to its variable. One line of $calctotal's final form looks like $tothours += $hours;. Next, a conditional provides two options for $calcavg. As a result, two successive lines in the final contents of $calcavg will appear as follows:

```
$avgwebhours = sprintf ('%.2f', $totwebhourrs / $num) if $num != 0;
$avgwebhourratio = sprintf ('%.2f', $totwebhourratio / $rationum) if $rationum != 0;
```

These statements will be executed later in the script. First, I'll explain the two new pieces of Perl that you see in the preceding examples.

The first new element is the += assignment operator. Much like the .= operator, += is a shortcut for a commonly performed task. In this case, $a += $b is the functional equivalent of $a = $a + $b. Perl has several "shortcut" assignment operators.

**See** "Operators," **p. 391**

The second new element is the function sprintf, which is used to set the average variables. This function takes a string representing a format and a list of values. The format contains a list of symbols and flags that tell the function how to deal with the listed values. In this case, the format tells the script to print the first value in the list as a floating-point number rounded to two decimal places.

**See** "Function List," **p. 423**

The next section of code from printcustomdata, shown in Listing 4.8, builds the actual statements that print the table shown in figure 4.3. The initial conditional ensures that the script will print data only for those fields that the user requested on the form. Remember that @fieldorder contains the exact names of the fields from the table section of the form shown in figure 4.2.

**Listing 4.8  Part 4 of the *printcustomdata* Script**

```
if ($fields{$_} eq 'y') {
        $tableit='y';
        $printtop .= "<td>$fieldtitles[$j]";
        $printrow .= "<td>\$$_";
        $printavg .= "<td>\$avg$_";
        if (/ratio/) {
          $printtot .= "<td>";
        }
```

```
      else {
        $printtot .= "<td>\$tot$_";
      }
    }
```

Each time through the loop, $_ contains one of these key fields. By checking to see whether $fields{$_} is y, the script is checking to see whether the user wanted that particular field in his table. After the loop finishes, $printrow contains the following:

```
print "<tr><td>$period[$i]<td>$hours<td>$webhours<td>$webhourratio<td>$sentmail
  <td>$receivedmail;
```

The purpose of this line should be clear: it prints one row of the table shown in figure 4.3. The line does not contain the variables $phonehours, $phonehourratio, and $waysused, because they were not checked on the form (the user didn't want them to be included in the resulting table).

$printtop, $printavg, and $printtot end up containing similar data. The major difference is that because a total would make no sense for a ratio, the conditional if (/ratio/) { is used to make the appropriate adjustments. If this conditional is true, the script appends the appropriate code to $printot so that it prints an empty table cell; otherwise, text is appended that puts the appropriate variable in the next cell.

The final section of the foreach(@fieldorder) loop shown in Listing 4.9 prepares the statements that print the graph that the user designed. These statements are somewhat more complex than the ones in the preceding section.

**Listing 4.9    Part 5 of the *printcustomdata* Script**

```
if ($fields{"gr$_"} eq 'y') {
      $graphit='y';
      $graph .= "\$gr${_}['.\"\$i\".']=\"<td valign=bottom><img src=\/bars\/
        ${_}bar.gif width=15 height=\$${_}hght['.\"\$i\".'] >\";";
      $calchght .= "if (\\\$max${_} != 0) {\\\$${_}hght[\$i] = int((\$$_
        / \\\$max${_})*200);} else {\\\$${_}hght[\$i] = 0;}\n";
      $printgraph .= "\$gr${_}[\$i]\n";
      $graphkey .= "<tr><td align=right>$fieldtitles[$j]=<td>
        <img src=\\\"\/bars\/$graphgifs[$j]\\\">";
  }
  $j++;
}
```

Like the code shown in Listing 4.8, Listing 4.9 first determines whether the user wants to display a given piece of data in the graph. This is where careful form design comes into play. When I created this form, I made sure to name the check boxes for the graph portion of the form identically to those in the table portion, but I appended gr to the beginning of each name. By doing this, I have to loop through only 8 values, rather than 15.

The opening conditional in Listing 4.8 checks to see whether $fields{"gr$_"} is equal to y. If so, the user wants that data to be used in the graph. The first time through the loop,

Part
II

Ch
4

$fields{"grhours"} would be checked. Because grhours is a piece of data that the user indicated on the form that he wanted to see on the graph, $fields{"grhours"} does indeed equal y, and we execute the block of statements.

The first thing that this block does is set $graphit to y. This variable tells later code that the script has at least one graph element. Then you reach what has to be one of the ugliest statements I've ever written in Perl:

```
$graph .= "\$gr${_}['.\"\$i\".']=\"<td valign=bottom><img src=\/bars\/${_}bar.gif
width=15  height=\$${_}hght['.\"\$i\".'] >\";";
```

To make this statement a little easier to understand, examine what $graph will contain after the first time through the loop:

```
$return='$grhours['."$i".']="<td valign=bottom><img src=/bars/hoursbar.gif
width=15
    height=$hourshght['."$i".']>";
```

Okay, the statement probably isn't much more clear immediately, but let's press on. Remember that in Listing 4.5, $graph was initialized with the string $return= \'. When you append the string to $graph as shown, you have the start of a new assignment statement. As you can see, you're going to be assigning a big string to $return.

When this statement is executed, the script won't be just assigning one long string enclosed in quotes; it actually will perform several append operations, using the . operator. The two instances of $i are enclosed in double quotes; thus, they will be interpolated when this statement is executed. The rest of the strings are enclosed in single quotes specifically to prevent interpolation when this statement is executed. The reason is that this step is actually two steps away from the final piece of code. $calchght also is two steps away from the final piece of code.

The last two variables—$printgraph and $graphkey—are similar to the print variables in Listing 4.8 and should be easy for you to figure out.

Listing 4.10 shows the final piece of code needed to complete this section. This code completes all the strings that will be executed as statements later in the script.

**Listing 4.10 Part 6 of the *printcustomdata* Script**

```
$printtop .= '\n";';
    $printrow .= '\n";';
    $printtot .= '\n";';
    $printavg .= '\n";';
    $graph .= '\';';
```

```
$calchght  .= '";';
$calctop   .= '";';
$graphkey  .= '\n";';
$printgraph .= '</table>";';
```

**Using *eval()* to Execute Dynamic Code Sections**   By now, you're probably wondering how the script is going to use all the mini-programs discussed in the preceding sections. The listings in this section should answer that question nicely. Listing 4.11 begins the answering process.

---

**Listing 4.11   Part 7 of the *printcustomdata* Script**

```
#print out the top of the page.

    print "<title>Web Use for $fields{'email'}</title>";
    print '<body bgcolor="#FFFFFF">';
    print "Following is the data you requested. Thank you for your continued
support. See you in another week or so.<p>";

    #Run the first mini-program to print out the top of the table.

    if ($tableit eq 'y'){
      print "<table border=1>\n";
      eval($printtop);
    }
```

---

Listing 4.11 begins by printing the top of the page, starting with a title and the <body> tag; it then prints a brief greeting message before executing the conditional if ($tableit eq 'y') {. If the $tableit variable is y, you know that you have at least one field requested for the table (refer to Listing 4.8), and you want to initialize the table. After the print statement that outputs the tag to open a table, you see the command that is going to take care of all the mini-programs: eval().

Just as you would expect, this command takes the string that you give it and executes the string as though the lines that it contains were typed at that point in the program. In Listing 4.11, this eval() command prints the top row of the table, which contains the column titles for the user-requested data. Listing 4.12 continues the process of printing the table.

---

**Listing 4.12   Part 8 of the *printcustomdata* Script**

```
$num=0;
   $rationum=0;

   #Loop through the data.

   for ($i=1; $i<9; $i++) {
     open (data, "printdatasup period$i $fields{'email'} |");
     $data=<data>;
```

*continues*

**Listing 4.12   Continued**

```
if ($data ne '') {
    $num++;
    $data=~s/:::::/::0::/g;
    $data=~s/:::::/::0::/g;
    $data=~s/^::/0::/;
    $data=~s/::$/::n\/a/;
    ($hours,$webhours,$phonehours,
    $sentmail,$receivedmail,$waysused)=split(/::/,$data);
    if ($hours != 0) {
        $rationum++;
        $webhourratio=sprintf('%.2f', $webhours/$hours);
        $phonehourratio=sprintf('%.2f', $phonehours/$hours);
    }
    else {
        $webhourratio='0';
        $phonehourratio='0';
    }
```

Listing 4.12 begins by initializing two counter variables—$num and $rationum—that will be used to calculate averages; then it starts a loop from 1 to 8. This loop is the same loop that was used to scan the data in Listing 4.1. The beginning of this loop uses the support script from Listing 4.2 to grab the appropriate data from the DBM file. After checking for data, the script performs a couple of substitutions on the data to make sure that the data contains zeroes instead of blank fields; then it splits the data into separate variables.

Notice that the variable names used here are the names of the fields in the original form. The mini-programs created earlier in the script depend on these variable names. After splitting the data, the script calculates the ratios (notice the use of sprintf()) for Web hours and phone hours. You could have created a string to run through an eval() to perform this calculation. You may want to see whether you can figure out what that would look like.

After the data is split into the appropriate variables and the ratio calculations are made, Listing 4.13 shows a series of eval() statements. As the comment at the top of this section of code indicates, this code performs several key steps.

**Listing 4.13   Part 9 of the *printcustomdata* Script**

```
#Run the mini-programs to print a row
        #recalculate totals and find the maximum
        #value of a column.

        eval ($printrow) if $tableit eq 'y';
        eval ($calctotal);
        eval ($findmax);
        $finalgraph .= eval($graph);
        $finalcalchght .= eval($calchght);
        $graphbottom .= "<td align=center>$period[$i]";
    }
  }
```

The first `eval()` prints a row of the table. Remember that `$printrow` contains the following:

```
print "<tr><td>$period[$i]<td>$hours<td>$webhours<td>$webhourratio<td>$sentmail
<td>$receivedmail;
```

When the script evaluates this string the first time through the loop, it prints the following:

```
<tr><td>Aug 5-11<td>50<td>45<td>0.90<td>30<td>200
```

The next two statements evaluate two strings that amount to a series of assignment statements. The first string adds the current value of each variable to the appropriate running total; the second string makes sure that the maximum value for each variable is still the maximum.

The functionality of the next two statements isn't as clear. Earlier in this chapter, I said that `$graph` and `$calchght` are two steps away from the final code. The next few paragraphs discuss the first step. If you use `eval()` on the right side of an assignment, it works just like a subroutine. The last value of the last assignment statement in the block of statements (a string, in the case of an `eval`) is returned to the variable on the left side of the assignment.

If you look at Listing 4.5, you'll notice that `$graph` and `$calchght` each contain a single assignment statement. Thus, when the script executes the `$finalgraph .= ...` statement in Listing 4.13, it repeatedly appends the data from `$graph`.

Remember that parts of `$graph` were single-quoted and other parts were not. If you look at what `$graph` contained, you see that by the time the script gets through this loop, the final graph contains a series of assignment statements that look like the following:

```
$grhours[1]= "<td valign=bottom><img src=/bars/hoursbar.gif width=15
height=$hourshght[1]>"; $grwebhours[1]= "<td valign=bottom><img
src=/bars/webhoursbar.gif width=15 height=$webhourshght[1]>";
```

Each variable that the user requested for the graph is represented by an array that contains as many members as the user has entries in the database. Similarly, `$finalcalchght` contains a series of statements that create the `hght` arrays for each variable. When each of these new strings is evaluated later (in Listing 4.15), the arrays are created, and all the appropriate data is assigned to the appropriate places.

This may not be entirely clear on first reading, but it's worth taking the time to wrap your brain around this concept. The `eval()` function is an extremely useful tool in high-end form processing.

After all that complexity, Listing 4.14 is a nice change of pace. This section of code starts with a conditional to make sure that the code executes only if some table data was selected in the original form. If the code passes that test, it prints a totals line, if the user selected it. The script then calculates the averages and prints the averages line, if needed. Then the script closes the table and prints a paragraph mark to separate the table from the graph that follows.

Part
II

Ch
4

**Listing 4.14   Part 10 of the *printcustomdata* Script**

```
if ($tableit eq 'y') {
    eval ($printtot) if $fields{'total'} eq 'y';
    eval ($calcavg);
    eval ($printavg) if $fields{'average'} eq 'y';
    print "</table>";
    print "<p>";
}
```

The last section of `printcustomdata`, shown in Listing 4.15, prints the graph portion of the page. Not surprisingly, the code first checks to make sure that the user actually requested a graph. With that task out of the way, the script opens the table. Then the script evaluates the `$finalcalchght` and `$finalgraph` strings, creating the arrays that the `eval($printgraph)` statement will use to print the graph.

**Listing 4.15   Part 11 of the *printcustomdata* Script**

```
if ($graphit eq 'y') {
    print "<table border=0><tr>";
    eval ($finalcalchght);
    eval ($finalgraph);
    for ($i=1; $i<9; $i++) {
        print "\n<td valign=bottom align=center>";
        eval ($printgraph);
    }
    print "\n<tr>$graphbottom";
    print "</table><p>";
    $graphkey=~s/<br>/ /g;
    print "<table>";
    print "<tr><td colspan=2 align=center><b>Key</b><hr>";
    eval ($graphkey);
    print "</table>";
}
}
```

You may be curious about why I had to go through the bother of creating two `eval`s for this section of code when everything else could be done in the loop started in Listing 4.12. The difficulty lay in the fact that I needed a maximum for each variable to set a scale for each section of the graph. Netscape scales images to the size indicated in the `<img>` tag to make the bars of the graph. The actual GIFs that make up the bars are 14 pixels high by 14 pixels wide. By calculating a height for each bar relative to the maximum for that variable over all of the periods, I am able to scale each bar appropriately. The Aug. 26-Sep. 1 total hours bar, for example, is all the way to the top. That period happened to have the highest number of hours, so all the rest of the hours bars were set relative to it. This method seemed to be the best way to present the data in one graph.

After finishing the loop, the script prints the labels for each period and closes the table. The final act that this script performs is to print a key so that the user knows what each bar means. By now, you should be able to figure out how this procedure works.

As you've seen, the eval() function is a useful tool for interpreting some kinds of form data into truly advanced dynamic pages. The following sections introduce some other high-end page-output options.

# Returning Data to a Form for Further Revision

Beginning CGI programmers often get stuck in the mindset that forms are a data source, not an output option. This is not always the case. Almost certainly, a user will need to change some data that he entered at your site. The ability to take data from your data files and return it to a form for editing is an important tool to have in your CGI toolbox.

## Filling in Text Fields and Selecting List Items

Consider the periodic data-entry field shown in figure 3.5. Not every user is going to get his data correct right off the bat, so you should allow users to select and edit a line of data. I changed two of the scripts that appear earlier in this chapter for this purpose. Now, after a user enters data, a screen like the one shown in figure 4.4 appears.

**See** "Advanced Form Processing and Data Storage," **p. 73**

Part II
Ch 4

**FIG. 4.4**
This form enables the user to edit previously entered periodic data.

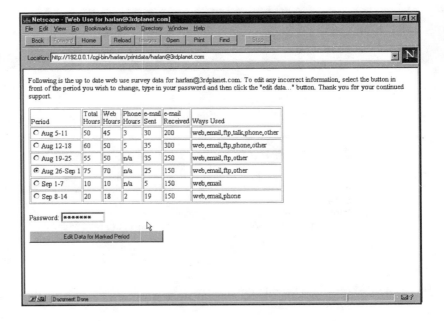

As you can see in the Location box in figure 4.4, this page was produced by a modified version of the printdata script shown in Listing 4.1. The new version of the script adds some code that makes the original table into an HTML form. The new code (PRINTDATA.PL) is on the CD-ROM that accompanies this book. To automatically direct the user to this script after entering data, I changed the postperioddata script (refer to Listing 3.8 in Chapter 3) to redirect the browser instead of printing a page directly; see POSTPERIODDATA.PL on the CD-ROM.

On the CD

When a user selects one of the periods and clicks the Edit Data... button in figure 4.4, a screen like the one shown in figure 4.5 appears. Notice that all the text boxes contain appropriate data and that the appropriate items in the Uses menu box are selected.

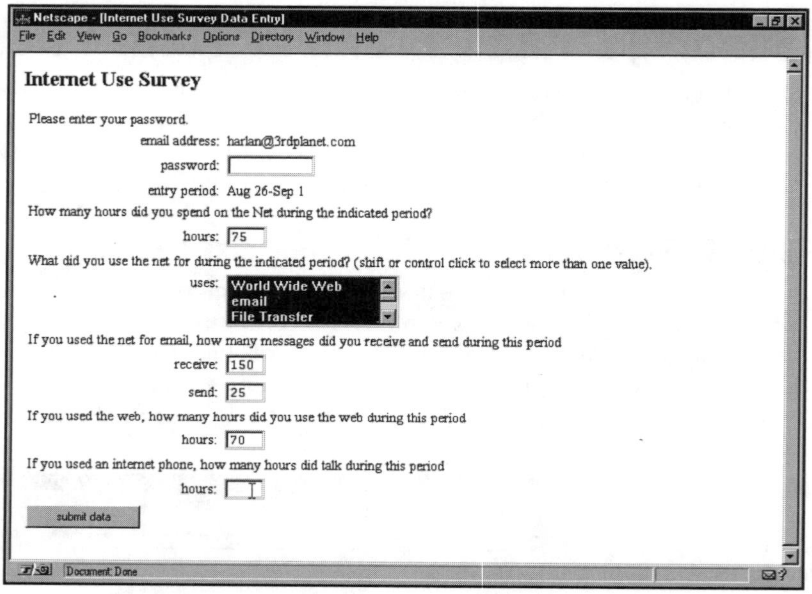

**FIG. 4.5**
The periodic data-entry form is generated on the fly for editing previously entered data.

Listing 4.16 shows the first key part of the code that creates this form. This block follows a straightforward initialization section that prints the header and initializes some variables.

---

**Listing 4.16   Partial Listing of *editperiod* (EDITPERIOD.PL)**

```
if (&check_pass($fields{'email'},$fields{'pass'})) {
  open (data, "printdatasup period$fields{'period'} $fields{'email'} |");
  $data=<data>;
  ($hours,$webhours,$phonehours,
  $sentmail,$receivedmail,$waysused)=split(/::/,$data);
  @waysused=split(/,/,$waysused);
  foreach (@waysused) {
    $dowaysused .= "\$${_}selected=\"SELECTED\";";
  }
  eval ($dowaysused);
```

---

The first thing that you should notice about Listing 4.16 is that it again uses the &check_pass() subroutine and printdatasup program. When the script gets the data back from the DBM file, it splits the data into the now-familiar variables. This time, however, the script splits one of those variables—$waysused—again. The script uses the resulting array in a foreach loop that builds a string that is evaluated in the last statement of Listing 4.16.

A closer look at $dowaysused clarifies what's happening. After the loop is complete, $dowaysused looks similar to this:

```
$webselected="SELECTED";
$emailselected="SELECTED";
$ftpselected="SELECTED";
```

When this string is evaluated, all the Web uses that the user selected have a corresponding selected variable set to SELECTED. When this process is complete, the script prints the actual form, as shown in Listing 4.17.

**Listing 4.17  Part 2 of *editperiod***

```
        print <<EOF
<title>Internet Use Survey Data Entry</title>
<body bgcolor=#FFFFFF>
<h2>Internet Use Survey</h2>
<form method=post action=/cgi-bin/harlan/postperioddata>
<table>
<tr><td colspan=2><p>Please enter your password.
<tr><td align=right>e-mail address:<td>$fields{'email'}<input type=hidden
name=email value="$fields{'email'}" size=30>
<tr><td align=right>password:<td><input type=password name=pass size=10
maxlength=10>
<tr><td align=right>entry period:<td>$period[$fields{'period'}]<input
type=hidden name=period value=$fields{'period'}>
<tr><td colspan=2><p>How many hours did you spend on the Net during the indi-
cated period?
<tr><td align=right>hours:<td><input type=text name=hours value="$hours" size=4>
<tr><td colspan=2><p>What did you use the Net for during the indicated period?
(Shift or Ctrl+click to select more than one value.)
<tr><td align=right valign=top>uses:<td><select name=uses multiple size=3>
<option value=Web $webselected>World Wide Web
<option value=e-mail $emailselected>email
<option value=FTP $ftpselected>File Transfer
<option value=Gopher $gopherselected>Gopher
<option value=IRC $ircselected>Internet Relay Chat
<option value=talk $talkselected>Talk (text based)
<option value=phone $phoneselected>Internet Phone (voice)
<option value=other $otherselected>Other uses
</select>
<tr><td colspan=2><p>If you used the Net for e-mail, how many messages did you
receive and send during this period?
<tr><td align=right>received:<td><input type=text name=receive
value="$receivedmail" size=4>
<tr><td align=right>sent:<td><input type=text name=send value="$sentmail"
size=4>
<tr><td colspan=2><p>If you used the Web, how many hours did you do so during
this period?
<tr><td align=right>hours:<td><input type=text name=webhours value="$webhours"
size=4>
<tr><td colspan=2><p>If you used an Internet phone, how many hours did you talk
during this period?
```

Part

II

Ch

4

*continues*

**Listing 4.17    Continued**

```
<tr><td align=right>hours:<td><input type=text name=phonehours
value="$phonehours" size=4>
<tr><td colspan=2><p><input type=submit value="submit data">
</table>
</form>
EOF
}
```

This listing presents a new piece of Perl syntax. The `<<EOF` after the `print` command tells the interpreter to print everything that follows until it runs into the label `EOF`. The next few lines are then treated as though they were a string—in this case, a double-quoted string. The primary advantage of this syntax in this application is that you don't have to worry about putting backslashes before any double quotes that you want to print. Variables are still interpolated, however. You can print single-quoted strings with this syntax by enclosing the label in single quotes. Had the script used the command `print <<'EOF'` instead, the variable references would not be interpreted, and instead of getting numbers in the form, the script would have printed the variable *names*.

Putting the values in the appropriate places in the form is easy. I put the values of text boxes after the appropriate `value=` attribute. When you set a selected variable for each Web use that occurs in the data, preselecting the list items is as simple as putting each selected variable next in the appropriate tag. If a particular Web use occurs in the data, the `<option>` tag ends up containing `SELECTED`, so that use shows up in the browser as being selected.

Although this block of text looks as though it may have been copied directly from the form's original HTML file, the code contains some significant changes. First, the code took away the user's capability to change the e-mail address and the period for which the data is being entered. Notice that the user sees these two pieces of information as straight text. In this new form, the appropriate data is also coded into a hidden field. Had the code allowed users to change this information, it would have created potential for confusion and perhaps lost data.

Also notice that the code requires the user to type his e-mail address again. Although I could have hard-coded the data into the form in a hidden field, I felt that the small inconvenience of having the user type the password again was offset by the added security. If this form resided on a site that had user authentication, I might have been able to prevent this repetitious password typing.

**See** "Understanding Basic User Authentication," **p. 215**

**TIP** One of the most important concepts for a CGI programmer to remember is the fact that Web applications are essentially stateless. The server makes no attempt to track a user's progress through a certain function, so if a function for your Web application is going to require three forms, you have to figure out a way to transmit the state of that function from one form to the next. The best CGI programmers understand this concept and develop an arsenal of tools (many of which are discussed in this chapter) to overcome this limitation.

## Saving and Editing User-Designed Pages

With some knowledge of editing previously entered data under your belt, now you can look for other kinds of data to store, retrieve, and edit. How about those user-designed pages that you created at the beginning of the chapter? Web users really appreciate sites that keep track of what they want to see. This section shows you a way to save a user's pages and enable the user to view and edit those pages.

**Saving the Custom Layout**  As you can see in figures 4.6 and 4.7, I have created scripts to store, retrieve, and edit the custom layouts that you spent so much time looking at earlier in this chapter.

**FIG. 4.6**

The bottom of a user-designed page gives the user the option to save this layout.

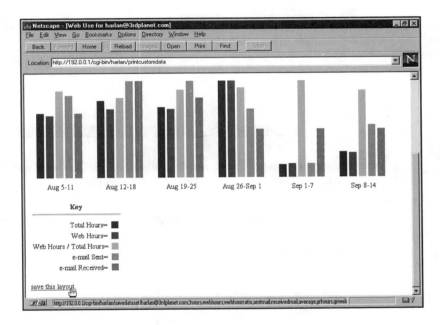

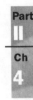

Figure 4.6 shows a good way to allow the user to save a layout. This link was a simple addition to the `printcustomdata` script that you examined in detail in Listings 4.4 through 4.15. I added the following line at the bottom of the script:

```
print "<p><a href=\"/cgi-bin/harlan/savedataset/$fields{'email'}::$saveit\">
    save this layout.</a>" if $direct ne 'y';
```

As you can see, the URL calls the script `savedataset`. You should also be able to tell that the script is going to get its data from the `PATH_INFO` variable. The variable `$fields{'email'}` should be familiar; `$saveit` should not. This new variable contains a list of the selections on the form. I built this variable in the same loop that built the dynamic code in `printcustomdata`. You can see exactly how this process works by looking at the code on the CD-ROM that accompanies this book (PRINTCUSTOMDATA.PL). I'll explain more about the conditional that controls this line later in the chapter.

**FIG. 4.7**

This listing of saved layouts is the result of selecting the link in figure 4.6.

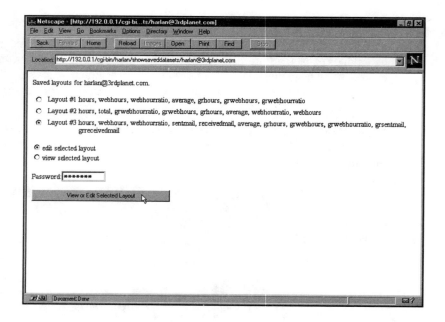

When the user selects the link shown in figure 3.6, the savedataset script saves the layout and prints the page shown in figure 4.7. Listing 4.18 shows the code.

**Listing 4.18    A Script to Save a User-Designed Page (SAVEDATASET.PL)**

```perl
#!/usr/bin/perl
require "process_cgi.pl";

if (&parse_input(*fields)) {
   $email=$fields{'email'};
   $pass= $fields{'pass'};
   $id= $fields{'layout'};
   delete($fields{'email'});
   delete($fields{'pass'});
   delete($fields{'layout'});
   foreach (keys(%fields)) {
     $data .= "$_,";
   }
   $data=~s/,$//;
   $data="NULL" if $data eq '';
}
else {
   $temp=&path_info;
   ($email,$data)=split (/::/,$temp);
}

dbmopen (%users,"users",0666);
if (!defined($users{$email})) {
   &print_header;
```

```
       print "The email address you entered does not exist in our
         database. Someone may be trying to fool us...";
   }
   else {
      system ("savegraph $email $data $id");
      &print_header ("http://192.0.0.1/cgi-bin/harlan/showsaveddatasets/$email");
   }
```

The first thing that you should notice in Listing 4.18 is the fact that this script checks for form input (if (&parse_input(*fields))...) before looking to the PATH_INFO variable for its data. I added this flexibility to avoid having to write another script to put edited data back into the database. When called from the link shown in figure 4.6, the script learns all that it needs to know from the PATH_INFO variable. The script splits the data into an e-mail address and the rest of the data: a list of fields that belong in this layout. The script then makes sure that the e-mail address exists in the user database. If the address doesn't exist, something has gone wrong, or someone is trying to fool the script.

You don't really need to check the password in this case, because the only way to get to this script is from scripts that check the password. A user could easily type some garbage to see what kind of result he would get. But because this data isn't very sensitive and the user can easily edit out any offending data, I didn't feel that the extra protection was necessary. By now, you probably can figure out how to add this protection on your own anyway.

After the script determines that the user exists, it makes a call to an outside program, savegraph (remember the limit of one dbmopen() call per script) to actually save the data. Listing 4.19 shows savegraph.

## Listing 4.19   Script to Save User Page Data to a DBM File (SAVEGRAPH.PL)

```perl
#!/usr/bin/perl

$email=$ARGV[0];
$data=$ARGV[1];
$id=$ARGV[2];
dbmopen (%graphs, savedgraphs, 0666);
if ($id ne '') {
   if ($data ne 'NULL'){
     $graphs{$email}=~s/\!\!\![\w,]+::$id/!!${data}::$id/;
   }
   else {
     $graphs{$email}=~s/\!\!\![\w,]+::$id//;
   }
}
else {
   $temp=$graphs{$email};
   $temp=~/(\d+)$/;
   if ($1 ne '') {
     $id=$1+1;
   }
   else {
```

*Part*

**II**

*Ch*

**4**

*continues*

**Listing 4.19  Continued**

```
    $id=1;
  }
  $graphs{$email} .= "!!${data}::$id"
}
```

Like its big brother in Listing 4.18, `savegraph` serves two purposes; it can deal with new data or edited data. The first thing that this script does is store the command-line arguments in `$email`, `$data`, and `$id`. The conditional `if ($id eq '')`... looks to see whether the script was called with a layout ID number on the command line. If not, the data that the script is given is for a new layout, and that processing takes place in the `else` section of the conditional.

This block begins by getting the current data for the given e-mail address from the DBM file `savedgraphs`, which was opened at the top of the script. The script then executes the command `$temp=~/(\d+)$/;`. This line of code places the number from the end of the data that the script just retrieved in the special variable `$1`. The script then checks for a number. If the script finds no number, this layout is the first saved layout, so the ID is set to 1. If the script does find a number, it adds 1 to that number to get an ID for the new saved layout. The script then appends the new data—with appropriate delimiters—to the data in the DBM file and exits, returning to `savedataset`.

On the CD

As you can see in Listing 4.18, only one command is left in the parent script: a call to the `&print_header` subroutine, with a location to direct the browser. The script at this location finally prints the form that you see in figure 4.7. The script, `showsaveddatasets`, is available on the CD-ROM that comes with this book (SHOWSAVEDDATASETS.PL). This script is a simple piece of code that you should be able to decipher without difficulty.

**Viewing and Editing the Saved Layouts**   With the data now safely stored, you need to act on the user's actions on the form shown in figure 4.7. Listing 4.20 shows the initial script that acts on the submission of this form.

**Listing 4.20  Script to Edit or View Selected Saved Layouts (EDITSAVEDLAYOUT.PL)**

```
#!/usr/bin/perl

require "process_cgi.pl";
require "check_pass.pl";

&parse_input(*fields);
&print_header;
if (&check_pass($fields{'email'},$fields{'pass'})) {
   open (data, "getlayoutdata $fields{'email'} $fields{'layout'} |");
   $data=<data>;
   if ($fields{'action'} eq 'edit') {
     open (out, "editlayout $fields{'email'} $fields{'layout'} $data |");
     @out=<out>;
     print @out;
   }
```

```
else {
    open (out, "printcustomdata $fields{'email'} $data |");
    @out=<out>;
    print @out;
  }
}
```

The basic format of the editsavedlayout script should be quite familiar to you by now. The script starts by requiring the CGI library and the password-checking script. The script then reads the input from the form, prints the header, and checks the password, just like many of the scripts in this chapter. When the password is confirmed, the script uses yet another support script (getlayoutdata, on the CD-ROM) to get the data for the chosen layout. If the user chose the Edit radio button, the script calls a new script called editlayout.

Listing 4.21 shows a partial listing of this script. Notice that the script again uses the eval function to create the variables that check the appropriate boxes on the form. Also, the script uses the print << syntax to ease the output of the on-the-fly form. The form that results from the submission of this form is almost identical to the original layout selection form shown in figure 4.2. The only differences are that the e-mail address is in plain text and that this version points to a different supporting script. Also, the layout number and the e-mail address are stored in hidden fields.

### Listing 4.21  A Partial Listing of *editlayout* (EDITLAYOUT.PL)

```perl
#!/usr/bin/perl
$email=$ARGV[0];
$number=$ARGV[1];
@data=split(/,/,$ARGV[2]);
foreach (@data) {
    eval ("\$${_}checked='CHECKED';")
}
print <<EOF;
<title>Data Display Choices</title>
```

When the user makes the desired changes to this layout, he can submit the form. The data is sent to the savedataset script (refer to Listing 4.18). I explained earlier how this script works with new data (and the PATH_INFO variable). With the edited data from this form submission, the information comes in through the normal POST-method channels, and the script accesses it through the &parse_input routine.

When the data is in the %fields hash, the script finds and saves the e-mail, password, and layout ID information. The script then uses a function that you haven't seen before— delete()—to delete those pieces from the %fields array. delete() does exactly what its name implies; it removes the indicated element from a hash. This function is useful in this case because you want to build your $data string from the remaining elements of the array. You use a foreach loop for this purpose, iterating over the keys of $fields. When $data is built, the script removes the extra comma from the end and then calls the savegraph script (refer to Listing 4.19).

Because the script calls `savegraph` with three command-line arguments this time, it knows that you are editing an existing layout. In most cases, the script performs a straight substitution, using the `s///` operator. Notice, however, that if the `$data` string is NULL, the script actually deletes the layout. If you refer to Listing 4.18, you'll notice that `$data` is set to NULL if it is empty at the end of the `foreach` loop that builds the string. This syntax provides a simple means of deleting unwanted layouts from the data file.

Why do I explicitly set `$data` to NULL instead of just allowing it to be empty? The problem is that if `$data` is empty, the script ends up calling `savegraph` with only two command-line arguments. The program would think that the ID is the data; it would see no ID, so it would create a new layout in the data file with bogus data.

When the processing of the edited data is complete, the program sends the user back to the listing of saved layouts.

If the user chose the View radio button in figure 4.7, the script calls `printcustomdata`, with the e-mail address and layout data as command-line arguments. The original version of this script did not account for dealing with command-line arguments, so I had to modify it slightly from what you saw in "Returning Data to a Form for Further Revision" earlier in this chapter. Listing 4.22 shows the most significant change.

### Listing 4.22   A Partial Listing of the New Version of *printcustomdata*

```
if (!(&parse_input(*fields))){
   $fields{'email'}=$ARGV[0];
   @layout=split(/,/,$ARGV[1]);
   foreach(@layout){
     $fields{$_}='y';
   }
   $pass="good";
   $direct='y';
}
else {
   &print_header;
   if (&check_pass($fields{'email'},$fields{'pass'})) {
     $pass="good";
   }
}
$j=0;
if ($pass eq 'good') {
```

As you can see in the listing, the modification was fairly simple. If `&parse_input` returned `false`, I knew that the script had been called directly. With that fact in mind, I put all the data in the appropriate places, building the `%fields` hash that would have come from `&parse_input`. Again, notice that careful form design and variable naming throughout this application helped immensely.

When `%fields` is built properly, the script sets two new variables. The first—`$pass`—substitutes for checking the password. Because the user has already authenticated to get this far, you needn't check again. The second variable— `$direct`—is used to prevent the `Save this layout` line from being printed at the end of the script. This option isn't necessary, and it would potentially cause confusion.

The `else` section of the conditional in Listing 4.22 performs password checking like the original version of the script and sets `pass` to `good`, if appropriate. The `if ($pass eq 'good') {` conditional replaces the password-checking line that you see at the top of Listing 4.5. If the password didn't pass muster, the script essentially stops at that point.

# From Here...

In the preceding two chapters, you got a detailed view of a relatively complex, user-driven Web application. Although you may not need a Web survey application, the concepts are applicable to a wide variety of programming chores. A good example is a companywide schedule book. Users would need to enter and edit data, and they would want to be able to view that data as flexibly as possible.

Now you're ready to find some new concepts to add to this knowledge. Following are some suggestions for further reading:

- Chapter 5, "Searching." These days, a Web site that doesn't have a search feature is almost sacrilegious. In this chapter, you find out how to implement your own search routines.
- Chapter 15, "Function List." By now, you should be thinking about things that you could do with Perl and CGI. If you're ready to branch out on your own, this chapter tells you everything that you ever wanted to know about Perl functions.

# CHAPTER 5

# Searching

*by David Harlan*

**T**he first part of this book spent a great deal of time looking at ways to deal with user input, parse it, view it, and return it to the user for editing. This chapter and Chapter 6, "Using Dynamic Pages," focus more on what CGI can do for pages that don't contain user data.

Web creators are always striving to put maximum content on a site. You know that the best sites out there are full of useful (or at least interesting) information. You also know that those sites make that information easy to find. This chapter closely examines a key feature that can make the data on your site more accessible: searching. ■

### Searching the full text of your site

Allowing a user to search for a single word or phrase is often the best approach for smaller sites. This section looks at a method that scans every word in every HTML document on your site to match the user's request.

### Indexing a Web site into a DBM file

For larger sites, scanning the entire directory structure for every search may be too much of a processing burden. This section examines a way to index every significant word on your site. The data is stored in a DBM file for almost instantaneous retrieval.

### Returning the documents

Sometimes, searching can create new frustrations when the user can't find the reference that he was looking for in the returned document. This section shows you a way to return the document to the user with the found words highlighted and referenced.

# Searching the Full Text of Your Site

If you've used the Web much, you've seen any number of Web-site search features. You've also discovered that some of these features are useful and that others aren't. But what makes the difference? From a user's perspective, the two main factors are speed and accuracy. A Web programmer has to weigh these two factors against the available resources to determine what kind of search feature is best for the site.

In many cases, simple search functionality is all that's required. If you have a small site and limited storage space on your server, for example, you can't afford to add several large files to your file structure just to support a search feature. But you might decide that you can afford to have a program search every file every time a request comes in, which is what you'll be doing in this first example.

## Scanning Directories Using a Recursive Subroutine

When an inexperienced programmer first examines the problem of scanning every file in a directory tree, he might be tempted to hard-code all those directories into the search script. You probably can guess that this action is a bad idea—it would not only make for ugly code, but also play havoc with the maintainability of your site. Fortunately, as with eval() and dynamic code in the preceding chapter, other options are available. The most obvious place to start is the search form, which at its simplest looks like figure 5.1.

**FIG. 5.1**
The user fills in and submits this form to perform a search of the site.

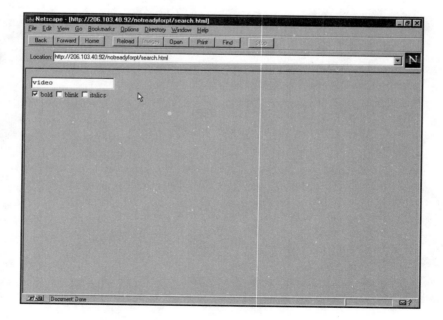

When a user enters a word or phrase into this form and presses Return, he hopes that the script will return the information that he's looking for. The only way that you can be sure to do this for the user is to make sure that you check every file on your site for that term, and fortunately, Perl provides some great tools that do just that. Listing 5.1 runs through a script that processes the form shown in figure 5.1.

**Listing 5.1   Part I of a Relatively Simple Search Script (search.pl )**

```perl
#!/usr/bin/perl

require "process_cgi.pl";

&parse_input(*fields);
$search=$fields{'word'};
&print_header;

if (length($search) < 4) {
 print "Search terms of less than four letters are not allowed.";
 exit 0;
}

$found=0;

@tag=split(/\0/,$fields{'tag'});
$tags=join ("::",@tag);

$directory='/usr/local/etc/httpd/htdocs/whitehorse';

print "<pre>";
&scan_files($directory,$search);
print "</pre>";
```

The code shown in Listing 5.1 is the entire main program for our search function. The first thing that this script does is read in the ubiquitous process_cgi library; it then prints the page header and reads the data from the form into variables. If the search term is shorter than four characters, the script tells the user a polite version of "Sorry, Bud" and exits; otherwise, it sets $directory to the desired starting point in the directory structure. Finally, the script calls &scan_files, and you can probably guess what goes on there. But instead of guessing, look at this subroutine in Listing 5.2.

**Listing 5.2   Part I of the &scan_files Subroutine from *search.pl***

```perl
sub  scan_files {
 my $dir=$_[0];
 my $st=$_[1];
 my (@dirs,@files,@results,$filename,$newdir,$list);
 opendir(dir,$dir);
 @dirs=grep {!(/^\./) && -d "$dir/$_"} readdir(dir);
```

*continues*

Part

II

Ch

5

**Listing 5.2 Continued**

```
rewinddir(dir);
@files=grep {!(/^\./) && /html$/ && -T "$dir/$_"} readdir(dir);
closedir (dir);
for $list(0..$#dirs) {
 if (!($dirs[$list]=[td]/temp/ ¦¦ $dirs[$list]=[td]/images/)) {
  $newdir=$dir."/".$dirs[$list];
  &scan_files ($newdir,$st);
 }
}
```

Right off the bat in Listing 5.2, you see a new piece of Perl. The first three lines of the subroutine begin with my. These lines aren't really being selfish; my actually is a call to the Perl 5 function by that name. The my function tells Perl that the listed variables should be treated as though they exist only in the current program block. This function allows you to set the variable at the same time as well (for example, my $dir=$_[0];) or to simply declare a list of local variables. The importance of these declarations will become clear to you soon.

After the variables are declared, you see a call to the opendir() function. This function creates a directory handle (similar to a file handle in the open() function) pointing to the specified directory. Directory handles are used by a set of Perl functions that allow the programmer to process directories in various ways.

**See** "opendir()," **p. 487**

One of these functions is readdir(), which appears in the next line. Having never seen the grep function, however, you likely are not too clear about what's going on there, so the following paragraphs examine that line in detail.

grep is named after a standard function on most UNIX-type operating systems that scans files for certain specified text. Perl's grep() function performs a similar but perhaps broader role. The function takes an expression and a list as arguments; it evaluates the expression for each element in the list and returns all the items from the list for which the expression evaluated as true.

The expression in this case—!(/^\./) && -d "$dir/$_"—has two parts, connected by Perl's and operator (&&). You should be able to decipher the first part; it says that you want the items from the list that don't start with a period. You may not recognize the second part of the expression, however. That part uses one of Perl's file-test operators: -d. This operator evaluates as true, if the argument to its right is a directory. In this case, the argument to the right is a string that, when the two variables are dereferenced, will contain each successive item in the list that you are checking, prepended with (the first time that the subroutine is executed) /usr/local/etc/httpd/whitehorse and a slash.

So here's what happens: readdir() returns an array that contains each item in the directory in a single element of that array. Because you are giving readdir() as an argument to the grep statement, the entire statement sets the array @dir to the list of all the directories within the original directory that do not start with a period.

The statement that follows—rewinddir (dir)—resets the pointer on the specified directory handle to the beginning of the directory, so that you can scan the listing again in the next line. This time, you are looking for files that do not begin with a period, that contain the string html at the end, and that are text files. The first two tests are accomplished by fairly obvious regular expressions. The third test is accomplished by another file-test operator: -T. The function is identical to its sibling described earlier in this section, with the obvious exception that it returns true for text files.

> **See** "Function List," **p. 423**

With the two arrays set, you now close the directory handle and move on to processing the information in the arrays.

The processing starts with the @dirs array, scanning through it by using a foreach loop. Although I could have accessed the data directly by using foreach $listitem(@dirs){, as you've seen before, in this case I used a different but equally valid syntax. This time, I told Perl to iterate from zero to the variable $#dirs. This variable is a special Perl variable that contains the index of the last item of the specified array. Because the script is iterating over the indices instead of the data, you'll notice that the code goes through a little more work within the loop to reference the data in the array itself. This syntax might be easier for some programmers to read and understand, however.

Within the loop itself, the first thing that the script does is determine whether the current item contains the string temp or the string images; if it does, the script skips that item. Why? Well, I know that in this site's directory structure, any directory called IMAGES contains only graphics files, and I don't want to waste processor time on those directories. I also know that any directories whose names contain the string temp do not have any documents that should be considered in the search. Any time I adapt this search script to a new site, I change this conditional accordingly. The new site may call its image directories by a different name; it might have other places where temporary documents are stored.

> **TIP** Searching is one good reason why Webmasters and CGI programmers want to pay close attention to their directory structures and what is contained in them. In my sites, I try to be as careful as possible in putting documents that are not intended for public consumption in places that search functions skip. I also like to place images in separate directories, mostly to keep them out of the way, but also so that I can cut (if even slightly) the processor time that a search may require.

After the first element passes these tests, I set the variable $newdir to that item, combined with the current directory and a slash. This means that $newdir contains the full directory path to the item. I then call &scan_files with $newdir and the same search string.

## Using Recursive Subroutines

This action of a subroutine's calling itself is known as *recursion*. Recursion is a common programming concept that is taught in almost every basic-to-intermediate programming class. If you aren't an experienced programmer, the concept may seem to be a bit odd, but trust me—it works. Recursion is most commonly used when a programmer needs some kind of looping but

Part

II

Ch

5

each successive iteration of the loop depends on some processing in the preceding iteration. In this example, you're scanning a directory tree. Obviously, you want to scan every subdirectory in that tree, but to do that, you have to scan every subdirectory's subdirectories. You get the idea. So you need to write a subroutine that keeps calling itself until it reaches a point at which there are no more subdirectories to scan.

When the subroutine is called the second time, it starts back at the top, just as described at the beginning of this section. This is where the importance of the my declarations comes in. If I hadn't made those variables local, each successive time the subroutine was called, the newer version of the subroutine would overwrite the data in those variables, and the results would be at best unpredictable and at worst garbage.

As it is, however, each successive call to the subroutine delves one branch deeper in the directory tree, creating a new list of directories and HTML files, and calling itself again for the first item in each new directory list. When a particular incarnation of the &scan_files subroutine calls itself, nothing further happens until the call to the subroutine "returns." This call can't occur until somewhere down the line the script finds a directory with no subdirectories. Then the latest incarnation of the &scan_files script moves on to process the @files array, as described later in this chapter. When that processing is finished, the subroutine returns successfully, and the preceding incarnation of &scan_files can move on to the next item in its directory list, calling itself again.

The processing moves on like this until all the results essentially cascade up from the bottom of the tree. When all the directories in @dirs from any incarnation of &scan_files are processed, the files from that particular incarnation can be processed. Finally, the script returns to the preceding &scan_files, and so it goes, back up the tree. When all the subdirectories in the original directory are finally processed, the files in that directory are processed—*last*. Again, it may seem to be odd at first, but if you take a simple directory tree and a paper and pencil, and trace out how it works, you'll see what I mean.

## Processing the Files in Each Directory

The actual processing of the files is relatively straightforward. As you can see in Listing 5.3, I use a foreach loop to iterate over the indices of the @files array. For each item in that array, I open the file that it points to and scan for the desired text by means of the while (<file>) { loop. You'll remember that this syntax places each successive line of the file in the Perl special variable $_. The first thing that this loop does is find the title of the document.

**Listing 5.3    Part II of &scan_files**

```
for $list(0..$#files) {
$filename=$dir."/".$files[$list];
$title=$files[$list];
open file, $filename;
while (<file>) {
 if (/<title>([^<]+)<\/title>/i) {
  $title=$1;
 }
```

```
  if (/$st/i) {
    s/<[^>]*(>|$)//ig;
    s/^[^>]*>//i;
    if (/$st/i) {
      my $urlsearch=$st;
      $urlsearch=[td]s/ /+/g;
      print "<a href=\"/cgi-bin/showfoundfile/$filename".".::",
        $urlsearch.".::"."$tags\">$title</a><br>\n";
      last;
    }
  }
 }
}
return 1;
 }
```

The conditional that accomplishes this task uses a match operator to check each line. This expression matches on any line that contains any text surrounded by `<title>` and `</title>`. One important thing to notice is that the expression is followed by `i`. This `i` tells Perl that I want it to perform a case-insensitive match. So whether the tags look like `<TITLE>`, `<Title>`, or `<title>`, the expression returns `true`. The characters between the title tags in the conditional (`[^<]+`) mean that I want to match one or more characters that *are not* less-than signs. Also, because this expression is enclosed in parentheses, this text is placed in the Perl variable `$1` when the expression matches. This fact explains `$title=$1;`—the line that is executed when the expression returns `true`. Thus, `$title` contains the text between the title tags in each scanned file.

The second conditional in the loop checks to see whether the current line contains the search text. If it does, the script does a little further checking. The two lines following this conditional remove any HTML tags from the line, using the `s///` substitution operator. The first of these lines removes any complete tags and any tag that begins but does not end on this line. The second line removes a tag that starts on the preceding line and ends in the current line.

Again, these expressions are followed by the `i` option to indicate case-insensitivity. The first expression also invokes the `g` option, which tells Perl to perform the substitution on the line as many times as possible. Notice also in the first substitution that the final element in the pattern that is being matched is `(>|$)`. The vertical-bar character (`|`) in a regular expression indicates alternation. This means that the pattern matches if it finds a > character or the end of the line in this position. This syntax allows you to match both complete tags and tags that start on this line with one expression.

After the script removes the tags from the current line, it checks again to see whether the line contains the search text. If so, you want the script to return a reference to this document to the user. Obviously, you could just return the title of the document, surrounded by an anchor tag and with an `href` attribute that points directly to the document. But I have a little something up my sleeve, so I don't do that. I want to refer the user to a script that processes and prints the document in a special way.

To do this, first I encode the search string so that any spaces in it become plus signs. Then I print the title of the document, with an anchor tag that refers the browser to a script with the search text and some extra information tacked onto the URL, so that this information ends up in the PATH_INFO variable. The final section of this chapter explains the method to this seeming madness.

The final command in this block, last;, simply saves a little processing time. After the first match in any file, this last; command ends the processing of that file completely. At this point you only need to know that the string was matched once in a file, so there's no need to go on after the first match. Efficient, eh?

Each file in the @files array is processed as described earlier in this section. A reference to any file that contains the search text is printed back to the user. When the processing of the @files array is complete, the subroutine returns, going back to the preceding incarnation of &scan_files to either process the next item in @dirs or (if this happened to be the last item in @dirs) to process its own @files array. When all is said and done, the user is presented with a complete list of files that contain the requested text.

# Using an Index Search

I hope you can see how effective the search that I just explained is. The search looks at every file on your site every time someone calls up the search function. You can probably guess one of the problems with this method: processing power. On a small site, a Web server running on "average" hardware can run through this search fairly quickly. But as a site gets bigger, the time that it would take to go through the each file and directory for every search request would become intolerable for the user (and, of course, would also bog down your server). For a bigger site, you want an alternative. One of the best alternatives is to index your site. To *index* means that you build a file that relates each significant word on your site to a list of the pages on which the word occurs.

Instead of scanning each and every file, this search method simply looks at the index file for its references. With the right structure for the index file, this process can be lightning-quick, taking very little processing power. The major processing takes place in the building of the index file, which would have to occur only once a day (or less frequently on a less dynamic site).

## Indexing Your Web Site into a DBM File

The process of indexing a Web site is accomplished with a script that is *not* technically a CGI script, because it will never be run by your Web server at the request of some remote user. The script is run from the command line by a Webmaster or is made to run automatically at specified times. Many parts of this script look quite similar to the CGI script described earlier in this chapter. Listing 5.4 shows how the script works.

**Listing 5.4  Part I of the Script to Index a Web Site (*indexsite.pl* )**

```perl
#!/usr/bin/perl

$directory='/usr/local/etc/httpd/htdocs/whitehorse';

dbmopen (%final, "index", 0666);
@time=localtime(time);
$time="$time[2]:$time[1]";
print "Scan started: $time\n";
scan_files($directory);
@time=localtime(time);
$time="$time[2]:$time[1]";
print "Scan complete: $time\n";
```

The first part of this script should be fairly familiar. Like `search.pl` in Listing 5.1, this script simply initializes some variables and then launches into its processing by calling a subroutine. Because you're not searching for any specific text here, you don't need to set a search string variable, and you don't need many of the CGI preliminaries. But as in the search script in Listing 5.1, you do set the starting directory. You also open a DBM file, which will be used to store the index information. With that done, the script does some basically unnecessary, but somewhat useful, printing before calling &scan_files. First, the script calls the `localtime` function, putting the results in the array @time. Then the script prints the time when the scan started, using two of the values from that array. This step is not strictly necessary, but it makes me feel better to see some output from the program as it's running.

Just like the first part of the script, the &scan_files subroutine in Listing 5.5 should look somewhat familiar.

**Listing 5.5  Part I of the *&scan_files* Subroutine of *indexsite***

```perl
sub  scan_files {
 my $dir=$_[0];
 my (@dirs,@files,@results,$filename,$shortfilename,$newdir,$list, %words);
 print "Scanning: $dir \n";
 opendir(dir,$dir);
 @dirs=grep {!(/^\./) && -d "$dir/$_"} readdir(dir);
 rewinddir(dir);
 @files=grep {!(/^\./) && /html/ && -T "$dir/$_"} readdir(dir);
 closedir (dir);
 for $list(0..$#dirs) {
  if (!($dirs[$list]=[td]/temp/ ¦¦ $dirs[$list]=[td]/images/)) {
   $newdir=$dir."/".$dirs[$list];
   &scan_files ($newdir);
  }
 }
```

I start the script by setting up my local variables, using the `my()` function just as I did in `search.pl`. Then, in an effort to give myself some peace of mind while the script is running, I print the name of the directory that the script is currently scanning. Why do this? By nature, I'm a cynic, and if I can't prove that something is working right, I assume that it's broken. Without the periodic update from the script, I would assume that the script is malfunctioning and that any moment, my server will go up in a ball of flames. Printing each directory name as I process it is an easy way to keep myself from worrying. In a more practical vein, if something does go wrong, the output can help point me to the problem.

The next few lines initialize the `@files` and `@dirs` arrays, just as `search.pl` did. With the arrays populated, the script iterates through `@dirs`, calling `&scan_files` for each directory found. Again, the only difference from `search.pl` is the fact that I don't need to look for any specific text, so I make the recursive call with the directory as the only argument. After all the directories are processed (refer to the description of *recursion* in "Using Recursive Subroutines" earlier in this chapter, if you haven't read it already), the script turns its attention to the files listed in the `@files` array.

Listing 5.6 shows where this script varies significantly from `search.pl`. The reason for this variation should be obvious. Whereas previously I was interested in finding one specific word or phrase, now I want to find *every* significant word in every document on the site.

**Listing 5.6   Part II of *&scan_files***

```
for $list(0..$#files) {
  undef(%words);
  undef(@results);
  $filename=$dir."/".$files[$list];
  $shortfilename=$filename;
  $shortfilename=[td]s/$directory//;
  open file, $filename;
  @file=<file>;
  $file=join(" ",@file);
  $file=[td]s/<[^>]*>/ /gs;
  $file=[td]tr/A-Z/a-z/;
  @results=split (/[^\w-']+/,$file);
  foreach (@results){
   s/^'//;
   s/'$//;
   s/^-//;
   s/-$//;
   if (length($_) > 3) {
    $words{$_}=1;
   }
  }
  foreach (keys(%words)) {
   $final{$_} .= "#$shortfilename";
  }
 }
return 1;
}
```

To do this, I iterate over the `@files` array. Each time through the loop, I initialize a few variables. First, I use the `undef()` function to make sure that the array `@results` and the hash `%words` are empty before I go any further. With that task accomplished, I append the directory name to the file name so that I can tell Perl exactly where to find the file. Then I set `$shortfilename` to contain the path from the original directory to the current file. I do this to keep the data that I will be storing in the DBM file as short as possible. Because I always know that I started with the directory in `$directory`, I don't need to put that information into the DBM file.

With all the necessary variables initialized, I open the specified file. Instead of using a `while` loop to look at each line, this time, I dump the entire file into an array. The line `@file=<file>` accomplishes this feat, putting each line of the current file (from the file handle `file`) into a field of the array `@files`. This method is an easy shortcut; use it so that you don't have to use the more common `while` loop syntax. From this new array, I then create one big string, using the `join` command.

Because I don't want to index any words that occur inside the actual HTML tags , I want to remove all the tags from the newly created string. The line `$file=[td]s/<[^>]*>//gs;` performs this task for me. The regular expression in this substitution matches anything that looks like an HTML tag. I tell Perl to substitute a space for each match. The `g` option that follows means that I want to perform this substitution as many times as possible. The `s` option tells Perl to treat the string as a single line. With this option enabled, the substitution operator allows new lines to match in the `[^>]*` portion of the pattern, which means that tags that span lines are removed. Finally, I use `"tr/A-Z/a-z/"` to translate all uppercase characters in the string to lowercase.

The `$file` variable now contains only the text of the document, with all words in lowercase. I now use the `split` function to put the words into the array `@results`. Although this is not the first time that you've seen `split()`, this instance is quite different from what I've shown you before. In previous uses, I split a string on some known character or simple string. In this case, I'm splitting based on a regular expression: `/[^w-']+/`.

What's going on here? I know that at this point in the processing, `$file` will contain only the text of the file, but I don't know exactly what that means. I might be tempted to split just on spaces, but that wouldn't take punctuation into account. So my next thought might be to split on any nonword character, using `/W`. That method would be a good option. I chose to go a little further, though. I wanted to include hyphenated words and words with apostrophes in my index; thus, I used the expression in the preceding paragraph.

In English, the split translates roughly to this: "Split the string `$file` on any series of one or more characters that do *not* belong to the set of word characters plus apostrophe and hyphen." What I end up with, then, is an array that contains (mostly) words. Of course, this result isn't perfect; I would end up indexing "words" such as *24-30* if I happened to have a document that referred to a week at the end of a month. But I can live with that result if someone can search for *Mason-Dixon* and find what she's expecting.

After building the array, I need to process it a little more before putting it in the DBM file. Processing each item in a `foreach` loop, I begin by deleting any leading or trailing single quotes or hyphens. With that task accomplished, I check to see whether the length of the item meets my criterion. If so, I make that item a key in the `%words` hash, with an arbitrary value of 1. I perform this processing until I've looked at all the members of `@results`.

When I'm done with this loop, `%words` contains keys for each significant word in the current file. Then I can iterate over these keys to put the appropriate information in the DBM file. For each word that occurs in `%words`, I append a delimiter and the current value of `$shortfilename` to the value of `%final` (which is the hash that points to the index DBM file), with the current word as the key. So if the current word is *that*, `$_` equals `that`, and I will append `#` and `$shortfilename` to `$final{'that'}`.

All this happens for each file that occurs in `@files`, for each instance of `@files`, and in each instance of `&scan_files`. The procedure sounds like a great deal of work, and it is. But when all is said and done, the result is a DBM file that has a list of words as its keys. Each of these keys points to a string that contains one or more file names delimited by the pound-sign character (#). Each of these files contains one or more occurrences of that key. Does that explanation make sense? I hope so.

## Performing a Search Using the Index File

All the work explained in the preceding section will be useless unless you find some use for this newly created DBM file, so I'd better show you the search function that goes along with the script. Assume that you're using the search form shown in figure 5.1 (refer to "Scanning Directories Using a Recursive Subroutine" earlier in this chapter). When the user enters some text and presses Return, he wants to see a list of documents that contain those words. Listing 5.7 shows the first part of a script that is intended to do just that.

---

**Listing 5.7   Script to Perform a Search Using a DBM Index File (*indexsearch.pl*)**

```perl
#!/usr/bin/perl
require "process_cgi.pl";
&parse_input(*fields);
$search=$fields{'word'};
&print_header;

@tag=split(/\0/,$fields{'tag'});
$tags=join ("::",@tag);

$urlsearch=$search;
$urlsearch=[td]s/ /\+/g;
$words=$search;
$words=[td]s/[^\w-' ]//g;
@words=split(/ +/, $words);

$directory='/usr/local/etc/httpd/htdocs';
dbmopen (%index,"index",0666);
$i=0;
```

The first section of this script performs all the preliminary steps needed before the bulk of the processing takes place. The script begins by parsing the input from the form and placing the search string in $search. The script then creates an array called @tag from the check boxes below the search-text box and then uses join() to create a single string that contains all the selected tags. Next, the script creates a string called $urlsearch. This string will be part of the URL that links to the returned pages. Then the script removes any characters from the search string that don't fit the criteria listed earlier in this chapter: any character that isn't a letter, a number, a hyphen, or a single quotation mark. After that, the script splits the search string into individual words in an array called (not surprisingly, I hope) @words.

TIP  You may notice that I silently ignore any illegal characters in the script shown in Listing 5.7. Some users may find this silence confusing or even annoying. Many Web users—particularly longtime Web users—expect to have complete control and knowledge of what's going on; they don't like things to go on behind the scenes (or, as they might say, behind their backs). If your site's target audience includes this type of user, you want to keep this attitude in mind. You probably will want to warn the user that he entered illegal characters in the search form instead of ignoring those characters.

Finally, the script sets the directory variable and opens the DBM file, ready to look for the search words. This process begins in Listing 5.8.

## Listing 5.8  Part II of the DBM Search Script

```
foreach $word(@words) {
 undef(%mark);
 undef(@files);
 $files=$index{$word};
 $files=[td]s/^#//;
 @files=split(/#/,$files);
 grep ($mark{$_}++,@files);
 if ($i > 0) {
  @combined=grep($mark{$_},@oldfiles);
  @oldfiles=@combined;
 }
 else {
  @combined=@files;
  @oldfiles=@files;
 }
$i++;
}
dbmclose (%index);
```

The processing of the @words array takes place in a foreach loop. (You should have been able to guess that by now.) The script begins by undefining two arrays to make sure that they are empty at the beginning of each iteration of the loop. Then the script sets $files to equal $index{$word}, which puts the list of files from the index DBM file for the current value of $word in $files. Next, the script removes the leading # before splitting $files into the array @files.

The following syntax is the key to this entire process. The intention of this script is to find all the documents that contain *all* the words supplied by the user in the form. To do this, the script needs to compare the @files array from each iteration of the foreach $word(@words){ loop with all the other @files arrays from all iterations of the loop. Unfortunately, Perl has no built-in logical-and function for arrays, so we use magic in this listing. Unlike most magicians, though, I'll explain the trick.

The first grep() creates a key in the hash %mark for each item in @files, assigning an arbitrary value to that key. How? Recall exactly what grep does: It evaluates the first argument for each item in the list in the second argument, returning an array that contains all the items for which the first argument evaluated true. In this instance, you really don't care whether the argument evaluates true; you're just using the grep as a quick way of giving %mark the appropriate set of key–value pairs, so you don't even assign the result anywhere. Notice that you could just as easily have set values for %mark by using a foreach loop.

As you can see by the conditional if ($i > 0) {, the first time through the loop, this hash doesn't get used at all. The script simply sets @oldfiles and @combined to equal the current value of @files, and moves on to the next word in @words. If the user happened to type only one word, the script is done. The array @combined contains the list of files that you want to return to the user.

But if the user typed more than one word, you go through the loop again. Again, you set the %mark as described earlier in this section. This time, though, you use it. You set @combined to equal the result of grep($mark{$_},@oldfiles). Don't blink, or you'll miss the slick part of this. Remember that %mark has a key associated with a 1 for each item in the current @files array. The second time through this loop, @oldfiles contains the @files array from the *preceding* iteration of the loop. So when grep evaluates $mark{$_}, for each item in @oldfiles, the expression is true only if the current $_ exists as a key in %mark. The value $_ exists as a key in %mark if that value was in @files this time through the loop. The result is that @combined contains only those values that existed in both @files and @oldfiles. Get it?

Each successive time through the loop, @oldfiles becomes @combined, so that when you do the grep($mark{$_}, @oldfiles), you're anding to the proper array. This process ands together arrays until the cows come home. In the end, when you run out of words in @words, @combined contains the list of files that contain all the words in @words.

Now all that is left to do is run through @combined so that the script can return a page to the user. Listing 5.9 shows this process.

**Listing 5.9    Final Section of *indexsearch.pl***

```
if ($#combined > -1) {
 foreach $list(@combined) {
  $title="${list}: No Title";
  $filename=$directory.$list;
  open file, $filename;
  while (<file>) {
   if (/<title>([^<]+)<\/title>/io) {
```

```
    $title=$1;
    last;
  }
 }
 close file;
 print "<a href=\"/cgi-bin/showfoundfile/$filename".":".$urlsearch.":",
  "$tags\">$title</a><br>\n";
 }
}
else {
 print "No matching documents found.";
 }
```

The script begins by checking to see whether there are any elements at all in @combined. If $#combined is greater than –1, there is at least one element, so the script starts a foreach loop over @combined. Initially in this loop, I set a default title for the document, in case one does not exist in the document itself. Then I set $filename equal to the current element of @combined appended to the value of $directory. Remember that the index script shown earlier in the chapter shortened the file names that it stored so as to save space. I have to add back here what I removed earlier so that Perl can find the file.

When the script has the full path to the file in $filename, it opens that file and searches for the title. This code is identical to the code that found the title of the documents in the preceding search script. Now, with the title of the document in hand, the script prints that title hyperlinked to a URL that sends the user to that document. This process occurs for each file found in @combined, so the result is a page that lists all the titles for the documents that met the user's search criteria.

There is one major functional difference between this search and the one that you saw earlier in this chapter. In this search, the text that the user enters is treated as a list of words. This search returns all documents that contain all the listed words anywhere in the document. By contrast, the first search treated the entered text as a string; it returned only those documents that contained the entire string, spaces, punctuation, and all. You will want to take this fact into consideration when you decide which search to implement on your site.

Part
II

Ch
5

# Printing the Resulting Pages

You may wonder why printing the resulting pages deserves its own section. As I said earlier, I have a bit of a trick up my sleeve that has the potential to enhance any search function significantly. Many times, when I have searched a site, I ended up going to pages where I couldn't even find the text that I searched for. I realize that most modern browsers have a command that allows the user to find text. But as a programmer, I wondered whether I could build this functionality into the search. The answer, of course, was yes. The following sections explain how.

# Returning Pages from the Nonindex Search

The first search function described in this chapter searched for a single word or phrase. A list of pages returned from that search might look like the page shown in figure 5.2.

**FIG. 5.2**

This page results from a user-initiated search.

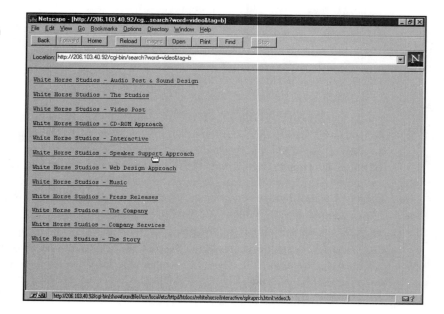

Figure 5.2 shows what is obviously a simple page—just a list of files. Select one of those links, however, and see what happens.

Figure 5.3 clearly shows the additional feature of this search function. The number of occurrences of the search term is indicated at the top of the page, and there is a link to each occurrence. Notice, also, that each occurrence in the text is marked with the tags that the user chose on the form shown in figure 5.1. Finally, a back link takes the user from the current occurrence back to the top of the page, should she want to go back. With this feature, the user gets not only the pages that contain her search term, but also direct links to every occurrence of that search term on every returned page. Listing 5.10 shows the first part of the script that accomplishes this minor miracle.

**Listing 5.10  Part I of a Script to Return a File from a Simple Search (*showfoundfile.pl*)**

```perl
#!/usr/bin/perl

require "process_cgi.pl";
&print_header;
$temp=&path_info;
($file,$st,$tag1,$tag2,$tag3)=split ("::",$temp);
```

```
$file=~m#/usr/local/etc/httpd/htdocs/whitehorse(/.*)/#;
$urlstart=$1;

$starttag="<$tag1><$tag2><$tag3>";
$endtag="</$tag3></$tag2></$tag1>";
$starttag=~s/<>//g;
$endtag=~s/<\/>//g;
```

**FIG. 5.3**

This page displays the information returned from the search.

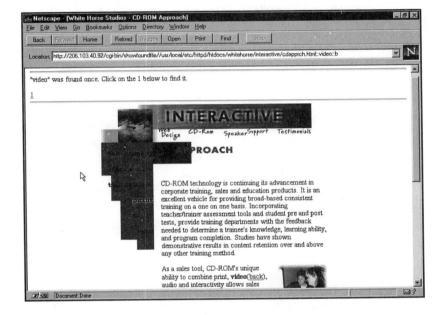

You shouldn't have too much trouble figuring out what's going on in Listing 5.10. The script begins by calling in the process_cgi library, printing the header, and grabbing the PATH_INFO variable; it then splits that variable into its components. Next, the script sets the variable $urlstart to contain the path to this file from the document root of the Web server. You may not recognize the m## pattern-match operator that I use for this purpose, but you have used this feature many times before. In those previous uses, you employed the standard delimiter, /. In such cases, you can (and normally do) leave off the m. I chose to perform this match in this fashion so that I wouldn't have to put backslashes in front of all the slashes in the string that I'm matching.

The final bit of processing in this section of the script sets up $starttag and $endtag. These variables function as their names indicate that they will: they contain the beginning and ending tags that mark the found text. You'll notice that the two substitutions that follow the initial assignments are necessary, because I don't know that any of the tag variables will contain any text at all. If any or all of the variables are empty, I have to get rid of the empty tags from the strings.

Part

II

Ch

5

The code shown in Listing 5.11 begins by initializing $page for later use and decoding the search text. Next, the script opens the file that the user selected and initializes a couple more variables. Then the script walks through the file, using the standard while loop. The first thing that this loop does is check to see whether the line contains the flag text EEENNNDDD. If so, the script sets $dontmark equal to y. You'll notice in the line that follows that if $dontmark equals anything but n, the script doesn't do any processing on the current line. This flag feature allows you to mark the ending portions of certain files as being off-limits to marking. This feature can be helpful if, for example, you have a footer on a page that might get mangled if you start pasting new anchors into it. To activate this feature, I simply put EEENNNDDD in an HTML comment at the point in the document where I wanted the marking to stop.

**Listing 5.11   Part II of *showfoundfile***

```
$page=' ';
$st =~ s/\+/ /g;
open (f,$file) ¦¦ print "couldn't open file ${file}:$!";;
$iteration=1;
$dontmark='n';
while (<f>) {
 $dontmark='y' if /EEENNNDDD/;
 if ((!(/<[^>]*$st/i)) && (!(/[^><]*$st[^>]*>/i)) && (!(/<title>[^<]+<\/title>/
i)) && ($dontmark
 eq 'n')) {
  if (/$st/i) {
   s/($st)/<a name=search${iteration}>${1}<\/a>(<a href=#searchtop>back<\/a>)/
gio;
   s/($st)/${starttag}${1}${endtag}/gio;
   $iteration++;
  }
 }
 s#(<[^>]+)(href¦src)(= *"*)(../)#$1$2$3$urlstart/$4#gi;
 s#(<[^>]+)(href¦src)(= *"*)(http:)#$1$2$3/$4#gi;
 s#(<[^>]+)(href¦src)(= *"*)([\w+])#$1$2$3$urlstart/$4#gi;
 s#(<[^>]+)(href¦src)(= *"*)(/)(http:)#$1$2$3$5#gi;
 push (@page,$_);
}
```

In addition to passing the $dontmark flag, the line has to pass three other tests before going on. The first two tests make sure that the line doesn't contain HTML tags that contain the search text. I choose to skip those lines that contain HTML tags, because they can cause significant confusion. I also don't want to do any additional marking inside the title tag, so I skip the line that contains the title.

After the line passes these tests, the script checks to see whether it contains the search text. If so, the script marks each occurrence of that text with a named anchor; it also adds a link that will take the user back to the top of the page. Finally, the script marks the found text with the tags that the user selected in the form. When the additional markup is complete, the script increments the $iteration variable, so that the next time the script finds the search text, the named anchor will have a unique identifier.

The next four lines are needed to change any URLs on the original page that are relative to that page's location into absolute URLs. If an image on the requested page is contained in the same directory as the page, for example, and is referred to by only its file name, without these substitutions, that picture would show up as a broken image on the page that this script outputs.

The first substitution takes care of any references to documents that are higher up in the directory structure. The second substitution temporarily puts a slash before any URLs that start with http:, so they are not affected by the line that follows. This line adds $urlstart before any references that begin with alphanumeric characters. (This situation would solve the problem in the example in the preceding paragraph.) The fourth substitution removes any slashes that were put before http: two lines earlier.

When all the appropriate substitutions are complete, the script adds the current line to the @page array, using the push function. When all the lines of the file have been processed, the script moves on to the code shown in Listing 5.12.

### Listing 5.12  Final Section of the *showfoundfile* Script

```
$header="<p>";
for ($i=1;$i < $iteration;$i++) {
 push (@header,"<a href=#search$i>$i</a>");
}
$iteration—;
$header=join(" ",@header);
$header="<a name=searchtop><hr>\"$st\" was found in $iteration lines. Click on
the numbers below to go to each occurrence.<p>".$header."<hr>" if $iteration >
1;
$header="<a name=searchtop><hr>\"$st\" was found once. Click on the 1 below to
find it.<p>".$header."<hr>" if $iteration == 1;
foreach $page(@page) {
 $page=[td]s/(<body[^>]*>)/$1$header/i;
 print $page;
}
```

The final section of showfoundfile begins by creating a header for the document. This header contains the links to each occurrence of the search text on the page. This process begins with a for loop that creates the list of numbered links, pushing each one into the @header array. When that task is finished, the script join( )s @header into a single string and then adds the explanatory text and formatting. You'll notice that if the search text occurs only once in the document, I use different text. Although this step isn't strictly necessary, it didn't cost much effort, and the result is better-looking output.

When it's done with the header, the script runs through the @page array created earlier and prints each line back to the user. When the script runs into the <body> tag for the document, it adds the $header text immediately after. The result is a page like the one shown in figure 5.3 earlier in this section.

As I described this script, you may have noticed that it is not perfect. The script requires all the HTML files to have a body tag, for example; it needs img and a tags to start on the same line as

Part

II

Ch

5

their `src` and `href` attributes. The script also may behave poorly if the search text was an HTML tag or an attribute to a tag. In the applications in which I've employed this system, these facts didn't matter, because the sites had solid HTML code to begin with—and also were sites whose users were extremely unlikely to search for HTML tags and attributes. You will want to take these limitations into consideration before you implement a search of this kind; you may need to modify it to fit your needs.

## Returning Pages from the Index Search

As in the nonindex search described earlier in this chapter, I want to be able to show the user where her search terms occurred in the returned documents. Unfortunately, I can't use the same `showfoundfile` script, because in the index search, the search string is interpreted as a list of words, rather than a single phrase. When a user executes a search and selects a file from the resulting list, figure 5.4 shows what she would see.

**FIG. 5.4**
This page shows the information returned from the index search through `showfoundindexfile`.

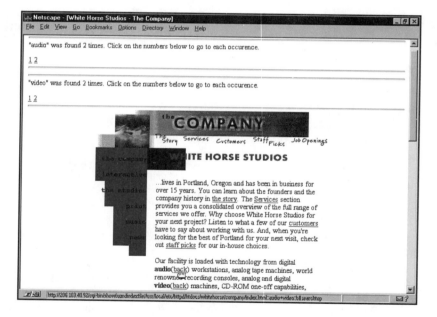

The first part of the `showfoundindexfile` script is identical to the code shown in Listing 5.10. The next section varies, as you might expect, because this script looks at the search text as a list of words. You can see the differences in Listing 5.13.

**Listing 5.13    Partial Listing of *showfoundindexfile.pl***

```
$page=' ';
$search =~ s/\+/ /g;
@words=split(/ +/,$search);
foreach (@words) {$iteration{$_}=1;};
```

```
open f,$file;
$dontmark='n';
while (<f>) {
 $dontmark='y' if /EEENNNDDD/;
 $i=1;
 foreach $st(@words) {
  if ((!(/<[^>]*$st/i)) && (!(/[^><]*$st[^>]*>/i)) && (!(/<title>[^<]+<\/title>/
i)) &&
   ($dontmark eq 'n')) {
    if (/$st/i) {
     s/($st)/<a name="search${i}$iteration{$st}">${1}<\/a>(<a
      href=#searchtop>back<\/a>)/gi;
     s/($st)/${starttag}${1}${endtag}/gi;
     $iteration{$st}++;
    }
  }
 $i++
 }
 s#(<[^>]+)(href¦src)(= *"*)(../)#$1$2$3$urlstart/$4#gi;
 s#(<[^>]+)(href¦src)(= *"*)(http:)#$1$2$3/$4#gi;
 s#(<[^>]+)(href¦src)(= *"*)([\w+])#$1$2$3$urlstart/$4#gi;
 s#(<[^>]+)(href¦src)(= *"*)(/)(http:)#$1$2$3$5#gi;
 push (@page,$_);
}
```

The first change that you'll notice is the splitting of the $st variable into the array @words. Immediately thereafter, the script initializes the hash %iteration. This hash performs the same function in this script that $iteration does in showfoundfile. After opening the file and setting $dontmark, the script runs through each line of the file with a while loop, just as the preceding script did.

Now, for each line, the script has to check for any occurrences of each word in @words. The code that checks for and marks the words is identical to that in showfoundfile; it's just embedded in a foreach loop that iterates over @words. The only change in the marking is the addition of the variable $i to the anchor name for each reference. This variable will contain one for the first word in @words, two for the second word, and so on. This makes each anchor name unique.

When the markup is complete, the script again has to resolve any partial URLs with the same four lines of code from showfoundfile. When that task is accomplished, the script pushes the line into the @page array and moves on. Listing 5.14 shows what goes on after the entire file has been processed.

## Listing 5.14  End of the Partial Listing of *showfoundindexfile*

```
$j=1;
$header="<a name=searchtop>";
foreach $st(@words) {
 undef(@header);
```

*continues*

Part

II

Ch

5

**Listing 5.14 Continued**

```
for ($i=1;$i < $iteration{$st};$i++) {
 push (@header,"<a href=#search$j$i>$i</a>");
}
$newheader = join(" ",@header);
$iteration{$st}—;
$newheader="<hr>\"$st\" was found $iteration{$st} times. Click on the numbers
below to go to each occurrence.<p>".$newheader."<hr>" if $iteration{$st} > 1;
$newheader="<hr>\"$st\" was found once. Click on the 1 below to find
it.<p>".$newheader."<hr>" if $iteration{$st} == 1;
$j++;
$header .= $newheader;
}
foreach $page(@page) {
$page=[td]s/(<body[^>]*>)/$1$header/i;
 print $page;
}
print $header
print @words;
```

After initializing $header, the script scans through @words. The processing that takes place in the loop builds the header for each word in @words. This process should look familiar. The major differences between this code and the same section in showfoundfile are the use of the hash %iteration in place of the scalar $iteration and the fact that I had to put the $j in front of $iteration{$st} in the anchor href for each occurrence of the current word. As soon as the header for each word is complete, I append it to the variable $header. So when this loop is finished, $header will contain a header for each word that the user searched for.

The end of this script is identical to showfoundfile. The script loops through the @page array, printing each line and adding the header text where appropriate.

# From Here...

This chapter exposed you to two effective methods for searching a Web site. For smaller sites, I demonstrated a full-text search that looks for a user-provided word or phrase in every file on a site. As an alternative for larger sites, you saw a method to index every significant word in the server's document structure. I also demonstrated a search method to go along with this indexing. Finally, I showed you an alternative method for returning pages from these searches to the user.

With these tools, you can implement your own search feature on your site. You may want to branch out in a different direction. Following are some suggested destinations:

■ Chapter 6, "Using Dynamic Pages." Netscape and Microsoft have implemented several innovative features in their browsers recently. This chapter demonstrates a few ways to take advantage of advanced features such as plug-ins, client pull, and server push.

- Chapter 11, "Database Interaction." Many people say that databases are key to the future of the Web. I agree. You may wonder how the average Webmaster can implement database technology on his or her site. Chapter 11 will help you take that leap.
- Chapter 14, "Operators." This chapter introduces several new Perl operators, but there are still many that you haven't seen yet. Head to Chapter 14 for the full details on all those nifty operators.

Part

II

Ch

5

# CHAPTER 6

# Using Dynamic Pages

*by Shelley Powers*

**P**eople are, by nature, dynamic and, for the most part, pre-fer a visually stimulating environment. Enter any scientific museum, and you will see that the displays that generate the most interest are those that do something. Given the choice of a static display or a changing one—or, better yet, one that allows interaction—most people will take the one with the interaction every time. Something about pressing a button to see what happens seems to be a fundamental human behavior.

*Dynamic Web sites* are those that change through anima-tion or interactive content while a person is accessing the site, or that change based on some factor each time the user accesses the site. Web page readers will access a dynamic, changing Web site more often than they will a static, unchanging one because of their curiosity about what the site will display next or do next, or about the information that it will provide next. Additionally, people are more likely to recommend a Web site that they visit often than they are to recommend a site that they visit only once or twice.

Webmasters understand these facts and work with their site's content accordingly. Examining many of the major Web sites, you can see that most companies change their Web sites at least once a week; in some cases, they change the sites daily. Companies use many Web capabilities to

### How to use Perl and CGI to generate an HTML page

You can generate HTML documents that change based on the time of day, the person who accesses the document, or some other factor.

### What can you find out from the environment using CGI?

Some environment variables are available for use by any CGI applica-tion.

### How to direct Web page read-ers to a Web page optimized for their browsers

With CGI, you can access the type of browser that the Web page reader is using and direct the reader's requests to the appropriate docu-ment.

### How to use client pull to create animation in a Web document

Client pull is a technique of using the Refresh response header to reload an HTML document after a specified period.

### How to use server push to create inline animation

Server push maintains a link be-tween the HTML document in the browser (after it has been loaded) and some application on the server that may change part of the document's contents on a periodic basis.

insert interactive and dynamic capabilities into their sites, including the use of animated GIFs, JavaScript and Java, plug-ins, and controls.

Perl and CGI can be used to add to the dynamic quality of a site. Web application developers can access variables and determine which Web page to open, embed animation in their pages, and personalize the Web pages based on time of day or some other factor. Best of all, these dynamic features can be set up once and not modified for some time, yet to the Web page reader, the site contents seem to be highly changeable. ■

# Generating HTML Pages

Generating HTML pages is a relatively simple process when you use Perl. When you have a basic idea of what you want to put on the page, you use Perl print commands to output the HTML tags. When the application is called, the program generates a response header and whatever HTML statements are necessary to create the Web page contents. The contents are sent to the server, which parses the results and displays them to the Web page reader.

Listing 6.1 contains a simple example of this process.

**Listing 6.1   Basic CGI-Generated HTML Document Page (*HelloWorld.cgi*)**

```
#!/user/local/bin/perl
#
# HelloWorld.cgi
#
# Application that will generate a dynamic HTML document.
# This simple example will create a document that contains
# a header, and a familiar message...
#
# response header - content-type, required
print "Content-type: text/html\n\n";
#
# redirect output, simplifies output of statements
print<<Page_Done;
<HTML>
<HEAD><TITLE>Listing 8.1</TITLE></HEAD>
<BODY>
<H1>And now, here is the document content...</H1>
<p>
Hello <FONT SIZE=5 COLOR="#FF0000">World!</FONT>
</BODY>
</HTML>

Page_Done

exit(0);
```

This CGI application prints the appropriate response header. Because the content that the application generates is HTML, the content type in the header is text/html. Next, the application outputs the HTML tags that create the Web page document: the HEAD section, the BODY section, a header (H1), and a message that probably is familiar to most programmers. The last statements finish the Web page document, and the application exits. Figure 6.1 displays the output from the CGI program.

**FIG. 6.1**
This Web document was generated by the CGI program HelloWorld.cgi.

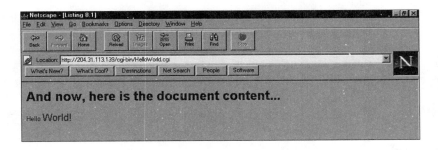

The CGI application has the extension .CGI, which is a relatively common approach to naming the application, especially if you do not maintain the traditional /CGI-BIN subdirectory for your CGI applications. The application can be called directly by the browser if the browser is configured to understand that documents with this extension are executable and can respond accordingly.

In addition, you can embed a reference to a CGI program directly into an HTML document by using the HREF anchor tag. Listing 6.2 contains the HTML statements to create a reference to the HelloWorld.cgi program. When the Web page reader clicks the link, the CGI application runs and outputs the results to the browser.

**Listing 6.2  HTML Web Page Document (*HelloWorld.html*) That Contains a Linked Reference**

```
<HTML>
<HEAD><TITLE> HelloWorld </TITLE>
</HEAD>
<BODY>
<H1> Link to CGI application </H1>
<p>
<a href="http://204.31.113.139/cgi-bin/HelloWorld.cgi">
  CGI Program</A>

</BODY>
```

Part
II

Ch
6

The HelloWorld.html document creates a link to the CGI application, and clicking the link executes the program.

**N O T E**  In Listing 6.2, the anchor references an URL that contains an IP address rather than a domain-name alias. The application was tested in UNIX and on Windows 95; and the Windows 95 test Web server—FolkWeb by ILAR Concepts, Inc.—was actually on my personal PC. To test

*continues*

*continued*

Web applications without having a full-time IP address, you can install some Web server (such as FolkWeb or Microsoft's Front Page) and then use the standard 127.0.0.1 loopback IP address. This IP address is always defined to mean "loop the request back to the site that is making the request." Changing the IP address was as easy as changing one field in a property sheet. After that, I was able to test the CGI applications locally on my machine, using Windows 95. ■

Although the sample presented in this section is an effective demonstration of using CGI to generate HTML pages, the results could easily have been created as a static document. The power of dynamically generated HTML pages is that they allow you to embed changing information in the document. The following section begins to cover this topic.

# Understanding the CGI Environment and HTML Generation

With the ability to use CGI to generate HTML documents, the Web application developer has access to the full programming power of the operating system on which the Web site resides and can use that power to create Web pages. In addition, information is available to help the developer determine what should be on the page or even what page should be displayed. Some of this information appears in CGI environment variables.

## CGI Environment Variables Using the *GET* Method

Chapter 3, "Advanced Form Processing and Data Storage," discussed using the GET and POST methods for form submission. This section lists out the CGI environment variables and displays their values based on using the GET HTTP request. The next section details the differences based on using the POST method.

When you use the GET method, the data for a form is appended to the URL of the CGI application when the form is submitted. Figure 6.2 displays a form with two text controls and a submit button. When the button is clicked, a document page appears, listing the values of several CGI environment variables (see fig. 6.3).

**FIG. 6.2**

envvar1.html is a form that contains a header, two text controls, and a submit button.

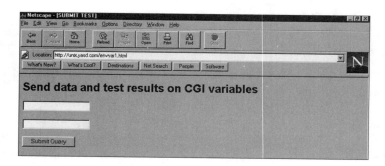

**FIG. 6.3**

This Web document was generated by `envvar.cgi`, which was run when the form in `envvar1.html` was submitted. The GET method was used for the submission.

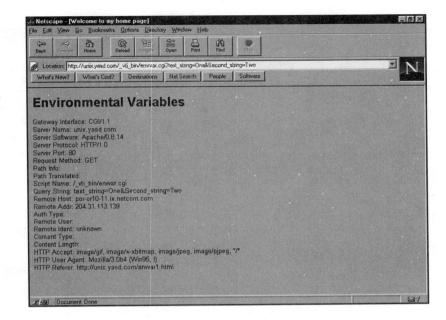

The document in figure 6.3 was generated by the CGI program shown in Listing 6.3.

**Listing 6.3   CGI Application (*envvar.cgi*) That Accesses and Prints Several CGI Variables**

```perl
#!/usr/local/bin/perl
# envvar.cgi
#
# Application will output CGI
# environment variables
#
# print out content type
print "Content-type: text/html\n\n";

# start output
print<<End_of_Homepage;
<HTML>
<HEAD><TITLE>Welcome to my home page</TITLE></HEAD>

<BODY>
<H1> Environmental Variables </H1>
<p>
Gateway Interface: $ENV{'GATEWAY_INTERFACE'}<br>
Server Name: $ENV{'SERVER_NAME'}<br>
Server Software: $ENV{'SERVER_SOFTWARE'}<br>

Server Protocol: $ENV{'SERVER_PROTOCOL'}<br>
Server Port: $ENV{'SERVER_PORT'}<br>
```

Part

II

Ch

6

*continues*

---

**Listing 6.3   Continued**

```
Request Method: $ENV{'REQUEST_METHOD'}<br>
Path Info: $ENV{'PATH_INFO'}<br>
Path Translated: $ENV{'PATH_TRANSLATED'}<br>
Script Name: $ENV{'SCRIPT_NAME'}<br>
Query String: $ENV{'QUERY_STRING'}<br>
Remote Host: $ENV{'REMOTE_HOST'}<br>
Remote Addr: $ENV{'REMOTE_ADDR'}<br>
Auth Type: $ENV{'AUTH_TYPE'}<br>
Remote User: $ENV{'REMOTE_USER'}<br>
Remote Ident: $ENV{'REMOTE_IDENT'}<br>
Content Type: $ENV{'CONTENT_TYPE'}<br>
Content Length: $ENV{'CONTENT_LENGTH'}<br>

HTTP Accept: $ENV{'HTTP_ACCEPT'}<br>
HTTP User Agent: $ENV{'HTTP_USER_AGENT'}<br>
HTTP Referer: $ENV{'HTTP_REFERER'}<br>

End_of_Homepage

exit(0);
```

---

The following list describes the variables displayed in figure 6.3 and explains their values:

- GATEWAY_INTERFACE: contains the CGI specification revision in the format CGI/revision. The example in figure 6.3 displays the value CGI/1.1 for this variable, which means that the specification revision of CGI that the server complies with is 1.1.

- SERVER_NAME: contains the IP address, the DNS alias, or the host name of the server. The example displays the value unix.yasd.com, which is the DNS alias for this site.

- SERVER_SOFTWARE: contains the type and version of the Web server software. The example displays the value Apache/0.8.14. (Time to upgrade.)

- SERVER_PROTOCOL: contains the name and revision number for the transportation protocol that the server uses. The example displays HTTP/1.0.

- SERVER_PORT: contains the port number that received the request. The demonstration displays 80.

- REQUEST_METHOD: contains the type of request made. In this case, the request method was GET, which means that when the form was submitted, the submission contents were appended to the URL. The impact of a POST request is explained later in this section.

- PATH_INFO: contains extra path information. This information is passed to the CGI program directly, after the URL of the CGI application and just before the question-mark character (?) that begins the list of data. The example does not show any value for this variable. If the HTML document contained the following line for defining the FORM submit action, the value in PATH_INFO would be /test:

```
<FORM ACTION="http://unix.yasd.com/book-bin/envvar.cgi/test" METHOD=GET>
```

This information is used in the PATH_TRANSLATED variable, which is discussed next.

- PATH_TRANSLATED: contains the value of PATH_INFO translated to an absolute address. This variable can be used to reference configuration files, or a subdirectory containing documents, or for other situations in which an absolute address is needed.

- SCRIPT_NAME: contains the script name and path as referenced from the URL. In the example, this variable contains /_vti_bin/envvar.cgi.

- QUERY_STRING: contains the information (still in a state that has not been decoded) that is passed after the ? when the URL of the CGI application is referenced. This variable has a value if the reference to the CGI program was accessed directly and if the ? values were coded directly into the URL reference. The variable also has a value when the CGI application is called as a result of a form submission when the GET method is used. The value is in name–value pair format; blanks are represented by plus signs (+), and name–value pairs are separated by an ampersand (&).

  The example displays the value text_string=One&Second_string=Two. This value indicates that the form had two text controls (which it does) and that the Web page reader entered the value **One** into the first control (which is named text_string) and the value **Two** into the second control (named Second_string).

- REMOTE_HOST: contains the name of the host that is making the request. In the example, this variable is set to por-or12-20.ix.netcom.com.

- REMOTE_ADDR: contains the IP address of the requestor. In the example, this value is 204.31.113.139.

- AUTH_TYPE: contains the authentication method if user authentication is deployed for the server and if the script is protected. (Chapter 8, "Understanding Basic User Authentication," discusses user authentication.) No authentication was used in the example, so this variable is empty.

- REMOTE_USER: contains the name of the user if authentication was required. In the example, this variable is empty.

- REMOTE_IDENT: contains the remote user name if the server is set up to use the identd identification daemon. This variable should be set only when logging in. In the example, this value is set to unknown.

- CONTENT_TYPE: contains the MIME content type of the data passed with the query, if the query was made with the POST or PUT method. Because the example used the GET method, this variable is empty. A demonstration of using the POST method appears in "CGI Environment Variables Using the POST Method" later in this chapter.

- CONTENT_LENGTH: contains the length of the data message if the data was sent with the POST or PUT method. Otherwise, the value is empty, as shown in the example.

- HTTP_ACCEPT: contains the MIME types that the client will accept, separated by commas. This variable helps the server program determine what it can return to the client. In the example, the value of this variable is image/gif, image/x-xbitmap, image/jpeg, image/pjpeg, */*. The format is in type–subtype order.

■ HTTP_USER_AGENT: contains the browser that the client used to send the HTTP request. This value is also the value from the User_Agent field. The example shows Mozilla/ 3.04b (Win95; 1) for this variable, with Mozilla (Netscape) being the software, 3.04b being the version, Win95 being the library, and 1 being the library version.

■ HTTP_REFERER: contains the URL that issued the HTTP request. The value in the example is http://unix.yasd.com/envvar1.html.

**ON THE WEB**

You can also find these descriptions at **http://hoohoo.ncsa.uiuc.edu/cgi/env.html**.

The GET method is losing popularity, primarily due to limitations on the length of the data string that can be sent to the server. GET is a handy choice, however, if the data string is not large and if you want to enable the user to record both the URL that contains the CGI application call and the data that is sent with the call. With this capability, the user can recall the program with the same content without having to access any preceding documents.

## CGI Environment Variables Using the *POST* Method

The POST method opens an input stream and uses this stream to send the data from the form to the CGI application. The application then uses standard input to access the data. When you use a browser that informs you when you are making an insecure transmission, you may get this notice when you use the POST method but not when you use the GET method. In addition, you could get server errors if your CGI application is not in a different subdirectory from the HTML document (as it should be).

Figure 6.4 displays a document page that is generated when the envvar.cgi program is called with the POST method instead of the GET method. The form contains two text controls and a submit button.

Listing 6.4 contains the form statements.

**Listing 6.4    Document (*envvar2.html*) That Calls *envvar.cgi* Using the *POST* Method**

```
<HTML>
<HEAD><TITLE>SUBMIT TEST</TITLE></HEAD>
<BODY>
<H1> Send data and test results on CGI variables </H1>
<p>
<FORM ACTION="http://unix.yasd.com/_vti_bin/envvar.cgi" METHOD=POST>
<INPUT TYPE="text" Name="text_string">
<p>
<INPUT TYPE="text" Name="Second_string">
<p>
<INPUT TYPE="submit">
</FORM>
</BODY>
</HTML>
```

**FIG. 6.4**
This Web document was generated by `envvar.cgi`, which was run when the form in `envvar2.html` was submitted. The POST method was used for the submission.

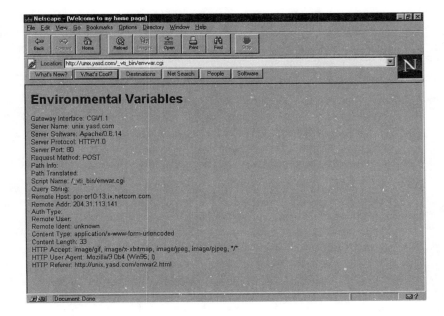

The following list describes the variables that change based on the different submission method:

- REQUEST_METHOD. The request method is now POST rather than GET.
- QUERY_STRING. The data string is passed via standard input by means of the POST method, so the variable QUERY_STRING is empty.
- CONTENT_TYPE. The content type of the data is displayed in this variable when the POST method is used. In the example shown in figure 6.3, the value would be application/ x-www-form-urlencoded.
- CONTENT_LENGTH. The length of the form data is recorded in this variable. The example displays the length 33 for the data string.

Well-behaved CGI applications never assume which method is used; they code for either method. A better technique is to use one of the established Perl libraries, such as `cgi-lib.pl` or `cgi.pm`, to access the query data.

# Referring the User to Browser-Specific Web Pages

The Internet and especially the Web are very dynamic and also very competitive. Web page readers can access a site with any of several browsers, among the most popular of which are

Part
II

Ch
6

Netscape, Mosaic, and Microsoft's Internet Explorer. One problem with this heterogeneous access is that if you can fine-tune your Web site for one browser, the site may break or look unattractive with another. Yet you want to provide a site that takes advantage of cutting-edge technology by using some of the newest techniques.

One option is to provide Web pages that are fine-tuned for only one browser and then to provide an alternative text-based Web page. A large number of sites display an icon for Netscape or Internet Explorer, for example, along with the information that the site is best viewed with that browser. This option can highly simplify the maintenance of the site. The downside of this approach, however, is that you are in effect opening the doors of your business or your home page to some customers and closing them to others. Most people would find this prospect to be unattractive.

Another option is to find the lowest common denominator among the most popular Web browsers and set your site to support the functionality defined by that browser. The advantages are the increased ease of maintaining the site and the knowledge that the Web site is readable by most people who access it. The downside is that people tend to embrace the newest technological advances on the Web and prefer Web content that takes advantage of what the new browsers allow. The popularity of frames highlights this fact. Businesses and Web page readers love frames, and a sophisticated site provides for content with and without frames, based on the reader's preference. If a browser cannot handle frames, the user is likely to see a message to this effect and little else, except maybe an annoying suggestion that the user get a different browser.

The third alternative is to test the browser before displaying any Web pages and then redirect the URL to a site that contains documents that the browser can display easily and attractively. This option, although not as easy to implement and maintain as the other two, is one of the better options from the viewpoint of the Web page reader. The reader has access to content that is fine-tuned to his or her browser, which in turn increases the reader's appreciation of the site and, perhaps, of what the site contains. Web page redirection is also popular for sending the Web page reader to the new URL of a page, if the URL has changed.

Figure 6.5 displays a plain-text Web page that is the best page for an unknown browser or a text-based browser.

The HTML statements that create this document appear in Listing 6.5.

### Listing 6.5   Simple Text-Only Web Page (*main.html*)

```
<HTML>
<HEAD><TITLE>Welcome!</TITLE><HEAD>
<BODY BGCOLOR="#FFEBCD" TEXT="#8B4513">
<H1>Welcome to my site! </H1>
<p>
This site will test your browser before opening up this page. Based
on the type of browser it determines, it will open a different page.
<p>
<H2>One page will be text only.</H2>
<p>
<H2>One page will be Netscape specific.</H2>
```

```
<p>
<H2>One page will be Microsoft Internet Explorer Specific</H2>
<p>
<H2>And one page will be Mosaic Specific</H2>
</BODY>
</HTML>
```

**FIG. 6.5**
This figure shows a basic text-based Web page.

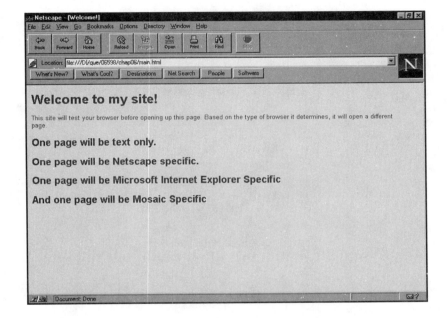

Figure 6.6 displays a basic Web page that contains one JPEG-type graphic. This type of page could be read by a graphical browser (such as Mosaic) but not by a text-based browser (such as Lynx).

The HTML statements that create the Web page with one embedded graphic appear in Listing 6.6.

Part
II
Ch
6

**Listing 6.6   Web Page (*maingrph.html*) with Text and One Embedded JPEG Graphic**

```
<HTML>
<HEAD><TITLE>Welcome!</TITLE><HEAD>
<BODY BGCOLOR="#FFEBCD" TEXT="#8B4513">
<H1>Welcome to my site! </H1>
<p>
<IMG SRC="garden2.jpg">
<p>
This site will test your browser before opening up this page. Based
on the type of browser it determines, it will open a different page.
```

*continues*

**Listing 6.6    Continued**

```
<p>
<H2>One page will be text only.</H2>
<p>
<H2>One page will be Netscape specific.</H2>
<p>
<H2>One page will be Microsoft Internet Explorer Specific</H2>
<p>
<H2>And one page will be Mosaic Specific</H2>
</BODY>
</HTML>
```

**FIG. 6.6**

This basic Web page contains one JPEG-style embedded graphic.

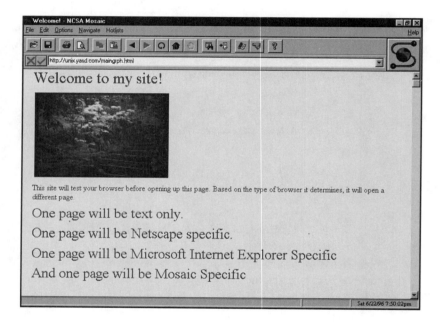

Figure 6.7 shows a more sophisticated Web page that contains five frames. The four top frames display JPEG-style graphics embedded in the documents that are opened in the frames; the bottom frame contains the main document. To read this page, the browser must support frames. Netscape version 2.x or later, Microsoft Explorer 3.x or later, and any other HTML-3.0-based browser can read frames. Trying to open this page without a frame-enabled browser results in a message stating that the browser is not capable of reading frames.

The HTML that creates the document that contains the FRAMESET document appears in Listing 6.7.

**FIG. 6.7**
This frames-based Web page has four JPEG images open in the four top frames.

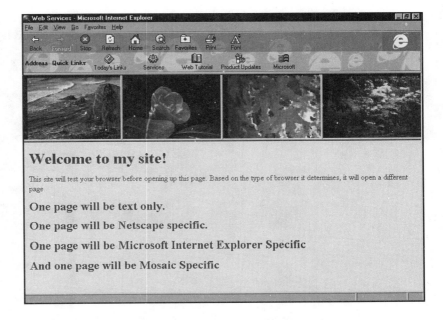

---

**Listing 6.7  Web Page (*frames.html*) That Creates Two Framesets Containing Two Rows and Four Columns**

```
<HTML>
<HEAD>
<TITLE>Web Services</TITLE>
</HEAD>

<FRAMESET ROWS="30%, *">
<NOFRAMES>
<p>You are using a browser that is not capable of working with
frames.

</NOFRAMES>

  <FRAMESET COLS="25%, 25%, 25%, 25%">
   <FRAME SRC="cliff2.jpg" NAME="Logo" MARGINWIDTH="0"
     MARGINHEIGHT="0" SCROLLING="no">
   <FRAME SRC="flower2.jpg" NAME="Stars" MARGINWIDTH="0"
     MARGINHEIGHT="0" SCROLLING="no">
   <FRAME SRC="leaves2.jpg" NAME="Stars" MARGINWIDTH="0"
     MARGINHEIGHT="0" SCROLLING="no">
   <FRAME SRC="garden2.jpg" NAME="Stars" MARGINWIDTH="0"
     MARGINHEIGHT="0" SCROLLING="no">
  </FRAMESET>
   <FRAME SRC="main.html" NAME="WorkSpace">
</FRAMESET>

</HTML>
```

Part
II

Ch
6

Finally, figure 6.8 displays a frames-based Web page that contains VRML files developed specifically for use with Netscape's Live3D plug-in. This document was developed for one and only one browser, at least at this time. If you try to open this document with another browser, such as Microsoft's Internet Explorer, the top part of the document will remain blank.

**FIG. 6.8**

This frames-based Web page contains four VRML files, one for each of the top-row frames.

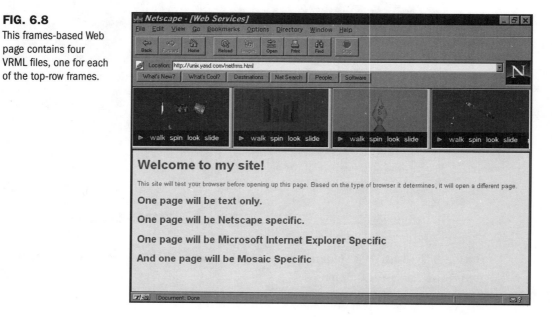

The HTML that creates this document appears in Listing 6.8. The code is virtually the same as that in Listing 6.7, except that files with the .WRL extension, rather than JPEG files, are open in the four top frames.

**Listing 6.8   HTML Document (*netfrms.html*) That Contains Five Frames, Four with VRML Files**

```
<HTML>
<HEAD>
<TITLE>Web Services</TITLE>
</HEAD>

<FRAMESET ROWS="30%, *">
<NOFRAMES>
<p>You are using a browser that is not capable of working with
frames.

</NOFRAMES>

  <FRAMESET COLS="25%, 25%, 25%, 25%">
   <FRAME SRC="box.wrl" NAME="Logo" MARGINWIDTH="0"
     MARGINHEIGHT="0" SCROLLING="no">
   <FRAME SRC="graph.wrl" NAME="Stars" MARGINWIDTH="0"
```

```
      MARGINHEIGHT="0" SCROLLING="no">
  <FRAME SRC="lava.wrl" NAME="Stars" MARGINWIDTH="0"
      MARGINHEIGHT="0" SCROLLING="no">
  <FRAME SRC="station.wrl" NAME="Stars" MARGINWIDTH="0"
      MARGINHEIGHT="0" SCROLLING="no">
 </FRAMESET>
  <FRAME SRC="main.html" NAME="WorkSpace">
</FRAMESET>

</HTML>
```

When the HTML documents are created, all that's left to do is create the simple (yes, simple) Perl program that chooses the correct Web page. The program accesses the CGI environment variable HTTP_USER_AGENT to find the Web page reader's browser. Then the program looks for a target substring within the string that contains the browser's name. Each target substring that the program looks at calls a different Web page, based on whether the substring is found. By default, if no substring match is found, the text-based Web page described in Listing 6.5— main.html—is called. The Perl code to determine the Web page appears in Listing 6.9.

**Listing 6.9   Perl Code (*choose.cgi*) That Accesses *HTTP_USER_AGENT* and Redirects the Browser**

```
#!/usr/local/bin/perl
#
# choose.cgi
#
# Application will check for the existing of certain
# key terms to determine which browser the web page reader
# is using.
#
# The CGI environment variable HTTP_USER_AGENT is accessed
# and certain substrings are matched against it. If
# a match occurs, the browser is re-directed to the
# document that matches the browser.
#
# If no match is found, the browser is directed to a text
# only web page.
#
# Access environment variable
$browser = $ENV{'HTTP_USER_AGENT'};
#
# check for Internet Explorer
if (index($browser,"MSIE") >= 0) {
   print "Location: ../book-html/frames.html\n\n";
} elsif (index($browser,"Mozilla") >= 0) {
   print "Location: ../book-html/netfrms.html\n\n";
} elsif (index($browser,"Mosaic") >= 0) {
   print "Location: http://unix.yasd.com/book-html/maingrph.html\n\n";
} else {
   print "Location: ../book-html/main.html\n\n";
}

exit(0);
```

Part

II

Ch

6

As I said previously, the application accesses the HTTP_USER_AGENT CGI environment variable and loads it into a variable. Then the application uses the index function to search for a substring in the environment string.

Notice, also, that some of the location paths are given with the full URL and others are given with a relative URL. This difference demonstrates one of the problems that can occur with this type of program. If you apply a relative URL to all the browser-specific paths, you receive an error message in Mosaic. Using a relative URL works without any problems, however, when you use Netscape or Internet Explorer. Coding to the standard of "if I don't, it will break," the best option is to add the full URL for all the browser types.

---

### Site Organization

You can organize your site in a way that helps with its maintenance when you use the redirection technique. If you call the script index.cgi and place it in your URL-based subdirectory, the CGI application is called automatically when your site is accessed by its IP address or DNS alias. Depending on the server and site, the server tries to access a file called INDEX.HTML or INDEX.HTM. If the server finds neither file, it probably will continue with others, such as INDEX.SHTML and, eventually, INDEX.CGI.

In addition, you can create subdirectories that are specific to content for each of the browsers, and name the main Web document page in each index.html. With this, you always have a default file of some form in all your public subdirectories.

Finally, once a month, check the main Web site of each browser for which you are providing direct support to see whether any changes have occurred. If so, test your content with the new browser; add any new features that interest you; and repair any existing features that no longer work. Then sit back and enjoy the accolades for providing a sophisticated and highly organized site.

---

# Using Client Pull with Perl

Client pull uses the Refresh response header to reload the HTML document automatically after a specified period. This technique originally worked only with Netscape; now it works with at least Internet Explorer 3.0 and Mosaic 2.1.1. Notice that with Mosaic, you are asked whether it is OK to reload the current document, which pretty much guarantees that you will not have smooth dynamic content.

Client pull uses the Refresh response header, which instructs the browser to load the same document or a different document after a certain period has passed. The response occurs only one time, so if the content is directed to a different page, the document does not continue to load. This technique is implemented by using the META tag of an HTML document. An attribute of the META tag is HTTP-EQUIV, which is a directive to the server that the META tag should be parsed by the server and converted to an HTTP response.

To use this directive, you set the HTTP-EQUIV attribute equal to Refresh and then assign the number of seconds to wait until the refresh to the CONTENT attribute. Following is an example:

```
<META HTTP-EQUIV="Refresh" CONTENT="5">
```

This example tells the server to refresh (reload) the current document in 5 seconds. When the document is reloaded, this directive again instructs the server to reload the document in 5 seconds, and the cycle continues.

You can have another document loaded by adding the URL to the document, as follows:

```
<META HTTP-EQUIV="Refresh" CONTENT="5; URL=http://www.your.com/doc.html">
```

This directive instructs the server to load the document located at **www.your.com/doc.html** in 5 seconds.

> **N O T E** The META element, which is contained in the HEAD section of an HTML document, contains three attributes. The META element must contain either a NAME or an HTTP-EQUIV attribute, but not both. The NAME attribute is defined by the browser that parses it. One use is to have the word *keywords* as a name; the CONTENT attribute will contain a list of keywords that describe either the document or the site. The HTTP-EQUIV attribute, used in combination with the CONTENT attribute, is parsed by the browser to provide response headers. ■

One popular use of this technology is to refresh screen cam sites, such as the famous FishCam site. If the site takes a static picture of an object at intervals of 30 seconds and uses the same name for this picture each time, refreshing the content of the document every 30 seconds results in the display of a new image, thereby providing dynamic content for the Web page.

Taking this concept one step further, you can call a CGI application in place of loading an HTML document, and the CGI application creates the document that is loaded. With each iteration of the program, the application can provide slightly different content.

Figure 6.9 shows a simple Web page that states that the Web page reader is there for the first time (at least for the current session). After about 30 seconds, a different page loads automatically, stating that the person has been at the page 1 time; the next iteration is 2, and so on. Figure 6.10 shows a Web page after two iterations of the refresh operation.

**FIG. 6.9**
This simple Web page contains a header that includes a META attribute to refresh the page automatically after 30 seconds.

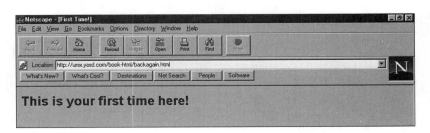

The first page is a standard HTML document that includes the HTTP-EQUIV attribute with its META tag. After 30 seconds, this directive has the server load a CGI application called `backagain.cgi`. The CGI application in turn creates a new HTML document with its own directive to refresh after 30 seconds. In addition, the number of iterations is passed as a query string in the URL for the application call. Listing 6.10 displays the HTML document statements, and Listing 6.11 displays the CGI application.

**FIG. 6.10**
This simple Web page was generated by a CGI application that displays the number of iterations of refresh and that includes its own META attribute to refresh again automatically in 30 seconds.

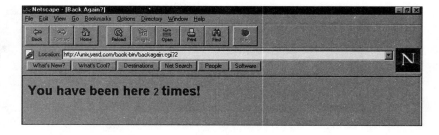

---

**Listing 6.10   HTML Document (*backagain.html*) That Contains the Refresh Response**

```
<HTML>
<HEAD><TITLE> First Time! </TITLE>
<META HTTP-EQUIV="Refresh"
CONTENT="30; URL=http://unix.yasd.com/book-bin/backagain.cgi?1">
</HEAD>
<BODY>
<H1>This is your first time here!</H1>
</BODY>
</HTML>
```

---

**Listing 6.11   CGI Application (*backagain.cgi*) That Includes the *HTTP-EQUIV* Refresh Response**

```
#!/usr/local/bin/perl
#
# backagain.cgi
#
# This application is called by the server based on
# a refresh response header embedded in a document.
# Each iteration is captured and printed out in the
# header of the new document that is generated.
#
$iteration=$ENV{"QUERY_STRING"};
$again=$iteration + 1;
#
# print out content type
print "Content-type: text/html\n\n";
# start output
print<<End_of_page;
<HTML>
<HEAD><TITLE>Back Again?</TITLE>
<META HTTP-EQUIV="Refresh"
CONTENT="10; URL=http://unix.yasd.com/book-bin/backagain.cgi?$again">
</HEAD>
<BODY>
<H1> You have been here
<FONT COLOR="#FF0000" SIZE=5>$iteration </font> times!
</FONT>
```

```
</BODY>
</HTML>

End_of_page

exit(0);
```

Informing Web page readers that they have been through the automatic refresh cycle a certain number of times is not very useful. You can, however, add content that increases the usefulness of this concept. The next example adds, to the end of the document, the information that at a certain time, the person who is designated as the Webmaster is either logged on to the system or logged out of the system. In addition, the CGI application is called directly from the browser, rather than being initiated by an HTML document. Listing 6.12 shows the Perl code.

**Listing 6.12   CGI Application (*backagain.cgi*) That Accesses the Time and Generates an HTML Document**

```
#!/usr/local/bin/perl
#
# backagain2.cgi
#
# This application is called by the server based on
# a refresh response header embedded in a document.
# Each iteration of this application will test to
# see if the webmaster is in and add this information
# to the document
#
# First, get the time and assign to variables
($sec,$min,$hour,$date,$month,$year) = localtime(time);
#
# Next, check for the webmaster
open(MASTER, "/usr/bin/w -h shelleyp |");
read(<MASTER>,$result,200);
if (index($result,"shelleyp") >= 0) {
   $status = "logged in.";
} else {
   $status = "logged out.";
}

close(MASTER);
# print out content type
print "Content-type: text/html\n\n";
# start output
print<<End_of_page;
<HTML>
<HEAD><TITLE>Back Again?</TITLE>
<META HTTP-EQUIV="Refresh"
CONTENT="30; URL=http://unix.yasd.com/book-bin/backagain2.cgi">
</HEAD>
<BODY>
<H1> Welcome to my site </H1>
<p>
```

Part

II

Ch

6

*continues*

### Listing 6.12    Continued

```
<H3>At $hour:$min:$sec The webmaster is $status </H3>
</BODY>
</HTML>

End_of_page

exit(0);
```

When the application is run, the time is accessed and output to variables. Then the application opens a pipe for the w UNIX command, which displays all the ongoing processes on a system and who owns those processes. Because the application is interested in only one person, the command is used with the -h flag, which directs the command to look only for the specified person. The handle is accessed with the Perl read function, and the results are output to the variable $result. Then this variable is used with the index() function to search for the Webmaster substring. The result of the search is output to the $status variable, which is printed in the HTML document.

Figure 6.11 displays the result of this CGI application while the Webmaster is logged in.

**FIG. 6.11**

This figure shows the output of backagain2.cgi while the Webmaster is logged in.

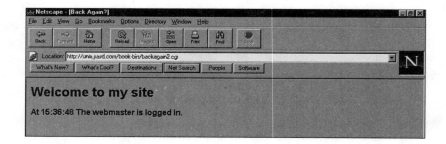

Figure 6.12 displays the result of the application after the Webmaster logs out.

**FIG. 6.12**

This figure shows the output of backagain2.cgi after the Webmaster has logged out and the HTML page has been refreshed.

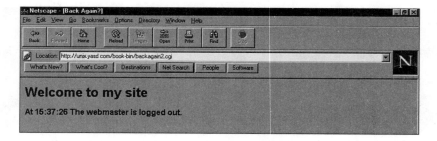

## ON THE WEB

Before the existence of Java, JavaScript, and ActiveX controls, client pull was one method of generating dynamic Web page content. This technique has lost popularity, however, primarily due to the rather clumsy refresh method of completely loading the Web page just to modify one portion of it. (For a rather humorous view of some sites that use client pull or server push, see the URL **http://www.chaco.com/useless/useless/auto-refresh.html**.) Although the technique is not effective for all uses, it can be effective for some uses, such as a timed demonstration that requires different Web pages to be loaded at certain times.

### Is CGI Dead?

When new technology is released, developers inevitably begin to talk about the death of existing technology. Sometimes, this prediction is true; many times, it isn't. A case in point is the release of Java. When Java was released, some Web application developers stated that CGI was "old" technology that was going to be "obsolete."

Any good Web application developer realizes that more than one tool can effectively and efficiently create the same functionality and that in most cases, it takes more than one tool to create a great Web site.

Does this mean that client pull is no longer a viable option? No—it just means that other options are available and that many of those options may be better.

# Using Server Push with Perl

*Server push* essentially means establishing a connection between the server and the client and then leaving that connection open. After the Web page document is downloaded, the connection is left open. After a certain period, the server sends more data to the browser, and that data is displayed. This cycle continues until the server stops sending data, the browser is closed, or the Web page reader moves to a different Web page or clicks the browser's Stop button.

Server push is based on an HTTP response containing a MIME type that is `multipart/x-mixed-remove`. What this means is that the data that the server sends could be of different types, such as text and a graphic image. Previously, the MIME type used for creating dynamic HTML pages has been `text/html`, meaning that the content is standard HTML format.

To use this MIME type, the CGI application needs to have a fairly rigid structure. The first part of the application has to turn off buffering if the data type is graphic images. Without this modification, the performance of your graphics will degrade to the point of being virtually useless. If you are like most developers (including the author), you don't think you will need to turn off buffering, but you will.

To turn off buffering, insert the following line as one of the first in your Perl application:

```
$|=1;
```

Part<br/>II<br/>Ch<br/>6

To increase the speed of the animation, the content is sent with the nonparsed header option. This option directs that the content be sent directly to the browser, rather than being parsed by the server. To use this option, precede the name of the file with nph-, as in nph-dynagraphics.cgi. Using this option means that you have to send the standard response header that normally is sent by the server.

Following is the standard HTTP header:

```
print "HTTP/1.0 200 Okay\n";
```

The Okay part of the message is the response that normally is transmitted when the document is successfully retrieved. The next line that your CGI application needs is the Content-type specifier. This line defines the content type and also defines the boundary of the data object that is being sent to the browser. This unique phrase is used to separate the data blocks.

The following line of code defines both the content type and boundary:

```
print "Content-type: multipart/x-mixed-replace;boundary=appboundary\n\n";
```

The x of the MIME type translates to *experimental*, and the replace instructs the server to replace the preceding block. The boundary in this example is set to appboundary.

Now that the boundary string has been defined, you need to print the boundary to start the data block, as shown in the following line of code:

```
print "—appboundary\n";
```

Next, you can output a graphic data block. You need to define the content type of the data object, which in this case is gif (for a GIF file). The type could also be text/html (for HTML format) or jpeg (for a JPEG file), as follows:

```
print "Content-type: image/gif\n\n";
```

The actual output is relatively simple. For a graphic, the graphic file is opened with the Perl open command; the file is printed with print; and the file is closed, as follows:

```
open(GRAPHIC, $member);
print <GRAPHIC>;
close(GRAPHIC);
```

Last, you must print the boundary string again to flush the buffers and to make sure that the content displays, as shown in the following code:

```
print "\n—appboundary\n";
```

If you remember each of these statements, the CGI application should perform as you expect it to. You can modify the types of the data blocks, and you can open and print the data blocks in a loop to enable animation. Figure 6.13 demonstrates a server push application that performs a relatively simple animation, using five GIF files.

Figure 6.14 demonstrates the same page, but now the graphic is different. Approximately every 3 seconds, the server loads a different data block into the GIF image. The image shown in the figure is actually the fourth image that was loaded.

**FIG. 6.13**

This figure shows the result of using server push to load an image just after the HTML document has been loaded.

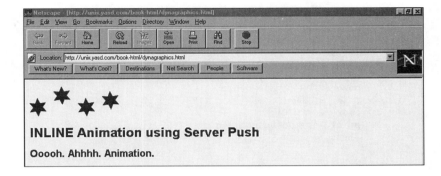

**FIG. 6.14**

This figure shows the result of using server push to load an image after the Web page document has been loaded for several seconds.

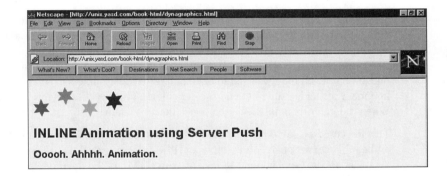

To create the type of effect shown in the figures, you need to create both a CGI application and an HTML document. Listing 6.13 shows the Perl code for the CGI application.

**Listing 6.13   CGI Application (*nph-dynagraphic.cgi*) to Implement Server Push to Create an Animation**

```
#!/usr/local/bin/perl
#
# dynagraphic.cgi
#
# This application uses server push to
# change the graphic that is displayed in
# an HTML document.
#
# create array of graphics
$|=1;
$count=1;
@grapharray = ("one.gif","two.gif","three.gif", "four.gif","five.gif");
# as file begins with nph-
# application needs HTTP directive
print "HTTP/1.0 200 Okay\n";
print "Content-type: multipart/x-mixed-replace;boundary=appboundary\n\n";
```

*continues*

Part

II

Ch

6

**Listing 6.13 Continued**

```
print "—appboundary\n";
while ($count <= 10) {
  foreach $member (@grapharray) {
   print "Content-type: image/gif\n\n";
   open(GRAPHIC, $member);
   print <GRAPHIC>;
   close(GRAPHIC);
   print "\n—appboundary\n";
   sleep 3;
  }
  $count++;
}
```

The Perl code contains the statements that have been discussed previously in this chapter. The names of five GIF files are loaded into an array. The HTTP response headers and MIME type are printed. Next, an outer loop that cycles 10 times is created. Finally, an inner loop is created; this loop cycles through the array that contains the names of the GIF files and accesses each one in turn. Each name is used to open and print the graphic file. After the file is closed, the boundary string is printed to end the data block. This process occurs for each of the GIF files. When the inner loop finishes, the outer loop runs again.

This file could be run directly from the browser, but a graphic by itself is not very helpful. To embed this server push animation in an HTML document, the application is actually called by means of an IMG tag. Listing 6.14 displays the HTML of the document that appears in figures 6.13 and 6.14.

**Listing 6.14 HTML Document (*dynagraphic.html*) To Create the Inline Animation**

```
<HTML>
<HEAD></HEAD>
<BODY BGCOLOR="#FFFFFF">
<IMG SRC="../book-bin/nph-dynagraphic.cgi">
<p>
<H1> INLINE Animation using Server Push"</H1>
<p>
<H2> Ooooh. Ahhhh. Animation.</H2>
</BODY>
</HTML>
```

Alternatives to using server push or client pull for animation are available now. You can create animated GIFs, for example, and you can use Java and JavaScript to change a graphic to create animation. However, server push is a fairly effective method of displaying different graphics when you are using JPEG format, or to display text or even data objects of different types. Additionally, after you create a server push application, you can reuse the same script to create other inline animations. Other techniques (such as animation GIFs) require tools that can create these types of files, or require you to be familiar with a language such as Java or JavaScript.

**ON THE WEB**

The example listed in this section is relatively simple; you can view more complex examples at **http://www.comp.vuw.ac.nz/~matt/serverpush.html**. For a humorous look at several sites that use this technique, check out **http://www.chaco.com/useless/useless/auto-refresh.html**. Just remember that the usefulness of a technique depends on the result.

# From Here...

Web page redirection, client pull, and server push are effective Web tools when they are used wisely. Each method requires resources, and each adds to the complexity of a Web site. In addition, server push can use valuable server resources to maintain the open link, and client pull loads a new document page for each iteration.

When used in the correct context, these techniques are very useful:

- To implement Web pages for more than one browser, use Web page redirection.
- To forward a Web page reader from one URL to another, use Web page redirection.
- To create a JPEG animation, use server push.
- To provide a demonstration in which each page changes after a certain interval, use client pull.
- To provide dynamic text banners without using Java, use server push.
- To implement Web pages for more than one remote user or host, use Web page redirection.
- To refresh a page dynamically (such as in a full-page stock-market display), use client pull.

For information on related topics, check out the following chapters:

- Chapter 7, "Dynamic and Interactive HTML Content in Perl and CGI," continues the discussion of dynamic and interactive documents by covering the process of creating Web page content dynamically, based on the reader and his or her preferences. The chapter also covers server-side includes (SSI), persistent cookies, and the shopping-cart application style.
- Appendix B, "Perl Web Reference," provides several sites that provide examples of this type of dynamic document content and that host discussions of the pertinent techniques.

Part
II

Ch
6

# Dynamic and Interactive HTML Content in Perl and CGI

*by Shelley Powers*

**C**hapter 4, "Advanced Page Output," contained some discussion of generating HTML content, and Chapter 6, "Using Dynamic Pages," extended this description with a detailed description of Web page redirection, the CGI environment variables, client pull, and server push. This chapter discusses additional aspects of using Perl to develop interactive and dynamic Web applications. ■

**Using the shopping-bin approach**

Develop a sophisticated shopping-bin approach to providing a customized interface for a Web page reader.

**Using server-side includes (SSI) to provide an access counter for a Web page**

Server-side includes are a quick and easy way to add an access counter to your Web site.

**Using SSI to provide a personalized greeting to the Web page reader**

Use server-side includes to add a personal greeting to the reader.

**Using persistent cookies to implement a shopping cart**

One common technique for maintaining a persistent link between the browser and the server is the use of Netscape cookies.

**Using hidden fields to implement a shopping cart**

A second technique for maintaining a persistent link between the browser and the server is the use of hidden form fields.

**Using Perl and CGI to implement an image map**

One technique for implementing an image map uses Perl and CGI.

# Creating User-Specific Pages

No matter how dynamic or interesting a page is, no one page can please all people or provide information that interests all people at all times. That old adage says you can please some of the people all of the time or all of the people some of the time, but you can never please all of the people all of the time. Application developers have always been acutely aware of this adage, particularly when they try to get the users of their application to buy off on a design or a deliverable.

Recent technology permits most of us to change our environments, at least on the computer. We have control of features as simple as what screen saver we use and what background we display; we can also control more complex features, such as what macros we install and what features we enable in the applications that we use.

In Web application development, the ideal approach is to present a list of options to a particular Web page reader and allow that reader to choose what content he or she wants to see and the way that the content is presented. Both Netscape and Microsoft implement some version of this approach with their personalized home pages.

You also can implement this approach by providing a shopping bin of components and allowing your users to select components from the bin. After a user makes his choices, the information is stored under his name or alias. When the user accesses the main document, such as INDEX.CGI, the application accesses the file that stores this information and basically builds the user's page, based on his preferences and including only the components that he picked. For a new user who does not have a previously defined preference, the application displays a generic Web page that includes an option allowing that person to define his own unique Web page. Creating user-specific pages usually implies two types of processing: one to allow the user to define what he wants on his page, and the second to actually create the page.

## Allowing the User to Shop for Options

The first technique to implement for the shopping-bin approach is to build a Web page that lists the options. This page must be accessible from your main Web site page. You also need to create the content bins. To do so, examine your Web site and determine what its major components are. If you are selling a product, you could organize the components in a catalog layout, or you could organize by department. If your site provides general information—such as the current weather, exciting events that are occurring that week, or major product announcements—you could classify each type of information as a major component.

For the example in this chapter, the major components are:

- **Company Announcements.** This section includes information about new products and company changes.
- **Product Announcements.** This section contains information about new and existing products, such as new releases and cost changes.
- **Product Announcements for Product X.** This section contains information that is specific to Product X.

- **Product Announcements for Product Y.** This section contains information that is specific to Product Y.

Normally, all these components would be available directly in the main Web page or as links from the main page. In the shopping-bin approach, part of the information will be listed in the user-specific Web page, and additional information will be listed as links.

After you determine the content of each section, the next step in creating a shopping bin is creating a form that asks for and processes the Web page reader's user name and password. Chapter 8, "Understanding Basic User Authentication," covers user authorization, and this form is covered in that chapter. After the user name and password have been processed, a second form opens, allowing the user to pick the options that he or she wants to see.

Figure 7.1 displays a form that allows the user to choose among the components listed earlier in this section. This form is generated by a CGI application that creates the HTML. The application also includes the new user name as part of a hidden field. The user name is sent along with the other form data. Listing 7.1 shows an example of this form.

**FIG. 7.1**
This Web document provides a form in which a Web page reader can choose preferences, enter a user name, and enter a password.

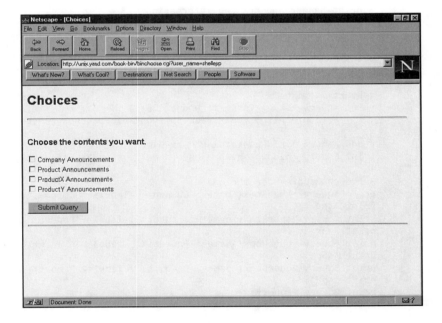

**Listing 7.1  HTML That Allows Web Readers to Specify Preferences (*binchoose.cgi*)**

```
#!/usr/local/bin/perl
#
# binchoose.cgi
#
# Application will generate an HTML document
```

*continues*

Part
II

Ch
7

**Listing 7.1 Continued**

```perl
# that contains the user name as a hidden
# field.  One method of implementing persistence across
# HTML documents.
#
# Application will also list content choices
#
# add location of CGI.pm
BEGIN {
    push(@INC,'/opt2/web/guide/unix/book-bin');
}
use CGI;
$query = new CGI;
#
# if existing parameters, get value for user_name
if ($query->param()) {
    $user_name = $query->param('user_name');
}
#
# print header and heading information
print $query->header;
print $query->start_html('Choices');
print $query->h1('Choices');
print "<hr>";
print $query->h3('Choose the contents you want.');
#
# start form
print $query->start_form(-method=>'POST',
    -action=>'http://unix.yasd.com/book-bin/process_request.cgi');
#
# add hidden field containing user name
print $query->hidden(-name=>'user_name',-value=>$user_name);
#
# add checkboxes for choices
print $query->checkbox(-name=>'Company',-label=>'Company Announcements');
print "<br>";
print $query->checkbox(-name=>'Products',-label=>'Product Announcements');
print "<br>";
print $query->checkbox(-name=>'ProductX',-label=>'ProductX Announcements');
print "<br>";
print $query->checkbox(-name=>'ProductY',-label=>'ProductY Announcements');
print "<p>";
print $query->submit;
print $query->end_form;
#
# finish document
print "<hr>";
print $query->end_html;
```

After the form is submitted, the application uses the user name and password to create an entry in the password file for the Web page reader. Chapter 8, "Understanding Basic User Authentication," goes into detail on this process, so it is not covered here. The application uses the rest of the contents to add an entry to a file that contains the user name.

The program that processes the contents adds an entry to a file called USERBIN.INP. Following is the format of the entry that will be added:

```
username::option1:option2:option3:…optionn
```

The user name is followed by two colons (::), which in turn are followed by a string that contains the options that the reader chose, with the options separated by single colons (:).

After the entry has been created in the USERBIN.INP file, the choices are processed. The resulting Web page displays the Web page reader's choices and a link to the site, as shown in figure 7.2.

**FIG. 7.2**

This page confirms that the Web page reader's choices have been saved and provides a link to the location that the reader needs to access.

The application uses the Perl 5.0 library CGI.pm to process the form after the Web page reader submits it. Listing 7.2 shows the code for this application.

**Listing 7.2   CGI to Process the Reader's Choices for a Dynamic Page (*process_request.cgi*)**

```perl
#!/usr/local/bin/perl
#
# process_request.cgi
#
# Application will access user name and
# check for it in password file.
# If name exists, reader will get a duplicate
# name response and a link back to try again.
#
# If name does not exist, name and choices are
# added to file.
#
BEGIN {
    push(@INC,'/opt2/web/guide/unix/book-bin');
}
use CGI;
$query = new CGI;
#
# if existing parameters, get value for user_name
if ($query->param()) {
    $user_name = $query->param('user_name');
```

*continues*

Part

II

Ch

7

**Listing 7.2  Continued**

```perl
}
print $query->header;
print $query->start_html('User Name Status');
#
# use grep to check for user name
$grep_string = "grep 'user_name=" . $user_name . "' userbin.inp |";
open(MASTER, $grep_string);
read(MASTER, $result, 100);
#
# if not found, add, else give message of duplicate
if (index($result, $user_name) > 0) {
    print $query->h1('Name already exists in system');
    print "<p> That name already exists.<p>";
    print "To try another go ";
    print $query->a({href=>"http://unix.yasd.com/unique/
add_user.html"},"here");
} else {
    &add_choices($query);
}
# finish document
print "<hr>";
print $query->end_html;

exit(0);

#
# Subroutine add_choices
#
# Access query sent from form with options
# Add user_name as first entry, then
# add each of the options, formatted
#
# output line to userbin.inp file
sub add_choices {
    my($query)=@_;
    $name=$query->param('user_name');
    $query_line = $name . ":";
    $company = $query->param('Company');
    if ($company) {
        $query_line = $query_line . ":Company";
    }
    $products = $query->param('Products');
    if ($products) {
        $query_line = $query_line . ":Products";
    }
    $prodx = $query->param('ProductX');
    if ($prodx) {
        $query_line = $query_line . ":ProductX";
    }
    $prody = $query->param('ProductY');
    if ($prody) {
        $query_line = $query_line . ":ProductY";
    }
```

```
      open(USER_FILE, ">> userbin.inp") ¦¦ die "Could not process request";
       $query_line = $query_line . "\n\n";
      print USER_FILE $query_line;
      close(USER_FILE);
      print $query_line;
      print $query->h1('Your page information has been added');
      print "<p> To try your page go ";
      print $query->a({href=>"http://unix.yasd.com/unique/index.cgi"},"here");
}
The application creates a line in the USERBIN.INP file that looks similar to any
one of the following:
joeg::Company:ProductY

tester::Products:ProductX

sallybrown::Company:Products:ProductX
```

An additional enhancement that you could make in this application would allow the Web page reader to modify his choices. Currently, the application does not allow modifications after the user makes his choices.

## Building an HTML Document Based on Options

When accessing his or her user-defined Web pages, the reader really is accessing the same CGI application as every other person who defined a user page. This application, called index.cgi, resides in a password-protected subdirectory. As stated previously, Chapter 8, "Understanding Basic User Authentication," provides the information necessary to set up this type of subdirectory.

Because the server is defined to look for certain files—such as INDEX.HTML, INDEX.HTM, INDEX.SHTML, and eventually INDEX.CGI—when a browser accesses a subdirectory, this application runs as soon as the subdirectory is accessed. First, the server determines that the file exists in a protected subdirectory and requests that the user enter his or her user name and a password. These entries are verified with the .HTPASSWD file; then the application runs.

Because the user's identity was verified by means of authentication, certain CGI environment variables are set. Chapter 6, "Using Dynamic Pages," contains a list and description of several CGI environment variables. In this case, the one variable that is of interest is REMOTE_USER. This variable contains the name that the user entered as his user name; it should also be the name that the user entered when he defined his Web page.

The index.cgi application accesses the REMOTE_USER variable and then accesses the options that the reader specified for his other_page. The application parses the options one at a time and then builds the page by accessing the subroutine that processes that particular option. Listing 7.3 shows the code for the main program of index.cgi.

**Listing 7.3 Application to Access User-Specified Options and Call the Appropriate Subroutines (*index.cgi*)**

```
#!/usr/local/bin/perl
#
# index.cgi
#
# Opens userbin.inp and pulls in user's choices.
#
BEGIN {
    push(@INC,'/opt2/web/guide/unix/book-bin');
}
use CGI;
$query = new CGI;
#
# printer document header
$user_name = $ENV{'REMOTE_USER'};
print $query->header;
print $query->start_html('The Unique Page');
print $query->h1("Some Software Company");
#
# use grep to check for user name
$grep_string = "grep '" . $user_name . "' userbin.inp |";
open(MASTER, $grep_string);
read(MASTER, $result, 100);
close(MASTER);
#
# if not found, return, else give pull in components
if (index($result, $user_name) >= 0) {
    &get_options($user_name);
} else {
    &not_found($user_name);
}
print "<ADDRESS> <a href='mailto:shelleyp\@yasd.com'>Webmaster</a></ADDRESS>";
print $query->end_html;

exit(0);
```

Notice that the Webmaster `mailto` is added at the bottom after all the components have been added and the page is complete.

At least two options determine how to add the components of each section of the Web page that is being built. One option is to use Perl to print the component content. The advantage of using this method is that you could use the same technique to generate all the sections of the document. The Perl library `CGI.pm` is particularly suited for this purpose, because it contains defined objects that can easily create whatever content is needed for the page.

Listing 7.4 shows the subroutine that creates the Company Announcements component.

**Listing 7.4  Subroutine That Generates the General Company Announcements (*index.cgi*)**

```
Sub print_company {
      print "<FONT SIZE=5 COLOR='#FF0000'>RECORD EARNINGS!</FONT>";
      print "<p>";
      print "Some Software Company has announced that they have exceeded all";
      print "industry experts and have made a whopping $50,000,000.00 this last";
      print "quarter.  When the news was announced, stockholders, all two of";
      print "them, collapsed in shock.  Some Software Company CEO Joe Software";
      print "has stated that this is the beginning only. He is quoted as saying";
      print "'Software today, the World tomorrow.'  This reporter is assuming";
      print "he is talking about distribution only.";
}
```

To pass the CGI object to the function, the first line of the subroutine is:

```
local($query)=@_;
```

The result of this code is the Web page shown in figure 7.3.

**FIG. 7.3**

This Web page displays the HTML generated from the majannounce CGI subroutine.

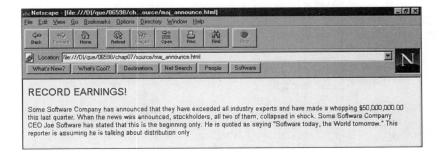

Another approach is to open a file containing the HTML statements and basically print the contents out as is. Listing 7.5 shows the subroutine that generates the Company Announcements section, using this technique.

**Listing 7.5  Subroutine to Read Company Announcements and Print Directly (*index.cgi*)**

```
#
# subroutine print_company
#
# Open and print the contents of the company announcements file.
sub print_company {
      open(COMPANY, "../book-html/maj_announce.html");
      print "<HR><p>";
      while (<COMPANY>) {
            print $_;
      }
      close(COMPANY);
}
```

The advantage of using this technique is that someone who is not proficient in using Perl can create the content independent of the application. Also, this approach is simpler to implement, because the HTML document basically opens, prints, and then closes an HTML document.

The second technique is used for the example presented in this section. Listing 7.6 shows the code for all the subroutines.

**Listing 7.6   Subroutines to Create the User-Defined HTML Document Contents (*index.cgi*)**

```
#
# subroutine get_options
#
# This subroutine will access the choices for the reader from
# the userbin.inp file. For each option, the subroutine that contains
# the handling of the option is called.
sub get_options {
    my($name)=@_;
    #
    # find options line and load into variable
    open(CHOICES, "userbin.inp");
    while (<CHOICES>) {
        $line=$_;
        if (index($line,$name) >= 0) {
            $data_string = $line;
            last;
        }
    }
    close(CHOICES);
    #
    # check for each option and call associated subroutine
    $line = $data_string;
    if (index($line, "Company") >= 0 ) {
        &print_company();
    }
    if (index($line, "Products") >= 0) {
        &print_products();
    }
    if (index($line, "ProductX") >= 0) {
        &print_productX();
    }
    if (index($line, "ProductY") >= 0) {
        &print_productY();
    }
}


#
# subroutine not_found
#
# If there were no options for this reader, a
# message is output and a link provided to
# allow the reader to add options
sub not_found {
    my($name)=@_;
    print "<HR><p>";
    print "There are no options for " . $name . ".<p>";
```

```perl
    print "set options <a href='http://unix.yasd.com/book-bin/binchoose.cgi'";
    print "?user_name=" . $name;
    print ">here</a> to create your dynamic page.";
}


#
# subroutine print_company
#
# Open and print the contents of the company announcements file.
sub print_company {
    open(COMPANY, "../book-html/maj_announce.html");
    print "<HR><p>";
    while (<COMPANY>) {
        print $_;
    }
    close(COMPANY);
}


#
# subroutine print_products
#
# Open and print the contents of the general products
# announcements file.
sub print_products {
    open(PRODUCT, "../book-html/prod_announce.html");
    print "<HR><p>";
    while (<PRODUCT>) {
        print $_;
    }
    close(PRODUCT);
}


#
# subroutine print_productX
#
# Open and print the contents of the product X file.
sub print_productX {
    open(PRODX, "../book-html/prodx_announce.html");
    print "<HR><p>";
    while (<PRODX>) {
        print $_;
    }
    close(PRODX);
}


#
# subroutine print_productY
#
# Open and print the contents of the product Y file.
sub print_productY {
    open(PRODY, "../book-html/prody_announce.html");
    print "<HR><p>";
    while (<PRODY>) {
        print $_;
    }
    close(PRODY);
}
```

The last step in creating the user-defined HTML document is creating the components that are used. Listing 7.7 shows the HTML that creates the Company Announcements component. This component contains a headline and an announcement of record earnings for the quarter.

**Listing 7.7   Company Announcements HTML Document (*maj announce.html*)**

```
<!-- Major company announcement -->
<FONT SIZE=5 COLOR="#FF0000">RECORD EARNINGS!</FONT>
<p>
Some Software Company has announced that they have exceeded all
industry experts and have made a whopping $50,000,000.00 this last
quarter.  When the news was announced, stockholders, all two of
them, collapsed in shock.  Some Software Company CEO Joe Software
has stated that this is the beginning only. He is quoted as saying
"Software today, the World tomorrow."  This reporter is assuming
he is talking about distribution only.
```

The next component to implement is the Product Announcements page. This page contains an announcement of a new product that is in production and is expected to be delivered by the end of the year. Listing 7.8 shows the HTML for this component.

**Listing 7.8   Major Product Announcement HTML Document (*prod_announce.html*)**

```
<!-- Product Announcement -->
<H2> New product, Product Z, to be released at year end </H2>
Some Software Company has announced a new product, Product Z,
that is expected to be ready for distribution. Unlike some
other software programs that do everything "but wash your windows,"
Product Manager Paula Produce states "Product Z will add
extensibility to any existing software products that will add
in window washing capability." Industry experts are awed.
```

The next component contains a product announcement related specifically to Product X. The announcement states that Product X is being recalled, because the government has found that it tends to erase hard drives if it is brought within 25 feet of a computer. Listing 7.9 contains the code for this component.

**Listing 7.9   Product X Announcement HTML Document (*prodx_announce.html*)**

```
<!-- Product X announcement -->
<H2> Product X recall </H2>
Product X, also know in the industry as Solv-Ur-Problems, is
being recalled by the Federal Government. Product X is an
all purpose software program guaranteed to solve all your
existing software problems. The government has found, though, that
Product X will erase any and all hard drives that it comes within
25 feet of.
```

```
<p>
Paula Product, Product Manager, is quoted as saying "While
we will comply with the government request to pull this product,
we want to re-assure people that Product X does live up to
it's claim of solving any software problem.."
```

The next component is for Product Y. There are no major announcements for Product Y, so the file is empty. The application can deal with empty files.

The result of all this effort is that a Web page reader with the user name sallybrown has chosen to read Company Announcements, Product Announcements, and Product X Announcements only. When she accesses the dynamic Web page site, her page looks like the one shown in figure 7.4.

**FIG. 7.4**

This dynamic Web page was generated for user sallybrown, listing Company and Product Announcements.

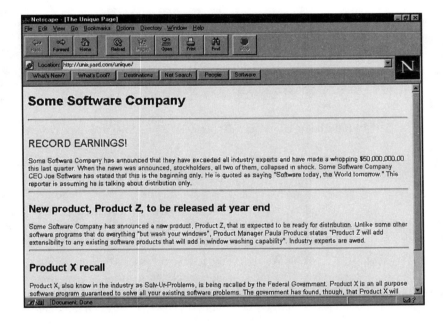

Another Web page reader with the user name joeg chose the Company Announcements and Product Y Announcements options. His page is similar to the one shown in figure 7.5.

No section is generated for Product Y, because the file that contains this information is empty. The file could have contained a line stating that there is no new information, or it could contain the most recent announcement, regardless of when it was made.

A Web page reader would follow these steps to set up a dynamic Web page:

1. Access the "Add user and password" Web page, which takes the contents of an HTML form and passes them to a CGI program. This CGI program adds the user and password to the .HTPASSWD file. You can find the HTML document and CGI application in Chapter 8, "Understanding Basic User Authentication."

**FIG. 7.5**
This dynamic Web page was generated for user joeg, listing Company Announcements only.

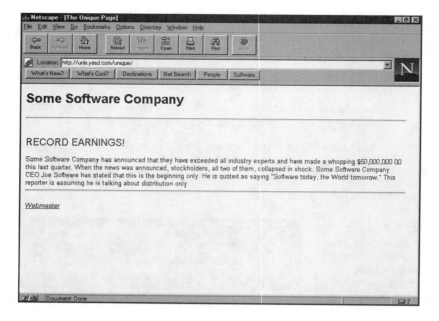

2. After being added as a dynamic-page user, the Web page reader is presented with another HTML document, which allows him to choose the content that he prefers to see on his page. This HTML document is a CGI-generated HTML program, `binchoose.cgi`, with a hidden variable that contains the user name.

3. After making his choices, the reader submits the Choices form. This form activates a CGI application called `process_request.cgi`, which appends the user name and the choices to the USERBIN.INP file. An HTML file is generated and displayed to the reader, confirming the reader's choices and providing directions for accessing his dynamic page.

4. To access his Web page, the reader accesses a specific subdirectory that is password-protected. After the user enters his user name and password, a CGI program called `index.cgi` is run, and the user name is accessed. This user name is used to access the choices from the USERBIN.INP file. The application then builds the Web page by accessing the chosen applicable components and printing them.

# Using Server-Side Includes

*Server-side includes* (SSI) are directives that are processed at the server before the HTML document is sent to the client. The server has to parse the file one line at a time, looking for something that it should process.

The good news about SSI is that they are very easy to use. The bad news about SSI is that they can be a burden on the server and can also decrease the performance of the Web site. The server normally adds a response header to a document and then sends the document to the browser. With SSI, the server then has to scan each line. Any time that the server has to perform additional processing or handling of the document before transmission, that server's task is going to take valuable resources and degrade the performance of the Web site.

Some judicious use of this technology, however, can make SSI an effective Web tool.

## Understanding the SSI Commands

If a site has 50 or 60 Web pages, and each Web page has the same images or text heading each page, you should consider implementing SSI. This technique allows the site to create one HTML document with the header that is then included in all the other documents. If that header is ever changed, the change would be reflected in all the documents.

One of the commands is the `include` command, which accesses a file and adds the contents of that file where the command is embedded in the document. With this type of command, the Web page developer for the hypothetical site could create one heading HTML file and use SSI to include this heading in each of the site's Web pages. The developer is spared from having to repeat the same statements again and again, and it is extremely easy to make changes in the heading and have those changes propagated across the entire site.

How difficult is it to use SSI? The format of an SSI command is:

```
<!-- #SSI_command arguments="values" -->
```

That's it, and that's why SSI is so popular. The following sections discuss setting up an environment for using SSI commands, the commands, and their arguments, and provide some examples of their use.

## Setting up an Environment for Server-Side Includes

Server-side includes are not implemented for all Web servers, but they are implemented with NCSA, and there is a workaround with CERN servers.

Setting up the site requires the modification of the file named SRM.CONF, which is the server configuration file. Add the extension of the file that will contain the HTML to be parsed by adding a line similar to the following:

```
AddType text/x-server-parsed-html .shtml
```

With this line, any file with the extension .SHTML will be parsed by the Web server to look for SSI commands. The most common file extension used is .SHTML. This extension prevents the server from parsing any file with the .HTML extension, which could slow performance on HTML documents that do not include SSI commands.

A line needs to be added to the ACCESS.CONF file to enable SSI. To enable SSI with the `exec` command option, add the following line:

```
Options Includes
```

To enable SSI without the `exec` command, add the following:

```
Options IncludesNoExec
```

To enable a CERN Web server, a file called FAKESSI.PL is used. This file enables the server to emulate server-side includes. With this file installed, the server can process everything but the cmd option on an exec SSI.

To install this file, copy it to the /CGI-BIN subdirectory, and change the permissions on it to make it executable. In the HTTPD.CONF file (which is located in the Web server configuration file subdirectory, as it is defined for your system), add the following line:

```
Exec /*.shtml /users/www/cgi-bin/fakessi.pl
```

After the server is restarted, SSI commands will be enabled.

## Understanding the Commands

The SSI commands are:

```
include

config

flastmod

fsize

echo

exec
```

The format of an SSI command is:

```
<!--command arg="value" -->
```

It is extremely important to notice the spacing in this command. There can be no spaces between the first two dashes and the command, and there must be a space between the value and the last two dashes.

**The _include_ Command**    This command has two arguments: virtual and file. Using file allows the developer to specify subdirectories relative to the current directory, where the HTML document is contained. An example of this command is:

```
<!--#include file="/support/top_main.html" -->
```

With the virtual argument, the command changes to:

```
<!--#include virtual="/main_grp/top/support/top_main.html" -->
```

The virtual argument defines the path relative to the root directory on the server.

The included file cannot be a CGI application, but it can be an HTML document that contains a reference to a CGI application.

Figure 7.6 shows an example of an include SSI. The Web page displayed in this figure includes an HTML document that in turn contains a general header that is included in all the documents.

**FIG. 7.6**
This HTML document contains an SSI include that in turn calls an HTML document containing a header message.

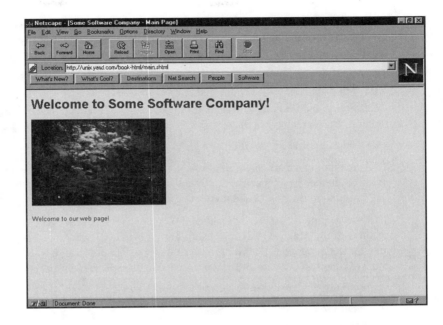

The main HTML document is called MAIN.SHTML. The .SHTML extension is the one that is defined for a SSI. Listing 7.10 shows the source code for this document.

**Listing 7.10  HTML Document Containing a Server-Side Include with the *include* Command (*main.shtml*)**

```
<HTML>
<HEAD><TITLE>Some Software Company - Main Page </TITLE>
</HEAD>
<!--#include file="support/top_main.html" -->
<p>
Welcome to our web page!
</BODY>
</HTML>
```

The included file contains the beginning of the BODY section, which also defines the page colors, a header, and a graphic. Listing 7.11 displays the HTML for this document.

**Listing 7.11  HTML Document Containing Header Section (*top_main.html*)**

```
<BODY BGCOLOR="#FFEBCD" TEXT="#8B4513">
<H1>Welcome to Some Software Company!</H1>
<p>
<IMG SRC="../images/garden2.jpg">
<p>
```

Part
II

Ch
7

**The *config* Command**  The `config` SSI is used to modify the results of other SSI commands. The following command line modifies the error message that is returned when an SSI directive fails:

```
<!--#config errmsg="We're sorry but we are temporarily having difficulty opening
this page." -->
```

Another argument to use with the `config` command is `sizefmt`. The following command line modifies the formatting of the size that is returned when the SSI `fsize` is used:

```
<!--#config sizefmt="bytes" -->
```

This command formats the return result of the `fsize` command in a display showing the full bytes of the file. An alternative argument is `sizefmt='abbrev'`, which returns the size of the file, rounded to the nearest kilobyte.

The last argument that can be used with the `config` SSI is `timefmt`, which formats the return result with the `flastmod` SSI command. The `flastmod` command returns the last-modification date for the document. Following is an example of this command, which displays the date as the weekday and the date as abbreviated decimals separated by a slash:

```
<!--#config timefmt="%A %m/%d/%y" -->
```

**The *flastmod* Command**  This SSI command displays the date when the HTML document was last modified. Like the `include` command, the `flastmod` command can be specified with the `file` argument or the `virtual` argument. Figure 7.7 shows an example of this command.

Listing 7.12 shows the HTML statements that generate this document.

**FIG. 7.7**
This HTML document contains three SSI commands.

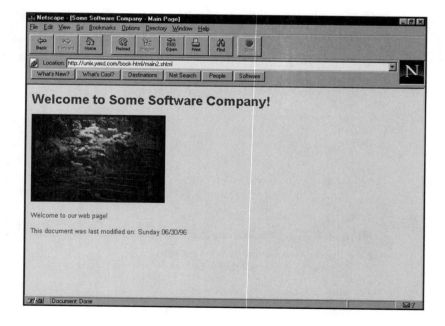

**Listing 7.12   HTML Document Containing Three SSI Commands (*main2.html*)**

```html
<HTML>
<HEAD><TITLE>Some Software Company - Main Page </TITLE>
</HEAD>
<!--#include file="support/top_main.html" -->
<p>
Welcome to our web page!
<p>
This document was last modified on:
<!--#config timefmt="%A %m/%d/%y" -->
<!--#flastmod file="main2.shtml" -->
</BODY>
</HTML>
```

**The *fsize* Command**   The `fsize` command returns the size of a file. Like the `include` command, `fsize` can access a file with the `file` argument or the `virtual` argument. To use this command, use the following syntax:

```
<!--#fsize file="main3.shtml" -->
```

**The *echo* Command**   This command allows the Web page developer to print certain variables that are specific to it. Table 7.1 lists these variables.

**Table 7.1   The *echo* SSI Command Variables**

| Command Variable | Definition |
| --- | --- |
| document_name | Main HTML document name |
| date_gmt | Current date in GMT (Greenwich Mean Time) format |
| date_local | Current date in local time zone |
| Document_uri | Virtual path of document |
| last_modified | Date document was last modified |
| QUERY_STRING UNESCAPED_ | Unescaped version of any search query that the client sent, with all shell-specific characters escaped with a backslash (\) |

Figure 7.8 shows an example of using `echo` and other SSI commands, and Listing 7.13 shows the HTML that creates this document.

Part

II

Ch

7

**FIG. 7.8**

This HTML document contains examples of the `include`, `echo`, `fsize`, and `config` SSI commands.

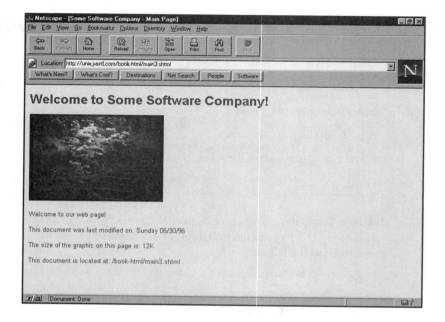

## Listing 7.13 HTML Document Containing Several SSI Commands (*main3.shtml*)

```
<HTML>
<HEAD><TITLE>Some Software Company - Main Page </TITLE>
</HEAD>
<!--#include file="support/top_main.html" -->
<p>
Welcome to our web page!
<p>
This document was last modified on:
<!--#config timefmt="%A %m/%d/%y" -->
<!--#flastmod file="main3.shtml" -->
<p>
The size of the graphic on this page is:
<!--#fsize file="garden2.jpg" -->
<p>
This document is located at:
<!--#echo var="document_uri" -->
</BODY>
</HTML>
```

**The *exec* Command**  By now, you may be beginning to wonder how SSI commands fit in with a book about Perl. Any good developer uses multiple tools to do a job, and server-side includes are an effective tool. Additionally, you can include a Perl-based application by using the `exec` command. This SSI command runs an application and returns the result to the HTML document. This method is an effective approach to embedding in an HTML document information such as page access counts, a list of other people logged in, or any other command or application that returns a result.

Based on the power of this little command, this directive involves all sorts of security risks, and there is a good chance that it may be disabled for your system. "Setting up an Environment for Server-Side Includes" earlier in this chapter discussed how SSI commands are enabled and disabled. If you have access to exec in your system, however, this command provides an easy way to implement an access counter in your Web page.

Creating an access counter with SSI starts with creating a simple CGI program to open a file, get the count, increment the count, write back out to the file, and print to output. Listing 7.14 contains the Perl code for this application.

**Listing 7.14   CGI Application to Increment Access Counter (*accesses.cgi*)**

```perl
#!/usr/local/bin/perl
#
# accesses.cgi
#
# Application will access a value in a file,
# increment it, write this new value out to the
# file, and print the current value out to
# standard output.
#
# print out content type
print "Content-type: text/html\n\n";

# get current count
open(COUNTER, "< access_counter") || die "BUSY";
$value = <COUNTER>;
close(COUNTER);

# increment count and write back out to file
$value++;
open(COUNTER, "> access_counter") || die "BUSY";
print COUNTER $value;
close(COUNTER);
#
print $value;

exit(0);
```

Next, access the CGI application by using the exec SSI command. Listing 7.15 shows the pertinent HTML statements.

**Listing 7.15   Document That Contains Several SSI Commands (*main4.html*)**

```html
<HTML>
<HEAD><TITLE>Some Software Company - Main Page </TITLE>
</HEAD>
```

Part

II

Ch

*continues*

**Listing 7.15 Continued**

```
<!--#include file="support/top_main.html" -->
<p>
Welcome to our web page!
<p>
This document was last modified on:
<!--#config timefmt="%A %m/%d/%y" -->
<!--#flastmod file="main3.shtml" -->
<p>
The size of the graphic on this page is:
<!--#fsize file="garden2.jpg" -->
<p>
This document is located at:
<!--#echo var="document_uri" -->
<p>
This site has been accessed <!--#exec cgi="accesses.cgi" --> times.
</BODY>
</HTML>
```

Each time the HTML document is accessed, the CGI application `accesses.cgi` is called. This application increments a count that is then returned to the HTML document.

---

**File Locking**

Now is a good time to talk about file locking. If the ACCESS_COUNTER file in this example were not locked, two people accessing the site at the same time would get the same number. The first access would result in the existing number's being incremented and output to the counter file. The second access would increment the same number and output it. The result is that one count on the access counter would be lost. Over time, this situation could affect a busy site.

One function to use is `flock()`, which locks the file and restricts two users from updating it at the same time. Unfortunately, this function uses the underlying operating-system command of the same name, and this command does not exist on many systems. In such a case, you could create a lock file when the file is opened. The application would test for the presence of this file when it wants to open the counter file. If the file exists, the application sleeps briefly. When the lock file does not exist, the application creates it, opens the target file, does what it needs to do with the file, and closes it. The last thing that the application does is remove the lock file.

---

# Understanding Shopping Carts

*Shopping carts* are applications that track information between several HTML documents. These applications usually use a combination of information stored at the client and information stored in a database or file at the server.

There are two approaches to shopping carts: storing information in form hidden fields or in client-side cookies. *Form hidden fields* are fields that store information and are not displayed to the Web page reader. *Client-side cookies* are small bits of information that are stored in a file (usually, COOKIE.TXT) at the client site. In both cases, the information that is stored usually is a file name or user name that is used to access the greater store of information at the server.

## Shopping Cart Using Hidden Fields

As stated in the preceding section, hidden fields are form fields that are used only for information storage and retrieval. Generating an HTML document with CGI allows input to these fields. Alternatively, you can set the fields by using a scripting language such as JavaScript.

One common use of hidden fields is to store a user name or file name that then can be used to reference and store information at the server. The information is passed when the form is submitted, and the CGI application that processes the form in turn uses the same information to set hidden fields on the next form that is displayed.

You also can send the information passed to the form by appending that information as name–value pairs in the URL of the document.

To demonstrate these concepts, the following listings create a small, simple electronic store called The Cyber Corner Market. This online store allows users to select fruits and vegetables, and stores the information in a file at the server. This file is created with the first order by using the user name and appending the day, month, and year to the name. The name and the user name are then passed to each of the documents and stored in hidden fields or processed directly.

Listing 7.16 contains code that creates the first HTML document of the market. The document contains a text field in a Web page reader can enter his name, as well as two radio buttons that allow the reader to specify whether he wants to order from the vegetable department or the fruit department.

**Listing 7.16  CGI Application That Creates the Beginning Market HTML Document (*market.cgi*)**

```
#!/usr/local/bin/perl
#
# market.cgi
#
# Creates HTML for beginning market order system.
# Will check to see if user name and file name
# are being passed into application.  If they are
# the values are stored in hidden fields.
#
#
BEGIN {
      push(@INC,'/opt2/web/guide/unix/book-bin');
}
use CGI;
$query = new CGI;
#
# if existing parameters, get value for user_name
if ($query->param()) {
```

Part

II

Ch

7

*continues*

**Listing 7.16 Continued**

```perl
        $user_name = $query->param('user_name');
}

if ($user_name) {
        $file_name = $query->param('file_name');
} else {
        $user_name = "your_name";
        $file_name = "your_name100.ord";
}


# print header and heading information
print $query->header;
print $query->start_html('Cyber Corner Market');
print $query->h1('Cyber Corner Market');
print<<end_of_page;
<HTML>
<HEAD><TITLE> The Cyber Corner Market </TITLE>

<SCRIPT LANGUAGE="JavaScript">
<!-- hide script from old browsers

// this JavaScript function will create the file name
function GenerateFileName(user_name) {

    var time = new Date()
    var time1 = time.getMonth()
    var time2 = time.getDay()
    var time3 = time.getYear()
    var filename = user_name + time1 + time2 + time3 + ".ord"

    document.MarketForm.file_name.value = filename
}

// this JavaScript function will access the appropriate CGI application
function SubmitNow(category) {

    var suserfile = "user_name=" +
        document.MarketForm.user_name.value
    suserfile = suserfile + "&file_name=" +
        document.MarketForm.file_name.value

    if (category == "fruit") {
        window.location.href=
            "http://unix.yasd.com/book-bin/fruit.cgi?" + suserfile
    }
    else {
        window.location.href=
            "http://unix.yasd.com/book-bin/veggies.cgi?" + suserfile
    }
}

// end hiding from old browsers -->
</SCRIPT>
```

```
</HEAD>
<BODY>
<H1> Welcome to the Cyber Corner Market </H1>
<p>
<hr>
<p>
<H3> Please enter your name below and check which category
you wish to shop from </H3>
<p>
<FORM name="MarketForm">
Your Name: <INPUT TYPE="text" size=30 name=user_name value=$user_name
     onChange="GenerateFileName(this.value)">
<p>
<INPUT TYPE="hidden" name="file_name" value=$file_name>
Fruit:<INPUT TYPE="radio" name="category"
     onClick="SubmitNow('fruit')">
<p>
Veggies:<INPUT TYPE="radio" name="category"
     onClick="SubmitNow('veggies')">
<p>
<hr>
<ADDRESS>
Webmaster
</ADDRESS>

end_of_page

print $query->end_html;

exit(0);
```

When the application is run for the first time, a default user name and file name are entered in the form fields, as shown in figure 7.9. When the Web page reader changes the user name, as shown in figure 7.10, a JavaScript function is called to create the new file name, which is then stored in a hidden field called file_name.

If the reader chooses the veggies option, the next form (see fig. 7.11) displays a selection of vegetables.

Notice from the Location toolbar that the user name and file name—in this case, customer and CUSTOMER6696.ORD—are passed to the new application. The application then stores this information in hidden fields. As the Web page reader enters the quantity that he wants, the total is calculated and placed in the Total field for each item. When the reader finishes and clicks the Send Order button, the form contents are processed by the next CGI application.

Listing 7.17 shows the CGI code for creating this form.

Part

II

Ch

7

**FIG. 7.9**

This figure shows the first form of the Cyber Corner Market application.

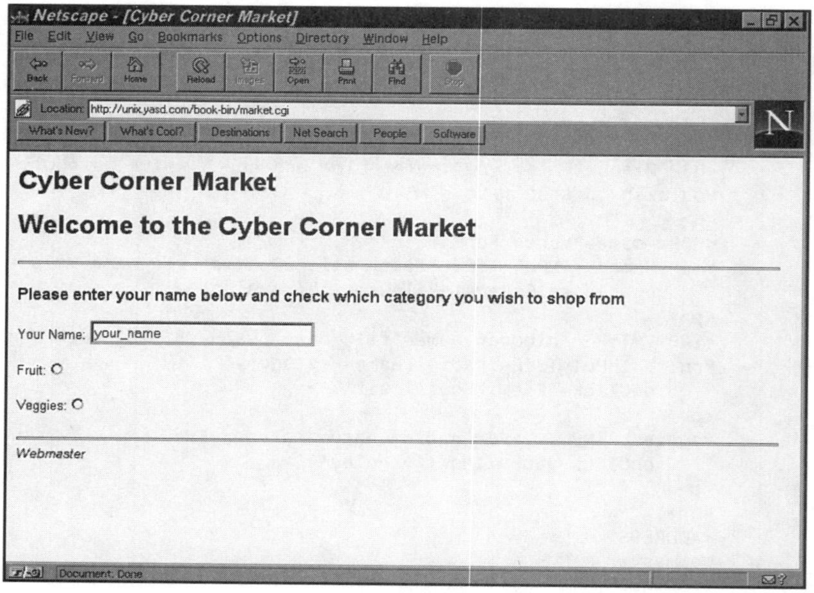

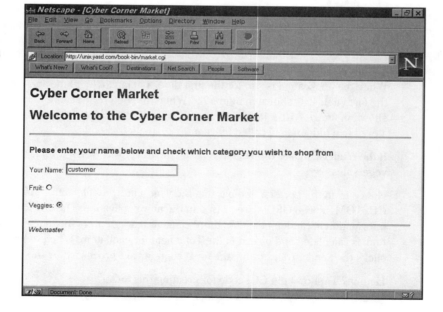

**FIG. 7.10**

This figure shows the Cyber Corner Market after the user name has been changed.

**FIG. 7.11**

This form allows the reader to select vegetables from the Cyber Corner Market.

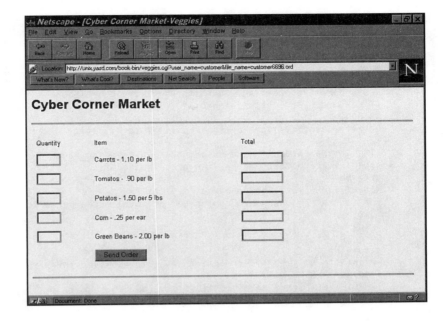

## Listing 7.17 CGI That Accesses the Passed-In File Name and User Name, and Generates the Form (*veggies.cgi*)

```perl
#!/usr/local/bin/perl
#
# veggies.cgi
#
# Application will generate HTML for Cyber Corner Market,
# vegetable section.
#
# Included in form will be hidden field containing
# user_name and a hidden field containing file name.
#
#
BEGIN {
    push(@INC,'/opt2/web/guide/unix/book-bin');
}
use CGI;
$query = new CGI;
#
# if existing parameters, get value for user_name
if ($query->param()) {
    $user_name = $query->param('user_name');
    $file_name = $query->param('file_name');
}
# print header and heading information
print $query->header;
print $query->start_html('Cyber Corner Market-Veggies');
print $query->h1('Cyber Corner Market');
```

*continues*

Part
II

Ch
7

**Listing 7.17  Continued**

```
print<<end_of_page;
<p>
<hr>
<p>
<FORM name="veggies" ACTION="http://unix.yasd.com/book-bin/process_order.cgi">
<TABLE width=600 cellpadding=5
<STRONG>
<tr><td>Quantity</td><td>Item</td><td>Total</td></tr></strong>
<p>
<INPUT TYPE="hidden" name="user_name" value=$user_name>
<INPUT TYPE="hidden" name="file_name" value=$file_name>
<tr><td>
<INPUT TYPE="text" name="carrot_qty" size=5
    onChange="document.veggies.carrot_total.value=parseFloat(this.value) *
1.10">
</td><td>
Carrots - 1.10 per lb
</td><td>
<right><INPUT TYPE="text" name="carrot_total" size=10></right>
</td><tr><td>
<INPUT TYPE="text" name="tomatoes_qty" size=5
    onChange="document.veggies.tomato_total.value=parseFloat(this.value) *
.90">
</td><td>
Tomatoes - .90 per lb
</td><td>
<INPUT TYPE="text" name="tomato_total" size=10>
</td><tr><td>
<INPUT TYPE="text" name="potato_qty" size=5
    onChange="document.veggies.potato_total.value=parseFloat(this.value) *
1.50">
</td><td>
Potatoes - 1.50 per 5 lbs
</td><td>
<INPUT TYPE="text" name="potato_total" size=10>
</td><tr><td>
<INPUT TYPE="text" name="corn_qty" size=5
    onChange="document.veggies.corn_total.value=parseFloat(this.value) * .25">
</td><td>
Corn - .25 per ear
</td><td>
<INPUT TYPE="text" name="corn_total" size=10>
</td><tr><td>
<INPUT TYPE="text" name="beans_qty" size=5
    onChange="document.veggies.beans_total.value=parseFloat(this.value) * 2.0">
</td><td>
Green Beans - 2.00 per lb
</td><td>
<INPUT TYPE="text" name="beans_total" size=10>
</td></tr>
<tr><td> </td><td>
<INPUT TYPE="submit" value="Send Order">
</td></tr>
</table>
```

```
<p>
<hr>
end_of_page
print $query->end_html;

exit(0);
```

When the Web page reader submits the form, all the information—including the information in the hidden fields—is passed to the next application. By default, the application processes the form results, using the GET form-posting method.

The next component of the Cyber Corner Market application processes the order by appending it to the file and then provides options that allow the reader to continue or to finish the order, as shown in figure 7.12.

**FIG. 7.12**
This document is displayed after the reader submits a vegetable order.

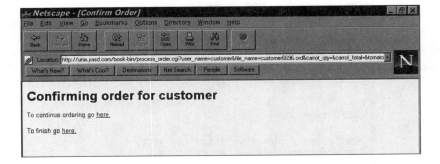

Listing 7.18 shows the code to create the HTML and to process the order.

**Listing 7.18  Application to Access the Order Elements That Are Passed in (*process_order.cgi*)**

```
#!/usr/local/bin/perl
#
# process_order.cgi
#
# Application will access user name and
# check for it in password file.
# If name exists, reader will get a duplicate
# name response and a link back to try again.
#
#
BEGIN {
      push(@INC,'/opt2/web/guide/unix/book-bin');
}
use CGI;
$query = new CGI;
#
# if existing parameters, get value for user_name
```

Part
II
Ch
7

*continues*

**Listing 7.18  Continued**

```perl
if ($query->param()) {
    $user_name = $query->param('user_name');
    $file_name = $query->param('file_name');
}
print $query->header;
print $query->start_html('Confirm Order');
#
# add order to file
$person = "user_name=" . $user_name;
$person = $person . "&file_name=" . $file_name;
&process_order($query, $file_name);
# finish document
print $query->h1('Confirming order for ' . $user_name);
print "<p>To continue ordering go ";
print "<a href='http://unix.yasd.com/book-bin/market.cgi?";
print $person . "'>here.</a>";
print "<p>To finish go ";
print "<a href='http://unix.yasd.com/book-bin/finish.cgi?";
print $person . "'>here.</a>";
print $query->end_html;

exit(0);

#
# Subroutine process_order
#
# Access query sent from form with options
# Add user_name as first entry, then
# add each of the options, formatted
#
# output line to userbin.inp file
sub process_order {
    local($query, $file_name)=@_;
    @fruits = (apple_total,grapes_total,pears_total,
        peaches_total,pineapple_total);
    @veggies= (carrot_total, tomato_total,potato_total,
        corn_total,beans_total);
    $name=$query->param('user_name');
    $output_string = "";
    @named_param=$query->param;
    if ($query->param()) {
        foreach $param_name (@fruits) {
            $val = $query->param($param_name);
            if ($val) {
                $output_string = $output_string . $param_name . "=" . $val .
":";
            }
        }
        foreach $param_name (@veggies) {
            $val = $query->param($param_name);
            if ($val) {
                $output_string = $output_string . $param_name . "=" . $val .
":";
            }
        }
```

```
        }

    }
    open(USER_FILE, ">> " . $file_name) || die "Could not process request";
     $output_string = $output_string . "\n";
    print USER_FILE $output_string;
    close(USER_FILE);
}
```

Notice in Listing 7.18 that the possible elements that can be passed to the application are placed in an array. Then each of these array elements is checked against the parameters passed to the application. If a parameter match is found, the value of the item and the item are output to file. Also notice that the file-name and user-name values are not maintained in hidden fields. These values are appended directly to URLs that are created for the document locations that the reader can access next.

If the reader were to continue ordering, he would return to the original document, shown in figure 7.13. This time, however, the name that the user specified is placed in the text field, and the created file name is placed in the hidden field.

**FIG. 7.13**

The application returns to the main Market form after processing the vegetable order.

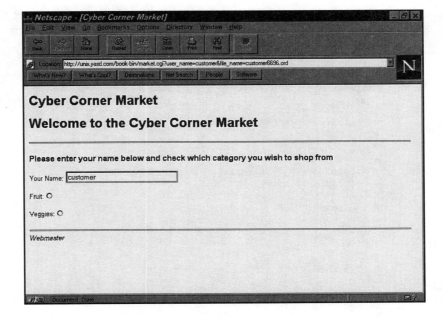

Accessing the fruit option next, the reader sees a list of fruits. As in the vegetable form, the reader types the quantities, and the total is created from a JavaScript function, as shown in figure 7.14.

Part
II

Ch

7

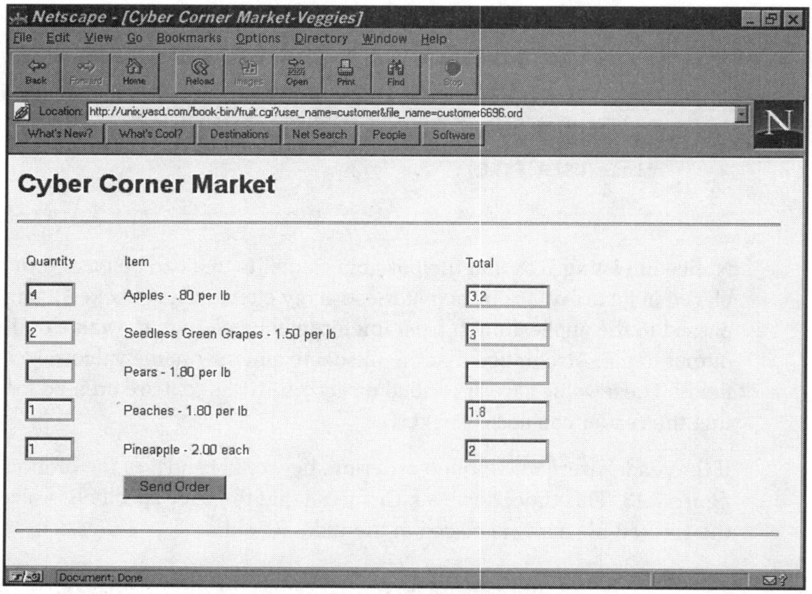

**FIG. 7.14**

This figure shows the Cyber Market fruit form after several quantities have been entered but before the form is submitted.

Listing 7.19 shows the CGI application for this form.

## Listing 7.19   Application That Generates the Fruit-Ordering Document (*fruit.cgi*)

```perl
#!/usr/local/bin/perl
#
# fruit.cgi
#
# Application will generate HTML for Cyber Corner Market,
# vegetable section.
#
# Included in form will be hidden field containing
# user_name and a hidden field containing file name.
#
#
BEGIN {
     push(@INC,'/opt2/web/guide/unix/book-bin');
}
use CGI;
$query = new CGI;
#
# if existing parameters, get value for user_name
if ($query->param()) {
     $user_name = $query->param('user_name');
     $file_name = $query->param('file_name');
}
# print header and heading information
print $query->header;
```

```
print $query->start_html('Cyber Corner Market-Veggies');
print $query->h1('Cyber Corner Market');
print<<end_of_page;
<p>
<hr>
<p>
<FORM name="fruit" ACTION="http://unix.yasd.com/book-bin/process_order.cgi">
<TABLE width=600 cellpadding=5
<STRONG>
<tr><td>Quantity</td><td>Item</td><td>Total</td></tr></strong>
<p>
<INPUT TYPE="hidden" name="user_name" value=$user_name>
<INPUT TYPE="hidden" name="file_name" value=$file_name>
<tr><td>
<INPUT TYPE="text" name="apple_qty" size=5
    onChange="document.fruit.apple_total.value=parseFloat(this.value) * .80">
</td><td>
Apples - .80 per lb
</td><td>
<INPUT TYPE="text" name="apple_total" size=10>
</td><tr><td>
<INPUT TYPE="text" name="grapes_qty" size=5
    onChange="document.fruit.grapes_total.value=parseFloat(this.value) * 1.50">
</td><td>
Seedless Green Grapes - 1.50 per lb
</td><td>
<INPUT TYPE="text" name="grapes_total" size=10>
</td><tr><td>
<INPUT TYPE="text" name="pears_qty" size=5
    onChange="document.fruit.pears_total.value=parseFloat(this.value) * 1.80">
</td><td>
Pears - 1.80 per lb
</td><td>
<INPUT TYPE="text" name="pears_total" size=10>
</td><tr><td>
<INPUT TYPE="text" name="peaches_qty" size=5
    onChange="document.fruit.peaches_total.value=parseFloat(this.value) *
1.80">
</td><td>
Peaches - 1.80 per lb
</td><td>
<INPUT TYPE="text" name="peaches_total" size=10>
</td><tr><td>
<INPUT TYPE="text" name="pineapple_qty" size=5
    onChange="document.fruit.pineapple_total.value=parseFloat(this.value) *
2.0">
</td><td>
Pineapple - 2.00 each
</td><td>
<INPUT TYPE="text" name="pineapple_total" size=10>
</td></tr>
<tr><td> </td><td>
<INPUT TYPE="submit" value="Send Order">
</td></tr>
</table>
```

Part
II

Ch
7

*continues*

**Listing 7.19 Continued**

```
<p>
<hr>
end_of_page
print $query->end_html;

exit(0);
```

As in the vegetable order form, clicking the Send Order button calls the `process_order.cgi` application, which appends the order to the file. At this point, the reader can choose to finish processing the file, which brings up a document listing his order (see fig. 7.15).

**FIG. 7.15**
The final document of the Cyber Market form lists the items ordered and their totals.

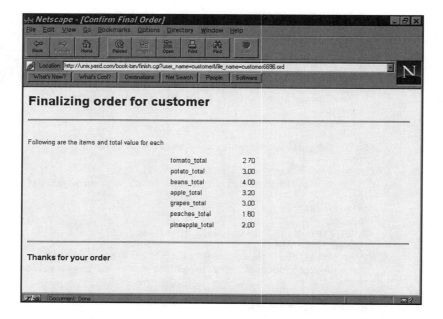

The application that generates this form accesses the file that contains the order information and displays the values. The application then uses the `unlink` Perl function to remove the link to the file. Because there is only one link to the file, the file is deleted.

Listing 7.20 shows the code for this component.

**Listing 7.20 Application to Finish Processing the Order and to Destroy the Order File (*finish.cgi*)**

```
#!/usr/local/bin/perl
#
# finish.cgi
#
```

```
# Finalized order for the Corner Cyber Market
#
# opens order file and loads each total into
# array and prints each one out
#
# When done, the file is closed and deleted.
#
BEGIN {
     push(@INC,'/opt2/web/guide/unix/book-bin');
}
use CGI;
$query = new CGI;
#
# if existing parameters, get value for user_name
if ($query->param()) {
     $user_name = $query->param('user_name');
     $file_name = $query->param('file_name');
}
print $query->header;
print $query->start_html('Confirm Final Order');
print $query->h1("Finalizing order for " . $user_name);


# open order file and print out totals
print "<p><hr><p> Following are the items and total value for each <p>";
open(USER_FILE, "< " . $file_name) || die "Could not open order file.";
print "<CENTER><TABLE width=200>";
foreach $line(<USER_FILE>) {
     @order_line = split(/:/,$line);
     print "<tr>";
     foreach $elem (@order_line) {
          ($object,$value) = split(/=/,$elem);
          if ($value <= 0) {
               last;
          }
          print "<td>" . $object . "</td><td>";
          printf "%7.2f", $value;
          print "</td></tr>";
     }
}
print "</TABLE></CENTER>";
close(USER_FILE);
unlink($file_name);
print "<p><hr><p><h3>Thanks for your order</h3>";
print $query->end_html;

exit(0);
```

The application described in this section is an extremely simplified version of more sophisticated ordering systems. This setup has several potential problems, including the following:

■ Entering more than one word as a name results in no file name being created. The name should be checked in the code.

- The order-entry system is not secure; it should be placed in a protected environment.

- The user is identified to the operating system as nobody, which is the standard user name for people accessing a site from the Web. For this user to create a file, the site where the file is created must be left open for write from the world.

- There is nothing to prevent the user from leaving while the ordering process is occurring, leaving extraneous files cluttering the system. The solution is to have a background application (cron) running that periodically cleans out the files that have not had any activity for a certain period.

# Shopping Cart Using HTTP Cookies

*Cookies* are an HTTP extension that began with Netscape. The concept is that a little bit of information is passed in the HTTP response header. The browser then processes the information and either stores it in a file (usually, COOKIE.TXT) on the client or accesses information in the same file to pass to the newly opened document or application.

The syntax for a cookie is:

```
Set-Cookie: name=value; expires= ; domain= ; path=\
```

Name is the name of the cookie, and Value is the value of the cookie. These values are the only required values. Expires is the expiration of the cookie, and by default, the cookie expires as soon as the current browser session terminates. The domain defaults to the server that generated the cookie, and the path defaults to the path of the Uniform Resource Identifier that sent the cookie.

Following is an example of setting a cookie:

```
Set-Cookie: user_name=test; expires=Tuesday, 12-Jun-96 10:00:00 GMT;
```

Cookies have limitations. There can be no more than 20 cookies from a domain or server, a cookie cannot be larger than 4K, and there can be only 300 cookies at the client.

When the cookie is set, each time the client requests a document in the path, it also sends the cookie, as follows:

```
Cookie: user_name=test
```

Using the CGI.pm Perl library, you set the cookie by using the cookie() method, as follows:

```
$cookie1=$query->cookie(-name=>"user_name",-value=>$user_name, expires=>"+1h");
```

The string is then sent in the header request, as follows:

```
print $query->header(-cookie=>$cookie1);
```

Multiple cookies can be sent using an array reference, as follows:

```
print $query->header(-cookie=>[$cookie1,$cookie2]);
```

To access the cookie, use the same cookie method, but this time pass in the name parameter, as follows:

```
$user_name = $query->cookie(-name=>'user_name');
```

**N O T E** Although cookies are handy and a highly effective way of passing information between document pages at a site, their biggest limitation is that Netscape Navigator and Microsoft's Internet Explorer are the only browsers that are capable of processing them at this time. ■

# From Here...

For information on related topics, you may want to read the following chapters:

■ For more information on form input, check out Chapter 3, "Advanced Form Processing and Data Storage."

■ Chapter 6, "Using Dynamic Pages," discusses other CGI-based applications.

■ For more information on security issues, including setting and maintaining the password file, see Chapter 8, "Understanding Basic User Authentication."

# Authentication and Site Administration

# CHAPTER 8

# Understanding Basic User Authentication

*by Paul Doyle*

**O**ne reason why the Web has grown so quickly is that it is a very open environment. Services are set up for anyone who cares to use them, quite often with the aim of attracting as many users as possible.

Sometimes, though, services need to be restricted so that only designated people can use them. Restrictions can apply to files or directories, with different levels of access for different users. With such restrictions in place, authenticating the identity of all users who attach to the server is a priority.

This chapter explains how user authentication works and tells you how to set up and administer user accounts on an Apache Web server. This chapter is not about Perl per se, but is intended primarily to serve as a foundation for the rest of the chapters in Part III, "Authentication and Site Administration." ■

### Basic user authentication

The Web server runs CGI programs on behalf of remote users. This situation may represent a security problem; at minimum, you need to verify the identity of users who are attaching to your server. This section looks into the mechanics of password protection of Web services, as well as securing the confidentiality and integrity of Web transactions.

### User authentication on the Apache Web server

This section examines how user authentication and security management operate on the Apache Web server. The principles apply on other servers, too. The section also takes an in-depth look at the syntax of configuration files and the meaning of the available configuration directives.

### User administration with Perl

Finally, this section develops some useful Perl scripts for managing Apache users and groups. These scripts complement the utilities supplied with the server and provide an in-depth explanation of the techniques involved.

# Basic User Authentication

A read-only Web service that is open to everyone presents no particular security problems. The files are made available in read-only mode, and the Web server process presents the files to any users who request them. As long as basic precautions are taken with regard to access rights to the files and the parent directory, the service is secure.

A service in which the user has write access to one or more files is a little more complex. The Guestbook example in Chapter 2, "Introduction to CGI," is an example of this type of service. Actually, the user does not really write to any files; the Web server process does that on the user's behalf. Making such a service secure means granting the Web server process the appropriate access restrictions (read-only to all files except the ones that it needs to write to) and making sure that your CGI program does not offer the end user any security loopholes, such as executing arbitrary strings involving user input through a HTML form.

The type of service with which this chapter is concerned has access restrictions that involve one or more of the following complexities:

- Only designated users can use the service, and only when they provide a valid user ID and password.

- Not all users who can access the service are allowed to use all functions. Some users may be able to update data files through a HTML form, for example; others can read data only.

- Users from some Internet addresses may be allowed to use the system; users from other addresses may not.

Restrictions such as these are more relevant when you are using CGI programs than when plain old HTML files are involved. To understand why, you need to look at the way in which a Web server works.

## Processes and User IDs

A Web server consists of a networked computer running special software under a special user ID. The fact that all three elements—hardware, software, and process—are referred to as Web servers in different contexts isn't very helpful. For clarity, I'll use the following definitions:

- The *Web server* is the entire system: hardware, software, and process.
- The *HTTP daemon (httpd)* is the Web server software.
- The *httpd process* is the process under which the Web server software is running.
- The *httpd user ID* is the user ID under which the httpd is executed.

So the *httpd* runs as the *httpd process* under the *httpd user ID* on the *Web server*.

## CGI Program Execution

The central issue here is that all file accesses on the Web server are performed by an httpd process. For this process to be capable of serving up files from many different directories, it must run under a user ID with relatively liberal access rights. If the process is to run CGI programs, too, it probably will require generous write access throughout the same directories.

This access is a security risk, however, because the process executes CGI programs under the httpd user ID on behalf of users from elsewhere on the Internet. In effect, you are allowing complete strangers to run programs on your system with a privileged user ID. A CGI program potentially can do anything on the server machine that a user who logged in under the httpd user ID could do, including reading, writing, creating, and deleting files. So if you're not careful, you can open your server to attack from anywhere on the Internet.

By default, the httpd user ID is the ID of the process that executes it. This user ID should not be root! Create a special user ID with limited privileges to start the httpd. Then you can start the httpd by using this user ID. Alternatively, if you are using the Apache httpd, use the User and Group configuration directives (described in "Apache Server Configuration Directives" later in this chapter) to get httpd to switch user IDs at startup time.

# Access Control

The server's user ID is, of course, subject to access restrictions in the same way that any other user ID on the system is. But because you need to give the server read and write access to so many places, and because you also allow it to perform tasks on behalf of complete strangers, you need to introduce an extra layer of access control.

It is important to note here that this extra layer involves user IDs and passwords that belong to the server, not to the host system. In other words, the Web server has a password file that is separate from the /etc/passwd file on UNIX systems. Having a logon account on a system does not guarantee that a user can use a restricted Web page on the server, even if the user has read access to that page when logged on interactively. The opposite also is true—a user who doesn't have a logon ID can access restricted Web pages on the server if that user has the appropriate Web server user ID and password.

The extra security layer takes a different form for each HTTP server package, but in essence, this layer has two strands:

- A mechanism for identifying all users who attempt to attach
- A set of rules governing access rights on the server (who can access which files and what they can do with those files)

The "User Authentication on the Apache Server" section later in this chapter describes how access restrictions work on the Apache server and how to implement restrictions that are appropriate for your site. First, however, you need to consider the issues that are involved in verifying a user's identity.

# User Identification

The effectiveness of your server's access restrictions depends on whether you can authenticate the identity of users who attempt to attach to your server. If you can't confirm that a user is who he says he is, you may as well make everything read-only and remove all sensitive information that you don't want to publish to the world.

Fortunately, you can check the identity of users in many ways. This section describes the most useful methods, starting with a simple unencrypted password check and moving to secure HTTP using public key cryptography.

**User ID and Password**   The most basic kind of authentication is a simple user ID and password check against a list of user IDs and passwords in a file. Users initially connect to a CGI script on the server that challenges them for a user ID and password. If a user enters a valid combination, the script displays another page or sends a HTTP redirect header to the browser to force it to load the other page.

This rather facile approach to authentication is weak for three reasons:

- **Privacy.** The user ID and password are transmitted over the network in plain text.
- **Verification.** There is no guarantee that the user ID and password were not sent by some user other than the person who is entitled to use them.
- **Manageability.** This method can make it difficult to manage access to multiple pages.

The following sections examine these reasons in detail.

*Privacy*   Given the openness of the Internet, you should assume that all transmissions— messages, Web pages, or (in this case) parts of a HTTP request—can be intercepted. If a transmission is sent in plain text and is intercepted, its contents become known to the person who intercepted it. If the transmission is encrypted in some way and is intercepted, the original content will not be known to the interceptor without substantial extra effort.

Encrypting the content of transmissions on the Internet is, therefore, a means of ensuring privacy. If a user ID and password are sent in plain-text mode, they might be used subsequently in a so-called impostor attack. This type of attack occurs when somebody other than the owner of the user ID–password pair attempts to use the pair to access the server. Encrypting the user ID and password before they are sent to the server protects them from the bad guys and helps ensure user authentication. Encryption by itself, however, does not provide authentication.

*Verification*   Assume that the user ID and password have been discovered by a person who should not have access to a service. This person may have made this discovery in any of several ways: intercepting a user ID–password pair sent as plain text; intercepting and successfully decrypting an encrypted user ID–password pair, although this event is unlikely; or watching the real owner of the pair type them, which is a more likely event. If no other checks are in place, this miscreant can then access the service from any Internet location.

You can encrypt transmissions in such a way that:

- Only the intended recipient can decrypt them
- The recipient can be sure that the transmission originated where it claims to have originated

These methods are described in detail in "Public Key Cryptography" later in this chapter.

*Manageability*   The simple user ID–password methodology outlined in the preceding section is simple only if it is used to control access to a single location. If this method is extended to several CGI programs that form a single system, coordinating the activities of all the CGI programs can be difficult. Users may have authenticated themselves upon accessing one CGI program, but they will have to authenticate themselves again if they access the same program a second time (or access a different CGI program that forms part of the same system).

The basic idea outlined here, however, can be developed to the stage at which a single CGI script manages access to a set of other files, so that users need to validate themselves only one time. This type of system is examined in detail in Chapter 9, "Understanding CGI Security."

**User ID and Password Summary**    A simple user ID–password mechanism has flaws. The basic principle is sound, though: Users must say who they are (user ID) and then prove it (password). The mechanism is adequate as it stands for services in which security is a low priority, but it needs to be developed a little to allow for really secure transactions. The following section, "Public Key Cryptography," outlines the current best technology to achieve secure user authentication and describes some of the products that use it.

**Public Key Cryptography**    The main problem with the simple user ID–password schema outlined in the preceding sections is the fact that the origin of the user ID–password pair cannot be verified. The problem of adequate verification extends to many other areas on the Internet, including the contents of messages themselves. But in this case, you're concerned only with ensuring adequate verification of a user's identity before allowing that user to access your CGI scripts or Web pages.

*Public key cryptography* is a method of transmitting data from a sender to a recipient in such a way that nobody other than the recipient can receive the data and the recipient can be certain of the identity of the sender.

The basic idea underlying public key cryptography is the use of a pair of keys:

- The *private key* is kept secret by its owner and is used to decrypt encrypted messages sent by other people.
- The *public key* is advertised widely and is used by people other than the owner to encrypt messages before sending them to the owner.

The public and private keys are derived simultaneously, using a special algorithm in such a way that messages encrypted with a person's *public* key can be decrypted only with that person's *private* key. Likewise, messages encrypted with a person's *private* key can be decrypted only with that person's *public* key.

**Key Pairs**    Suppose that I want to send a message to you, using public key cryptography. You have a public and a private key. You tell me your public key, perhaps by including it in your e-mail signature, but you keep your private key to yourself. This is what happens:

1. I encrypt the original message text, using your public key, and then send the encrypted message to you.
2. You receive the message in encrypted form and then decrypt it, using your private key.

**N O T E**    The details of how messages are encrypted and decrypted with particular key strings are beyond the scope of this book. ■

This transmission is secure in the sense that anybody else who receives the message while it travels across the network in encrypted form will be unable to determine the original content of the message without knowing the value of your private key. In theory, someone could crack the code and read the message, but the amount of effort required runs into so many thousands of hours on a powerful computer that the possibility is a concern only if you are, say, a major world power. Even then, cracking a single transmission is of no use for cracking other transmissions if you change your key pair on a regular basis.

**Certificate Authorities**   The problem with the scheme described in the preceding section is the fact that your public key is unverified. How do I know that the public key really is your public key and not a public key generated by some impostor who wants to intercept messages to you? When public key cryptography is used to protect mail messages, this problem is not too serious—the impostor would have to establish e-mail communication with me for long enough to convince me that he is you, before he transmits the fake public key. This situation is possible, though.

The problem is much more acute when public key cryptography is used to automatically verify transmissions between two Internet hosts, such as a Web server and a client running a Web browser. The reason is that the public key is transmitted during the same dialogue as the transmission of the secure message that is encrypted with that key value. No opportunity exists to develop trust through a person-to-person dialogue, such as an exchange of e-mail messages.

That's where certificate authorities come into the picture. *Certificate authorities* are companies that are trusted to issue certificates to Internet users and to verify the contents of those certificates at a later stage.

A certificate contains the following information:

- The identity of the certificate-issuing authority
- The identity of the person or organization on whose behalf the certificate is issued
- The public key of the person or organization on whose behalf the certificate is issued

Certificates cost money and are issued at the request of the person or organization to which they refer. The certificates are used as a trusted point of referral by the recipient of an encrypted message, to verify that the sender really is who he or she claims to be.

In terms of the earlier example, here's how I would go about sending you an encrypted message, using certificate verification:

1. I send a message to you, asking for your certificate.
2. You send your certificate to me.
3. I check with the certificate issuer to see whether the certificate is valid. Specifically, I want to know that the issuer really did issue the certificate on your behalf and that your public key is the same as the public key stated in the certificate.
4. I receive confirmation from the certificate issuer that the certificate is valid.
5. I encrypt the original message text, using your public key, and then send the encrypted message to you.
6. You receive the message in encrypted form and then decrypt it, using your private key.

As is true of all Internet communications, the possibility always exists that someone will attempt to impersonate the entity with which you are dealing, so as to eavesdrop on your communications. When you deal with a certificate authority, that company's reputation is your guarantee. Attempting to impersonate a certificate authority brings tremendous wrath down on the head of any malefactor—a great deterrent to that form of impersonation.

Now suppose that you receive a message from me, encrypted with my private key, and you want to decrypt it while making sure that it really did come from me. This is what would happen:

1. I encrypt the original message text, using my private key, and then send the encrypted message to you, along with details of my certificate.
2. You receive the message in encrypted form.
3. You check with the certificate issuer to verify that my public key is correct.
4. You decode the message, using my public key.

Remember—all this works because of the unique properties of the public–private key pair. In this example, information on my public key is freely available and verifiable. Only messages that are encrypted with the corresponding private key can be decrypted with this public key. That fact means that nobody can fake messages from me without knowing my private key.

Public key cryptography is an algorithmic method. The algorithms that do the real work—deriving public and private keys, and encrypting and decrypting data—were developed by RSA Data Security, Inc. RSA does not produce any end-user software for performing authentication; instead, it licenses its algorithms to other companies for incorporation into their products.

To ensure secure communications between a server and a browser, you need both the server and the browser to execute these algorithms automatically, behind the scenes, acting under an agreed protocol. The next two sections, "Secure HTTP" and "Secure Sockets Layer," discuss two products that use RSA's public key cryptography technology to authenticate Web communications.

**Secure HTTP**   Secure HTTP (S-HTTP) is an extension of the HTTP protocol developed by Enterprise Integration Technologies (EIT); the National Center for Supercomputing Applications (NCSA); and RSA Data Security, Inc. S-HTTP uses public key cryptography to guarantee the authenticity of signed transmissions, allowing for comprehensive user verification. Although the S-HTTP protocol specification is public, the toolkit necessary to build applications that use it is a commercial product. S-HTTP has not yet become prominent on the Web.

**Secure Sockets Layer**   Netscape Communications has approached the authentication issue from a different angle. Netscape has licensed RSA's public key cryptography technology and used it to developed a security protocol called Secure Sockets Layer (SSL). This layer resides between TCP/IP (the communications layer) and HTTP (the applications layer). Netscape states that SSL will support other application protocols, such as NNTP, but that support has not materialized yet.

Netscape has developed another proprietary extension of the HTTP protocol to support SSL on Web servers. This extension is called *https*, and URLs that are to be delivered through SSL need to have the prefix `https:` instead of `http`. A Web server that supports SSL normally watches for `http` requests on port 80 and `https` requests on port 443. The use of two separate ports makes it possible for a server to communicate securely with clients that support https while providing normal, unauthenticated communications with other browsers.

**User Verification Summary**  The fields of cryptography and secure communications are much too vast to cover in detail in this book, and doing so wouldn't be appropriate anyway— this is a Perl book, after all. But understanding the different types of user authentication is important, especially if you're going to introduce user authentication on your Web server. The last few pages should be enough to give you a flavor for the various types of user authentication and the current trends in authentication technology.

If your server uses S-HTTP or SSL technology, authentication becomes a matter of server configuration, so your Perl programs don't need to concern themselves with it. If your server doesn't use either technology, you must provide authentication yourself, in your Perl programs. Your Internet Service Provider may not be able or willing to provide support of this kind on its server, for example. Chapter 9, "Understanding CGI Security," describes a method for implementing user authentication on a Web server entirely by means of Perl. This method works with or without an authentication-aware protocol such as https or S-HTTP.

If you need to be absolutely certain of the identity of anyone who is accessing your CGI/Perl programs, you have to use a certificate authority via S-HTTP, SSL, or some other method. If you want to make it difficult for people to fake their identity, a simple user ID–password system may be more appropriate. You may decide to combine the two approaches, requiring a user ID and password for your Perl script even if it runs on a secure server. Ultimately, the level of security that you choose depends on the sensitivity of your data and your estimate of the risk involved.

# User Authentication on the Apache Server

Assuming that you can satisfactorily verify the identity of all users who attach to your server, you need to implement a strategy that gives users of your server enough access to do the things that you want them to be able to do, but not enough access to do the things that you *don't* want them to be able to do. This section describes the specific details of user authentication on the Apache server.

> **N O T E**  This section focuses on access restrictions for the Apache httpd server only; the chapter can't cover all features of all Web servers. Apache is fairly representative, being a superset of the NCSA httpd server. Apache also is an excellent piece of work and currently is the most popular Web server software in the world. ▧

## Access Restrictions

You can use two basic parameters to restrict access to a service:

- **Host IP address.** Access can be restricted to individual Internet nodes or subnets by IP address. Users who access the service from these nodes do not need to provide a user ID or password.

■ **User.** Access can be restricted to individual users or groups of users. All users who attempt to access the service are challenged for a user ID and password. Those who enter a valid combination are allowed to access the requested file; those who enter invalid combinations are denied access.

Access can be restricted for one or more HTTP access methods (GET, PUT, POST, and so on) for users, groups, IP addresses, subnets, or a combination.

## Apache Configuration Files

All aspects of configuration of the Apache server are controlled by a number of configuration files. Each file contains several configuration directives, each of which controls a specific aspect of Apache behavior in a specific directory tree. Table 8.1 lists the configuration files, in the order in which they are processed by the server. The default file specs shown in the table are relative to the server root directory.

**Table 8.1    Apache Server Configuration Files**

| File | Default File Spec | Override With | Controls |
|------|-------------------|---------------|----------|
| Server configuration | conf/httpd.conf | httpd's -d command-line switch | Server daemon |
| Resource configuration | conf/srm.conf | ResourceConfig directive | Document provision |
| Access configuration | conf/access.conf | AccessConfig directive | Access permissions |

Additional configuration directives can be stored in a special file in each directory to provide a fine level of access control. The per-directory configuration file is called .htaccess by default, but you can override this name with the AccessFileName directive (described in "Apache Server Configuration Directives" later in this chapter).

**Filtering of Rights**    The directives in the .htaccess files control server behavior with regard to files in the directory tree in which the .htaccess file is stored. Notice that the directives in a .htaccess file propagate through subdirectories. An attempt to access a file causes the server to look for a file called .htaccess in the directory in which the file is stored, in the parent directory of that subdirectory, in the parent's parent directory, and so on up to the server's document root directory. The .htaccess files found in this fashion are parsed in sequence, with directives in .htaccess files in lower-level subdirectories overriding directives in higher-level directories.

**Realms, Users, and Groups**    The information used to determine whether a user has access to a particular directory on the server is specific to the httpd server. The access-control mechanism used by the system on which httpd executes is not involved. So on UNIX systems, the contents of /etc/passwd are not relevant.

Instead, user information is stored in several user and group files, which can be either plain text or DBM files. Group definitions can be omitted if access is to be defined on a user-by-user basis.

> **CAUTION**
>
> User and group files should be stored in a location that is not exported by the Web server. Otherwise, users may be able to download them and thereby breach your server's security.

User and group definitions apply to a particular authorization realm. An *authorization realm* is a set of directories for which access rights are evaluated as a unit. The concept of authorization realms allows a user to access any directory in a designated set on the basis of a single authentication pass. This means that users are prompted for their user ID and password only one time during a session: the first time that they attempt to access a URL within the realm.

**Configuration Delimiters**   Configuration directives appear, one per line, in any of these configuration files. Directives can be grouped by means of the <Directory>...</Directory> and <Limit>...</Limit> delimiters, as follows:

- The `<Directory>` and `</Directory>` delimiters enclose a set of directives that apply to the named directory. The following configuration statements, for example, allow the server to follow symbolic links in the /usr/local/projects directory:

  ```
  <Directory /usr/local/projects>
  Options FollowSymLinks
  </Directory>
  ```

  The `Options` directive is explained later in this chapter.

- The `<Limit>` and `</Limit>` delimiters enclose a set of directives that apply only to certain access methods (`GET`, `POST`, and so on). The following configuration statements allow the server to follow symbolic links in the /usr/local/projects directory for `GET` requests only:

  ```
  <Directory /usr/local/projects>
  <Limit GET>
  Options FollowSymLinks
  </Limit>
  </Directory>
  ```

Directory groups can contain `Limit` groups, but no other nesting of delimiters is permitted. This means that `Limit` groups may not contain either `Limit` or `Directory` groups, and `Directory` groups may not contain `Directory` groups.

# Configuration Directives

The authentication-related configuration directives for the Apache httpd are listed in tables 8.2 through 8.4. Directives related to server configuration are listed in Table 8.2; directives that can be used in local .htaccess files are listed in Table 8.3; and directory-specific configuration directives are listed in Table 8.4.

Notice that a certain amount of overlap occurs among these tables, because some directives can be used in more than one context. Those directives that are relevant to user authentication and access restriction are described in separate sections after each table. Refer to the Apache server documentation for detailed information on all directives, including the ones described in this chapter.

**Apache Server Configuration Directives**   Table 8.2 lists the directives that can be used in the server configuration files.

**Table 8.2   Apache HTTPD Server Configuration Directives**

| Directive | Argument Type | Default Value | Purpose |
|---|---|---|---|
| AccessConfig | File name | conf/access.conf | Name of file containing access-control directives |
| AccessFileName | File name | .htaccess | Name of per-directory access-control file |
| BindAddress | IP address | * (all IP addresses) | IP address of server to listen on |
| DefaultType | MIME type | text/html | Default type for documents with no MIME type specifier |
| DocumentRoot | Directory name | /usr/local/etc/ httpd/htdocs | Name of top-level directory from which files will be served |
| ErrorDocument | Error code | — | Specifies which document to return in the event of a given error code |
| ErrorLog | File name | logs/error_log | Name of server error log file |
| GroupUnix | Group ID | #-1 | Name or number of user group under which server will run |
| IdentityCheck | on/off | off | Whether to try to log remote user names |
| MaxClients | Number | 150 | Maximum number of clients that the server will support |
| MaxRequests➡ PerChild | Number | — | Maximum number of requests that the server will handle simultaneously for any one client |

*continues*

**Table 8.2  Continued**

| Directive | Argument Type | Default Value | Purpose |
|---|---|---|---|
| MaxSpare➥Servers | Number | 10 | Maximum number of desired idle processes |
| MinSpare ➥ Servers ➥ | Number | 5 | Minimum desired idle options |
| Options ➥ | List of options | — | Defines which server features are allowed |
| PidFile | File name | logs/➥<br><br>httpd.pid | Name of file where server daemon process ID is stored |
| Port | Port number | 80 | Port number where server listens for requests |
| ResourceConfig | File name | conf/ ➥<br>srm.conf | Name of file to read for server resource config-uration details |
| ServerAdmin | E-mail address | — | E-mail address quoted by server when reporting errors to client |
| ServerName | IP address | — | Server's host name |
| ServerRoot | directory name | /usr/local/➥<br>etc/httpd | Name of directory where httpd is stored |
| ServerType | inetd/ standalone | standalone | Whether to run as one process per HTTP connection (inetd) or one process to handle all connections (standalone) |
| StartServers | Number | 5 | Number of child processes to create at startup |
| TimeOut | Number | 200 | Maximum server wait time |
| User | User ID | #-1 | User ID under which server will run |

The server configuration directives that are relevant to user authentication are explained in the following sections.

**AccessConfig** This directive overrides the default access configuration file specification, `conf/access.conf`, where access-control directives (such as directory-specific restrictions) are supposed to be stored. In fact, you can store these directives either in the access configuration file or in the resource configuration file.

The following directive in the server configuration file tells the server to read `access_test.conf` for directives instead of `conf/access.conf`:

```
AccessConfig conf/access_test.conf
```

You can tell the server not to look for an access configuration file by using the file spec `/dev/null` with the `AccessConfig` directive.

**AccessFileName** Before the server sends any file to a client, it looks in the directory in which the file is stored for that directory's optional local configuration file. You can override the default file name, .htaccess, by using the `AccessFileName` directive.

**Group** Use the `Group` directive in conjunction with the `User` directive to control the access rights of the server process. If you start the httpd server process as root, the `Group` and `User` directives cause the server to become the designated user in the designated group before answering any requests. By specifying a user ID and group that has access only to those files that you want to export onto the Web, you can avoid accidental exposure of sensitive information.

Apache recommends that you set up a special user ID and user group to run the server process. This user ID normally should have access only to the documents directory within the httpd directory tree (normally, /etc/local/http/htdocs). You may want to grant read access to the users' home directory tree as well if you want to allow your users to maintain Web material in their home areas.

**IdentityCheck** Some Web clients run a daemon that allows the client to provide the user name of the remote user to the Web server on request. This identification is not secure and should not be taken seriously; it may be useful in some cases for crude access counts, but such counts will be incomplete, because most clients do not provide identification of this sort.

Setting the `IdentityCheck` directive to on instructs httpd to ask clients to identify the remote user and, if an identity is provided, to log this information in the server log file.

**Options** The Apache httpd allows a great deal of control of the use of extra server features on a directory-by-directory level. The `Options` directive allows you to turn extra server features on for all directories (if used outside a `Directory` group) or for a specific directory (if used within a `Directory` group).

The `Options` directive takes any combination of the arguments in the following list and turns on the specific feature described by that argument. The directive has two special arguments: `All` turns on all extra server features, and `None` turns them all off.

- **ExecCGI**: allows execution of CGI scripts in the designated directory. Use this directive for all directories in which you intend to run Perl scripts.

- **FollowSymLinks**: allows the server to follow symbolic links in the designated directory.

- **Includes**: allows the server to parse server-side includes in HTML files.

- **IncludesNOEXEC**: allows the server to parse server-side includes in HTML files, with the exception of the #exec and #include commands.

- **Indexes**: allows the user to browse this directory. If a browser requests a URL that points to a directory, and if no index.html file is found in that directory, the server returns a directory listing of the directory to the browser.

- **MultiViews**: allows content-negotiated MultiViews, a feature that allows the server to return data in one of several formats, depending on the capabilities of the browser.

- **SymLinksIfOwnermatch**: allows the server to follow symbolic links in the designated directory only if the link points to a file or directory owned by the same user who owns the link. This security precaution is useful, because it prevents users from making files available on the Web unless they own those files.

**ResourceConfig**   This directive is quite similar to AccessConfig and is provided largely for backward compatibility. ResourceConfig overrides the default resource configuration file specification, conf/srm.conf, which is where resource control directives are supposed to be stored. In fact, you can store the directives either in the resource configuration file or in the server configuration file.

The following directive in the server configuration file tells the server to read srm_test.conf for directives instead of conf/srm.conf:

```
AccessConfig conf/srm_test.conf
```

You can tell the server not to look for a resource configuration file by using the file spec /dev/null with the ResourceConfig directive.

**User**   Use the User directive in conjunction with the Group directive to control the access rights of the server process. If you start the httpd server process as root, the Group and User directives cause the server to become the designated user in the designated group before answering any requests. By specifying a user ID and group that has access only to those files that you want to export onto the Web, you can avoid accidental exposure of sensitive information.

The argument to the User directive can be either a user ID or a user number preceded by a pound sign (#).

Apache recommends that you set up a special user ID and user group to run the server process. This user ID normally should have access only to the documents directory within the httpd directory tree (normally, /etc/local/http/htdocs). You may want to grant read access to the users' home directory tree as well if you want to allow your users to maintain Web material in their home areas.

**Apache Directory Directives**   Table 8.3 lists the directives that may be applied to individual directories. These directives are used in server configuration files to override default settings for a particular directory.

**Table 8.3  Apache HTTPD Directory Authorization Directives**

| Directive | Argument Type | Default Value | Purpose |
|---|---|---|---|
| allow from | List of hosts | — | Allows access to this directory from the designated IP hosts |
| deny from | List of hosts | — | Denies access to this directory from the designated IP hosts |
| order | Evaluation order | deny,allow | Sets the order in which deny and allow directives are applied. |
| require user | List of user IDs | — | List of IDs of users who can access a directory |
| require group | List of groups | — | List of groups that can access a directory |
| require ➡ valid-user | — | — | Allows access to all users who provide a valid user ID and password |
| AuthName | Domain name | — | Name of authorization domain for a directory |
| AuthType | Basic | Basic | Type of user authorization (only Basic available) |
| AuthUserFile | File name | — | Name of text file containing list of users and passwords |
| AuthDBM ➡ UserFile | File name | — | Name of DBM file containing list of users and passwords |
| AuthGroupFile | File name | — | Name of text file containing list of user groups |
| AuthDBM ➡ GroupFile | File name | — | Name of DBM file containing list of user groups |
| Options | List of options | — | Defines which server features are allowed |
| Allow | Override list | All | Specifies which directives can be overridden by local .htaccess file |

The directory configuration directives that are relevant to user authentication are explained in the following sections.

**allow from**   Use the allow from directive to specify which IP hosts are allowed to access a given directory. This directive takes a series of host names as arguments, and allows access from each of the designated hosts. Host names may be fully qualified (as in bilbo.tolkien.org) or partially qualified (as in .tolkien.org). A partially qualified host name (such as `tolkien.org`) allows access from all hosts whose name ends in the string supplied (`bilbo.tolkien.org`, `gandalf.tolkien.org`, and so on).

Use the `order` directive (described later in this chapter) to determine the sequence in which the `allow from` and `deny from` directives are evaluated.

**deny from**   Use the `deny from` directive to specify which IP hosts are not allowed to access a given directory. This directive takes a series of host names as arguments and denies access to the directory from each of the designated hosts. Host names may be fully qualified (as in `bilbo.tolkien.org`) or partially qualified (as in `.tolkien.org`). A partially qualified host name (such as `.tolkien.org`) denies access from all hosts whose name ends in the string supplied (`bilbo.tolkien.org`, `gandalf.tolkien.org`, and so on).

Use the `order` directive (described in the following section) to determine the sequence in which the `allow from` and `deny from` directives are evaluated.

**order**   The `allow from` and `deny from` directives have opposite effects; they can be used in tandem to control exactly which IP hosts can and cannot access a particular directory. The order in which these directives are evaluated for a particular directory is significant, however.

Consider the effect on `frodo.tolkien.org` of `allow from .tolkien.org` followed by `deny from frodo.tolkien.org`. The net result is to allow access from all hosts in `.tolkien.org` *except* `frodo`. Now consider the effect of `deny from frodo.tolkien.org` followed by `allow from tolkien.org`. The net result in this case is to allow access from all hosts in `tolkien.org`, *including* `frodo`.

The `order` directive allows you to specify whether the `allow from` or `deny from` directives are evaluated first. The first argument is either `allow,deny` or `deny,allow`. In the first case, `deny from` directives can override `allow from` directives; in the second case, `allow from` directives can override `deny from` directives.

The following example allows access to `frodo.tolkien.org` but to no other hosts within the `tolkien.org` domain:

```
order deny,allow deny from .tolkien.org allow from .frodo.tolkien.org
```

**require**   Use the `require` directive to restrict access to a directory to one or more designated users. Any user who attempts to access a restricted directory is challenged; the user must provide a valid user ID and password before the server returns the requested URL.

The `require` directive can be used to restrict access in three distinct ways:

- **require valid-user**. All users in all user groups are allowed access. Users who attempt to attach and who cannot provide a valid user ID and password are denied access.
- **require group**. All users in a set of named user groups are allowed access. Users who cannot provide a valid user ID and password, or who are not members of one of the named groups, are denied access.
- **require user**. Named users in a specific set are allowed access. All other users are denied access.

The following directive restricts access to users JohnB and DaveD only:

```
require user JohnB DaveD
```

This set of directives restricts access to the membership domain to members of the leaders group:

```
AuthType Basic
AuthName membership
AuthUserFile /www/staffmembers
AuthGroupFile /www/staffgroups
require group leaders
```

**AuthName**   Used with the AuthType, require, and AuthUserFile directives, the AuthName directive sets the authorization realm of the current directory when used inside a Directory group. For an example of using AuthName, see the section on the require directive earlier in this chapter.

**AuthType**   Apache currently has only one type of user authentication: Basic. The AuthType directive was introduced to allow for the anticipated introduction of other methods at a later stage.

Use the AuthType directive with the AuthName and require directives. For an example, see the require directive section earlier in this chapter.

**AuthUserFile**   Use the AuthUserFile directive to specify the name of the text file containing user IDs and passwords that is to be used to verify access to the current directory.

Each line of a user definition file contains a user ID, followed by a colon and a password encrypted with the crypt() function, as in the following example:

```
jeremiah:sn/A4bkdRjylI
ruth:1H.yzi5xcMPbk
```

This directive should be used in conjunction with the AuthName, AuthType, AuthGroupFile, and require directives.

**AuthDBMUserFile**   UNIX DBM files are a more efficient way than plain text files of storing user IDs and passwords. Use DBM files if you are dealing with more than a handful of users. Use the AuthDBMUserFile directive to specify the name of the DBM file containing user IDs and passwords that is to be used to verify access to the current directory. This directive should be used in conjunction with the AuthName, AuthType, AuthDBMGroupFile, and require directives.

**AuthGroupFile**   Use the AuthGroupFile directive to specify the name of the text file containing group definitions.

Each line of a group definition file contains a group name, followed by a colon and a list of the users in the group, as in the following example:

```
admin:  henry martha dave
```

**AuthDBMGroupFile**   The group file for a given directory may be a UNIX DBM file rather than a plain text file. If so, use the AuthDBMGroupFile directive, rather than the AuthDBMFile directive, to specify the group definition file.

**Options**  The Options directive described earlier in this chapter can also be used within a Directory group to control behavior for that directory. For details, refer to the "Options" section earlier in this chapter.

**AllowOverride**  Directives in the server configuration files can be overridden by directives in local .htaccess files, as described in the following section. As a server administrator, you may not want users to override all server directives. In such a case, use the AllowOverride directive in a Directory group to specify which directives can be overridden.

The default behavior is to allow the user to override all directives, which is the equivalent of using AllowOverride with an argument of All. Using an argument of None has the opposite effect, telling the server to ignore the contents of any .htaccess files. You can use the following arguments to fine-tune override behavior related to access control:

- **AuthConfig**: allows overriding of the AuthDBMGroupFile, AuthDBMUserFile, AuthGroupFile, AuthName, AuthType, AuthUserFile, and require directives.
- **Limit** (not to be confused with the <Limit> and </Limit> delimiters): allows overriding of the allow from, deny from, and order directives.
- **Options**: allows overriding of the Options directive.

The directive AllowOverride Limit in the server configuration file, for example, allows local .htaccess files to control which hosts can access files.

**Apache .htaccess Directives**  Table 8.4 lists the directives that can be used in the local .htaccess files. These files override server configuration directives for the directory in which they reside.

**Table 8.4   Apache httpd .htaccess Configuration Directives**

| Directive | Argument Type | Default Value | Purpose |
|---|---|---|---|
| allow from | List of hosts | — | Allows access to this directory from the designated IP hosts |
| deny from | List of hosts | — | Denies access to this directory from the designated IP hosts |
| order | Evaluation order | deny,allow | Sets the order in which deny and allow directives are applied. |
| require user | List of user IDs | — | List of IDs of users who can access a directory |
| require group | List of groups | — | List of groups that can access a directory |
| require ➡ valid-user | — | — | Allows access to all users who provide a valid user ID and password |

| Directive | Argument Type | Default Value | Purpose |
|-----------|---------------|---------------|---------|
| AuthGroupFile | File name | — | Name of file containing list of user groups |
| AuthName | domain name | — | Name of authorization domain for a directory |
| AuthType | Basic | Basic | Type of user authorization (only Basic available) |
| AuthUserFile | File name | — | Name of file containing list of users and passwords |
| Options | List of options | — | Defines which server features are allowed in a given directory |

These directives can be used in the .htaccess files as well as in the server configuration files. For details on each of these directives, refer to "Apache Directory Directives" earlier in this chapter.

**CAUTION**

Be careful not to give users too much leeway with .htaccess files. Local .htaccess directives can be used for purposes such as exporting files that would not otherwise be available. The best way to provide security is to use the AllowOverride directive in the server configuration file. The following example provides reasonable protection against accidental or deliberate security breaches:

```
<Directory>
AllowOverride None
Options None
<Limit GET PUT POST>
allow from all
</Limit>
</Directory>
```

This code prevents any overriding of directives by means of .htaccess files; explicitly turns off extra server features by means of the Options directive; and allows accesses from all hosts, but only by means of the GET, PUT, and POST methods.

# User Administration

The extra layer of access control required on a Web server that uses user-related access restrictions has a certain amount of maintenance overhead. Aside from setting up the configuration files that define a realm (and the users and groups that have access to it), you need to be able to add and delete users in the various realms, change passwords for users who lose or forget them, and so on.

Fortunately, that task is just the kind of task for which Perl was brought into this world. The remainder of this chapter describes some sample Perl scripts that make it easy to administer the httpd's user accounts.

**N O T E** The code for the samples in this chapter is available on the CD-ROM that comes with this book. Copy these files into a directory in your path, and make sure that `UserUtil.pl` is in your Perl library directory (/usr/local/perl/lib, for example). This file contains the shared subroutines that do all the work. ■

On the CD

# Adding Users

The first task is to define a user, which means adding a line to a user file that contains the user name, a colon, and the user's password in encrypted format.

**Encrypting Passwords** Getting the password into encrypted form is fairly straightforward when you use Perl. This task is one that you're going to want to perform again (in your script for setting passwords for existing users), so write a subroutine to do the job for you and then store it in UserUtil.pl, where it can be shared by several scripts.

Listing 8.1 shows the source for the `GetPWord()` subroutine. The subroutine takes no arguments, prompts the user for the password (twice, to prevent errors), and returns the encrypted password.

**Listing 8.1   The *GetPword* Subroutine**

```
# Subroutine to prompt for and return (encrypted) password.
sub GetPword {

    my ( $pwd1, $pwd2, $salt, $crypted );
    my @saltchars = (a .. z, A .. Z, 0 .. 9);

    print "Enter password: ";
    $pwd1 = <STDIN>;
    chop($pwd1);
    length($pwd1) >= 8 ||
        die "Password length must be eight characters or more.\n";

    print "Enter the password again: ";
    $pwd2 = <STDIN>;
    chop($pwd2);

    # Check that they match:
    ($pwd1 eq $pwd2 ) || die
        "Sorry, the two passwords you entered do not match.\n";

    # Generate a random salt value for encryption:
    srand(time || $$);
    $salt = $saltchars[rand($#saltchars)] . $saltchars[rand($#saltchars)];

    return crypt($pwd1, $salt);
}
```

## The *crypt()* Function

In the UNIX world, the `crypt()` function looks after the job of encrypting passwords. The function takes two arguments:

- A password in raw text
- A random salt argument, consisting of two characters

The `crypt()` function applies an encryption algorithm to the password, using the `salt` value. Then the function returns the encrypted password, which consists of the `salt` value followed by 11 other characters. The password `password`, encrypted with the `salt` Xb, is `Xbs.myqnmA.bI`.

Decrypting a password from the encrypted form of the password is almost impossible, but comparing a given string with the password is easy.

The following list steps through the code to show you how it works:

1. An array (`@saltchars`) of characters suitable for use in the `salt` value is defined.
2. The user is prompted for a password, which is stored in `$pwd1`. If the password has fewer than eight characters, the subroutine dies.
3. The user is prompted to re-enter the password. If the two passwords do not match, the program aborts with an error message.
4. The random-number generator is seeded with a Boolean or combination of the current time and perl's process ID.
5. A character from the set of `salt` characters is selected at random, using the expression `$saltchars[rand($#saltchars)]`.
6. A second character is similarly selected, and the two are combined with the . (period) concatenation operator. The result is the two-character encryption `salt` value.
7. Finally, the password specified by the user and the `salt` value that you generated are passed to Perl's `crypt()` function. The value returned by `crypt()` is passed, intact, back to the calling subroutine.

**Adding a User** Adding a user amounts to no more than adding a line that contains the user name and password to the user definition file. You can perform this task by using the SetPword() function, the code for which appears in Listing 8.2.

### Listing 8.2 The *SetPword* Subroutine

```
# Store a user's password in a user definition file
# Arguments:
# - user file spec
# - user name
# - password
sub SetPword {
    my( $filespec, $user, $pword ) = @_;

    # Open user file for appending:
```

*continues*

**Listing 8.2   Continued**

```
    open(USERFILE, "+>>$filespec") ||
     die "Could not open user file \"$filespec\" for appending: $!\n";

    # Write to the user file
    print USERFILE "$user:$pword\n" ||
     die "Failed to write the user/password to file \"$filespec\".\n";

    # Tidy up:

    close USERFILE;
}
```

This code opens the named user definition file for appending by including the >> append operator in the file specification argument to the open() function. If the file does not already exist,
perl creates it.

The code then writes the supplied user ID and encrypted password (with a colon between
them and a new line at the end), closes the user definition file, and returns.

**Putting It All Together: *Aaddu***    The script that you invoke when you actually want to add a
user is relatively simple, because most of the work has been separated out into reusable subroutines. Listing 8.3 shows the code for Aaddu.

**Listing 8.3   The *Aaddu* Script**

```
#!/usr/local/bin/perl -I. -T

# Script to add a user to an Apache user file.

require "UserUtil.pl";  # Need utilities

# Takes two arguments:
# - username to add
# - file to add to

# Get the arguments:
($user, $file) = @ARGV;

# Check that we got two arguments:
$file ||
    die "Aaddu: Add user utility for Apache (text) user files.\n",
    "Usage: Aaddu username filespec\n";

$file =~ /(.+)/;
$safefile = $1;

# Get the encrypted password:
$password = &GetPword;
```

```
# Store the new username and password:
&SetPword($safefile, $user, $password);

# End
```

This script simply takes the user name and user definition file as arguments; gets the password interactively, using the GetPWord() subroutine; and then calls SetPWord() to add the users.

One more detail here. Examine the following mysterious lines:

```
$file =~ /(.+)/;
$safefile = $1;
```

These lines are here because the script turns on Perl's taint checking with the -T switch. In this mode, Perl does not allow you to pass an argument from the command line—namely, $file—to a function such as open(), because doing so might compromise security. Making a copy of $file won't work either, because it will be similarly tainted.

So how do you get the file name from $file in a way that won't upset Perl's taint-checking sensibilities? One way is to perform a regular expression match on the contents of $file and then store what was matched. Perl allows this method because it assumes that if you go to this much trouble in your own code, you know what you're doing.

The statement $file =~ /(.+)/ carries out a regular expression match on $file, using the expression (.+). This expression simply matches the entire contents of $file and returns what it found as $1. The script then stashes this result in the new variable $safefile. If you are writing scripts to be executed by other users, you may want to use a more elaborate regular expression to eliminate any suspicious characters from the variable before passing it to open.

**See** "Regular Expressions," **p. 39**

**Avoiding Duplicate User Names**   The major difficulty with simply appending new users to a user definition file is that there is no safeguard against the possibility of adding the same user name more than once. The procedure would be much safer if the Aaddu script determined whether a user already existed in a user definition file before trying to add the user.

The UserDefined() function in UserUtil.pl makes just that determination. Listing 8.4 shows the code.

---

**Listing 8.4   The *UserDefined* Subroutine**

```
# Return 1 if user defined in named text file
sub UserDefined  {

    my ( $username, $filespec ) = @_;

    # No file, no user
    open(USERFILE, $filespec) || return 0;
```

*continues*

**Listing 8.4   Continued**

```
    # Check each line for username:
    while (<USERFILE>)  {
     if ( /^$username:/ )  {
         close USERFILE;
         return 1;
     }
    }
    close USERFILE;
    return 0;
}
```

The function takes a user name and a user definition file specification as arguments; it returns 1 if the user exists in that file and 0 if the user doesn't exist. This function will also be useful in the opposite context when you want to change the passwords of existing users.

The operation of this function is quite straightforward: It opens the user definition file for reading, and checks each line in the file. If the line starts with the user name followed immediately by a colon, the function returns 1 to confirm that the user is defined.

Notice the use of the close() function before both return 1 and return 0. Placing a single close() statement at the end of a subroutine is not sufficient, because a return statement earlier in the subroutine may prevent the close() statement from being reached. It is, therefore, important to place close() statements immediately before every return point in the subroutine.

Listing 8.5 shows the new, improved Aaddu script.

**Listing 8.5   The *Aaadu* Script with Duplicate Checking**

```
#!/usr/local/bin/perl -I. -T

# Script to add a user to an Apache user definition file.
# Prevents duplicate entries.

require "UserUtil.pl";  # Need utilities

# Takes two arguments:
# - username to add
# - file to add to

# Get the arguments:
($user, $file) = @ARGV;

# Check that we got two arguments:
$file ||
    die "Aaddu: Add user utility for Apache user definition files.\n",
    "Usage: Aaddu username filespec\n";

$file =~ /(.+)/;
$safefile = $1;
```

```
# First check that the user does not already exist:
&UserDefined($user, $safefile) &&
    die "User \"$user\" already exists in file \"$safefile\".\n";

# Get the encrypted password:
$password = &GetPword;

# Store the new username and password:
&TextSetPword($safefile, $user, $password);

# End
```

The only change from the earlier version of Aaddu is the addition of a call to UserDefined() to check for the existence of the user.

# Deleting Users

Deleting users is a little less straightforward than adding them. Adding a user is simply a matter of sticking a new user line at the end of a file. Deleting a user, however, involves finding that user in the file and then rewriting the file without that user line but with all others left intact.

The simplest way to perform this task in Perl is to read the entire contents of the user definition file into an associative array, delete the entry that corresponds to the user that you want to drop, and then write the whole array out to the same file. This approach may not be immediately intuitive if you're not used to working with associative arrays, but it will become familiar to you in a short time, as you learn to leverage the power of associative arrays.

Listing 8.6 shows the code for the DeleteUser() subroutine.

### Listing 8.6   The *DeleteUser* Subroutine

```
# Subroutine to delete a user from a user file
# Input: Username, filespec

sub DeleteUser  {

    my ($user, $filespec) = @_;
    my ($thisusr, $thispw, $elem, %passwords);

    # Open the file for reading:
    open(USERFILE, "$filespec") ||
        die "Could not open user file \"$filespec\" for reading: $!\n";

    # Grab the contents of the user file in an associative array:
    while (<USERFILE>)  {
        chop;
        ($thisusr, $thispw) = split(':', $_) ;
        $passwords{$thisusr} = $thispw;
    }
    close USERFILE;
```

*continues*

**Listing 8.6   Continued**

```
# Check that the named user exists:
$passwords{$user} ||
    die "User \"$user\" not found in file \"$filespec\".\n";

# Now delete the user from the array:
delete $passwords{$user};

# Now write the whole user/password array to the user file:

# First re-open the user file for writing:
open(USERFILE, ">$filespec") ||
    die "Could not open user file \"$filespec\" for reading: $!\n";

# Now write each element of the array in the correct format:
foreach $elem ( keys %passwords )  {
    print USERFILE $elem, ":", $passwords{$elem}, "\n" ||
        die "Failed to write user/password to file \"$filespec\": $!.\n";
}

close USERFILE;
}
```

The following list goes through this script a step at a time:

1. The named user definition file is opened for reading.

2. The contents of the file are read into the %passwords associative array by the following three lines, in a while(<>) loop:

```
chop;
($thisusr, $thispw) = split(':', $_) ;
$passwords{$thisusr} = $thispw;
```

The chop statement drops the new-line character from each line as it is read in. The split() function breaks the line into the user name ($thisusr) and password ($thispw) components. Then a new entry is created in the %passwords associative array, with $thisusr as the key and $thispw as the value.

3. With the associative array complete, the script throws away the entry that corresponds to the user that you want to drop, using the delete command.

4. The script re-opens the user definition file for writing and iterates through all elements of the %passwords array, writing one at a time in the correct user:password format.

# Changing Passwords

Changing the password of an existing user is trivial now; you've already written the code that does all the work. All you need is the following simple wrapper, Asetpw, to call the UserDefined() and SetPWord() subroutines, as shown in Listing 8.7.

**Listing 8.7   The *Asetpw* Script**

```
#!/usr/local/bin/perl -I. -T

# Script to change a password in an Apache user file.

require "UserUtil.pl";  # Need utilities

# Takes two arguments:
# - username to change
# - file containing userid, password

# Get the arguments:
($user, $file) = @ARGV;

# Check that we got two arguments:
$file ||
    die "Asetpw: Change password utility for Apache user definition files.\n",
    "Usage: Asetpw username filespec\n";

$file =~ /(.+)/;
$safefile = $1;

# First check that the user exists:
&UserDefined($user, $safefile) ||
    die "User \"$user\" does not exist in file \"$safefile\".\n";

# Get the encrypted password:
$password = &GetPword;

# Store the new username and password:
&SetPword($safefile, $user, $password);

# End
```

This listing illustrates just how useful a modular approach to code design can be.

## Adding Users to Groups

A group definition file consists of a series of lines, one per group, each of which contains the name of the group, followed by a colon and a list of space-separated member names. This format is somewhat similar to the format of a user definition file, but the task of adding or deleting a user is more complex, because user definition lines have a single name and a single password—ideal material for an associative array. Group definition files, on the other hand, have a single group name and multiple member names.

You will still use associative arrays to deal with groups, but you need to do a little extra work to allow for the storage of a list of members as a single value. The approach that you take in this section is to deal with a group file as a whole, reading its contents to and from an associative array. This approach allows you to modularize your code into neat functional elements. This method lends itself particularly well to working with UNIX DBM files, should you decide to use them at a later stage.

**Reading Groups**    Listing 8.8 shows the source code for GetGroupMembers( ), which is stored in UserUtil.pl. GetGroupMembers( ) is a subroutine that reads the entire contents of a group file into an associative array.

### Listing 8.8    The *GetGroupMembers* Subroutine

```
# Subroutine to extract group member list from group file
# Input: file spec of group membership file
# Returns: Associative array of groups, members.

sub GetGroupMembers {
    my( $filespec ) = @_;
    my ($thisgrp, $grpmembers, %groupmembers);

    # Just return now if file does not exist:
    -e $filespec || return;

    # Open the group file:
    open(GFILE, "$filespec") ||
     die "Could not open user file \"$filespec\" for reading: $!\n";

    while (<GFILE>)  {
     chop;
     ($thisgrp, $grpmembers) = split(':' , $_);
     $groupmembers{$thisgrp} = $grpmembers;
    }

    close GFILE;

    return %groupmembers;
}
```

When the input file has been opened, each line is read and split at the colon into a group name ($thisgrp) and a member list ($grpmembers). The member list is a single string containing the user names of all group members, separated by spaces. The associative array %groupmembers is built by adding $thisgrp as a key and $grpmembers as a corresponding value for each line read from the file. Then the entire associative array is returned to the calling routine.

**Writing Groups**    Listing 8.9 shows the source code for SetGroupMembers( ), which is stored in UserUtil.pl and which is similar to SetPword( ).

### Listing 8.9    The *SetGroupMembers()* Subroutine

```
# Subroutine to store group member list in group file
# Input: file spec of group membership file,
#        associative array of groups/users

sub SetGroupMembers {
    my( $filespec, %groups ) = @_;
    my ($grp);
```

```
    # Open the group file:
    open(GFILE, ">$filespec") ||
      die "Could not open group file \"$filespec\" for writing: $!\n";

    foreach $grp ( keys %groups )  {
     print GFILE "$grp: $groups{$grp}\n";
    }

    close GFILE;
}
```

This function does the opposite of GetGroupMembers(): It opens the group definition file for writing and writes out one line per entry in the %groups associative array. Each line is written as the key, followed by a colon and then the corresponding value.

**Putting It All Together: *Agrpaddu***   The source code for Agrpaddu is relatively short, making use of the functionality in UserUtil.pl, as shown in Listing 8.10.

**Listing 8.10   The *Agrpaddu* Script**

```
#!/usr/local/bin/perl -I. -T
# Script to add a user to a group in an Apache group file.
require "UserUtil.pl";  # Need utilities

# Takes two arguments:
# - group to add to
# - username to add
# - file to add to

# Get the arguments:
($group, $user, $file) = @ARGV;

# Check that we got three arguments:
$file ||
    die "Agrpaddu: Utility for adding users to Apache group files.\n",
    "Usage: Agrpaddu groupname username filespec\n";

# Extract filename:
$file =~ /(.+)/;
$safefile = $1;

# Read the current group membership into an associative array:
%groups = &GetGroupMembers($safefile);

# Check if user already in group:
$groups{$group} =~ /\b$user\b/ &&
    die "User \"$user\" is already a member of group \"$group\".\n";

# Add the user to the group:
$groups{$group} .= " $user";
```

*continues*

**Listing 8.10   Continued**

```
# Write the array out to the groups file:
&SetGroupMembers($safefile, %groups);

# End
```

The following list describes what this script does:

1. The script reads the designated group definition file into the %groups associative array.
2. The script checks to see whether the user is already in the named group.
3. If the user is not in the named group, the script appends a space and the user name to the value of the entry in %groups that has the group name for a key. (If the group was not defined, this step defines it.)
4. The script writes the %groups associative array out to the group definition file.

# Deleting Users from Groups

The task of deleting users from groups is a little more involved  than adding them. Listing 8.11 shows the source for Agrpdelu.

**Listing 8.11   The *Agrpdelu* Script**

```
#!/usr/local/bin/perl -I. -T

# Script to delete a user from a group in an Apache group file.

require "UserUtil.pl";  # Need utilities

# Takes two arguments:
# - group to delete from
# - username to delete
# - file to delete from

# Get the arguments:
($group, $user, $file) = @ARGV;

# Check that we got three arguments:
$file ||
    die "Agrpdelu: Utility for deleting users from Apache group files.\n",
    "Usage: Agrpdelu groupname username filespec\n";

# Extract filename:
$file =~ /(.+)/;
$safefile = $1;

# Read the current group membership into an associative array:
%groups = &GetGroupMembers($safefile);
```

```
# Check if user is in group:
$groups{$group} =~ /\b$user\b/ ||
    die "User \"$user\" is not a member of group \"$group\".\n";

# First make an array of all members of this list:
(@oldmembers) = $groups{$group} =~ /(\w+)/g;

# Clear down the current member list for this group:
$groups{$group} = "";

# now add all but the member to be deleted to a new string:
foreach $member (@oldmembers)  {
    if ( $member ne $user )  {
      $groups{$group} .= " $member";
      }
  }

# Write the array out to the groups file:
&SetGroupMembers($safefile, %groups);

# End
```

The following list shows the essential steps:

1. The script reads the group definition file into the %groups associative array.

2. The script stores the membership of the named group in the @oldmembers array, using this statement:

   ```
   (@oldmembers) = $groups{$group} =~ /(\w+)/g;
   ```

   This statement is worth examining. $groups{$group} is the string that contains all group member names, separated by spaces. Applying the /(\w+)/g operator performs a pattern match on the member list, saving all full words in $1, $2, and so on. Then these values are stored in @oldmembers.

3. The script obliterates the group membership for the named group by setting it to an empty string.

4. The script rebuilds the member list for the named group— $groups{$group}—by looping through all elements of the @oldmembers array, adding each element to $groups{$group} unless it matches the user name that is to be dropped.

5. The script writes the %groups associative array back out to the group definition file.

Again, you get to reuse the GetGroupMembers() and SetGroupMembers() functions.

# From Here...

This chapter describes how user authentication combines user verification with access restrictions to ensure that your server is as open as it needs to be, and no more. This book has a great deal more to say about server security and Perl:

■ Chapter 9, "Understanding CGI Security," explains how you can maintain the state of an authenticated session across several Perl scripts.

■ Chapter 10, "Site Administration," has more information on how you can use Perl to assist in the management of your Web server.

# Understanding CGI Security

*by Paul Doyle*

**P**roviding a secure but open Web service is a balancing act. You want to make your site as easily accessible as possible so that the maximum number of people can use it, but you also want to make sure that access is not so open that your service can be harmed, accidentally or deliberately, due to a lack of security.

Achieving the correct balance between security and openness is easier if you simply eliminate all write access on the server. Often, however, the nature of the service that you are providing dictates that users have write access to files on the server.

This chapter deals with one approach to providing a secure Web service that permits writing of data on the server. The chapter examines the security issues in detail and shows how you can accept data from users and store it on the server while protecting the integrity of your service. To illustrate the techniques, a sample Web-based ordering system using shopping-cart logic is developed in the course of the chapter. ■

### CGI security

CGI applications are executed by the server on behalf of the end user. This chapter explains how the server acts as a proxy, running programs for users, and why this behavior can present a threat to the integrity of your server.

### Session management

A user may execute a CGI program many times in the course of what appears to her to be a single session. The server generally needs to store information for the user temporarily between executions of the CGI script. We'll examine the techniques behind session management and the programming issues that it raises.

### Sample CGI wrapper script

Finally, we'll develop a working, session-managed sample application in Perl. This shopping-cart program allows users to browse through some menus of products and build an order. The application illustrates the principles and methods involved in temporary session storage.

# Understanding the Security Issues

Previous chapters (particularly Chapter 8, "Understanding Basic User Authentication") dealt with the general issues involved in verifying the identity of users who access your Web server and in restricting access to files on the server by using the HTTP daemon's configuration mechanism. Before you get started using CGI wrapper scripts, take a closer look at the specific security issues that arise when you decide to accept input from users.

## Tracing the Chain of Command

The transparency of the Web's infrastructure is one thing that has contributed to the enormous growth in its popularity in recent years. The user clicks a button in his browser, and a server somewhere on the planet sends him whatever his little heart desires.

**The Browser As Interface**    Users feel as though they are interacting directly with the material that they read on the Internet, with only their browsers between them and the words or images that they see. A browser picks up files for a user and displays images. From time to time, the user may need to enter a user ID and a password to access a special service. To most users, their browsers appear to be logging them on to the server. If a user notices that a program on the server is being executed, the impression is that the browser is executing the program for the user.

**Beneath the Surface**    In fact, looking just below the surface of the action in a typical point-and-click operation, you can see that what actually happens is considerably more complex. The sequence of events can be summarized as follows:

1. The user selects a location on the Web, using a browser.
2. The browser locates the server that stores the requested item.
3. The browser sends a request to the server for the contents of the location.
4. The server examines the request and decides, based on its access restrictions, whether access to the location is allowed from the IP address at which the request originated.
6. If access is allowed from that IP address, the server decides whether its access restrictions mean that user authentication is required for the requested location.
7. If so, the server challenges the browser to provide a valid user ID and password for the authentication domain that contains the requested location.
8. If the user ID and password are verified, and if that user ID is entitled to access the authentication domain that contains the requested location, the server reads the contents of the location.
9. If the location is a CGI program, the server executes it and sends the results to the browser. If the location is not a CGI program, the contents of the location are sent as they are to the browser.
10. The browser displays the content sent to it by the server.

This schema could be broken down into much finer levels of detail, but for now, the points of interest are:

- The server decides whether a user ID and password are required.
- The server validates the user ID and password.
- The server executes the CGI program.
- The server transmits the contents of the requested location.

In short, all the action takes place on the server, and all of it is done by the Web server (httpd) process. The user sends a request to the server and receives the result from the server; everything that happens in between involves activity carried out by the server process on behalf of the user.

**N O T E**    Browser extensions such as Java and SafeTcl are exceptions to this rule. They are executed by the browser after the browser downloads script files from a server. ▪

**The Server As Interface**    This execution by the server on behalf of the user presents a serious security issue. If the user were logging in to the server interactively and running a program in a shell that was governed by the user's own private account privileges, matters would be simpler. It would be relatively easy to ensure that the user did not have privileges that endangered the integrity of the rest of the system. Many system administrators would protest that it is far from easy to restrict privileges in this way on even a moderately large system. The difficulty, however, certainly pales in comparison with the effort involved in maintaining the integrity of data in a directory to which everyone on the Internet has some form of write access.

The fact is, users do not log in to the Web server. The Web server responds to requests from anyone on the Internet, reading files on the server on the user's behalf or even executing programs on the server on the user's behalf. The same httpd process generally executes programs for all users who access the server, so the system that works on interactive systems—containing the activities of the user at the operating-system level based on the user's process ID—will not work on Web servers.

Instead, the httpd process uses its own verification mechanisms to ensure that users are who they say they are, and it interprets its access restriction rules to determine who can do what (and where). From the point of view of the operating system, everyone who accesses a service shares the same process ID and has the same privileges to all files. The following sections explain why sharing a process is a problem.

# Reading Files

All Web servers make files available for reading. If your server does nothing else, you can concentrate on making sure that the http daemon has no write access anywhere on your server, with the exception of its log files.

But even then, you need to take care. Some files may be intended for the eyes of a particular group of people only. In that case, creating Web server user groups and carefully planning authentication domains (containers for the files) can protect the data from unwelcome attention.

It is also important to avoid exporting files that should not be visible over the network. A classic example is exporting the server's password file so that anyone on the Internet can have a crack at it. Restricting the exported area on the Web server to a particular, specially designated directory tree can help you avoid security holes such as this, but you also must prevent users from placing links or aliases to sensitive files in the exported area. Chapter 8, "Understanding Basic User Authentication," explains how to secure against this kind of security breach.

# Writing to Files

The primary area of concern in this chapter is allowing users to write files, not just read them. When you decide that it is necessary to allow the httpd server to write to files on behalf of remote users, you must take great care to limit the circumstances under which the httpd writes data to disk.

You may need to allow the server to write files on behalf of users for several reasons:

- **Accepting user input.** The guestbook example in Chapter 2, "Introduction to CGI," stores data entered by users who visit a site. Other examples include name and address or customer feedback fields in Web forms.

- **Taking orders.** The same concept can be extended to cover actual orders for goods. The Web server acts as a front end for an ordering database, with the order data being read from a form filled in by users on their browsers. Although it is similar in many technical respects to survey-type data collection (user feedback, for example), this type of input is conceptually quite different. The data received by the server in this way is not simply stored on disk; it directly initiates a sequence of events that leads to the delivery of a product and the generation of an invoice.

- **Providing temporary storage.** The page-based nature of Web services raises a special difficulty for the Web programmer. Each screen that the user sees on his browser is a separate Web location. If a user is presented with a menu on one page and chooses one of the menu options, the menu choice generally leads to a separate location. In the case of CGI programs, a separate program is invoked for each menu choice. And that fact, to the dismay of programmers, unfortunately means that variables must be stored on disk between pages.

# Storing Variables

This section takes a closer look at providing temporary storage. Suppose that you, the CGI programmer, want to implement a system that involves three screens. Screen A presents a form that contains the usual elements: fill-in boxes, drop-down menus, and such. When form A is submitted, assuming that no essential data is missing, screen B appears. This screen is also a form, but it picks up additional information from the user. When form B is submitted, screen C appears—another form, this time summarizing the user's entries in forms A and B.

When I fill in form A and click the submit button, the ACTION parameter of the FORM statement in form A contains the name of a CGI program that generates form B. This CGI program—call it MakeB.c—receives the values that I entered in form A through the process environment, as described in earlier chapters. The program then generates form B with a FORM statement that has an ACTION parameter specifying that another program—call it MakeC.cgi—should be invoked when form B is submitted. So I fill in form B and click the submit button. MakeC.cgi receives the values that I entered in form B and generates form C appropriately.

## Losing the Data

Just one thing is missing in form C: the data that I entered in form A! This data was held in two places: in the form where I entered it and in MakeB.cgi, which received it. That's as far as the data goes unless you take explicit steps to pass it along.

So you need to make sure that all values that I enter or select in both forms A and B arrive safely in MakeC.cgi.

**Overloading the *ACTION* Parameter**   One way is to make sure that the data gets passed along is to add the cgi variable information to the ACTION parameter of the FORM statement in form B. The value of ACTION is a hyperlink, so it can take CGI parameters in the usual way. This example invokes MakeC.cgi, with the variables Name, ColorChoice, and Horsepower equal to Kurt, Blue, and 0, respectively, when the user submits the form:

```
<FORM ACTION="MakeC.cgi?Name=Kurt&ColorChoice=Blue&Horsepower=0">
```

Notice that a statement such as this must be generated by a CGI program. The values Kurt, Blue, and 0 are decided only when the user fills in form B, so these values cannot be hard-coded into a HTML file on disk.

This method ensures that the designated values get to MakeC.cgi. Unfortunately, the contents of form B will be lost, replaced by these manually imposed values. This method may be useful in limited circumstances, but beware—it can get out of hand quickly. Consider a case in which a group of HTML forms are used to build up a set of data over a series of transactions, with the user being allowed to go back and forth between forms at will. Consider the number of variables that you need to put on the ACTION parameter's hyperlink, and consider the impossibility of keeping everything straight. Then read on.

**Saving It to Disk**   Another approach is to store the values of all such variables to a file as the filled-in forms are received. This type of method is easier to manage when you have multiple pages and when flow between pages is not strictly linear—that is, in virtually all Web services. From the point of view of the Web programmer, writing pages and scripts to use such a system is not terribly arduous; the main requirement is that you store to disk all data that you may want to see again later.

Although saving data to disk is the preferred option for all but the most trivial cases, it has some drawbacks:

■ You need to allow write access in CGI directories. This situation is not a security risk in itself, but it does make security risks more likely, and it certainly precludes the possibility of a watertight, read-only Web server.

■ A good deal of programming overhead is involved in setting up a system of this sort. You need to write low-level storage management functions that other, higher-level scripts will invoke; you need to decide on a user authentication strategy; and you may have to write a primitive interpreter to allow stored values to reappear in HTML pages. (Fortunately, I've done all that work for you.)

■ Finally, you must do a certain amount of minor housekeeping work on a regular basis with a system of this type—deleting stale data from time to time, reviewing access restrictions, and so on.

These disadvantages are easily outweighed by the flexibility of a solid intermediate storage system, especially when you consider that most of the work has already been done. The system described in the rest of this chapter has all the essentials that you need to get up and running quickly. Just finish this chapter, copy some files from the CD-ROM that comes with this book, and prepare to amaze and astound your friends!

# Managing Sessions

The type of write-to-file system described in the preceding sections is a session-based system. A solid understanding of the way in which such a system works is essential before you can start writing code, so this section examines the building blocks of a session-based Web service.

## The Nature of a Session

A URL is the basic unit of Web access. You want to allow users to access several such locations—CGI scripts and HTML pages—on your server in a linked sequence, in such a way that you can track users' actions and any data that they enter. Therefore, you need to identify the user when she makes contact initially, and if she follows a link within our service, you want to regard the new access as being a continuation of the initial one. That means identifying her when she requests the second and subsequent locations, and making the logical connection between these accesses and the initial one. This logical sequence of connected accesses is what I refer to as a *session*.

This section is concerned with tracking the user's access over a sequence of steps *within* the service, not with gathering historical data over an extended period. If the user attaches to your service and follows links between pages for a few minutes one day, and then does something similar the next day, those accesses count as two sessions, not as two parts of one session.

**The End** The preceding section's definition of a session contains a loose end: when does a session finish?

In some cases, you may want to provide the user an explicit menu option for logging off and terminating the session. This approach makes sense in the case of password-protected services, in which a dangling open connection may represent a security risk.

In other cases, in which services are open to all users, an explicit disconnect or logout button may not be necessary. You simply follow the user's actions until she stops using the service, at which time any data stored on a temporary basis is deleted by a housekeeping process of some sort.

This open-ended approach can be messy. How do you know whether your user has really left your service and is not just reading what you displayed on her screen or handling some other business, with the intention of resuming the session later?

The answer lies in a time-out mechanism. You decide on a reasonable upper limit to the length of a pause between accesses to your service, and you regard as abandoned any sessions that pause for longer than that duration. A separate housekeeping process—a Perl script executed as a cron job at regular intervals, for example—deletes session files that have not been modified within the designated time.

A time-out system is also useful in systems that use an explicit logout option. If the connection goes down or the user forgets to log off, the session was not terminated properly and remains active until you kill it. You can use a time-out mechanism to put these suspended sessions to sleep.

**The Session Identifier**    Tracking each user separately from one CGI script or HTML page to the next is essential. You may have dozens of users accessing your page simultaneously, and you don't want one person's data becoming confused with that of another.

The key to keeping track of users is the *session identifier*—a unique number or string that your service assigns to a user when she first connects to the service. This identifier is automatically included in all subsequent requests made by the user during that session, allowing the service to determine which session file to use for the user when she reconnects.

You can pass the key between the server and the client in several ways. If you can guarantee that all clients who access your server are capable of supporting cookies, you can set a cookie to the value of the key, as described in Chapter 7, "Dynamic and Interactive HTML Content in Perl and CGI." The simplest approach—and the one that you'll use for your sample application—is to store the key in a HTML form as a hidden value.

The following HTML statement, for example, results in a CGI variable called `sessionkey`, with a value of `clef`:

```
<input type="hidden" name="sessionkey" value="clef">
```

The value is not displayed on the browser in any way, but when the user submits the form, `sessionkey` and `clef` are included in the list of CGI variables and values that the CGI script on the server receives.

To summarize, a *session* is a set of connected accesses of a service by one user. A session is terminated when the user explicitly sends a termination request or when a designated time-out period elapses. The service—your Perl program—tracks the user throughout the session by checking for the user's unique session identifier on each access request.

# The Wrapper

So far, so good. The user has a session ID, which she provides with each new request for a location within your service. Using this ID, she hops from one page, form, or CGI program to another, and you keep track of all her data for her.

This process should be managed by a single CGI program rather than by a series of interconnected scripts, for a few good reasons:

- If you use several CGI scripts—one to handle each distinct task carried out within your service—you must take great care to ensure that all scripts deal with session files in a coherent way.

- Managing the hyperlinks between a series of interconnected scripts can be a real nightmare. Suppose that you have a link from script A to script B to script C and another link from script X to script B. Then you decide to edit script A to go directly to script C, and delete script B. You don't realize that you've broken the connection between X and B until a customer runs script X, tries to follow the link to B, and gets a nasty error message. If you use a single CGI program, there is only one link to follow.

- If you want to send to the browser a HTML page that is mostly static, but that has a few simple text substitutions based on values from the user's session file, you have to write an entire CGI program to do the job. If you can get your single CGI program to perform those substitutions for you, you can write plain HTML where appropriate.

- Using many scripts is too much work. Remember, laziness is officially a virtue in the Perl world.

In short, a single program is easier to manage, and it makes the HTML and associated hyperlinks easier to develop, too. This single script is called a *CGI wrapper*, and it's how you'll write your sample application.

### CGIWrap

A public-domain utility called CGIWrap (included on the CD-ROM that comes with this book) uses a CGI wrapper script for a different purpose. The problem that CGIWrap seeks to address originates in the fact that HTTP daemons (httpds) execute CGI programs on behalf of the end user. The httpd process runs on the server under a user ID that has privileges that are not available to the ordinary user of the server, such as write access to database files. Accordingly, a user on your Web server can write a CGI program to perform tasks that the end user cannot carry out. Examples include printing configuration or password files that you prefer to keep confidential and overwriting data. It would be relatively easy for one user to attack another by overwriting the data in the other user's CGI directory, for example, but damage of this kind can occur accidentally, too.

The best solution to this kind of risk is to have each CGI program execute by using the user ID of the owner of the script, rather than using the user ID of the httpd process. The httpd process runs as root (on a UNIX machine) and gets the httpd to run each CGI program under a separate process, with the user ID of the script owner.

CGIWrap, written by Nathan Neulinger, is a utility program that farms out CGI executions to a separate process in this way. The program also performs some other basic security checks on the CGI script before deciding whether it should allow the script to execute.

Some HTTP daemons now have this type of functionality built in. If your HTTP daemon does not provide this feature, you may want to consider installing CGIWrap to enhance the security of your Web server.

Part

III

Ch

9

# Generic Substitutions

The list in "The Wrapper" earlier in this chapter discussed substitutions in HTML files. This process is best explained by means of a simple example. Suppose that you want to greet your user by using her first name, which she has already entered in a form. The relevant line of the HTML would look something like this:

```
<h3>Welcome, Jean!</h3>
```

Assuming that you stored the user's name in the Perl variable $firstname, you can produce this HTML by using a Perl statement such as the following:

```
print "<h3>Welcome, $firstname!</h3>";
```

This statement could go in a special CGI script that prints out the welcome page, or it could appear in a special subroutine in your wrapper script. You don't want to adopt that approach, though—you would find yourself writing special scripts or subroutines for every bit of HTML that is not completely static.

A much more elegant solution would be to have your variable name embedded in the HTML file and to have the variable replaced automatically just before the page is sent to the user. You can't use that method, of course; a HTML file is not a Perl program, so there's no point in sticking Perl variable names in there. The principle is sound, however, and you can achieve the same result by using a slightly different mechanism.

Instead of embedding Perl variable names in the HTML file, you can embed special placeholders that your script will translate for you as it sends the page. The placeholder needs to be identifiable as such to the wrapper script; you need to make sure that the wrapper replaces all placeholders without altering any of the HTML. You can identify your placeholders in several ways—by inventing a new HTML tag, for example. (That method is risky, though, because you never know what tag names will appear in the next version of the HTML standard.)

The method in this section uses simple syntax. Placeholders in your HTML files start and end with a backslash. The part between the placeholders indicates the name of the variable whose value is to go in the placeholder's position. The welcome line, for example, would appear in the HTML file as follows:

```
<h3>Welcome, \personalname\!</h3>
```

Your wrapper script will spot the backslashes, extract the `personalname` token, and look it up in a table in memory. Because you're using Perl, that table is implemented as an associative array. (The section called "Parsing an HTML File" later in this chapter explains exactly how that implementation is achieved.) The wrapper script then spits out the original line, minus the backslashes and the token name, which it replaces with the value in the associative array for that token.

You probably will want to develop your own simple syntax for your application. The syntax used in this chapter is deliberately simple, so as to keep the sample code easy to follow.

> **CAUTION**
>
> If you want to do anything more complicated than simply replace values, you probably should design proper syntax for your embedded commands before you start, because adding features as you go along will almost certainly result in obscure, confusing syntax. You may even want to add looping and other flow-control capabilities. If your needs really extend to features of that sort, you may want to consider server-side includes or Java for an out-of-the-box solution.

# Flow Control

The essential components of your managed system are:.

- Sessions
- Session keys
- Session management functions
- HTML files with placeholders for variable values
- A substitution mechanism to replace those placeholders with real values
- A wrapper script that manages all accesses within your system

Before you start to develop this application, you need to know how you're going to manage program flow.

This type of system is state-based in the sense that the current state of the system—the aggregate of the values of all the system's variables—dictates the next action taken by the system. Looking at the system from the server side, a set of variables and values are provided by the browser, and the CGI script decides what to do based on these values. From the point of view of the browser, the CGI program is directed by a sort of remote-control mechanism, by which the browser sets CGI values to control the action on the server.

**Pointing the Way**   The most direct way to tell the wrapper script which location to display next is to state it in the CGI values. You can accomplish this task quite easily by inserting into the outgoing form a hidden value that contains the URL of the next location, such as this:

```
<input type="hidden" name="location" value="wrap.cgi">
```

Then the wrapper script can check the CGI values for a `location` setting when it tries to decide what to do next.

**Directing the Action**    Although a `location` setting is adequate in many cases, you may not always know which location will come next. You may need the server to do some processing of the session-state values before deciding which location to return next.

In some cases, the CGI program can determine the next action by examining particular CGI values. If there is no session-key value, for example, the only valid action is to force the user to log on. In most cases, however, the number of values to be checked and the possible combinations of values will get out of control quickly. Statements of the form "if (A=B and X=Y) but not ((C=B or Y=Z) and A=D)" will start to appear.

A neat, direct way to implement this type of remote control is to have a special CGI value—call it `action`—that specifies the next action to be taken. This value is not always required but is very useful in most cases.

Suppose that your welcome screen is to be followed by a product menu. The following line, placed inside the form on the welcome page, will tell the wrapper that the next action to be taken should be `product_menu`:

```
<input type="hidden" name="action" action="product_menu">
```

Notice that this mechanism merely indicates a state to the wrapper script; it does not dictate which Perl function should be invoked in the event that a particular state arises.

**Walking Through the Wrapper**    Figure 9.1 illustrates the chain of events that take place during a typical session.

The following list provides a detailed explanation:

1. The user begins a new session by accessing the wrapper script without a session key.
2. The wrapper script sends back the logon screen (a simple HTML form).
3. The user enters a user ID and password, and submits the form. The ACTION parameter of the FORM statement ensures that the wrapper is invoked again when the form is submitted.
4. The wrapper script determines whether the user ID and password match; if they don't, the script sends a failure message back to the user.
5. If the authentication succeeds, a new session key is generated, and a welcome screen is displayed. This screen contains several links or submit buttons, each of which points to the wrapper script. The screen also contains a hidden field that stores the session key for this user.
6. The user enters data, if the screen is a form, and then selects a link or clicks a submit button.
7. The browser sends the user's CGI values to the wrapper script. These values *always* include the user's session key. Generally, there also is an action value to direct the wrapper script, as explained in "Directing the Action" earlier in this chapter.

**FIG. 9.1**

The typical program flow through the wrapper.

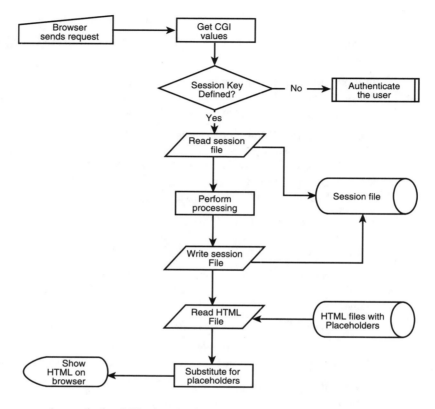

8. The wrapper script reads the CGI values and extracts the session key from them.

9. The wrapper script reads the user's current session state from the user's session file, using the session-key value.

10. Depending on the value of the location and action variables (or on a combination of other CGI values, if these values are not defined), the wrapper invokes a subroutine to perform whatever processing is required. This subroutine usually involves making changes in the user's session-state values.

11. The wrapper script saves the new session state to the user's session file.

12. If a location was set, either by the location value in the incoming CGI data or internally by the wrapper script, the wrapper script starts to read the file that corresponds to that location. Alternatively, the script can generate HTML to go directly to the browser. In either case, the user's session key is included in the HTML.

13. If a HTML file is being sent by the wrapper, each line of the file is sent to the browser, with any placeholders being filled in based on the user's session values.

14. The new location is displayed on the browser, and the entire process starts again from step 6.

Notice the overall level of program flow. The browser sends CGI values to the wrapper script; the wrapper script process the values, updates stored values, and returns HTML to the browser. The process starts again when the user submits the form or follows a hyperlink that leads back into the system.

# Designing the Sample Application

The example application in this chapter is a shopping-cart-style ordering system for Camels 'R Us, which sells three types of products: food, vacations, and accessories. You will develop an interface that allows authorized users to browse product menus; build up a list of purchases; review the order; and, finally, submit the order. At that point, your program simply writes the order details to a file. In real life, the order could be passed on to an ordering database.

## Program Flow

Start creating the application by outlining the sequence of events that take place from the user's point of view. This outline is not the same as the outline of the wrapper-script internals in the walk-through section earlier in this chapter, but a description of the functionality required of your application. The sequence of events from the user's point of view is as follows:

1. The action starts when a user accesses the wrapper script for the first time—that is, without a currently valid session key. The wrapper script sends a logon menu to the user's browser.

2. If the user provides a valid user ID and password, the main menu is sent. This menu (see fig. 9.2) allows the user to choose one of the three product categories.

**FIG. 9.2**
The main menu.

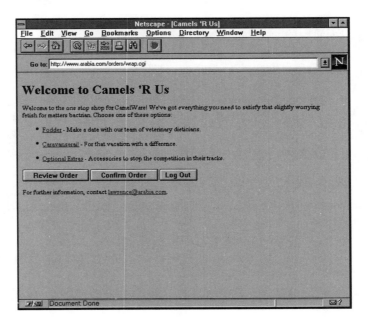

3. When the user makes a choice from the main menu, an order form for the chosen category appears. This form lists all the available products and allows the user to enter the numbers of all the products that she wants to order. A blank for any product means that the user does not want to purchase the product.

Figures 9.3, 9.4, and 9.5 show the order screens for the three product categories.

**FIG. 9.3**

The Feeds menu.

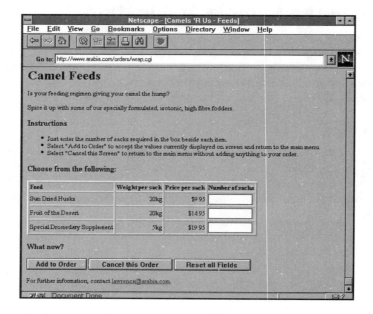

4. The user either submits or cancels the order form. If the user submits the form, the order details from the form are added to the user's session file, and the main menu reappears. If the user cancels the form, the session file is unmodified, and the main menu reappears.

5. The user can choose another product category to add to the order list for this session. If she wants, she can revisit a product category and amend the number of items ordered.

6. A submit button in the main menu allows the user to review her order for the session so far. When the user clicks this button, a form appears, showing the number of items of each type ordered and the total cost of the order.

Figure 9.6 shows a sample order-review screen.

7. When the user finishes adding items to the order list, she can click a submit button in the main menu to confirm the order. Her order details for this session are appended to an order file.

Alternatively, the user can choose to cancel the entire order. This action clears the order list contained in her session file.

**FIG. 9.4**

The Vacations menu.

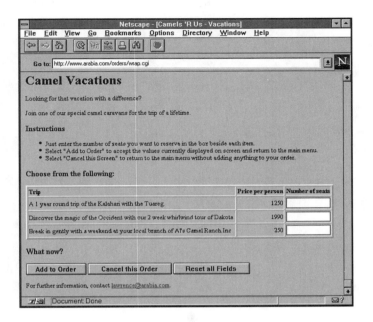

**FIG. 9.5**

The Extras menu.

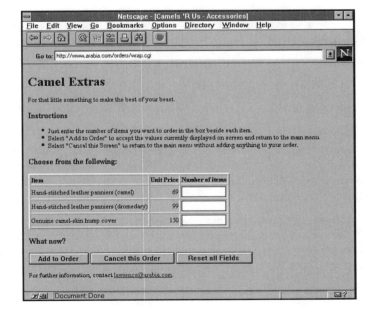

**FIG. 9.6**

The order-review screen.

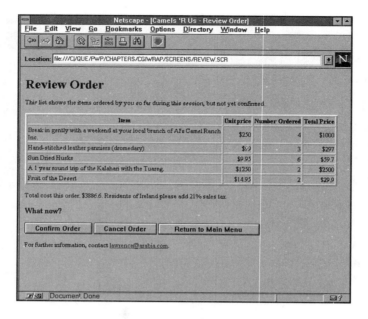

8. Finally, the user selects the log-off option from the main menu to terminate the session. Her session file is deleted at this point, and an appropriate end-of-session message is displayed.

The main menu acts as a sort of anchor for the application, offering three menu options and three submit buttons. A more hierarchical system may be appropriate for a larger system, but this level of complexity is fine for a simple example such as this one.

## Data Issues

Next, you need to consider how data is to be stored by the application, both internally (in Perl data structures) and externally (in session files and raw data files). There are two principal data elements. The first is the set of data representing the available products and prices; the second is the order list built up by the user in the course of a session.

**Product Data**   The price list consists of a list of product names and corresponding prices. You're writing this application in Perl, so the obvious candidate for storing this data is an associative array, with the product names being keys and the prices being values. An expression such as `$Price{"Camelskin"}` returns the unit price of the named product.

The data can be stored externally in several ways. On a UNIX system, a simple products-to-prices lookup list would be most efficiently stored in a DBM file, using a tied hash. You'll use this technique to store the session information. In the case of the product data, however, you will have two arrays indexed by product name: an array of prices and an array of product descriptions. The best approach for an application this simple is to store the data items in a flat text file, one product per line. More complex programs could interface with a relational database of product information, if necessary.

Each record contains three items of information about a single product: the product name, the product price, and a brief description. In this application, use the separator : : : between items so that Perl can easily split the lines as it reads them.

On the CD

Listing 9.1 shows the sample data file, which is stored in the file products.dat on the CD-ROM that comes with this book.

### Listing 9.1   The Contents of products.dat, the Data File

```
feed_desertfruit:::14.95:::Fruit of the Desert
feed_driedhusks:::9.95:::Sun Dried Husks
feed_dromspecial:::19.95:::Special Dromedary Supplement

travel_kalahari:::1250:::A 1 year round trip of the Kalahari with the Tuareg.
travel_dakota:::1990:::Discover the magic of the Occident with our 2 week
➥whirlwind tour of Dakota.
travel_alranch:::250:::Break in gently with a weekend at your local branch of
➥Al's Camel Ranch Inc.

extras_pancam:::69:::Hand-stitched leather panniers (camel)
extras_pandrom:::99:::Hand-stitched leather panniers (dromedary)
extras_covers:::150:::Genuine camel-skin hump covers
```

The first line in this file describes a product called feed_desertfruit, which is described as "Fruit of the Desert" and which has a unit price of $14.95. The product name is used as the key in the price and description associative arrays—%Price and %Desc, respectively. So $Price{'feed_desertfruit'} is "14.95", and $Desc{'feed_desertfruit'} is "Fruit of the Desert".

The three product categories are denoted by the feed_, travel_, and extras_ prefixes. These prefixes make maintaining the product data file easier; they have no significance for the program.

**Order Data**   Orders are built up over the course of a session, with the partial order being saved in a session file until it is complete. You'll save the order as part of the session data, in the form of an associative array. The keys of order elements in the session data array are the product names, and the values are the numbers of the items ordered by the user.

Internally, the wrapper program stores all session values in an associative array called %state. If the user orders three extras_covers items, $state{'Order_extras_covers'} is set to 3. The Order_ prefix here is used when you're scanning the session file to pick up ordered items.

One advantage of storing this data internally in the form of an associative array is that it makes the job of storing the data externally very simple indeed. You'll use Perl's tied-hash functionality to create a link between the internal storage (associative array) and the external storage

(DBM file), and leave it to Perl's innards to keep the two in sync. Session files are stored in the LOG subdirectory and called $Sessionid.DB. ($Sessionid is the user's session ID.)

# Implementing the Sample Application

On the CD

Now you're ready to implement your wrapper program. In this section, you develop a working wrapper system in Perl from scratch. This application is not highly sophisticated, but it is fully functional, and it is intended primarily to be an illustration of the techniques involved. The source code for the program is explained along the way; all source code for this basic wrapper program appears on the CD-ROM that comes with this book.

## Getting Started: The Main Routine

The main routine is the best place to start. This code dictates the overall program flow; it is also the only routine that is guaranteed to be executed every time. Listing 9.2 shows the code for the main routine.

**Listing 9.2    The Wrapper Script's Main Routine**

```
#!/usr/local/bin/perl -TI.


# Import methods for DBM files:

require SDBM_File;
require Fcntl;


# Global variables:

%Price, %Desc, %cgivals;


# Read any form values passed in.

&GetCGIVals(%cgivals);


# Extract the settings which dictate program flow:

$SessId = $cgivals{'sessionid'};
$Loc    = $cgivals{'location'};
$Action = $cgivals{'action'};


# Read the product details:

&ReadProductData("products.dat");


# Now decide what to do. First check if session id supplied:
```

```
if ( $SessId ) {

    # Session Id supplied: perform action and/or show location.

    $Action && &DoAction($SessId, $Action);
    $Loc && ShowLoc($SessId, $Loc);
}
else {

    # No session id supplied: login is only valid action.

    # Error check: session id required if location or action requested.

    ( $Loc || $Action ) &&
     HTMLError("Location/action requested but no session ID provided.<br>",
            "Please <a href=\"./wrap.cgi\">log in</a> ",
            "and follow the instructions on screen.");

    # Default action: log in.

    &DoLogin;
}
```

The main routine performs these tasks:

1. Reads the contents of SDBM_File.pm and Fcntl.pm, which are Perl modules that contain functions related to DBM files and file access modes, respectively.

2. Declares three global associative arrays to store prices, descriptions, and CGI values, respectively.

3. Calls &GetCGIVals to read the CGI values. (The &GetCGIVals function is described in "Getting the CGI Values" later in this chapter.)

4. Picks out the user's session ID, as well as the location to be loaded next or the action to be carried out.

5. Reads the product data from the data file by using the &ReadProductData function (described in "Reading the Product Data" later in this chapter).

6. If the session ID is defined and an action has been requested, the &DoAction function is called to carry out that action. (For details, see "Invoking a Specific Function" later in this chapter.)

7. If the session ID is defined and a location has been requested, the &ShowLoc function (described in "Parsing an HTML File" later in this chapter) is called to display that location.

8. If no session ID is defined, the only valid action is to display the logon screen.

9. The wrapper determines whether a location or action was requested. If no location or action was requested, the wrapper terminates the session with an error message. Otherwise, it calls the &DoLogin function to initiate a login. (The &DoLogin function is described in the "Initiating a Login" section later in this chapter.)

The subroutines called by the main routine are described in the following sections, in the sequence in which they appear.

### Error Messages and HTML Headers

The &HTMLError function, which appears from time to time in the following code, is a utility function that displays an error message on the user's browser in HTML format. You could simply write error messages to STDOUT, knowing that the messages will get to the browser. If an error message is sent before the browser receives a Content-type: HTML header line, however, the browser reports a server error, and the user does not get to see your error message. For this reason, send a Content-type: text/html line first.

Another problem arises if you send the HTML header twice; the user sees the second header line on-screen along with the error message. This arrangement is a little untidy, so use a second utility function— &HTMLhead—to write the header for you, as follows:

```
# A utility routine to print the HTML header once only.

sub HTMLhead {
    if ( !$header_printed ) {
     print "Content-type: text/html\n\n";
     $header_printed = 1;
     }
}
```

The variable $header_printed is 0, or false, initially. The first time that you call this function, the HTML header is printed, and $header_printed is set to true; thereafter, the if statement is false and the header is not printed.

Following is the &HTMLError function, which uses &HTMLhead:

```
# Utility routine to show a HTML error message

sub HTMLError   {

    my @ErrMsg = @_;

    &HTMLhead;

    print "<title>wrap.cgi Error</title>\n";
    print "<h1>Error</h1>\n";

    print @ErrMsg;

    print "<p>Execution aborted.";
    exit;
}
```

# Getting the CGI Values

The CGI values returned by the browser represent the sum of the wrapper's knowledge about the user when the program starts. Other information about the user and his or her previous actions is contained in the user's session file, but that information cannot be accessed without the session ID—a CGI value. Your first priority, then, must be to interpret the CGI information and save the values of all CGI variables.

The &GetCGIVals subroutine queries the httpd's environment values and saves the CGI values in the global %cgivals associative array. These values can arrive in two forms, depending on whether the form data was transmitted by means of the GET or POST method:

- If the GET method was used, the CGI values are contained in a single environment variable called QUERY_STRING.
- If the POST method was used, the CGI values are available on standard input, and the length of the string that contains those values is provided by the environment variable CONTENT_LENGTH.

Part
III

Ch
9

The &GetCGIVals routine checks for both the GET and POST methods and saves the CGI information in either case. Listing 9.3 shows the source code for &GetCGIVals.

### Listing 9.3  The *GetCGIVals* Subroutine

```perl
# Get the CGI Values

sub GetCGIVals {

    my (@settings, $set, $name, $value, $formvalues, $postlength);

    # First decide if GET or POST used:

    $postlength = $ENV{'CONTENT_LENGTH'};

    if ( $postlength ) {
       read (STDIN, $formvalues, $postlength);
    }
    else {
       $formvalues = $ENV{'QUERY_STRING'};
    }


    # Store settings in an associative array:

    # First split into "A=B" parts:
    @settings = split('&', $formvalues);

    # Now store each name and value in the associative array:
    foreach $set ( @settings )  {
     ($name, $value) = split('=', $set);
     $cgivals{$name} = $value;
    }
 }
```

The code shown in Listing 9.3 carries out the following steps:

1. Saves number of characters of CGI information waiting on standard input in the $postlength Perl variable.

2. If `$postlength` is nonzero, reads exactly `$postlength` characters from standard input and stores them in the `$formvalues` Perl variable.

   If `$postlength` is zero, sets `$formvalues` to the value of the QUERY_STRING environment variable.

3. The `$formlength` variable contains one or more CGI settings and is of the form `"A=X&B=Y&C=Z"` — a series of single settings concatenated with ampersands. The `&GetCGIVals` routine saves these individual settings in the `@settings` array by means of the `split` function.

4. Splits each element of the `@settings` array at the equal sign (=) into a key and a value, and stores the key and value in the `$name` and `$value` Perl variables, respectively.

5. Adds a new element to the `%cgivals` associative array, with `$name` as the index and `$value` as the value.

This last section may seem to be unnecessarily complicated. Why not split `$formvalues` into `%cgivals` in one step by using a statement like the following, which would replace the entire `foreach` loop in `&GetCGIVals`?:

```
%cgivals = map( split('='), split('&', $formvalues) );
```

The problem is that there may be "empty" CGI values, which would disrupt the mapping shown in the single statement. Suppose that a session ID was missing, for example. The `$formvalues` string might look like this:

```
sessionid=99353&action=Validate&userid=&pass=www
```

In this case, the first `split` function would break `$formvalues` into these substrings:

```
sessionid=99353
action=Validate
userid=
pass=www
```

The second `split` operation carried out within the map operation would break these substrings into the following list of substrings: `sessionid`, `99353`, `action`, `Validate`, `userid`, `pass`, and www.

Finally, the assignment of `%cgivals` would result in the following key/value pairs being stuffed into `%cgivals` (www would be empty):

```
sessionid=99353
action=Validate
userid=pass
```

Breaking the operation into two steps is marginally more complicated, but much safer.

# Reading the Product Data

Having read the CGI values, you next read in the product data. This data is stored in the `%Price` and `%Desc` associative arrays by the `&ReadProductData` subroutine, which takes a single argument: the name of the product data file. Listing 9.4 shows the code for `&ReadProductData`.

## Listing 9.4    The *ReadProductData* Routine

```perl
# Read in the product data:

sub ReadProductData {

    my ($infile) = @_;
    my $product, $price, $desc;

    # Check parameters:

    $infile || HTMLError("ReadProductData requires data file name.");

    # Open the data file:

    open (PRODUCTS, $infile)
     || HTMLError("Unable to open product data file $infile (!$).");

    # Read each line:

    while (<PRODUCTS>) {

     $line = $_;

     # drop trailing newlines:

     chop($line);

     if ( $line =~/:::/) {    # Ignore lines without separator

         # Split on ":::" separators:

         ($product, $price, $desc) = split(':::', $line);

         # Store price and description using product name as key:

         $Price{$product} = $price;
         $Desc{$product} = $desc;
     }
    }

    # tidy up:

    close PRODUCTS;
}
```

If the named product file exists and is opened successfully, it is read in one line at a time, and the following processing occurs for each line:

1. The new-line character at the end of the line is dropped by means of the chop function.
2. If the line does not contain the separator string, Perl skips to the next record in the file.

   If the line contains the separator string, it is split into the product name, price, and description fields by means of Perl's split function.

3. The product's price and description fields are stored in the %Price and %Desc arrays, respectively, using the product name as the key.

4. Finally, the data file is closed.

# Invoking a Specific Function

The next subroutine that the main routine may call is &DoAction—a function that encapsulates all specific processing functions other than parsing and displaying a HTML file. &DoAction consists primarily of a list of if clauses, as you can see from the source code in Listing 9.5.

**Listing 9.5   The *DoAction* Subroutine**

```
# Subroutine to perform a named action for a given session Id.
# Branches to required subroutine.

sub DoAction {

    my ($SessId, $Action ) = @_;


    # Argument check:

    $Action ¦¦ &HTMLError("DoAction called but no Action specified!");

    # Now a branch for each possible action -

    ( $Action eq "Validate" ) &&
    &Validate($cgivals{'userid'}, $cgivals{'pass'});

    ( $Action eq "Add+to+Order" ) &&
    &AddToOrder($SessId, %cgivals);

    ( $Action eq "Cancel+Order" ) &&
    &ShowLoc($SessId, "mainmenu.htmw");

    ( $Action eq "Return+to+Main+Menu" ) &&
    &ShowLoc($SessId, "mainmenu.htmw");

    ( $Action eq "Review+Order" ) &&
    &ReviewOrder($SessId);

    ( $Action eq "Confirm+Order" ) &&
    &ConfirmOrder($SessId);

    ( $Action eq "Log+Out" ) &&
    &DoLogout($SessId);

}
```

The $DoAction subroutine takes two arguments: the user's session ID and the name of the action to be taken. After a quick check for valid arguments, the subroutine checks the action name against a list of possible actions and, if it finds a match, calls the appropriate subroutine. The available subroutines are described in their own context later in this chapter.

## Parsing an HTML File

If the main routine finds that a location was specified with the $location variable, it invokes the &ShowLoc subroutine to show the contents of that file on the browser. Any tokens found in the file (denoted by means of the syntax described in "Generic Substitutions" earlier in this chapter) are filled in by means of the contents of the %State, %Price, and %Desc arrays.

This function is, in many ways, the core of the wrapper script. Listing 9.6 shows the code.

Part III

Ch 9

### Listing 9.6 The *ShowLoc* Subroutine

```perl
# Show a HTML file, filling in values using the supplied session ID

sub ShowLoc  {

    my ($ID, $URL) = @_;
    my %SessionValues, @matches;


    # Open the requested file for reading:

    open(RETURNFILE, $URL) ||
     &HTMLError("Unable to open file \"", $URL, "\" for reading.");


    # Send HTML header:

    &HTMLhead;


    # Load all session values for this ID:

    %SessionValues = &GetSessValues($ID);


    # Process each line of requested file:

    while(<RETURNFILE>) {

     # Store this line ($_ will be overwritten):
     $currentline = $_;

     # Check for prices, e.g. "\\Price\itemname\":
     if ( @matches = /\\\\Price\\(\w+)\\\/g ) {
         # Interpolate each match on this line:
         foreach $match ( @matches ) {
          $currentline =~ s/\\\\Price\\$match\\/$Price{$match}/;
         }
     }
```

*continues*

**Listing 9.6   Continued**

```
    # Check for descriptions, e.g. "\\Desc\itemname\":
    if ( @matches = /\\\\Desc\\(\w+)\\/g )  {
        # Interpolate each match on this line:
        foreach $match ( @matches )  {
         $currentline =~ s/\\\\Desc\\$match\\/$Desc{$match}/;
        }
    }

    # Check for tokens, e.g. "\tokenname\" => tokenvalue:
    if ( @matches = /\\(\w+)\\/g )  {
        # Interpolate each match on this line:
        foreach $match ( @matches )  {
         $currentline =~ s/\\$match\\/$SessionValues{$match}/;
        }
    }

    # Now print the line, including any substitutions:
    print $currentline;
    }


    # Tidy up:

    close RETURNFILE;
}
```

The code is simpler than it looks. Step through the code to see how it works:

1. The designated file is opened.
2. The HTML header line is sent by means of the &HTMLhead function (described earlier in this chapter).
3. All session state values for the supplied session ID are read in by means of the &GetSessValues subroutine (described in detail in "Retrieving Session Data" later in this chapter).
4. Each line of the input file is read in and printed to standard output.
5. The input file is closed.

The fourth step is actually slightly more complicated. Each line is checked for substitution tokens before being printed to standard output. If any tokens are found, they are replaced by the appropriate session-specific values.

Each line is checked for description, price, and other tokens. The mechanism is very similar in each case. Start with looking at the substitution of simple tokens, which are denoted by a token name surrounded by single backslashes (\sessionid\, for example).

The following steps are involved in replacing this value with the actual session ID value:

1. A regular-expression match is carried out. The regular expression is /\\(\w+)\\/ and has a trailing g to denote that all such patterns within the string are to be matched.

2. This pattern looks for a backslash, followed by at least one alphanumeric character, followed by another backslash. The backslash has special meaning within regular expressions, so it must be escaped by means of a second backslash.

3. The "at least one alphanumeric character" is the token name, which is saved because it is surrounded by parentheses.

4. All such tokens are saved in the @matches array, because the regular expression takes place in the context of an array assignment.

5. The foreach clause replaces all matched patterns on the current line with the actual value of the token in the session-state array. This replacement is made by making a regular-expression substitution; the matched token, surrounded by backslashes, is replaced by a value in the %SessionValues associative array. The index into this array is the current token name, $match.

The steps for replacing price and description tokens are quite similar. In the case of price tokens, the pattern match is /\\\\Price\\(\w+)\\/g, which looks for an additional \\Price\ before the token. The replacement operation is similar, too, but the %Price array is used instead of the %Price%SessionValues array. The procedure for descriptions is identical, except for the fact that the %Desc associative array is used.

## Initiating a Login

The final subroutine that may be invoked from the main routine is &DoLogin. This subroutine assigns a session ID and displays the login screen, which challenges the user to enter a valid user ID and password. Listing 9.7 shows the source code for &DoLogin.

**Listing 9.7  The *DoLogin* Subroutine**

```
# Subroutine to perform login.

sub DoLogin {

    # Generate a pseudo-random session id:

    $SessId = time || $$;


    # Store this id in its own session file:

    $sessvals{'sessionid'} = $SessId;
    &SetSessValues($SessId, %sessvals);


    # Show the login page

    &ShowLoc( $SessId, "login.htmw" );
}
```

The code carries out the following three simple steps:

1. Generates a unique session ID for this session. This ID consists of the system time on the httpd server combined with the process ID of the process that is running the wrapper program.

2. Stores the session ID in the session values file. This ID can be used at a later stage as a cross-check on the validity of a session file, but this wrapper program does not use it in this way. The value is stored by means of the &SetSessvalues function (described in "Storing Session Data" later in this chapter).

3. Displays the login menu, using the &ShowLoc function (described earlier in this chapter).

The mechanics of initiating and manually terminating a session are explained in the following section.

# Logging In and Out

The first time that the user runs `wrap.cgi`, &DoLogin is invoked and displays the login screen on the user's browser. The user enters a user ID and password and then sends them to the server by submitting the form. Then the wrapper program calls &Validate to authenticate the details provided by the user.

Notice that &DoLogin does no more than initiate the login. After the user fills in the user ID and password and submits the form, the wrapper program is invoked again. At that point, the &Validate function is called to perform the actual authentication of the user.

## Logging In

Listing 9.8 shows the HTML file `login.html`.

### Listing 9.8 The *login.html* File

```
<html>
<head>
<title>Camel's 'R UsLog in</title>
</head>

<body>
<h1>Camels 'R Us Log in</h1>

You must log in as a registered user before you can use the system.
<p>

<ul>

<li>
Click <a href="http://www.camelsrus.com/register.html">here</a> to register as
➥an on-line customer with Camels 'R Us.
<p>
```

```
<li>
If you have already registered, enter your userid and password and click "Log
➥on":

</ul>

<form method="post" action="wrap.cgi">

<input name="sessionid" type="hidden" value="\sessionid\">

<input name="action" type="hidden" value="Validate">

<table>

<tr>
<td>User ID:</td>
<td><input name="userid" type="text" size=20></td>
</tr>

<tr>
<td>Password:</td>
<td><input name="pass" type="password" size=20></td>
</tr>

<tr>
<td></td>
<td><input name="logon" value="Log on" type="submit"></td>
</tr>

</table>

</form>

</body>
</html>
```

Following are the critical lines of this file:

- `<form method="post" action="wrap.cgi">`
  This statement tells the browser what location to request when the form is submitted (`wrap.cgi`) and to submit its CGI data via the POST method.

- `<input name="sessionid" type="hidden" value="\sessionid\">`
  The session ID is inserted into this line by the wrapper program before the browser sees it, so to the browser, the line will look more like the following:
  `<input name="sessionid" type="hidden" value="838604689">`
  This statement tells the browser to store the CGI value sessionid=838604689 but not to display it. This value will be sent to the server with the other CGI values when the form is submitted, allowing you to identify the user.

■ `<input name="action." type="hidden" value="Validate">`
Another hidden value, `action=Validate`, is present in this form. The CGI data that goes back to the server instructs `wrap.cgi` what step to take next: validation of the user ID and password provided by the user.

■ Finally, the `userid` and `pass` fields create the text boxes where the user enters her authentication details.

## Validating the User

When the user submits the login form, the resulting CGI data contains two items that are of interest to the wrapper program: the user's session ID and a CGI value called `action`, which has the value `Validate`. The `&DoAction` function sees this value and invokes the `&Validate` function, which is shown in Listing 9.9.

### Listing 9.9 The *Validate* Subroutine

```
# Validate: Given a userid and password, check against
# a user database and if valid, show main menu.

sub Validate {

    my ($uid, $pwd) = @_;
    my %userdb;

    # Argument check: both userid and password are required.

    $pwd ¦¦ return 0;

    # userid/password pairs are stored in the user db file:

    tie(%userdb, 'SDBM_File', ".userdb", Fcntl::O_RDONLY(), 0664) ¦¦
     HTMLError("Unable to open user database (!$).");

    # Success if password given matches password in file.
    # Note check that a password was actually given...

    if ( $pwd ne "" && $userdb{$uid} eq $pwd ) {

      # Add customer name to session data:

      %sessvals = &GetSessValues($SessId);
      $sessvals{'customerid'} = $uid;
      &SetSessValues($SessId, %sessvals);

      # Show the main menu:

      &ShowLoc($SessId, "mainmenu.htmw");
    }
    else {
      &ShowLoc($SessId, "failedlogin.htmw");
```

```
    }

    # tidy up:

    untie(%userdb);
}
```

&Validate takes two arguments—the user ID and password—and attempts to match them with the contents of a DBM file that contains user ID–password pairs by following these steps:

Part III
Ch 9

1. &Validate first determines that a password has been provided.

2. The tie statement creates a link between an associative array (%userdb) and the DBM file that contains the valid user IDs and passwords. The arguments are:

    • The name of the associative array (%userdb).

    • The method to be used by Perl to associate external and internal storage. You'll use SDBM_File so that Perl will use the methods defined in SDBM_File.pm to connect the associative array with a DBM file.

    • The name of the DBM database in which the user data is stored.

    • The file-access mode. You'll use Fcntl::RDONLY(), which returns a read-only flag.

    • The default file protection for the database.

    If this call to tie is successful, the %userdb array serves as an interface to the contents of the DBM file.

3. If the password field is not empty, it is compared with the password for the specified user ID. If the user does not exist, the match fails. Likewise, if the user exists but the password is not the same as the one in the authentication DBM file, the match fails.

4. If the match succeeds, the authentication details are valid. The user ID is added to the session file, and the main menu is displayed; the user is logged in.

    If the match fails, the file failedlogin.htmw is displayed. This file explains what happens and allows the user to try logging in again.

5. Finally, the untie command breaks the connection between the %userdb array and the DBM file.

# Logging Out

Logging out is much simpler than logging in. If the user clicks a submit button called action, with a value of Log Out, the wrapper script's &DoLogout function is called by &DoAction. Listing 9.10 shows the code for &DoLogout.

## Listing 9.10   The *DoLogout* Subroutine

```
# Perform a logout. Deletes session file and shows log off screen.

sub DoLogout {
```

*continues*

**Listing 9.10   Continued**

```
my ($sessionid) = @_;


# zap the session file: two parts, *.pag and *.dir
# taint checking => need to save file name via a pattern match:

$sessionid =~/(\w+)/;
unlink("./log/$1.DB.pag", "./log/$1.DB.dir");


# show the farewell screen:

print "Content-type: text/html\n\n",
"<html><head>",
"<title>End of session</title>",
"</head>",
"<body>",
"<h1>Session Terminated</h1>",
"you have logged out from the Camels 'R Us Web ordering system.<p>",
"<a href=\"wrap.cgi\">Call again</a> soon!<p>",
"</body></html>";
}
```

This subroutine performs two simple steps: deletes the DBM file associated with the session and displays a farewell message. The latter task is simple, but the former is complicated somewhat by the fact that you have turned on Perl's taint checking by using the -T option in the command line.

There are, in fact, two DBM files for each session: one with a .pag extension and one with a .dir extension. Given a session ID stored in the Perl $sessionid variable, the most direct way to delete these two files is to pass them as a literal string to the unlink function, as follows:

```
unlink("./log/$sessionid.DB.pag", "./log/$sessionid.DB.dir");
```

This statement fails, however. Perl can see that $sessionid was passed in to the program via the environment and is, therefore, not to be trusted. In this instance, a hacked session ID value might result in the deletion of arbitrary files.

You need to extract the value contained in $sessionid to another variable that Perl does not regard as being tainted. Simply assigning a new variable to $sessionid does not work; Perl will see that the new variable is tainted by such close association with the old one.

Instead, perform a pattern match on $sessionid, looking for all alphanumeric characters and saving the result, as follows:

```
$sessionid =~ /(\w+)/;
```

The expression /(\w+)/ tells Perl to match the first set of alphanumeric characters in $sessionid and store them. Then this stored value—$1—is used in the arguments to the unlink command.

This method works, because Perl assumes that you know what you are doing when you save the results of a pattern match. The assumption is based on the fact that you got hold of the tainted variable and extracted something from it in a very specific way. It would be quite difficult for a suspect value to survive a pattern match of this sort.

# Managing Session Data

After you come this far, the management of session data becomes relatively simple. You use associative arrays to store the session data internally, and you use tied hashes to associate these arrays with DBM files for external storage. You've already seen how to use DBM files for user ID–password pairs; the principle is identical for session data.

## Storing Session Data

The current session data is stored by calling the &SetSessValues subroutine. Listing 9.11 shows the code for &SetSessValues.

**Listing 9.11   The *SetSessValues* Subroutine**

```
# Store values for a given session id
# Takes an associative array as argument, saves to session file

sub SetSessValues {

    my ($Sessionid, %DBMdb) = @_;

    my %tiedDB;


    # Open the session file and set values:

    tie(%tiedDB, 'SDBM_File', "./log/$Sessionid.DB",
      Fcntl::O_RDWR()|Fcntl::O_CREAT(), 0644) ||
      HTMLError("Unable to open session file for sessionid ",
            $Sessionid, " for writing ($!).");


    # Set the values in the DB to values passed as argument:

    %tiedDB = %DBMdb;


    # Store the new values:

    untie(%tiedDB);
}
```

The code does the following things:

1. Passes the user's session ID and the current session state as arguments to the function.

2. Using the `tie` statement, creates the relationship between an associative array (`%tiedDB`) and the session file. The arguments are:

   - The name of the associative array (`%tiedDB`).

   - The method to be used by Perl to associate external and internal storage. You use `SDBM_File`, just as you did for the user-authentication database.

   - The name of the DBM database in which the session data is to be stored.

   - The file access mode. You use a Boolean or combination of `Fcntl::RDWR()` and `Fcntl::O_CREAT()`, which are methods that return file access flags. The flags used here indicate that the file is to be opened in read/write mode and created if it does not already exist.

   - The default file protection for the database.

   If this call to `tie` is successful, the `%tiedDB` array serves as an interface to the contents of the DBM database. Making a change in `%tiedDB` has the same effect as making the same change directly in the DBM file.

3. Copies the entire contents of the session state, represented by `%DBMdb`, to the tied array (`%tiedDB`).

4. Closes the DBM database and breaks `%tiedDB`'s connection with it by calling the `untie` function. The contents of `%tiedDB` are written in full to the DBM file at this point.

That's the beauty of using tied hash arrays; they look after all the storage implementation details for you. Simply assign a normal associative array to a tied hash array, and you've stored the contents of the normal array.

## Retrieving Session Data

The principle for retrieving session data that has already been stored to a DBM file is analogous. You can retrieve the session state for a given session ID from DBM storage by using the `&GetSessValues` function, the code for which appears in Listing 9.12.

**Listing 9.12   The *GetSessValues* Subroutine**

```
# Retrieve session values for a given session ID
# Return them as an associative array

sub GetSessValues {

    my ($Sessionid) = @_;
    my %DBMdb, %returnvalue;


    # No session file, no values so just return.
```

```
    return unless -e "./log/$Sessionid.DB.pag";


    # Open the session file and get values:

    tie(%DBMdb, 'SDBM_File', "./log/$Sessionid.DB", Fcntl::O_RDONLY(), 0664) ||
      HTMLError("Unable to open session file for sessionid ",
            $Sessionid, " for reading ($!).");

    # Save the array before closing the file:

    %returnvalue = %DBMdb;

    untie %DBMdb;

    # Pass the associative array back to the calling routine:

    return %returnvalue;
}
```

All the action in this code is contained in the tie and untie statements; the rest is error checking. The following steps show how &GetSessValues works:

1. The user's session ID is passed in as the sole argument to the function.
2. If no session file exists for the supplied session ID, the function simply returns control to the calling function.
3. The tie statement creates the relationship between an associative array (%DBMdb) and the session file. The arguments are:
   - The name of the associative array (%DBMdb).
   - The method to be used by Perl to associate external and internal storage. You use SDBM_File again.
   - The name of the DBM database in which the session data is stored.
   - The file access mode. You use Fcntl::RDONLY(), which is a method within the Fcntl package that returns a read-only flag.
   - The default file protection for the database.

   If this call to tie is successful, the %DBMdb array behaves as though it contains all the values stored in the associated DBM file.
4. Next, the code copies the entire contents of %DBMdb into an array called %returnvalue, effectively making a local copy of the entire database.
5. The code closes the DBM database and breaks %DBMdb's connection with it by calling the untie function. The contents of %DBMdb are undefined after the code closes the DBM file by means of the untie function, which is why you needed to make the local copy of the database in %returnvalue before calling untie.
6. Finally, the code passes the contents of %returnvalue back to the calling function.

Again, the tied hash looks after the storage implementation details for you. These two functions allow you to store and retrieve an entire set of session data quite easily.

# Managing the Orders

You now have the necessary infrastructure to carry out the core business of this application, which is to give the user an interface to an ordering system. You need to allow the user to build an order in stages during the course of a session; review that order at any stage; cancel the entire order, if desired; and confirm the order, at which point the order will be written to permanent storage.

## Building an Order

A user builds an order by using the three order forms shown in figures 9.3, 9.4, and 9.5 (refer to "Program Flow" earlier in this chapter). These forms work in the same way, so this section focuses on only one: the Feeds form. The source for the form is stored in `feeds.htm`. The relevant lines for the first product are as follows, with the other products being set up in an identical fashion:

- `<form method="post" action="wrap.cgi">`
  The `form` statement tells the browser to send its CGI data to the server by using the POST method and to request the location `wrap.cgi` when the data is returned.

- `<input name="sessionid" type="hidden" value="\sessionid\">`
  The session ID is written to this line before the browser sees the form. Just as in the case of the login menu, this line ensures that the session ID is contained in the form as a CGI value, so that the browser can pass it back to the server with the rest of the CGI data.

- `<td>\\Desc\feed_driedhusks\</td>`
  The first data cell in the table contains the token `\\Desc\feed_driedhusks\`, which will be replaced in the `&ShowLoc` function by the current value of `$Desc{'feed_driedhusks'}`.

- `<td align=right>$\\Price\feed_driedhusks\</td>`
  Similarly, `\\Price\feed_driedhusks\` is replaced by `$Price{'feed_driedhusks'}`.

- `<td><input name="Order_feed_driedhusks" type="text"`
  `value="\Order_feed_driedhusks\" size=10></td>`
  This line appears in the browser with the final token filled in. If the number of items of this type that have been ordered so far is 3, the line appears as follows:
  ```
  <td><input name="Order_feed_driedhusks" type="text"
      value="3" size=10></td>
  ```
  This line gives the text input field for this item an initial value of 3.

- `<input name="action" type="submit" value="Add to Order">`
  The submit button labeled Add to Order is called `action`. If the user clicks this button, a CGI value of `action=Add+to+Order` is sent to the server. This value is trapped by `&DoAction`, and the appropriate function is called.

After filling in the desired quantity of each product, the user clicks the Add to Order submit button. A set of CGI data goes back to wrap.cgi, containing an action value that is caught by &DoAction and that in turn invokes the &AddtoOrder function.

&AddtoOrder takes two parameters: the user's session ID and the associative array of CGI values. Notice that these values are the CGI values, not the session values. You want to extract some of the CGI information and discard the rest; the data that you extract will be saved with the session data for later use.

Listing 9.13 shows the code for the &AddtoOrder function.

### Listing 9.13   The *AddToOrder* Subroutine

```
# Given the cgi values from a form, add fields starting
# with "Order_" to the order for the current session.

sub AddToOrder {

    my ($SessId, %cgivals) = @_;
    my %state;


    # Get current session state first:

    %state = &GetSessValues($SessId);


    # Add order items and quantities to state:

    foreach $item (keys %cgivals) {
     if ( $item =~ /^Order_/ && $cgivals{$item} ) {
         $state{$item} = $cgivals{$item};
     }
    }


    # Save state after adding order:

    &SetSessValues($SessId, %state);


    # Now drop back to main menu:

    &ShowLoc($SessId, "mainmenu.htmw");
}
```

This code takes the following actions:

1. The current session values are retrieved from the DBM file by means of &GetSessVals and stored in %state.

2. Each item in the `%cgivals` array is checked. If an item begins with `Order_`, it is an order and is saved in the `%state` array. If one of the CGI values is `Order_feed_driedhusks=4`, for example, `$state{'Order_feed_driedhusks'}` is set to 4.

3. The updated `%state` array is saved back to the DBM file.

4. The main menu is displayed again, allowing the user to continue building the order, review it, or commit it.

# Reviewing the Order

It is reasonable to expect that the user may want to review the order before confirming it. She can do so by selecting `Review Order` from any of the menus. This option passes a CGI value of `action=Review+Order` to the wrapper script. This value is trapped by `&DoAction`, causing `&ReviewOrder` to be invoked.

Listing 9.14 shows the code for `&ReviewOrder`.

---

**Listing 9.14    The *ReviewOrder* Subroutine**

```
# Review the order for the current session

sub ReviewOrder {

    my ($sessionid) = @_;
    my %state = GetSessValues($sessionid);


    # Use &ShowLoc to display start and end parts of form:
    # We'll build the list manually in this subroutine.

    # Print the form up to the start of the list:

    &ShowLoc($sessionid, "review_head.htmw");


    # Show the current order in a table:

    print "<table border=2>",
    "<tr>",
    "<th>Item</th>",
    "<th>Unit price</th>",
    "<th>Number Ordered</th>",
    "<th>Total Price</th>",
    "</tr>";


    # Keep a running total of price as we go

    $grand_total = 0;
    foreach $item ( keys %state ) {
```

```
    # If it starts with "Order_", it's an order.

    if ( $item =~/^Order_(\w+)/ ) {
        $thisprice = $state{$item} * $Price{$1};
        print "<tr>",
        "<td align=left>$Desc{$1}</td>",
        "<td align=right>\$$Price{$1}</td>",
        "<td align=right>$state{$item}</td>",
        "<td align=right>\$$thisprice</td>",
        "</tr>\n";
        $grand_total += $thisprice;
    }
}

print "</table><p>";

print "Total cost this order: \$$grand_total. ",
"Residents of Ireland please add 21\% sales tax.";

# Now show the rest of the form:

&ShowLoc($sessionid, "review_tail.htmw");

}
```

This code builds a HTML table that shows the current order details, one item at a time. To create this table, the code follows these steps:

1. Gets the current session state and stores it in %state.
2. Calls &ShowLoc to display the header part of this page. This header does not vary from one invocation to the next, so it is stored in a HTML template file.
3. Prints the table header. The columns are Item, Unit Price, Number Ordered, and Total Price.
4. Checks each item in the %state array and, if the key starts with Order_, prints the details for that item.
5. Finishes the table.
6. Calls &ShowLoc to display the standard footer for this page.

You need to look closely at the code that displays the order information for a given item. Notice first that the regular-expression match that determines whether the item is an order item stores the text after Order_. This backreference is available as $1 after the match takes place. If the item's key is Order_feed_driedhusks, for example, $1 will be feed_driedhusks. You need to store this backreference so that you can reference values in the %Price and %Desc arrays.

For each item, &ReviewOrder does the following:

1. Multiplies the number of items ordered ($state{$item}) by the unit price of this item ($Price{$1}). The result is stored in $thisprice.

2. Prints an HTML table cell that contains the product description: $Desc{$1}.

3. Prints the unit price of this product: $Price{$1}. The \$ before $Price produces a real dollar sign on-screen.

4. Prints the number of these items ordered: $state{$item}.

5. Prints the total price for this product, in dollars.

6. Keeps a running tally of the grand-total price for this order. This total is printed below the table.

Figure 9.6, earlier in this chapter, shows an example of the resulting table.

# Placing the Order

Finally, the order that you have so carefully built must be confirmed by the user and written to a file. Order confirmation is triggered when the user clicks one of the many Confirm Order buttons that you have helpfully scattered around the various forms. The CGI data that arrives back at wrap.cgi then contains the setting action=Confirm+Order, which is caught by &DoAction; then &ConfirmOrder is invoked.

Listing 9.15 shows the source code for &ConfirmOrder.

### Listing 9.15  The *ConfirmOrder* Subroutine

```
# Confirm the order and write it to file.

sub ConfirmOrder {

    my( $sessionid ) = @_;

    my %state = GetSessValues($sessionid);

    # Write a record to the orders file:

    open(ORDFILE, ">>./orders.dat") ||
     &HTMLError("Unable to open orders file for appending.");


    # Print a header line for this order:

    print ORDFILE "Order for customer $state{'customerid'} at ",
                scalar(localtime(time)), ":\n";


    # Each order item:

    foreach $item ( %state ) {
     $item =~ /^Order_(\w+)/ &&
         print ORDFILE "$1 ($state{$item});\n";
```

```
    }

    # Finish:

    print ORDFILE "End of order for customer $state{'customerid'}.\n";
    close ORDFILE;

    # Inform the user:

    &ShowLoc($sessionid, "confirm.htmw");
}
```

&ConfirmOrder does the following things:

1. Retrieves the current session values from DBM storage into the %state associative array.

2. Opens the orders file (orders.dat) in append mode.

3. Prints a header line for this order in the orders file. This line contains the customer name ($state{'customerid'}) and the current time.

4. Recognizes any state item that begins with Order_ as an order item. The product name and number of items ordered are recorded in the orders file for each item.

5. Closes the orders file.

6. Notifies the user that the order has been accepted.

# Wrapping Up

The example wrapper application shown in this chapter, while primitive, is functional. You could easily develop this application into a practical package. Among the issues that need to be addressed to make this application production-ready are:

■ The user authentication used in this example is for illustrative purposes only. If you have authority to control httpd user authentication on your server, you probably should delegate the responsibility for user authentication to the httpd. You can create user databases, using standard tools, and know that you are benefiting from years of development of secure user authentication technology.

■ You need a regular procedure for clearing orphaned session files—files that remain on disk after a session is abandoned without the user's explicitly logging out. A simple Perl script run as a cron job should suffice.

■ The entire system, as it stands, will take orders but not process them. A real system will feed directly into an ordering database, so that orders are processed the same way as orders that are taken by telephone or any other medium.

# From Here...

You can learn more about the issues raised in this chapter by reading the following chapters:

- Chapter 1, "Perl Overview," provides more information on some of the Perl syntax used in this chapter.

- Chapter 2, "Introduction to CGI," provides more information about passing CGI values between browser and server.

- Chapter 8, "Understanding Basic User Authentication," provides background material on user authentication and Web security.

# CHAPTER 10

# Site Administration

*by Shelley Powers*

**P**revious chapters discussed creating both static and dynamic content as well as security. Two facts arise from this file creation: Files are generated, and maintenance must be maintained on your site if it is to perform at peak efficiency.

Depending on your Web server, you need to perform some configuration when you install the server, and you need to perform periodic maintenance. A detailed description of what is involved is beyond the scope of this book, but some maintenance tasks can be performed by Perl programs. This chapter discusses configuring the Apache Web server (from the Apache Group) and NCSA's httpd Web server.

The most useful tool for understanding how and when your Web site pages and applications are being accessed is the log file that your Web server generates. This log file can show, among other things, which pages are being accessed, by whom (usually, in a generic sense), and when.

Additionally, if your site runs Common Gateway Interface (CGI) or other applications, you most likely need applications that remove orphaned files from processes that the Web page reader began but never finished.

Your site may be visited by something other than humans. Web robots—also known as Web bots, spiders, and wanderers—may visit your site. This technique is how search engines, such as WebCrawler **(http://www.webcrawler.com)**, search for sites to add to their collections. Sometimes, these visitors take a quick peek around and leave quietly, and sometimes, they don't. ■

**Log-file capabilities of some common Web servers**

The log files contain several types of information, such as the HTTP access method and the IP address that made the HTTP request.

**File-maintenance issues**

For a site to be effective, it must, for the most part, be one that can be maintained automatically. You should be aware, however, of certain problems when you set up a site's maintenance routines.

**Web robots**

This section discusses what Web robots are, what they can do, and how you can prevent them from entering your site.

**Configuration tasks**

This section discusses some common configuration tasks that are involved in installing the Apache Web server and the NCSA httpd Web server.

# Working with Web Server Log Files

Each Web server provides some form of log file that records who and what accesses a specific HTML page or graphic. A terrific site called WebCompare (**http://www.webcompare.com/**) provides an overall comparison of the major Web servers. From this site, you can see which Web servers follow the CERN/NCSA common log format, which is detailed next. In addition, you can find out which sites can customize log files or write to multiple log files. You may be surprised by the number of Web servers that are on the market.

Most major Web servers provide certain information in their access log files. You can find the format for this information at **http://www.w3.org/pub/WWW/Daemon/User/Config/ Logging.html#common-logfile-format**. That site contains the following line:

```
remotehost rfc931 authuser [date] "request" status bytes
```

The items listed in the preceding line are:

- `remotehost`: host name or IP address of remote host
- `rfc931`: remote log name of the user
- `authuser`: user name (if authentication occurs)
- `date`: date and time of request
- `request`: full HTTP request, including any data associated with the request
- `status`: HTTP status code
- `bytes`: content length of requested document

Following is an example of a log-file listing from a log file generated by O'Reilly's WebSite Web server in Windows NT:

```
204.31.113.138 www.yasd.com - [03/Jul/1996:06:56:12 -0800] "GET /PowerBuilder/
Compny3.htm HTTP/1.0" 200 5593
```

Figure 10.1 shows an example of a log file generated by the Apache Web server.

Both Web servers provide the date and time when the HTTP request was made, the HTTP request, and the status. The first example does not have access to DNSLookup, which would pull up the DNS alias for the IP address, if available. The second example shows the DNS alias. In addition, the first example displays the site that is accessed (in this case, **www.yasd.com**). The second example would display the remote log name if the Web server could access it; because it cannot, it displays unknown. Finally, because none of the HTTP requests were made to a secure site, there is no authorized user name that would have displayed where the dash (—) is.

Each HTTP request is logged. The first request is for an HTML document, and the second is for a JPEG-format graphic. If a site has several graphics and pages, the log file can get rather large. In addition, pulling useful information from the log file is difficult if you try to read the file as it is.

To pull useful information out of log files, most people use one of the existing log-file analyzers or create their own. These utilities can generate a text-file analysis based in HTML and even display results in graphic form. A good place to look for existing freeware, shareware, or commercial log-analysis tools is the Yahoo subdirectory **http://www.yahoo.com/Computers_and_Internet/Internet/World_Wide_Web/HTTP/Servers/Log_Analysis_Tools/**.

**FIG. 10.1**

This log file was created by the NCSA Apache Web server.

The following two sections provide samples of Perl code that can access a log file and generate two types of output: an HTML document and a VRML (Virtual Reality Modeling Language) document.

## Generating HTML Output from a Log File

Regardless of the type of output, you must open a log file and read in the entries. You can read an entry into one variable for processing, or you can split the entry into its components. To read an entry as-is in Perl, you use the following code sample:

```
open(LOG_FILE, "< " . $file_name) || die "Could not open log file.";
foreach $line(<LOG_FILE>) {
    // do some processing
    .
    .
    .
}
```

This code opens the log file for reading and accesses the file one line at a time, loading the line into the variable $line. To split the contents of the line, use the following code, which is the same as the preceding code sample except for the addition of a split command:

Part

III

Ch

10

```
open(LOG_FILE, "< " . $file_name) ¦¦ die "Could not open log file.";
foreach $line(<LOG_FILE>) {
    // do some processing
    ($dns, $rfcuser,$authuser,$dt1,$dt2,$commethod,$comnd,$stat,$lnth) = split('
',$line);
  .
  .
  .
}
```

The preceding code splits the access log entry in either of the log-file examples shown in "Working with Web Server Log Files" earlier in this chapter. You can also load the entry elements directly into an array, as follows:

```
open(LOG_FILE, "< " . $file_name) ¦¦ die "Could not open log file.";
foreach $line(<LOG_FILE>) {
    // do some processing
    ($dns, $rfcuser,$authuser,$dt1,$dt2,$commethod,$comnd,$stat,$lnth) = split('
',$line);
  .
  .
  .
}
```

When you have access to the log entries, you can use the values to generate HTML, based on several factors. If you want to generate an HTML file that lists the number of accesses by document, you can code something like the following:

```
#!/usr/local/bin/perl
.
.
.
use CGI;
$query = new CGI;
.
.
.
open(LOG_FILE, "< " . $file_name) ¦¦ die "Could not open log file.";
foreach $line(<LOG_FILE>) {
    // do some processing
    ($dns, $rfcuser,$authuser,$dt1,$dt2,$commethod,$comnd,$stat,$lnth) = split('
',$line);
  .
  .
    if (index($comnd, "somedoc.html") >= 0) {
        $counter++;
      .
      .
      .
    }
}
```

Then you can output the variables by using standard HTML output procedures, as follows:

```
print $query->header;
print $query->start_html('The Access Page');
print $query->h1("Accesses Per Page");
.
.
print "<p> Page somedoc.html was accessed " . $counter ." times";
```

An alternative method that can provide some graphics output is to print an asterisk (*) for each access. This method provides output similar to that shown in figure 10.2.

**FIG. 10.2**
This figure shows the log-file analysis results.

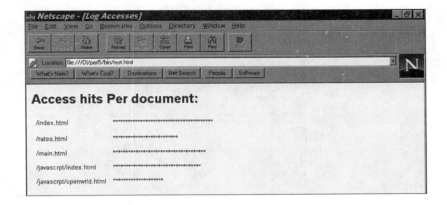

To do something like creating a text-based graphic, you should modify the code to output the results by using an HTML table, as in the following example:

```
print $query->header;
print $query->start_html('The Access Page');
print $query->h1("Accesses Per Page");
.
.
print "<table cellpadding=5>";
print "<tr><td> somedoc.html </td><td>";
for (i = 1; I <= $counter; i++) {
    print "*";
    }
print "</td></tr>";
.
.
print "</table>";
```

# Reviewing the AccessWatch Log Analyzer

On the CD

Several excellent log-analysis tools, written in a variety of programming languages, are available free or for a small fee. A particular favorite of mine is AccessWatch, by Dave Maher. Access Watch—a simple-to-use, easy-to-understand Perl application that provides sophisticated output with minimal complex, convoluted coding—is accessible on the CD-ROM that comes with this book. This tool is a favorite of mine not only because of its unusual and colorful output (see figs. 10.3, 10.4, and 10.5), but also because of how well the author documented the installation and configuration procedures.

**FIG. 10.3**

This figure shows AccessWatch's summary statistics.

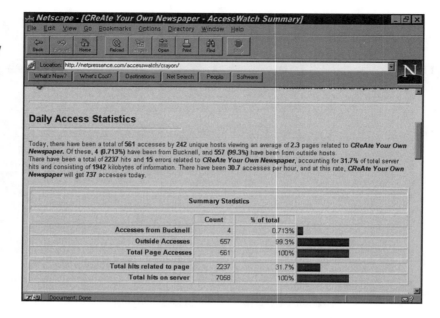

**FIG. 10.4**

This figure shows AccessWatch's hourly statistics.

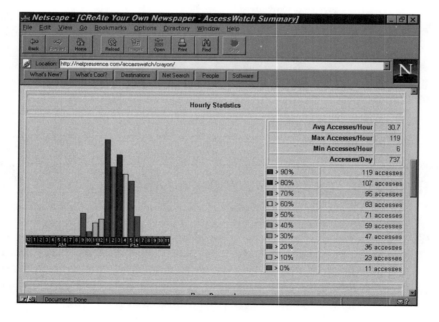

AccessWatch is not a CGI application; it is meant to be run manually or set to run as a `cron` job (more on `cron` later in this chapter). The application generates an HTML document called `index.html`, which can then be accessed with a Web browsing tool. AccessWatch analyzes the current day's accesses and provides statistics such as the number of accesses by hour and a projection of the total count for the day based on previous access patterns. In addition, the application displays a graphic representing the number of accesses for each target file; you can display the detailed access information, if you want.

**FIG. 10.5**
This figure shows AccessWatch's page demand.

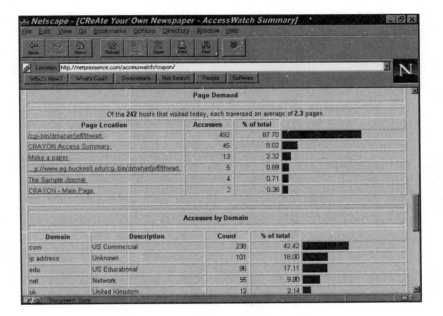

Part

III

Ch

10

One innovative aspect of AccessWatch is the graphics. Other applications use one technique or another to generate a graphics-based log analysis. The program 3DStats, written in C, generates VRML commands to create a 3-D model of log accesses. You can access this application at **http://www.netstore.de/Supply/3Dstats/**. Another program, Getgraph, is a Perl application that uses tools such as GIFTrans and gnuplot to create GIF files for display. You can find Getgraph at **http://www.tcp.chem.tue.nl/stats/script/**. Other log-analysis tools that provide graphical output are gwstat (**http://dis.cs.umass.edu/stats/gwstat.html**), which uses Xmgr; and Raytraced Access Stats (**http://web.sau.edu/~mkruse/www/scripts/access3.html**), which uses the POV-Ray raytracer.

AccessWatch creates small GIF files that form the bars of the display. The application includes a subroutine that generates the HTML to display the appropriate GIF file as a vertical bar (see Listing 10.1) or as a horizontal bar (see Listing 10.2).

---

**Listing 10.1   Displaying a GIF File as a Vertical Bar (*accesswatch.pl: PrintVertBar*)**

```
#- - - - - - - - - - - - - - - - - - - - - - - - - - - - - - - - - - - - - - - - - - - - - - - - - - - - - - - - - - - - -#
#  AccessWatch function - PrintBarVert
```

*continues*

**Listing 10.1 Continued**

```
#    Purpose : Prints a vertical bar with height as specified by argument.
#----------------------------------------------------------------------------#
sub PrintBarVert {
    local($pct) = $_[0];
    local($colorbar) = $vertbar{$_[1]};

    local($scale) = 0;
    $scale = $pct/$stat{'maxhouraccess'} * 200 if ($stat{'maxhouraccess'});

    print OUT "<IMG SRC=\"$colorbar\" ";
    printf OUT ("HEIGHT=%d WIDTH=10 BORDER=1 ALT=\"\">", $scale);
}
```

**Listing 10.2 Displaying a GIF File as a Horizontal Bar (*accesswatch.pl: PrintBarHoriz*)**

```
#----------------------------------------------------------------------------#
#   AccessWatch function - PrintBarHoriz
#    Purpose : Prints a horizontal bar with width as specified by argument.
#----------------------------------------------------------------------------#
sub PrintBarHoriz {
    local($pct) = $_[0];
    local($colorbar) = $horizbar{$_[1]};
    local($scale) = 1;

    $scale = ($pct*8)/log $pct + 1 if ($pct > 0);
    print OUT "<IMG SRC=\"$colorbar\" ALT=\"";
    print OUT "*" x ($pct/3 + 1) . "\" ";
    printf OUT ("HEIGHT=15 WIDTH=%d BORDER=1>", $scale);
}
```

To use the `PrintBarVert` subroutine, the height is calculated and passed as an argument. This process is demonstrated in the subroutine `PrintTableHourlyStats` (see Listing 10.3), which prints the hourly statistics.

**Listing 10.3 HTML Generating the Hourly Access Statistics (*accesswatch.pl: PrintTableHourlyStats*)**

```
#----------------------------------------------------------------------------#
#   AccessWatch function - PrintTableHourlyStats
#    Purpose : Prints bar graph of accesses over the course of the current
#              day. Thanks very much to Paul Blackman for his work on
#              this function.
#----------------------------------------------------------------------------#
sub PrintTableHourlyStats {

local($hourBar) = "img/hourbar.gif";
local($hour, $pct);
```

```
    print OUT <<EOM;
<TABLE BORDER=1 WIDTH=100%>
<TR><TH COLSPAN=3><HR SIZE=5>Hourly Statistics<HR SIZE=5></TH></TR>
<TR>
EOM
    print OUT "<TD ROWSPAN=11>";
    foreach $hour ('00'..'23') {
     if ($stat{'hr'.$hour} > 0.9*$stat{'maxhouraccess'}) {
         &PrintBarVert($stat{'hr'.$hour}, 9);
     }
     elsif ($stat{'hr'.$hour} > 0.8*$stat{'maxhouraccess'}) {
         &PrintBarVert($stat{'hr'.$hour}, 8);
     }
     elsif ($stat{'hr'.$hour} > 0.7*$stat{'maxhouraccess'}) {
         &PrintBarVert($stat{'hr'.$hour}, 7);
     }
     elsif ($stat{'hr'.$hour} > 0.6*$stat{'maxhouraccess'}) {
         &PrintBarVert($stat{'hr'.$hour}, 6);
     }
     elsif ($stat{'hr'.$hour} > 0.5*$stat{'maxhouraccess'}) {
         &PrintBarVert($stat{'hr'.$hour}, 5);
     }
     elsif ($stat{'hr'.$hour} > 0.4*$stat{'maxhouraccess'}) {
         &PrintBarVert($stat{'hr'.$hour}, 4);
     }
     elsif ($stat{'hr'.$hour} > 0.3*$stat{'maxhouraccess'}) {
         &PrintBarVert($stat{'hr'.$hour}, 3);
     }
     elsif ($stat{'hr'.$hour} > 0.2*$stat{'maxhouraccess'}) {
         &PrintBarVert($stat{'hr'.$hour}, 2);
     }
     elsif ($stat{'hr'.$hour} > 0.1*$stat{'maxhouraccess'}) {
         &PrintBarVert($stat{'hr'.$hour}, 1);
     }
     elsif ($stat{'hr'.$hour} > 0) {
         &PrintBarVert($stat{'hr'.$hour}, 0);
     }
     else {
         &PrintBarVert(0, -1);
     }
    }

    print OUT <<EOM;
<BR>
<IMG SRC="$hourBar" WIDTH=288 HEIGHT=22 BORDER=0 HSPACE=0 VSPACE=0 ALT="">
</TD>
<TD COLSPAN=2><TABLE BORDER=1 WIDTH=100%>
<TR><TH ALIGN=RIGHT>Avg Accesses/Hour</TH><TD
ALIGN=RIGHT>$stat{'accessesPerHour'}</TD></TR>
<TR><TH ALIGN=RIGHT>Max Accesses/Hour</TH><TD
ALIGN=RIGHT>$stat{'maxhouraccess'}</TD></TR>
<TR><TH ALIGN=RIGHT>Min Accesses/Hour</TH><TD
ALIGN=RIGHT>$stat{'minhouraccess'}</TD></TR>
<TR><TH ALIGN=RIGHT>Accesses/Day</TH><TD ALIGN=RIGHT>$stat{'accessesPerDay'}</
```

*continues*

---

**Listing 10.3    Continued**

```
TD></TR>
</TABLE></TD></TR>
EOM

foreach $pct (0..9) {
    $img = 9 - $pct;
    print OUT "<TR><TD ALIGN=LEFT><IMG SRC=\"$vertbar{$img}\" HEIGHT=8 WIDTH=10
BORDER=1 ALT=\"\"> &gt ";
    printf OUT ("%d%%</TD>", (9 - $pct)*10);
    printf OUT ("<TD ALIGN=RIGHT>%d accesses</TD></TR>\n", (1 - $pct/10) *
$stat{'maxhouraccess'});
    }

    print OUT <<EOM;
</TABLE><P>
EOM

}
```

---

The value of $hour that is passed to the PrintBarVert subroutine is captured in the
RecordStats subroutine, shown in Listing 10.4.

---

**Listing 10.4    *RecordStats* Stores from One Log Input Line *(accesswatch.pl)***

```
#--------------------------------------------------------------------------#
#  AccessWatch function - RecordStats
#    Purpose   : Takes a single access as input, and updates the appropriate
#                counters and arrays.
#--------------------------------------------------------------------------#
sub RecordStats {
    #tally server information, such as domain extensions, total accesses,
    # and page information

    local($hour, $minute, $second, $remote, $page) = @_;

    $remote =~ tr/[A-Z]/[a-z]/;

    if ($remote !~ /\./) { $remote .= ".$orgdomain"; }
      #takes care of those internal accesses that do not get fully
      # qualified in the log name -> name.orgname.ext
    local($domainExt) = &GetDomainExtension($remote, 1);

    $stat{'accesses'}++;
    $domains{$domainExt}++;
    $hosts{$remote}++;
    $pages{$page}++;
    $stat{"hr".$hour}++;

    push (@accesses, "$hour $min $sec $remote $page") if $details;

}
```

The rest of the code for this application is on the CD-ROM that comes with this book, in the zipped file ACCESSWATCH_TAR.GZ. You can open the file in UNIX and use WinZip in Windows 95 and NT.

# Understanding File Maintenance

Unless a Web site is very simple, containing only one level of HTML documents and no CGI or other applications, you need to establish procedures and probably create code for file maintenance. The preceding section demonstrated some techniques for analyzing the log files that are appended by the Web server. If an application has CGI applications that generate file output, you also need to manage those files, in addition to any database files with which the site may interact.

In Chapter 7, "Dynamic and Interactive HTML Content in Perl and CGI," you learned how to create a simplified version of a shopping-cart application. One side effect of this application is the creation of a temporary file to hold the contents of the shopping cart while the cart user is accessing items. When the user finishes the shopping process, the file is deleted. What happens if the shopping-cart user exits the site before reaching the finishing stage? The way that the application is written, it would leave this file on the system, which will eventually fill any free space allocated for the file.

Additionally, a CGI application may create a file that needs to be moved to a protected subsite for other forms of processing. The CGI application cannot move the file, because it could be running under the standard user name nobody—the user that most Web servers assign for Web-page access. This "user" does not have permission to move a file to a restricted area.

The most popular way to handle these types of file-management issues is to use a scheduler that performs maintenance activities at predefined times. In the UNIX environment, this daemon is cron. (A version of cron also is available for the Macintosh.) In Windows NT, you can use at. Alternatively, you can use NTCRND21, which is available at **http://www.omen. com.au/Files/disk12/a04fa.html**.

Using the UNIX version as an example, the site administrator can access or create a shell script that will access the date and time when a file was last accessed. (If the file is older than a specified age, the script removes it.) In the case in which the file is being moved, the script could access a particular subdirectory; move its contents (or only the files that have a certain extension); and kick off another application that will process them when they have been moved.

After you create the script, you need to set it up as a cron job. In UNIX, you accomplish this task by using the crontab, batch, or at command. The crontab command schedules a job to be run at a regular time for every specified period—such as once a day, week, month, or year. The at and batch commands are for batch jobs and are not used as commonly as crontab is.

For more information on schedulers, check your operating-system documentation, and check with the system administrators at your site.

Part
III

Ch
10

# Understanding Robots and the Robot-Exclusion Standard

A Web robot (also known as a wanderer or spider) is an automated application that moves about the Web, either on your local site or in a broader domain, by accessing a document and then following any URLs that the document contains. A well-known example of this type of robot is WebCrawler, which traverses the Web to add documents to its search engine.

Robots can be handy little beasties; they can perform functions such as testing the links in all the HTML documents on a specific Web site and printing a report of the links that are no longer valid. As a Web page reader, you can understand how frustrating it can be to access a link from a site, only to get the usual HTTP/1.0 404 Object Not Found error.

Robots also can be little nightmares if you have one that is not well written or intentionally not well-behaved. A robot can access a site faster than the site can handle the access and overwhelm the system. Or a robot can get into a recursive loop and gradually overwhelm a system's resources or slow the system until it is virtually unusable.

In 1994, the participants in the robots mailing list (**robots-request@nexor.co.uk**) reached a consensus to create a standard robot-exclusion policy. This policy allows for a file called ROBOTS.TXT, which is placed at the local URL **/robots.txt**. The file lists a user agent (which is a particular robot) and then lists the agent's disallowed URLs. The following forbids all robot entry to any site whose URL begins with **/main/**:

```
# robots.txt for http://www.somesite.com/

User-agent: *
Disallow: /main/
```

When the preceding format is used, any robot that honors the robot-exclusion standard knows that it cannot traverse any site whose URL begins with **/main/**.

Following is an example that excludes all robots except a particular robot with the user agent someagent:

```
# robots.txt for http://www.somesite.com/

User-agent: *
Disallow: /main/

# someagent
User-agent: someagent
Disallow:
```

The preceding code forbids entry to **/main/** to any robot that honors the robot-exclusion standard except someagent. Using the term disallow with no URL would remove any previous disallow statements.

Finally, to forbid access to any robot that honors the robot-exclusion standard, you would use the following:

```
# go away
```

```
User-agent: *
Disallow: /
```

You can see when a robot that honors the robot-exclusion standard accesses your site, because you will have a recorded HTTP entry similar to the following:

```
204.162.99.205 www.yasd.com - [04/Jul/1996:15:30:43 -0800] "GET /robots.txt HTTP/
1.0" 404 0
```

This entry is from an actual log file. Using the Windows Sockets Ping client application (which you can download from **http://www.vietinfo.com/resource/html/networks.html**), I found that the robot was from the DNS alias `backfire.ultraseek.com`. From my browser, I accessed **http://www.ultraseek.com/** and found that the company maintains the search engine of InfoSeek, which is available at **http://www.infoseek.com/**. The fact that the robot attempted to access the ROBOTS.TXT file shows that this robot program is complying with the no-robots exclusion standard, and because my site performance has never degraded when this robot visits, I can also assume that it is a well-behaved robot.

Following is another entry in the log file for the same month:

```
204.62.245.168 www.yasd.com - [11/Jul/1996:19:33:47 -0800] "GET /robots.txt HTTP/
1.0" 404 0
```

Again using the Ping program, I found that the IP address had the DNS alias `crawl3.atext.com`. Using this alias as a URL, I accessed **http://www.atext.com** and found that the robot belongs to the people who bring us the Excite search engine (**http://www.excite.com/**). The people at Excite also have a nice, clean, and easy-to-traverse Web site and maintain city.net, a knowledge base of information about communities around the world (**http://www.city.net/**).

In the past few paragraphs, I have mentioned those robots that comply with the robot-exclusion standard. This standard is not enforced. A robot does not have to access this ROBOTS.TXT file.

Following are some of the well-known robots that support the exclusion standard:

- The Ahoy Homepage Finder (**http://metacrawler.cs.washington.edu:6060/doc/home.html**) searches out personal home pages on the Web.

- The FunnelWeb Search Agent (**http://funnelweb.net.au/**) provides searches in the South Pacific, including Australia and New Zealand.

- The ht://Dig application (**http://htdig.sdsu.edu/**) provides search capabilities and an index for intranet use only.

- The Hyper-Decontextualizer tool (**http://www.tricon.net/Comm/synapse/spider/**) takes the words that you enter and links them to some random site. The tool is fun to play with, and the site is worth a visit.

- The InfoSeek robot (**http://www.infoseek.com**), mentioned previously in this section, is a general Web-search service tool.

- The Inktomi Slurp (**http://inktomi.berkeley.edu/**) has an irresistible name and is a well-known search engine.

Part

III

Ch

10

The list could go on and on. You can see these and other sites listed in the Web Robots Database (**http://info.webcrawler.com/mak/projects/robots/active.html**), which is maintained by WebCrawler.

# Configuring Some Common Web Servers

Other site-administration and site-maintenance tasks have to do with the configuration of the Web server. You may need to create permissions for users, start servers running, kill processes that are causing problems, and perform other administrative tasks. Additionally, you need to perform upgrades not only on the Web server software, but probably also on all the supporting software (compilers, databases, and so on).

The following sections discuss some of the installation and configuration tasks involved in creating Web applications (particularly with Perl) for some common Web servers.

## O'Reilly's WebSite

WebSite (**http://website.ora.com/**) is a popular Windows NT and Windows 95 32-bit Web server, due to its features and price. After you install this application, a tabbed property sheet allows you to configure such aspects as CGI access, user access, mapping, and logging. The details on setting up the site for CGI applications are provided in a book that comes with the installation software.

## NCSA httpd

NCSA httpd is a popular UNIX-based Web server; you can download it for free from **http://hoohoo.ncsa.uiuc.edu/**. After installation, a subdirectory called CONF contains the configuration file HTTPD.CONF, which you access and change to customize the installation.

The configuration file contains several directives, including the following:

- `AccessConfig`: global access configuration file. The access configuration file establishes what server-side includes (SSI) are allowed and which directive controls can be overridden by a subdirectory-based access control file.
- `ErrorLog`: file in which the Web server will log errors.
- `AuthUserFile`: file that contains users and passwords.
- `AuthName`: file that sets the authorization realm.
- `AuthType`: authorization type.
- `AuthGroupFile`: user groups for authentication.
- `VirtualHost`: multiple responses for multiple IP addresses.

Several other directives are allowable for the configuration file; you can review them at **http://hoohoo.ncsa.uiuc.edu/docs/setup/httpd/Overview.html**.

In addition to the server-configuration file, you'll find a file for configuring the server resources (SRM.CONF). This file contains the `AddType` directive, which adds MIME types for the server. Without this directive, the server does not know how to process a file that has a certain extension. Another important directive is the AddEncoding directive, which allows you to add file-encoding types, such as x-gzip encoding for the .GZ file extension.

Access for the Web server is maintained in the global access configuration file and in individual access files that are created for specific directories.

Setting up CGI for a NCSA httpd Web server is a simple process. First, you define which subdirectory contains scripts that will be executed by means of the ScriptAlias server directive. As documented by NCSA, the disadvantage of using this technique is that everyone would need to access and use the same subdirectory. In a virtual-host situation, this situation is highly unlikely.

Another technique for defining CGI executables is to define the MIME types for the CGI applications as executable by using the AddType resource directive and the extension, as in the following example:

```
AddType application/x-httpd-cgi .cgi
```

This code instructs the Web server to execute the file instead of attempting to read it when a Web page reader accesses a file that has this extension. My UNIX-based virtual Web site uses this technique.

To learn more about installing and configuring an NCSA httpd Web server, go to **http://hoohoo.ncsa.uiuc.edu/docs/Overview.html**.

# Apache

The Apache Group's Web server, Apache, is available at **http://www.apache.org/**. Apache has a configuration setup that is very similar to that of NCSA httpd. Three files are used to configure the Apache Web server: SRM.CONF, ACCESS.CONF, and HTTPD.CONF.

The directives that Apache supports are listed in Table 10.1. Reading the directives in the table (and accessing more information about them at **http://www.apache.org/docs/directives.html**) is a demystifying experience. If you are a Web-application developer but not necessarily a Webmaster, the information in this table allows you to communicate with your Webmaster in a more meaningful manner. If NCSA httpd has a corresponding directive, Y appears in the NCSA httpd column; if not, N appears in that column; if unclear, ? appears in the column.

**Table 10.1  Apache Web Server Configuration Directives**

| Directive | Purpose | NCSA httpd? |
| --- | --- | --- |
| AccessConfig | Access configuration file name | Y |
| AccessFileName | Local access file name | Y |
| Action | Action to activate CGI script for a specific MIME type | ? |

*continues*

**Part**
**III**

**Ch**
**10**

**Table 10.1 Continued**

| Directive | Purpose | NCSA httpd? |
|---|---|---|
| AddDescription | Description of file if FancyIndexing is set | Y |
| AddEncoding | Allows the Webmaster to add file-encoding types, such as x-gzip encoding | Y |
| AddHandler | Maps handler to file extension | ? |
| AddIcon | Icon to display if FancyIndexing is set | Y |
| AddIconByEncoding | Icon to display next to encoded files with FancyIndexing | Y |
| AddIconByType | Icon for MIME type files if FancyIndexing is set | Y |
| AddLanguage | Adds file extension to describe the language content | ? |
| AddType | Adds MIME-type extension | Y |
| AgentLog | File in which UserAgent requests are logged | Y |
| Alias | Allows alias path | Y |
| allow | Which hosts can access what directories | ? |
| AllowOverride | Indicates whether local access file can override previous access file information | ? |
| Anonymous | User name that is allowed access without password verification | ? |
| Anonymous_ Authorative | Must match Anonymous directive, or access will be forbidden | ? |
| Anonymous_LogEmail | Indicates whether anonymous password is logged | ? |
| Anonymous_NoUserID | Can leave out user name and password | ? |
| Anonymous_ VerifyEmain | Indicates whether verification of anonymous password occurs | ? |
| AuthDBMGroupFile | DBM file containing user groups for authentication | ? |

| Directive | Purpose | NCSA httpd? |
|---|---|---|
| AuthDBMUserFile | DBM file containing users and passwords | ? |
| AuthDigestFile | Digest authentication file containing users and passwords | ? |
| AuthGroup | File containing user groups for user authentication | Y |
| AuthName | Authorization realm name | Y |
| AuthType | Authorization type (basic only) | Y |
| AuthUserFile | File containing names and passwords for user authentication | Y |
| BindAddress | * for all IP addresses or a specific IP address | Y |
| CacheDefaultExpire | Expire time default if document is fetched via protocol that does not support expire times | ? |
| CacheGcInterval | Time factor for determining whether files need to be deleted due to space constraints | ? |
| CacheLastModified Factor | Factor for expiration calculation | ? |
| CacheMaxExpire | Maximum time that cached documents will be retained | ? |
| CacheNegotiatedDocs | Allows content-negotiated documents to be cached by proxy servers | ? |
| CacheRoot | Directory for cached files | ? |
| CacheSize | Space use for cache | ? |
| CookieLog | Allows for Netscape cookies | ? |
| DefaultIcon | Icon to display by default when FancyIndexing is set | Y |
| DefaultType | For handling unknown MIME types | Y |
| deny | Indicates which host is denied access to specific directories | ? |
| <directory> | Encloses a group of directives | ? |

*continues*

**Table 10.1   Continued**

| Directive | Purpose | NCSA httpd? |
|---|---|---|
| DirectoryIndex | Indicates which documents to look for when requester does not specify a document | ? |
| DocumentRoot | Directory where httpd will serve files | Y |
| ErrorDocument | Document to display when a specific error occurs | N |
| ErrorLog | Log in which server will log errors | Y |
| FancyIndexing | Indicates whether fancy indexing is set for a directory | Y |
| Group | Group where server will answer requests | Y |
| HeaderName | File inserted at top of listing | Y |
| IdentityCheck | Enables logging of remote user name | Y |
| ImapBase | Default base for image-map files | ? |
| ImapDefault | Sets default used in image maps if coordinates have no match | ? |
| ImapMenu | Action if no valid coordinates are in image map | ? |
| IndexIgnore | Files to ignore when listing a directory | Y |
| IndexOptions | Options for directory indexing | Y |
| KeepAlive | Number of requests to maintain persistent connection from one TCP connection | Y |
| KeepAliveTimeout | Seconds to wait for additional request | Y |
| LanguagePriority | Precedence of languages | ? |
| Limit | Enclosing directive for HTTP method | ? |
| Listen | Indicates whether to listen to more than one port or IP address | ? |

| Directive | Purpose | NCSA httpd? |
|---|---|---|
| LoadFile | Links in files or libraries on load | ? |
| LoadModule | Links to library and adds module | ? |
| Location | Provides for access control by URL | ? |
| LogFormat | Indicates format of log file | Y |
| MaxClients | Number of simultaneous client accesses | ? |
| MaxRequestsPerChild | Number of requests for child server | ? |
| MaxSpareServers | Number of idle child processes | Y |
| MetaDir | Directory containing meta information | ? |
| MetaSuffix | File suffix of file containing meta information | ? |
| MinSpareServers | Minimum number of idle child processes | ? |
| NoCache | List of hosts and domains that are not cached by proxy servers | ? |
| Options | Indicates which server features are available in which directory | ? |
| order | Order of allow and deny directives | ? |
| PassEnv | Passes CGI environment variable to scripts | ? |
| PidFile | File in which the server records the process ID of the daemon | Y |
| Port | Network port to which the server listens | Y |
| ProxyPass | Maps remote proxy servers into local address space | ? |
| ProxyRemote | Defines remote proxies to proxy | ? |
| ProxyRequests | Indicates whether the server functions as a proxy server | ? |
| ReadmeName | Name of file appended to end of listing | Y |
| Redirect | Maps old URL to new one | Y |

Part
III

Ch
10

*continues*

**Table 10.1    Continued**

| Directive | Purpose | NCSA httpd? |
|---|---|---|
| RefererIgnore | Adds to strings to ignore in the headings of *referers* (sites that contain your site as a link and refer a Web page reader to your site) | Y |
| RefererLog | Name of file in which the server will log referer headings | ? |
| Require | Indicates which users can access a directory | ? |
| ResourceConfig | Name of file to read after HTTPD.CONF file | Y |
| Script | Action that activates cgi-script after specific method | ? |
| ScriptAlias | Same as Alias; marks directory as cgi-script | Y |
| ServerAdmin | Sets the e-mail that the server includes in any error message | Y |
| ServerAlias | Alternative names for the host | ? |
| ServerName | Host name of the server | Y |
| ServerRoot | Directory in which the server lives | Y |
| ServerType | Value of inetd or standalone | Y |
| SetEnv | Sets environment variable passed to CGI scripts | ? |
| SetHandler | Forces matching files to be passed through a handler | ? |
| StartServers | Number of child server processes started at startup | Y |
| TimeOut | Maximum that time server will wait for completion and receipt of a request | Y |
| TransferLog | File in which incoming requests are logged | Y |
| TypesConfig | Location of MIME-type configuration file | Y |
| User | User ID for which the server will answer requests | Y |

| Directive | Purpose | NCSA httpd? |
|---|---|---|
| UserDir | Sets real directory to use when processing a document for a user | Y |
| VirtualHost | Groups directives for a specific virtual host | Y |
| XBitHack | Controls parsing of HTML documents | ? |

Reading through this table, a Web-application developer can see several directives that affect what she or he can do, as well as what actions result in what behavior.

# Examining Some Other File- and Site-Administration Issues

In addition to the files that are created and maintained by the Web server, the site needs to have access to the tools required for running the Web applications. On a UNIX site, this requirement could mean having access to C and C++ compilers and to any run-time libraries that your code may access, if you use either of those languages. If your site does not have a C++ compiler, you can access a GNU C++ compiler, g++, at **ftp://ftp.cygnus.com/pub/g++/**. To find out more about the GNU CC compiler, go to **http://www.cl.cam.ac.uk:80/texinfodoc/gcc_1.html**.

If you are using Perl (and I assume that you are, or this book would not have much appeal to you), you need to have access to the Perl executable, as well as to any Perl support files, such as CGI.pm. Appendix A, "Perl Acquisition and Installation," provides instructions on accessing Perl, and Appendix B, "Perl Web Reference," lists several sites from which you can access support files.

If you are working with any database access, you need to have the files and permissions to make this type of access. If your site does not contain a database, and you want to have access to a relational database access, visit the Hughes Technologies site at **http://Hughes.com.au/**. This site has a relational database engine, called mSQL or Mini SQL, that is very inexpensive and that has a large amount of support and utilities for the UNIX environment.

For Windows NT or Windows 95, you may need run-time files, such as those required by Microsoft's Visual Basic.

If you are using Java, you need to have the Java tools in the environment in which you will compile your application into byte code, but you do not need to have the Java development environment on your server. The byte code will be interpreted by a Java-compatible browser (such as Netscape's Navigator 2.0 and later, and Microsoft's Internet Explorer 3.0 and later). To download the Java Developers Kit, go to **http://java.sun.com/products/JDK/**.

If you are implementing security, you need to set up password security in whatever directories need to be secure. For some Web servers, additional security, installation, and configuration issues may arise. Check with your Webmaster on those issues.

# From Here...

If you are planning to develop Web applications and are not the Webmaster for your site, you should discuss your options with the Webmaster before you do any coding. You also should view the configuration files, if possible, to better understand what options you have when programming.

In addition, if you are developing Web applications that create files, you must provide some mechanism to clean up after the applications, or your site will quickly get full. Using cron to schedule a job that periodically performs cleanup operations is an effective solution.

The log files that your Web server generates are your most useful tool for understanding which documents are being accessed and by whom. If you have a page that is rarely accessed, you may want to drop it or provide access to it from a more prominent location.

For more information, you can check the following chapters:

- Chapter 7, "Dynamic and Interactive HTML Content in Perl and CGI," discusses source code that creates and accesses several dynamic files.
- Chapter 8, "Understanding Basic User Authentication," discusses some of the security issues for users accessing the site.
- Chapter 9, "Understanding CGI Security," discusses some of the security issues related to CGI applications.

# Databases and Internal Web Sites

# CHAPTER 11

# Database Interaction

*by David Harlan*

Throughout this book, I have persistently reminded you that if you want people to come back to your Web site, you have to give them a good reason to return. And I've said all along that fresh, dynamic content is one such reason. You've seen some good ways to add some dynamic elements to your site: server-side includes, client pull, server push, and others. This chapter introduces one of the best methods for maintaining large amounts of dynamic data on a Web site: databases.

You may remember reading earlier about DBM files, which are a simple form of database functionality accessible through Perl. I showed you some useful, if simple, examples and explained their limitations. This chapter examines some optional add-on functionality to Perl that allows for interaction with full-fledged relational database management systems (RDBMS), such as Informix, Sybase, and Oracle. Then I'll demonstrate the capabilities of one of these systems in detail. ■

**Justifying Perl/database interaction**

Before you go too far into this chapter, I'll give you my pitch in favor of using an RDBMS for Web-site data. In my mind, there is no better way to maintain complex data than in a real database.

**Examining the database/Perl options**

A wide variety of packages allow Perl to interface with an RDBMS. Your choice among these packages will be determined by the resources at your disposal. This section takes a brief look at the options.

**Using Oraperl**

One of the packages available to interface with the Oracle RDBMS is a set of extensions to Perl 4.036 called Oraperl. This section looks at the functionality of Oraperl, using a threaded-message database as an example.

# Justifying Perl/Database Interaction

In the Web survey example in Chapter 2, "Introduction to CGI," and Chapter 3, "Advanced Form Processing and Data Storage," I used Perl's built-in database functionality to store and retrieve some relatively complex data. Using DBM files was effective in this example, but barely so. You may have noticed that I had to work around some functional limitations of Perl's built-in DBM file handling. Also, you should have noticed that these DBM files had little advanced functionality—no relating between tables, for example, and no way to distinguish between fields in a given record.

Had I used an RDBMS, I would have been able to access the data more easily. I could have averaged and totaled data much more readily. In fact, that Web survey would have been an excellent candidate for a relational database application.

This last statement, of course, begs the question "How do I decide whether I should use a high-end database on my site?"

The easiest answer is this: If you have access to an RDBMS, use it on your Web site. You will find that many common tasks become much easier in a database environment. User tracking is a breeze. Summarizing Web logs can be simplified, and the data from the logs can be analyzed extensively if you transfer your logs to a database.

But what if you don't have an RDBMS and are wondering whether you should invest in one? Then the decision (like any business decision) comes down to a cost/benefit analysis.

The costs for an RDBMS can be significant. In addition to the initial outlay for the software, you have to calculate installation and configuration time, time to integrate the software with your Web server, time to learn the new system, and additional administrative effort that comes with any complex piece of software.

But keep in mind that all these tasks can be accomplished by a single person; I know this from experience. The effort can be a little draining at first, but it worked out well for me.

So, then, what are the benefits? As I said before, an RDBMS is capable of storing and retrieving large amounts of complex data with extraordinary speed and reliability. A Webmaster can, obviously, use a database to track users and analyze logs. But you could go so far as to keep your entire site in a database, accessing the whole thing through CGI. Why? This setup would allow you to use the built-in search features of an advanced RDBMS instead of adding search functionality, as I demonstrated in Chapter 4, "Advanced Page Output." This kind of setup would also allow you to create a rotation of pages, so users see fresh content every time they come to the site.

My best advice is this: If you wish that your users could more easily find, retrieve, and even create discrete pieces of data on your site, you may want to look into adding database functionality to your Web system.

# Examining the Database Options

Most manufacturers of database software have jumped onto the Web bandwagon recently. Some manufacturers have built their own Web servers to work directly with their database systems. Almost all of the major players have built add-on tools that give a Webmaster the means to access their databases from a stand-alone Web server.

Given the fact that this book is about Perl, however, we're not interested in those options right now. This section examines the options for accessing databases from Perl.

## DBI and DBD Database Access Modules for Perl 5

At this writing, the largest development effort in database–Perl integration is a set of modules called *DBperl*. This project is an effort by a group in this Internet community to standardize the methods for accessing a database from Perl.

The interface actually consists of two parts: DBI and DBD.

*DBI*, which is the actual Perl interface, defines a standard set of functions that (theoretically) allow a programmer to access any database from Perl. The goal is to make Perl code independent of the database that it is accessing.

The second part of this system, *DBD*, essentially is a driver for a specific database. Currently, 10 DBD modules are in some state of development. Most of these modules still are considered to be alpha software, which means that the developers don't recommend their use in production environments. Several Web sites, however, are using these tools fairly rigorously.

If you are looking for the future of Perl–database integration; are willing to take the risks (which perhaps are minimal at this point) of using alpha software; and have the time, inclination, and ability to get DBI up and running on your system, this latest technology is the way that you want to go.

## mSQL and mSQLPerl

At the other end of the spectrum from a high-end database and DBI are mSQL and mSQLPerl.

*mSQL* is a lightweight relational database server that supports a subset of the Structured Query Language (SQL), which is standard to the large relational databases. mSQL was created and is sold by Hughes Technologies in Australia. Although its functionality is somewhat limited compared with systems from the major database providers, mSQL does nearly everything that a Webmaster needs it to do, and it costs a fraction of the prices of Oracle, Sybase, and Informix.

*mSQLPerl* is a Perl 5 module that gives the Perl programmer full access to the mSQL database. Anything that you can do to the mSQL system from the command line, you can do from mSQLPerl. The manufacturer reports that the database itself is being used on Web sites around the world. The mSQLPerl module is reported to be quite stable.

mSQL and mSQLPerl might be a good first step for Webmasters who are not sure whether they need a database. The mSQL server itself is quick and easy to install, and so is the mSQLPerl module. The documentation included with the package is lucid and complete. With this combination, a Webmaster could add significant database capabilities to a Web site in just a few days, with minimal capital expense.

## Oracle RDBMS and Oraperl

The third and final option that I talk about here is my personal favorite, Oraperl. *Oraperl* is a set of extensions to Perl 4.036 that provides complete access to an Oracle database server. One obvious drawback of this package is the fact that it is built on an old version of Perl, but its positive traits are many and, in my mind, outweigh the few negatives.

First and foremost, the code is quite well-tested and stable. I have used it on a production Web site and have never had any problems with it. As with mSQL and mSQLPerl, the documentation included with Oraperl is quite good. Finally, installation is well-documented, as are all the additional functions.

If you can afford to purchase an Oracle database server, or if you have access to one already, Oraperl is an excellent database interface option.

The rest of this chapter examines an Oraperl example in detail. Even if you don't think that an RDBMS is in your Web future, you may want to continue reading, if only to see the functionality that databases add to Perl and CGI.

# Creating a Threaded Message Database

One of the most compelling aspects of the Internet is the ability of people around the world to interact with very few limitations. In the one-on-one communication arena, unfortunately, the Web has not caught up with its older siblings: Usenet, e-mail, and talk. Because many of the newest Internet users are solely Web users, the Web's weakness in the interactivity department has occasionally made new users wonder what the big deal is.

As browser technology advances, and as more specialized plug-ins and add-ons are created, the Web is catching up. Unfortunately, this new technology does not help people who are tied to older browser technology—people who are accessing the Web through online services or who simply don't have the hardware horsepower to run the big new browsers. The obvious answer to the interactivity question right now is CGI, and one of the best CGI methods available to support interactivity is the subject of this chapter: databases.

This section examines a threaded message database built in CGI, using Oraperl. You will see how using a database enabled me to produce a relatively simple and quite reliable application.

## Starting a New Message Thread

Figure 11.1 shows a typical opening screen to a threaded message database. Each row on the page represents a *thread*—a series of messages on a single topic. You notice that the subject of each thread is a link, and you probably can guess that selecting that link brings up a listing of that thread. Also, in the graphic at the top of the page is an image-map link that allows the user to create a new thread.

**FIG. 11.1**
This screen shows the opening page of a threaded message database.

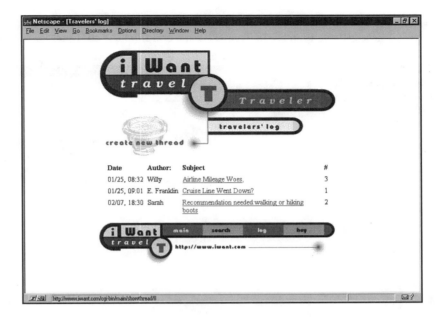

When the user selects the create new thread link, he or she goes to the form shown in figure 11.2.

**FIG. 11.2**
The user fills out and submits this form to create a new message thread.

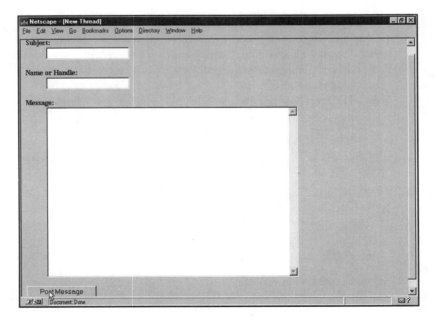

When the user completes the form and submits it, the server returns the user to the thread listing. As you can see in figure 11.3, the new thread is added to the bottom of the list.

**FIG. 11.3**

After submitting a new thread, the user returns to the thread-listing screen.

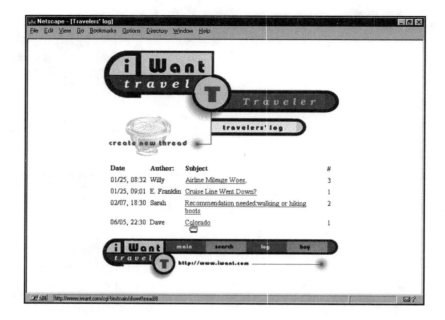

Listing 11.1 shows `newthread.pl`, the script that processes the user input into a new thread. The first thing that you should notice about this script is the top line. In all the scripts that you've seen up to this time, that line has read `#!/usr/bin/perl`. Remember that this line tells the operating system that the rest of the file is a program that should be passed to /USR/BIN/PERL for processing. As I said earlier, this example uses an extended version of Perl 4.036 called Oraperl. To parse the extended functionality, you have to call a different interpreter. The interpreter for Oraperl is (not surprisingly) called Oraperl—thus, the first line.

**Listing 11.1  Script (*newthread.pl*) to Parse Information into a New Message Thread**

```
#!/usr/bin/oraperl

require "process_cgi.pl";

#Login to oracle
$lda=&ora_login('oracle_sid','oracle_user','oracle_pass') || die $ora_errstr;

#Get a new messageid
$csr=&ora_open($lda, 'select max(msgid) from msghome');
if (($msgid)=&ora_fetch($csr)) { $msgid=$msgid+1; } else {$msgid=1;}
&ora_close ($csr);
```

```
#find the message id for the last message in the database
$select="select max(msgid) from msghome where threadid = (select max(threadid)
from msghome)";
$csr=&ora_open($lda,$select);
($previd)=&ora_fetch($csr);
```

As you move farther down the script, you see a call to the function &ora_login. This function is the first example of the extended functionality of Oraperl. The function requires an Oracle System ID, an Oracle user name, and a password as its arguments; it returns a scalar that uniquely identifies this particular Oracle session.

Notice that I follow this statement with Perl's | | (or) operator. If the login fails for some reason, I want to know about it. So on an unsuccessful login, the program exits, using the die function to print the variable $ora_errstr to STDERR. The variable $ora_errstr contains the text that describes the most recent Oracle error that Oraperl encountered. Recall that most Web servers direct STDERR from CGI scripts to the daemon's error log. If I'm conscientious about checking the error log, I'll discover this error and track down the problem.

Every Oraperl script has at least one call to &ora_login—usually near the beginning of the script, and always before any other Oraperl functions are used. Every Oraperl function requires a valid login identifier as an argument or requires another value that depends on a login identifier.

One such function, &ora_open, is used in the next statement in the script. This function takes a login identifier and a Structured Query Language (SQL) statement as its arguments; it returns a statement identifier, also known as a *cursor*.

SQL is the standard language of major relational databases. In its simpler forms, SQL reads very much like English. The statement that you see in this first use of &ora_open has the fairly obvious function of finding the maximum value of the field msgid in the table msghome. The basics of SQL are beyond the scope of this book, so from here on, I assume that you have some knowledge of the language.

The function &ora_open is the most commonly used Oraperl function. You use &ora_open whenever you want to submit an SQL statement to the database.

After you have the statement identifier, you need to get the data from it. This function is performed by &ora_fetch. Near the top of Listing 11.1, you can see that the result of &ora_fetch is being assigned to $msgid. You should take careful note of the syntax here, however. The result is being assigned to $msgid as the only member of a list; the parentheses create this syntax. This distinction is important, because &ora_fetch returns different data if it is asked for a scalar.

When called in a scalar context, &ora_fetch returns the number of fields returned by the SQL statement. Without the parentheses, this statement always returns 1, which is not the result that you are looking for. In an array context, however, the function returns a row of data returned from the statement. Upon each successive call to &ora_fetch, the function returns a row of data. When there is no data to return, the function fails.

Now you can see why this particular statement is embedded in an `if` statement. You know that `msgid` can have only one maximum value, and if it exists, `&ora_fetch` returns it successfully. Then you want to increment `msgid` by 1 to create your new message ID. If the function fails, you know that no data exists in the `msghome` table, because no row in this table can exist without an `msgid` field. Therefore, you set your new message ID to `1`.

With that processing out of the way, you get rid of the statement ID by calling `&ora_close`. This act is simply a matter of housekeeping and not strictly necessary in this script; any statement identifiers from this script are disposed of properly when the script ends. I habitually close the identifiers when I finish, however, to avoid any unnecessary memory use.

The next section of the script finds the message ID of the last message in the database. Understand that you can define the last message in the database in several ways—as the message with the highest ID number, for example. But for purposes of this example, the last message in the database is the message from the highest-numbered thread with the highest message ID.

You need this last message ID to set the preceding message ID for the message that you are creating. To understand this situation, it probably would help to know a bit about the structure of the table that this data is going into. The table, called `msghome`, consists of eight fields:

- `msgdate`, which contains the date and time when the message was posted
- `msgid`, which contains an integer that uniquely identifies this message in the table
- `subject`, which contains the Subject line typed by the user
- `author`, which contains the name given by the user
- `threadid`, which contains an integer ID of the thread to which this message belongs
- `previd`, which contains the integer ID of the message before this one in the database
- `nextid`, which contains the integer ID of the next message in the database
- `parentid`, which contains the integer ID of the message to which this message is a reply

**NOTE** This table is relatively simple, but it stores all the necessary data for this application. If you want to use the scripts on the CD-ROM that accompanies this book to put this message database on your own Web server, you first have to create the `msghome` table in your Oracle database. ■

To find the message ID of the last message in the database, you use the SQL `select` statement, which you can see near the bottom of Listing 11.1. This statement is more complex than the one used earlier in this section but still is fairly easy to understand. If you look at the part of the statement after `threadid=`, you see a complete `select` statement embedded in the main `select` statement. This embedded `select` is looking for the highest-thread ID in `msghome`. When you look at the statement as a whole, you see that it is looking for the highest message ID that belongs to the thread with the highest thread ID.

Now that you know the ID number of the new message and last message in the database, you can insert that information into the database and create the HTML for this new message. Listing 11.2 shows this part of the process.

**Listing 11.2  Part 2 of the Script to Update the *msghome* Table and Create the HTML Display**

```
&parse_input(*fields);

#parse out illegal characters and HTML
$fields{'body'} =[td] s/<[^>]+>//g;
$fields{'body'} =[td] s/\n/<br>/g;

$fields{'subject'} =[td] s/<[^>]+>//g;
$fields{'subject'} =[td] s/\'/&#039;/g;

$fields{'author'} =[td] s/<[^>]+>//g;
$fields{'author'} =[td] s/\'/&#039;/g;

#insert the new message information into msghome
$insert="insert into msghome
    (msgdate, msgid,subject,author,threadid,previd)
    select sysdate, '$msgid',
    '$fields{'subject'}','$fields{'author'}',
    '$msgid','$previd' from dual";
$csr=&ora_open($lda,$insert);
&ora_commit($lda);
&ora_close ($csr);

#update nextid for the previous message
$csr=&ora_open($lda,"update msghome set nextid = '$msgid' where msgid =
'$previd'");
&ora_commit($lda);

#print out the HTML file for this message
open(F, ">/opt/lib/httpd/htdocs/traveler/log/$msgid.html");
print F "<title>$fields{'subject'}</title>";
print F "<body bgcolor=\"FFFFFF\"><center>";
print F "<table width=480 border=0 cellpadding=3>\n";
print F "<tr><td colspan=2><img src=\"/traveler/tra211a.gif\">";
print F "<tr><td><b>Subject:</b><td>$fields{'subject'}";
print F "<tr><td><b>Author:</b><td>$fields{'author'}";
print F "<tr><td valign=top><b>Message:</b><td>";
print F $fields{'body'};
print F "</table><p><hr width=480><a href=\"/cgi-bin/main/msgnext/$msgid\"><img
src=\"/traveler/log/nextmsg.gif\" border=0></a>";
print F "<a href=\"/cgi-bin/main/msgprev/$msgid\"><img src=\"/traveler/log/
prevmsg.gif\" border=0></a>";
print F "<a href=\"/cgi-bin/main/showthread/$msgid\"><img src=\"/traveler/log/
showthrd.gif\" border=0></a>";
print F "<a href=\"/cgi-bin/main/msgreply/$msgid\"><img src=\"/traveler/log/
msgreply.gif\" border=0></a>";
close F;

#Send the browser back to the main threads screen
print "Location: http://www.iwant.com/traveler/log/log.cgi\n\n";

#close the last cursor and logout from oracle
&ora_close ($csr) || die $ora_errstr;
&ora_logoff ($lda) || die $ora_errstr;
```

Part
IV

Ch
11

The first thing that you see in Listing 11.2 is the standard call to `&parse_input`, processing the data from the form into the associative array `%fields`. After that processing is done, the next section attempts to process out any HTML coding from the fields that comprise the message. These lines also add `<BR>` tags in place of new lines in the body of the message. Finally, in `$fields{'subject'}` and `$fields{'author'}`, any single-quote characters are changed into the appropriate HTML-entity reference for that character. This process is necessary because the single quote is a special character in Oracle. If the data included any single-quote characters, the `insert` statement (described in the following paragraph) would fail.

The SQL `insert` statement placed in the variable aptly named `$insert` places the data from the new message into the database. Like the `select` statement described in the preceding paragraph, this `insert` uses an embedded `select` statement to perform its function. This embedded `select` may look strange at first, but its function actually is simple: to get the date and time from the system, which it does by selecting `sysdate` from the table `dual`. `sysdate` is an Oracle function that returns the date and time from the computer that is running the Oracle server. `dual` is a special system table in Oracle that contains only one field: a dummy field called (appropriately enough) `dummy`. `dual` is often used in situations such as this one, when you want to get the result of a function without an actual call to a real table.

The rest of the items that are being `selected` from `dual` in this statement actually are constants; notice that they are all enclosed in single quotes. Selecting constants in this way simply tells Oracle to return those constants with each row returned from the `select` statement. This syntax is an easy way to insert the user data, along with the system date and time, into `msghome` with only one Oracle call.

**TIP** Errors in my SQL statements tripped me up quite often when I was learning to use Oraperl. These errors frequently are difficult to track down. Nowadays, when I get unexpected results, I print the actual SQL statement that I'm using to my HTML page (during testing only, of course). Then I copy that text and paste it into Oracle's command-line SQL parser, SQL*Plus. This program gives me direct feedback on any errors, usually leading to a quick fix for my problem.

After defining the `insert` statement, the script immediately submits it to the database, using `&ora_open()`. Then the script commits the change that was just made, using `&ora_commit()`. This Oraperl function takes a login identifier as an argument. When called, `&ora_commit()` makes any changes to the database performed under the provided login identifier permanent.

The next step in this process tells the database that the message whose ID is stored in `$previd` should have its `nextid` field set to the message ID of the new message. This process is performed by `&ora_open()` and the SQL `update` statement that you see in Listing 11.2. Again, after sending this change to the database, the script immediately commits the change, using `&ora_commit()`.

When all the database changes are complete, the next section of the script prints the HTML file for this message. In this case (as in any case in which your CGI is writing to files on the server), you have to carefully set file permissions to allow `file creation`. The creation of the

HTML file completes the processing of the new message. All that is left to do is print a Location header to point the browser back to the script that shows the current threads in the database—including, of course, the one that the user just added. The final two lines of the script close the last cursor used and log the user out of the database.

# Listing Threads and Displaying the Contents of a Single Thread

Now that you have seen how to create a new message thread, the logical next step is to learn how to list the threads as shown in figures 11.1 and 11.3. Listing 11.3 shows the script that performs this task.

---

**Listing 11.3   Script (*showthreads.pl*) to List All the Thread Subjects in the Message Database**

```
#!/usr/bin/oraperl

require "process_cgi.pl";

#Login to oracle
$lda=&ora_login('oracle_sid','oracle_user','oracle_pass') || die $ora_errstr;

#print out the standard header and the top of the page
&print_header;
print "<title>Travelers' log</title>";
print "<body bgcolor=\"FFFFFF\">";
print "<center><table border=0 cellpadding=0 width = 450>";
print "<tr><td><a href=\"/cgi-bin/imagemap/log\">
    <img src=\"/traveler/tra210a.gif\" border=0 ISMAP></a></table>";
print "<table border=0 cellpadding = 3 width=450>";
print "<tr><td><b>Date</b><td><b>Author:</b><td><b>Subject</b><td><b>#</b>";

#Select all threads
$datemask='MM/DD, HH24:MI';
$query= "select msgid, subject, author, to_char(msgdate, '$datemask') from
    msghome where parentid is null order by msgdate";
$csr=&ora_open($lda, $query);

#run through the data returned from the select statement, printing
#out a row in the table per row returned.
while (($msgid, $subject, $author, $date)=&ora_fetch($csr)) {

    #Get the number of messages in a given thread
    $csr2=&ora_open($lda,"select count(msgid) from msghome where threadid =
$msgid");
    ($msgcount)=&ora_fetch($csr2);
    &ora_close($csr2);
    print "<tr><td valign=top>$date<td valign=top>$author<td valign=top>
        <a href=\"/cgi-bin/main/showthread/$msgid\">";
    print "$subject</a><td valign=top>$msgcount<br>"
}
```

*continues*

> **Listing 11.3   Continued**
>
> ```
> #print out the bottom of the page and close out the Oracle login.
> print "</table>";
> print "<p><a href=\"/cgi-bin/imagemap/navbar2\"><img src=\"/navbar2.gif\" ISMAP
> border=0></a>";
>
> &ora_close ($csr) || die $ora_errstr;
> &ora_logoff ($lda) || die $ora_errstr;
> ```

Listing 11.3 begins just as Listing 11.1 did, calling in the code for the CGI library and logging into the Oracle database. The script then prints the top of the thread-display page. With those details out of the way, the script moves on to print the threads themselves.

First, of course, you have to create a `select` statement that gets the proper data. You know that any message that has a null parent message ID is the start of a thread, so you select the messages that meet that criterion, as you see in the line of Listing 11.3 that begins with `$query=`.

This `select` statement grabs the message ID, the subject, and the author. The script also uses the Oracle function `to_char()` to get the message date in the format that you want. This function, which can be used within SQL statements in Oracle, takes a column name and a mask as arguments. In the listing, I defined the mask in the variable `$datemask`, telling Oracle that I wanted the date to be printed as a two-digit month–day combination, followed by the time in 24-hour notation. (For complete details on date masks, see your Oracle documentation.) Notice also that this `select` statement uses an `order by` clause to put the messages in order by date.

After submitting the `select` statement to Oracle, using `&ora_open`, the script begins a `while` loop to process all the data that is returned. Remember that `&ora_fetch` returns `true` as long as rows that meet the criteria of the `select` statement remain to be processed.

Each time through this loop, another SQL `select` statement is used to get the number of messages in the thread. This statement uses the function `count()` to determine the number of messages in the database that have a thread ID equal to the message ID that is currently being processed. This function works because the script is looping through all the message IDs that don't have parent messages. Messages without parent IDs are always the beginning of threads, and their message IDs are also their thread IDs. Each time through the loop, therefore, `$msgid` actually contains a thread ID, and you can use that message ID/thread ID to get the number of messages in that thread.

Notice that when you print each row of the table, you link each subject to a script called `showthread`. When users follow this link, they see a listing of the messages in that thread. Figure 11.4 shows an example of the output of `showthread`.

In figure 11.4, you should notice that the Subject lines of replies are indented from those of the original messages. If any of the replies had subsequent replies, they would be further indented. Listing 11.4 shows the script that prints this thread listing.

**FIG. 11.4**
Users see a thread listing like this one when they select a thread subject from the screen shown in figure 11.3.

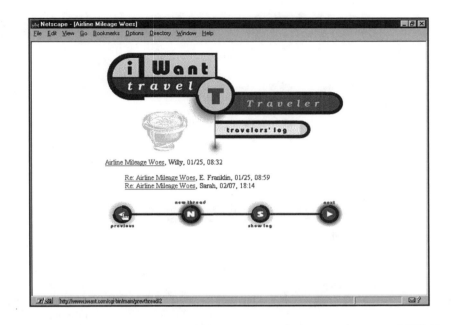

## Listing 11.4  Script (*showthread.pl*) to Query the Database and Print a Thread Listing

```
#!/usr/bin/oraperl

require "process-cgi.pl";
$msgid=&path_info;

#Login to oracle
$lda=&ora_login('oracle_sid','oracle_user','oracle_pass') || die $ora_errstr;

#Get the data for the first message in the thread
$datemask='MM/DD, HH24:MI';
$query= "select author, subject, to_char(msgdate, '$datemask') from msghome
where msgid='$msgid'";
$csr=&ora_open($lda, $query);
($threadauthor,$threadsubject,$threaddate)=&ora_fetch($csr);

#print the header and the top of the page
&print_header;
print "<title>$threadsubject</title>";
print "<body bgcolor=\"FFFFFF\">";
print "<center><table border=0 cellpadding=0 width = 450>";
print "<tr><td><img src=\"/traveler/tra211a.gif\" alt= \"Travelers' Log\"><br>";
print "<tr><td><a href=\"/traveler/log/$msgid.html\">$threadsubject</a>,
$threadauthor, $threaddate<br>";
```

*continues*

**Listing 11.4 Continued**

```
#Get and print the rest of the messages in the thread
&showreplies($msgid);

#print the end of the table
print "</table>";
print "<a href=\"/cgi-bin/main/prevthread/$msgid\"><img src=\"/traveler/log/
prevthrd.gif\" border=0 alt=\"Previous Thread\"></a><a href=\"/traveler/log/
threadform.html\"><img src=\"/traveler/log/newthrd.gif\" border=0 alt=\"New
Thread\"></a><a href=\"/traveler/log/log.cgi\"><img src=\"/traveler/log/
showlog.gif\" border=0 alt=\"Show Log\"></a><a href=\"/cgi-bin/main/nextthread/
$msgid\"><img src=\"/traveler/log/nextthrd.gif\" border=0 alt=\"Next Thread\"></
a>";

#Close final cursor and log out from Oracle
&ora_close ($csr) ¦¦ die $ora_errstr;
&ora_logoff ($lda) ¦¦ die $ora_errstr;
```

Listing 11.4 starts by calling in the process-cgi.pl library. The script then uses the
&path_info subroutine from that library to get the ID number of the thread that the user wants
to see. You can see, in Listing 11.3, that the URL for the link to showthread includes the thread
ID tacked to the end of it. After logging into the database, the script makes a call to the database to get the author, subject, and date for the message that begins the requested thread.
With that data in hand, the script prints the top of the page and the first item in the thread
listing. As in showthreads, the Subject line is a link. This time, however, instead of going to a
script, the listing in the thread links to the HTML file created when the message was posted.

When the top of the page is printed, you need to print the rest of the messages in the thread.
This processing takes place in the call to the subroutine &showreplies (explained in the following paragraphs). When &showreplies is finished, the script prints the bottom of the page,
including a button bar that allows users to go to the following and preceding threads, go back
to the thread listing, and create a new thread. Finally, the script closes the last cursor and logs
out of Oracle.

You still have &showreplies to deal with, however. Listing 11.5 shows this subroutine.

**Listing 11.5 Subroutine (*showreplies*) That Recursively Prints All Replies to a Given Thread**

```
sub showreplies {
   local ($msgid)=$_[0];
   local ($csr, $csr2, $query, $i);

   #select all replies to this message
   $query= "select msgid, subject, author, to_char(msgdate, '$datemask')
     from msghome where parentid='$msgid' order by msgdate";
   $csr=&ora_open($lda, $query);
   print "<menu>";
```

```
   #iterate through those replies
   while (($newmsgid, $subject, $author, $date)=&ora_fetch($csr)) {
      print "<a href=\"/traveler/log/$newmsgid.html\">$subject</a>, $author,
$date<br>\n";
      $csr2=&ora_open($lda, "Select count(msgid) from msghome where
parentid='$newmsgid'");

      #if there are replies to this message, make a recursive
      #call to get and print those replies.
      ($replycount)=&ora_fetch($csr2);
      if ($replycount > 0) {&showreplies($newmsgid);}
   }
   print "</menu>";
   &ora_close ($csr);
   return 0;
}
```

After the subroutine definition line, the first task at hand is to place the message ID that was passed to the subroutine in a local variable called $msgid. With that definition accomplished, the script defines four more local variables and moves on to select the replies from the database.

The select statement that gets the replies is shown in Listing 11.5 in the line that begins with $query=. This statement looks for messages whose parent message ID equals the value in $msgid; this condition is what makes them replies to the current message. After opening a cursor for this select statement and printing a <MENU> tag to indent the replies, the script begins a while loop to iterate through the data.

Each time through the loop, in addition to printing the appropriate line of data, the script checks to see whether the message currently being processed by the loop has any replies. If the message does indeed have replies, the script makes a recursive call to &showreplies to get them. If you trace through this process by hand, you see that the replies for each message follow that message and are indented from below that message. If any of those replies have replies themselves, those messages are treated similarly, creating a standard threaded-message database display.

## Navigating Through Messages and Posting Replies

When a user selects one of the messages to view, he or she sees a screen like figure 11.5. This message comes from an HTML file created by a script when a user replied to a message. Notice that this screen has a button bar along the bottom that allows users to navigate within the thread and gives them a chance to reply to the message.

After the user reads the message in figure 11.5, he or she may want to perform any of the functions in the button bar below the message. The following paragraphs discuss the buttons in left-to-right order.

To view the next message, the user clicks the Forward button. When this occurs, the button calls a script that figures out what the next message is and sends the user there. Listing 11.6 shows this script.

**FIG. 11.5**
After selecting a message to view, the user sees a message formatted like this.

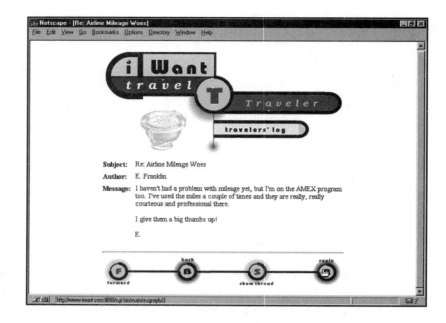

## Listing 11.6 Code (*msgnext.pl*) That Sends the User to the Next Message in the Database

```perl
#!/usr/bin/oraperl

require "process-cgi.pl";

#Login to oracle
$lda=&ora_login('oracle_sid','oracle_user','oracle_pass') || die $ora_errstr;

#Get the message ID from the PATH_INFO variable
$msgid=&path_info;

#Find the next message from the database
$csr=&ora_open($lda,"select nextid from msghome where msgid='$msgid'");
($nextid)=&ora_fetch($csr);

#print out the appropriate location header.
if ($nextid ne '') {
    print "Location: http://www.iwant.com/traveler/log/$nextid.html\n\n";
}
else {
    print "Location: http://www.iwant.com/traveler/log/$msgid.html\n\n";
}

#logout from Oracle
&ora_close ($csr) || die $ora_errstr;
&ora_logoff ($lda) || die $ora_errstr;
```

The msgnext script shown in Listing 11.6 is very simple. After reading in the process-cgi library and logging into Oracle, the script gets the message ID from the PATH_INFO variable. Then the script uses an SQL select statement and &ora_open to get the next message ID from the database. Using &ora_fetch to place the returned number in $nextid, the script uses an if...else conditional to make sure that the user is sent to the right place. If $nextid is not equal to the null string (' '), the script prints a location header pointing to the HTML file indicated by the $nextid variable. If $nextid *is* equal to the null string, you know that it currently is the last message in the database.

When I developed this application, I had several options at this point. I could have sent the user back to the first message in the database, essentially wrapping around to the top, or I could have sent some HTML to indicate that the user was already at the end of the database. Instead, I chose simply to stop the user at this point. If $nextid is null, the script sends a Location header back to the browser, pointing back to the message that the user is already viewing.

If the user chooses the Back button in figure 11.5, he or she follows a link that calls the script msgprev. Listing 11.7 shows this script.

---

**Listing 11.7    Script to Display the Previous Message in a Thread (*msgprev.pl*)**

Part

IV

Ch

11

```perl
#!/usr/bin/oraperl

require "process-cgi.pl";

#Login to oracle
$lda=&ora_login('oracle_sid','oracle_user','oracle_pass') ¦¦ die $ora_errstr;

#Get the message ID from the PATH_INFO variable
$msgid=&path_info;

#Find the previous message from the database
$csr=&ora_open($lda,"select previd from msghome where msgid='$msgid'");
($previd)=&ora_fetch($csr);

#print out the appropriate location header.
if ($previd ne '') {
    print "Location: http://www.iwant.com/traveler/log/$previd.html\n\n";
}
else {
    print "Location: http://www.iwant.com/traveler/log/$msgid.html\n\n";
}

#logout from Oracle
&ora_close ($csr) ¦¦ die $ora_errstr;
&ora_logoff ($lda) ¦¦ die $ora_errstr;
```

---

The msgprev script shown in Listing 11.7 is nearly identical to msgnext (refer to Listing 11.6). Like msgnext, msgprev calls in process-cgi.pl, logs into Oracle, and gets the message ID from the PATH_INFO variable. Instead of selecting the nextid from the database, however, this script calls for previd and then uses a similar conditional to determine what Location header to print. If $previd is not null, it sends the browser a Location header that points to the HTML for the $previd message. If $previd is null, the user is looking at the first message in the database. Again, I could have wrapped around or sent some warning HTML, but I chose to simply leave the user where he or she is. The script ends by closing the last cursor and logging out of Oracle.

The next button in the button bar shown in figure 11.5—Show Thread—goes back to the thread listing. This button links to the showthread script that appears in listings 11.4 and 11.5. Were the user to select this button, he or she would see the screen shown in figure 11.4.

The final option for a user who is viewing the message in figure 11.5 is to reply to that message. If the user selects the Reply button, the form shown in figure 11.6 results.

**FIG. 11.6**
The user enters a message reply on this form.

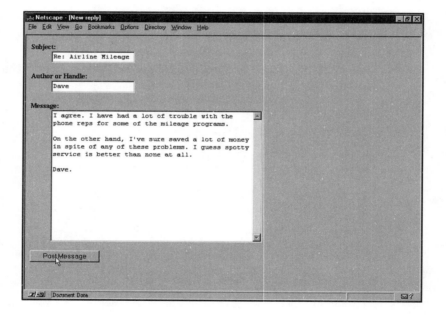

This reply form is produced by a script called msgnext, shown in Listing 11.8. After the normal preliminary steps, this script calls out to the database to get the subject of the message to which this new message is replying. The script then prints the form. You can see in the fourth print statement that the value of $subject is included, preceded by Re:. After printing the rest of the form, the script logs out of Oracle and exits.

When the user submits the new message, another script processes the entered data and returns the page shown in figure 11.7. This script, called newreply, is shown in Listing 11.9.

**FIG. 11.7**
The thread listing is printed back to the user after he or she replies to a message.

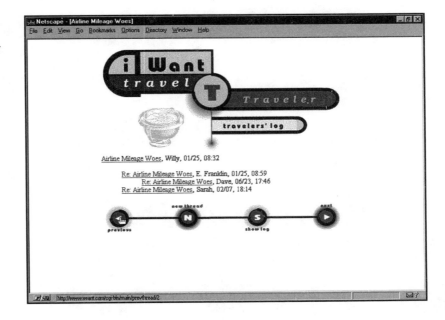

Part
IV
Ch
11

**Listing 11.8  Script (*msgreply.pl*) to Print a Form for the User to Reply to a Message**

```
#!/usr/bin/oraperl

require "process-cgi.pl";

&print_header;
$parentid=&path_info;

#Login to oracle
$lda=&ora_login('oracle_sid','oracle_user','oracle_pass') || die $ora_errstr;

#Get the subject from the database
$csr=&ora_open($lda,"select subject from msghome where msgid='$parentid'");
($subject)=&ora_fetch($csr);

#Print out the reply form with the subject filled in
print "<title>New reply</title>";
print "<form method=\"post\" action=\"/cgi-bin/main/newreply\">";
print "<b>Subject:</b><br>";
print "<dd><input type=\"text\" name = \"subject\" value= \"Re: $subject\"><p>";
print "<b>Author or Handle:</b><br>";
print "<dd><input type=\"text\" name = \"author\"><p>";
print "<b>Message:</b><br>";
print "<dd><textarea name=\"body\" WRAP=PHYSICAL rows=15 cols=50></
textarea><p>";
```

*continues*

**Listing 11.8 Continued**

```
print "<input type=\"submit\" value=\"Post Message\">";
print "<input type=\"hidden\" value=\"$parentid\" name=\"parentid\">";

&ora_close ($csr) ¦¦ die $ora_errstr;
&ora_logoff ($lda) ¦¦ die $ora_errstr;
```

**Listing 11.9 Script to Process a User's Reply (*newreply.pl*)**

```
#!/usr/bin/oraperl

require "process-cgi.pl";

#Login to oracle
$lda=&ora_login('oracle_sid','oracle_user','oracle_pass') ¦¦ die $ora_errstr;

#Get a new messageid
$csr=&ora_open($lda, 'select max(msgid) from msghome');
if (($msgid)=&ora_fetch($csr)) { $msgid=$msgid+1; } else {$msgid=1;}
&ora_close ($csr);

$insert="insert into msghome
     (msgid) values ('$msgid')";
$csr=&ora_open($lda,$insert);
&ora_commit($lda);
&ora_close ($csr);

&parse_input(*fields);
&print_header;

$csr=&ora_open($lda, "select threadid from msghome where msgid =
'$fields{'parentid'}'");
($threadid)=&ora_fetch($csr);
&ora_close($csr);

$previd=&findlast($fields{'parentid'});
$csr=&ora_open($lda,"select nextid from msghome where msgid = '$previd'");
if (($nextid)=&ora_fetch($csr)) {
   $csr2=&ora_open($lda,"update msghome set previd = '$msgid' where
msgid='$nextid'");
}
&ora_commit($lda);
&ora_close($csr);
$csr2=&ora_open($lda,"update msghome set nextid = '$msgid' where
msgid='$previd'");
&ora_commit($lda);
&ora_close($csr);
```

The first part of newreply shown in Listing 11.9 performs all the preliminary steps that all the previous scripts in this chapter do. When those steps are out of the way, the script goes to the database to get a new message ID for this reply. The process is similar to what I described in Listing 11.1. The script finds the maximum message ID and then adds 1 to it. After getting this message ID, the script inserts it into the database. I created this insert at this point in the script to prevent the possibility that another user would insert a message into the database while the script does the rest of the processing on this message, thereby coming up with the same new message ID.

After the new message ID is taken care of, the script gets the data from the form and begins processing it. First, the script finds out the ID of the thread to which this message belongs by selecting the thread ID of the parent message ID, which is a hidden field in the reply form. The script saves this value in $threadid for later insertion into the database.

The next piece of information that you need is the ID of the preceding message in the database. On its face, this proposition may seem to be simple, but in reality, it requires quite a bit of processing, as I'll explain later in this section. When this script has the previous ID, it places that message's nextid value and places it in $nextid for later insertion into the database.

Finally, near the end of Listing 11.9, you see two SQL update statements. The first of these statements sets the previd of the next message to point to this new message. Similarly, the second statement sets the nextid of the preceding message to point to this new message.

Now consider how the script found the ID of the preceding message in the first place. First, think about how this database is set up. The messages have been printed in hierarchical and chronological order. When a user steps through a particular thread, he or she goes in chronological order, *unless there is an appropriate hierarchical step to take*. In the listing shown in figure 11.7, for example, the new message is (obviously) the last one chronologically, but it does not come last when the user is stepping through the database. In fact, you want users to be able to step through a thread as though they were reading the messages one after another, from top to bottom, in the listing. Thus, you need to be careful in finding the appropriate preceding message. The code in Listing 11.10 accomplishes this task.

Part
**IV**
Ch
**11**

**Listing 11.10** Subroutine from *newreply.pl* That Determines What Message Precedes the New Message in the Database

```
sub findlast {
   local ($parentid,$select1);
   $parentid=$_[0];
   $select1="select max(msgid) from msghome where parentid = '$parentid'";
   $csr=&ora_open($lda,$select1);
   ($possible)=&ora_fetch($csr);
   if ($possible ne '') {
     $lastid=&findlast($possible);
   }
   else {
     $lastid=$parentid;
   }
}
```

The &findlast subroutine in Listing 11.10 is intended to find the last message in the thread of replies to the new message's parent message. At first, you might think that the script could find this last message by finding the maximum message ID of all the messages whose parent ID is equal to the parent ID of the new message. This process would work...sometimes. But if the highest-numbered message in that group has replies, the order is messed up. Remember that when users are stepping through messages, you want them to step down the hierarchy as far as they can before they go to the next chronological message on the current level. Therefore, this new message has to come after the last existing reply to its parent message and all of the replies to that reply.

The &findlast routine accomplishes this task by finding the maximum message ID of the parent ID. If this ID exists (if there are already replies to the new message's parent message, for example), the script calls &findlast recursively to see whether that message has any replies itself. If so, &findlast is called again, and so on until there are no replies. Then the routine simply returns the ID of the message being checked as the last message in this subthread. Then this value is assigned to $previd, as shown in Listing 11.9.

When the IDs of the next and preceding messages are taken care of, the rest of the processing can take place. Listing 11.11 shows the remainder of newreply.

### Listing 11.11  Final Section of the Script to Process a User Reply

```
$fields{'body'} =[td] s/<[^>]+>//g;
$fields{'body'} =[td] s/\n/<br>/g;

$fields{'subject'} =[td] s/<[^>]+>//g;
$fields{'subject'} =[td] s/\'/&#039;/g;

$fields{'author'} =[td] s/<[^>]+>//g;
$fields{'author'} =[td] s/\'/&#039;/g;

$update="update msghome
    set (msgdate,subject,author,threadid,parentid,nextid,previd) =
    (select sysdate,
    '$fields{'subject'}','$fields{'author'}',
    , '$threadid','$fields{'parentid'}','$nextid','$previd' from dual) where
msgid='$msgid'";
$csr=&ora_open($lda,$update);
&ora_commit($lda);
&ora_close ($csr);

open(F, ">/opt/lib/httpd/htdocs/traveler/log/$msgid.html");
print F "<title>$fields{'subject'}</title>";
print F "<body bgcolor=\"FFFFFF\"><center>";
print F "<table width = 480 border=0 cellpadding=3>\n";
print F "<tr><td colspan=2><img src=\"/traveler/tra211a.gif\">";
print F "<tr><td><b>Subject:</b><td>$fields{'subject'}";
print F "<tr><td><b>Author:</b><td>$fields{'author'}";
print F "<tr><td valign=top><b>Message:</b><td>";
print F $fields{'body'};
print F "</table><p><hr width=480><a href=\"/cgi-bin/main/msgnext/$msgid\"><img
```

```
src=\"/traveler/log/nextmsg.gif\" border=0></a>";
print F "<a href=\"/cgi-bin/main/msgprev/$msgid\"><img src=\"/traveler/log/
prevmsg.gif\" border=0></a>";
print F "<a href=\"/cgi-bin/main/showthread/$threadid\"><img src=\"/traveler/
log/showthrd.gif\" border=0></a>";
print F "<a href=\"/cgi-bin/main/msgreply/$msgid\"><img src=\"/traveler/log/
msgreply.gif\" border=0></a>";
close F;

print "Location: http://www.iwant.com/cgi-bin/main/showthread/$threadid\n\n";
&ora_close ($csr) || die $ora_errstr;
&ora_logoff ($lda) || die $ora_errstr;
```

The third section of the newreply script begins by processing HTML markup and single quotes out of the fields submitted by the user. Then the script updates the record in the database for the new message, using an SQL update statement. The script gets the message date and time from the Oracle function sysdate; it finds the subject, author, and parent ID in the data from the form. Finally, the script gets the thread ID, next message ID, and previous message ID from values calculated earlier in the script.

When the database is updated, the script creates the HTML file for the new message and prints a Location header to send the browser back to the thread listing. Finally, the script closes the last cursor and logs out of Oracle.

# From Here...

This chapter barely scratched the surface of database integration, but it covered some extremely valuable concepts. The chapter demonstrated how a database can be used to ease the implementation of a fairly complex application. The chapter showed the basic syntax of Oraperl, which is one of the most common Perl–database integration tools; it also showed that a database can be an excellent addition to your Web arsenal. Finally, the chapter whetted your appetite (I hope) for more highly interactive Web applications.

Following are some chapters where you may want to go to whet your appetite even further:

- Chapter 12, "Database Application Using CGI," further explores the process of integrating a database into your Web site, examining an internal database application built with Web tools.

- Chapter 16, "Subroutine Definition," presents more information on Perl libraries and modules for applications ranging from database integration to graphics.

# Database Application Using CGI

*by Matthew D. Healy*

**A**lthough an increasing proliferation of commercial tools for World Wide Web/database integration exist, there still is a place for custom-written Perl CGI scripts in database work. By using CGI scripts to access an existing internal SQL database, you can provide controlled access for outside users without having to redesign the database itself and without purchasing any proprietary software. As a bonus, your WWW front end will automatically be platform- and location-independent: All that your users need is a WWW browser. Building a good Web/database application is not easy, but the results can be well worth the effort. ■

**Fundamental design and security issues**

Some fundamental principles of Web/database programming apply to any application.

**The client/server architecture**

This section provides an overall description of how information passes from each layer to the others.

**A simple Web/database application in Perl**

This section provides a simple but functional example.

**Perl tools for database work**

Several useful tools for Perl database work are available on the Internet.

**What to do when things go wrong**

Debugging and performance tuning can be rather difficult. This section provides some techniques that I have found to be useful.

**The future of WWW/database integration**

Some of the technical limitations of the Web discussed in this section may soon become far less troublesome.

# Fundamental Design and Security Issues

Figures 12.1 and 12.2 show how information flows between the various programs that together constitute a complete Web/database application. Each layer hides many internal details from the other layers and presents the layers above and below it with standardized protocols. This information-hiding is the great advantage that a Web front end has over conventional client/server systems; the numerous, widely distributed users need nothing but standard Web browsers on their computers. The Web server and the database server could reside on one machine, or they could reside on different machines, in which case your CGI program talks over a network to the database server.

**FIG. 12.1**

This schematic of Web/database interaction shows how information flows between the programs that make up the application when the database server and Web server are on the same machine.

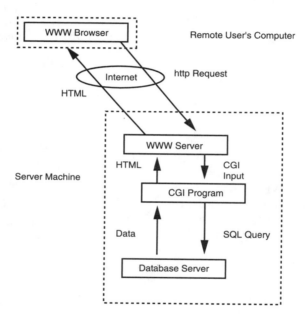

More complex possibilities exist. One application running at my site talks to several database servers, integrating information from a local database with several remote databases. Indeed, users may not even realize how many computers are cooperating to answer their queries; with a well-written database application, all a user needs to know is what information to request. Your job as a Web/database developer is to build tools that allow users to find information without their knowing or caring where the information is actually stored. Security access controls, although often important, should be as unobtrusive as possible, especially for users who are accustomed to the wide-open Internet.

**FIG. 12.2**
This schematic shows how information flows between the programs that make up the application when the database server and the Web server are on different machines.

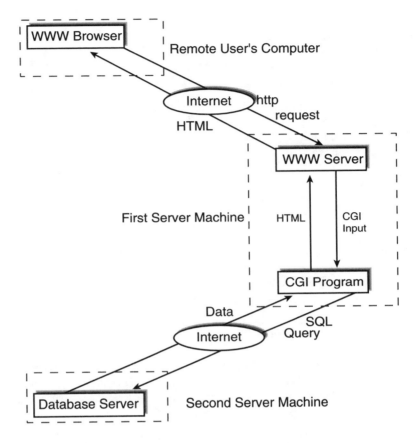

## Advantages and Disadvantages of a Web/RDBMS Interface

Building a Web interface to an existing relational database management system, or RDBMS, isn't simple. You need to be familiar with both your relational database and CGI scripting to plan their integration.

You may also need to do much more "roll-your-own" work than you would with a conventional client/server design, because you need to polish the rough edges off the available tools for Web gateways to relational databases. Many of the most powerful products are freeware or shareware, and all the commercial products are very new. Just about every database vendor now has some kind of Web offering, but most products are either in beta or just barely out of beta. In short, if you do Web/database development, you'll be on the cutting edge.

So why do it? For one thing, the Web is a hot field, so you may feel a compelling desire to be in the vanguard. You may also see the neat tricks that other people do at their Web sites and wonder how you can duplicate such effects—especially if the WWW site doing the neat tricks belongs to a competitor.

I believe that some very good technical reasons exist for putting databases on the Web. Your existing relational database serves as a robust repository for your data, with all the maintenance and security features that you have come to expect from your RDBMS, and the WWW front end provides the open access and user-interface flexibility that your users have come to expect from desktop applications.

I won't try to teach relational design in this chapter, because that's beyond the scope of this book. Many excellent books on relational database design are available; I recommend practically anything by C.J. Date, David McGoveran, Joe Celko, George Tillman, and Andrew Warden (pseudonym for Hugh Darwen; some of his works have appeared under both names at different times). Any large technical library or bookstore should have works by most of these authors. At a more advanced level, the writings of E.F. Codd, who invented the relational model, will reward prolonged study. If more RDBMS programmers had read Codd's works with care, the RDBMS implementations that are now on the market would be far better.

After reading what these people have to say, I hope that you'll share my passionate conviction that the relational model is both an elegant mathematical formalism and a powerful tool for solving real-world database problems in a manner that no other approach can match. As is true of any type of front end, no CGI application can replace a good database design, but you probably know that already. End of sermon.

---

### SQL and Its Dialects

SQL has become the *lingua franca* of relational database work. Starting at IBM in the mid-1970s as a research project called SEQUEL, SQL has grown in popularity over the intervening decades. Today, SQL is by far the most important database query language, with probably hundreds of implementations in use. ANSI has published several official standards (in 1986, 1989, and 1992) and is now working on a new version, informally known as SQL3.

Though official SQL standards exist, few implementations follow them strictly. Every implementation that derives from one or another ANSI-standard dialect of SQL has its own extra features that are deemed useful by those who built it—a situation that creates a big mess. Fortunately, in a typical CGI application, you'll mostly use a rather small subset of SQL that appears (in nearly the same form) in all commonly used dialects of the language.

---

# Limitations of HTTP in a Database Context

With a CGI front end to an RDBMS, you have multiple programs cooperating to accomplish a task. The remote browser is a client to your HTTP server, but the CGI script launched by the HTTP server is itself a client to the RDBMS server. Furthermore, the HTTP protocols are stateless—the browser connects to the server, sends one query, and waits for the reply. After the server sends its reply, it closes the connection. There's no concept of a current connection, so there's no simple mechanism for keeping client-state information around on the server.

For most searches, you can get around the statelessness of the server by keeping all client-state information on the client. Suppose that a user has just performed a search that returned the list of employee records shown in figure 12.3.

**FIG. 12.3**
In this sample query-results screen, each item in the results list is a hot link that performs another search.

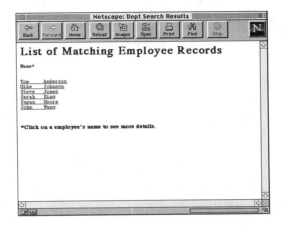

Encoded in the URL behind each hot link in a list like that shown in figure 12.3 is sufficient information for the CGI script to perform a database lookup that will return more details to the user. This technique—sending program-generated HTML that contains enough state information to perform the next search—is known as *dynamic HTML*. The URLs listed in a search-results screen, such as the one in figure 12.3, typically look something like the following:

```
<a href=/cgi-bin/EmpSrch?id=503">Tom     Anderson</a>
<a href=/cgi-bin/EmpSrch?id=229">Mike    Johnson</a>
<a href=/cgi-bin/EmpSrch?id=507">Steve   Jones</a>
<a href=/cgi-bin/EmpSrch?id=917">Sarah   King</a>
<a href=/cgi-bin/EmpSrch?id=467">Susan   Moore</a>
<a href=/cgi-bin/EmpSrch?id=327">John    Wang</a>
```

id is the primary key in the employees table that is to be searched. (By *primary key*, I mean that the database designer has set things up so that a given key value uniquely identifies a single record.)

How does this allow the database server to display a detail view without any information beyond that in the URL? You may recall from Chapter 3, "Advanced Form Processing and Data Storage," that when an URL contains a question mark, the part that follows the question mark is passed to the CGI program as the environment variable QUERY_STRING. The SQL code generated in response to a QUERY_STRING that contains a primary key value of 503, as in the first sample URL in this section, might look something like Listing 12.1.

**Listing 12.1   Sample SQL Query Generated by Clicking a Hot Link**

```
select
     employees.first_name,
     employees.last_name
     employees.salary,
     employees.startdate
     depts.name,
     depts.locid
```

*continues*

Part

**IV**

Ch

**12**

**Listing 12.1  Continued**

```
     emp_dept.empid,
     emp_dept.deptid
from
     employees,depts,emp_dept
where
     employees.id = 503
     and depts.id = emp_dept.deptid
     and employees.id = emp_dept.empid
```

**TIP**  Look at the bottom of any Yahoo (**http://www.yahoo.com**) search-results screen for an elegant example of how URLs can pass information from query to query. The links below the heading "Other Search Engines" automatically search other databases.

When you're updating a database, the use of a CGI interface presents some serious difficulties if more than one user is allowed to make changes to the database. If you aren't careful, the following sequence of events may occur:

- User 1 downloads the form to edit a record.
- User 2 downloads the same record for editing.
- User 1 submits an edited version of the record.
- User 2 submits an edited version of the same record.

In a conventional client/server database system, each user maintains an active connection with session-specific state information. If a user downloads a record for editing, the server can keep that record locked until the user who downloaded that record for editing either submits the changes or cancels the editing. Any other user who tries to change the locked record will be told that it's locked by the user who is editing it. With a stateless HTTP server, there's no concept of a current connection; thus, there is no simple mechanism for locking a record.

**TIP**  One way to handle updates in a CGI program is to place a time-stamp field in each record. You must update this field every time the record changes. In your editing forms, include hidden time-stamp fields so that the CGI program can detect conflicting updates.

Another significant limitation of HTML forms for database work is the lack of field-level validation. A conventional client/server database typically allows the designer to specify various constraints for each field—this one must be an integer between 5 and 99, that one must be in telephone-number format, and so on. When a user tries to type a name in a phone-number field, for example, the program immediately beeps and displays an error message. But an HTML form is sent to the server all at once when the user clicks the submit button, so your script must handle the errors all at once. As you'll see near the end of this chapter, new technologies such as Java and JavaScript can remove this limitation.

# Security Issues

Remember that any CGI script is being executed on the same machine as your HTTP server to fulfill a request from an untrusted client browser. Although this situation is true of any CGI script, with a CGI RDBMS application, your script is itself a trusted client to your RDBMS server. Accordingly, you must be even more careful about what you allow users to do through your CGI interface than you do when you write other types of CGI programs.

I said that your CGI program is a trusted client to your RDBMS server. How does the RDBMS server know that your script is to be trusted? Database servers commonly use two mechanisms to authenticate client programs. Both of these mechanisms have important security implications.

One approach is for the database server to implement its own user name and password system, independent of your operating system's or Web server's user names and passwords. In this case, your program source code must contain a database password, which it transmits every time that it tries to connect. When you use this approach, you must be careful to prevent strangers from seeing your actual program code.

Also, to limit the damage in case someone does manage to see the password contained in your program, you should create a user account on your database server, with only the access rights needed for your CGI program to function, and use that account in all your CGI programs. If most of your CGI programs perform only searching, and if only one updates the database, only that program should have update rights in the database.

> **CAUTION**
>
> A particular trap in the CGI-database context is the use of file extensions to tell your HTTP server which files are CGI executables and which are documents. If your text editor makes a backup copy in the same directory with a different extension (such as NAME.BAK or NAME.CGI˜), a wily cracker might be able to download your actual code. For this reason, I strongly advise anyone who uses CGI scripts with hard-coded passwords to configure the HTTP server so that certain directories are defined as CGI directories. Files in those directories can be executed but never displayed. In my experience, any time you mix documents and programs in the same directory, you're asking for trouble.

Part
IV

Ch
12

The other common mechanism for the database server to decide whether a client can be trusted is to define database access rights for specified operating-system user names. In this approach, the database server must trust the operating system to authenticate users. In the CGI context, the use of operating-system user names for authentication presents an especially tricky issue, because most HTTP servers run all CGI scripts under a special, low-privilege user name. (Most UNIX HTTP servers, for example, run all CGI scripts under the name nobody or the name www.) Therefore, you must trust every person who writes CGI scripts on your HTTP server.

One alternative provided in some operating systems is the capability to have a CGI program run as the user name of its owner, with all rights that the owner would have. This method eliminates the need to have your database server trust every CGI script, but it creates its own security problems—now your CGI program has significantly more access rights to the rest of your system than does a CGI running under a special, low-privilege ID. If your HTTP server is running under a single-user operating system that lacks the concept of user names, of course, you must trust every CGI program in any case.

If you use a UNIX server, the program cgiwrap (available at **ftp://ftp.cc.umr.edu/pub/cgi/cgiwrap/**) provides an excellent way to run a script as a given user name. This program is better than others for this purpose because it was designed to plug some CGI-specific security holes.

To handle multiple classes of users with one script, put symbolic links (aliases) to your script in multiple directories with different access policies. Your script checks the SCRIPT_NAME environment variable to see which version was called.

# A Simple Working Example in Perl

I often find vague generalities and isolated code snippets to be frustrating, because they don't tell me how the various pieces fit together to form a complete application. To show you how a Web/database gateway works, in this section I'll build a small working application that maintains a hotlist of Web sites, which remote users can search.

First, you see how a Perl script talks to the database. I'll demonstrate the specific calling conventions of two database engines; then I'll show you how to make the code much more portable. The sample application is written with this portable interface.

## Accessing a DBMS from Perl

As I noted in the sidebar "SQL and Its Dialects" earlier in this chapter, the subset of SQL that is needed for most CGI/database programming is nearly universal; the same SQL code can often be ported from one database engine to another with little or no change. The details of sending that SQL to the database server and getting the results back from the server, however, are much more varied. Most SQL database servers provide some form of C API for this purpose—typically, a set of functions that can be linked into a C client program. Because Perl, with its strong string manipulation and I/O facilities, lends itself so well to database manipulation, Perl wrappers have been written for most of the common database-server APIs. The use of such a Perl wrapper permits database access from within Perl programs but limits portability, because each database server API is unique; therefore, its Perl wrapper is also unique.

**Two DBMS APIs**   To illustrate the variation in database APIs, listings 12.2 and 12.3 show two short sample programs written in the Perl wrappers for Sybase and mSQL (mini-SQL) servers. The Perl wrapper for Sybase is called SybPerl, and the Perl wrapper for mSQL is called msqlPerl; Perl wrappers for other database engines typically follow the same naming convention. Each of the following two programs connects to the server, asks for a database called `test`, sends a single SQL statement, and prints the results.

### Listing 12.2 An Example of a Simple SQL Query with SybPerl

```
#!/usr/local/bin/perl
require sybperl;
#
#This code tested with Sybase 4.9.1 and Sybase 10.0.1 under SunOS 4.1.2
#
#NOTE: for Perl4, or for Statically loaded Perl5 versions
#of sybperl, you must edit the first line to replace
#the name 'perl' with the name of your sybperl version

#raw_syb_perl_demo.p
#A simple demonstration of Sybperl in action
#
#Must define $USER,$PWD,$SERVER here!
    $dbproc = &dblogin( $USER,$PWD,$SERVER);
    $dbproc != -1 || die "Can't connect to $server ...\n";
    &dbuse( "test" ) || die "Can't use $database ...\n";

#Create the SQL statement & send to the server
$SQL = "select last_name,salary,id from employees";
&dbcmd( $SQL ) || die "Error in dbcmd.\n" ;
&dbsqlexec || die "Error in dbsqlexec.\n" ;
$result = &dbresults($dbproc);

#and get the resulting rows
%row = &dbnextrow($dbproc, 1); #get first row
while (%row = &dbnextrow($dbproc, 1))
    {
        print "last_name:$row{'last_name'}\t";
        print "salary:$row{'salary'}\t";
        print "id:$row{'id'}\t";
        print "\n";
    }
```

### Listing 12.3 The Same Query as Listing 12.2, but Using mSQL

```
#!/usr/bin/perl
#raw_msqlperl_demo.p
#
#This code has been tested with Msql 1.0.6 under SunOS 4.1.4
#
#A simple demonstration of Msqlperl in action
require "Msql.pm";$host = shift || "";
package main;
#Connect in two steps: (1) Connect and (2) SelectDB...
if ($dbh = Msql->Connect($host))
    {print "Connected\n";} else {die "failed to connect\n";}
```

*continues*

**Listing 12.3    Continued**

```
if ($dbh->SelectDB("test"))
    {print("Test db\n");} else {die "Select db failed\n";}

$SQL = "select last_name,salary,id from employees";
$sth = $dbh->Query($SQL) or die $Msql::db_errstr;
#get the hash associating fieldnames and numbers:
@fieldnum{@{$sth->name}} = 0..@{$sth->name}-1;
# %fieldnum is now a list of fieldnums, indexed on names
#and get the rows
while (@row = $sth->FetchRow())
    {
        print "last_name:$row[$fieldnum{'last_name'}]\t";
        print "salary:$row[$fieldnum{'salary'}]\t";
        print "id:$row[$fieldnum{'id'}]\t";
    print "\n";
    }
```

The output of either program looks something like the following:

```
last_name:Smith      salary:21000     id:123
last_name:Huskins     salary:19500      id:124
last_name:Williams     salary:51075       id:125
last_name:Jones      salary:27000     id:126
last_name:Hill       salary:17500     id:127
```

Notice in listings 12.2 and 12.3 that the SQL code string is exactly the same for either database server and that the output is also the same (assuming identical data in the table, of course). Also, the structure of the two programs is similar: connect to the database, send the query, and get the rows. But the details of how the client communicates with the server are different. If your code is to be portable, you need some kind of abstraction layer that insulates the programmer from most database-specific details. Fortunately, such a layer has been written.

**A Simple DBMS Abstraction Layer**    Bo Frese Rasmussen, the author of the excellent WDB database forms-generation package (discussed in detail in the section "WDB" later in this chapter) has written a simple database interface, or *dbi layer*. By isolating most of the database-specific details to one Perl function library, he made the entire package easy to port, and various database programmers have written versions of the dbi library. As of late August 1996, versions of WDB (and, therefore, of the dbi library) were available for Sybase, Informix, mSQL, Oracle, and Postgres95.

Listing 12.4 shows a dbi version of the simple Sybase and mSQL clients from listings 12.2 and 12.3.

## Listing 12.4 The Same Query as Listings 12.2 and 12.3, Using the dbi Layer

```perl
#!/usr/local/bin/perl
#Either_dbi_demo.p
#
#This works with either Sybperl or Msqlperl

#AS SHOWN HERE, this works with Msqlperl.
#To make it work with Sybperl, change the
#     $dbFlag line below.
#
#Also, if you are using the Perl4 version of sybperl
#then you must change the first line of this program

$dBFlag = 'MSQL';  ## OR $DbFlag = 'SYBASE'
#this is the msql version!

if ($DbFlag eq 'MSQL') {require 'msql_dbi.pl';}
elsif ($DbFlag eq 'SYBASE') {require 'syb_dbi.pl';}
else {die "unsupported database\n";}

$database = "test"; #define $User, etc here!
&dbi_connect( $user, $pswd, $server, $database );

$Query = "select last_name,salary,id from employees";
&dbi_dosql($Query);

if ($DbFlag eq 'MSQL') #one extra thing needed for Msql
{&dbi_fieldnames( 'last_name', 'salary','id');}

while( %row = &dbi_nextrow  ) {
        print "last_name:$row{'last_name'}\t";
        print "salary:$row{'salary'}\t";
        print "id:$row{'id'}\t";
        print "\n";

    }
```

Part

IV

Ch

12

If you have either Sybase and Sybperl or mSQL and MsqlPerl installed on your system, you can run the code in Listing 12.4 on either platform by editing it as indicated by the comments in the program. Revising the code to work with the other versions of the dbi library shouldn't be much more difficult. All Perl examples in the rest of this chapter use the msql_dbi.pl interface, so they can easily be ported to any other database for which WDB has been ported.

# Defining the Database Schema for the Working Example

This example, as I said in "A Simple Working Example in Perl" earlier in this chapter, is a simple interactive hotlist of Web sites, providing the URL and a description for each site. Remote users can search the hotlist and submit new entries for potential inclusion. The administrator (who knows the appropriate password) can review submissions, adding approved submissions to the hotlist for public viewing. Think of the example as being a rudimentary equivalent of Yahoo (just as the Wright brothers' flying machine of 1903 was a rudimentary equivalent of an airliner).

**Database Tables and Fields** This database has three tables. The UIDs table shown in Table 12.1 is used for generating UIDs, so that each record in the other tables has a unique identifier that can be used as a primary key.

**Table 12.1  The UIDs Table**

| Column | Type | Length | Not Null | Key |
|---|---|---|---|---|
| TableName | char | 40 | Y | Y |
| MaxUID | longint | 4 | Y | N |

This technique is commonly used by database designers. You create one row in the UIDs table for each table that needs to have UIDs generated. MaxUID then records the highest UID yet assigned. Each time you create a new row for a data table, you increment the MaxUID value for that table and use this value for the new row of data.

The Hotlist table, shown in Table 12.2, contains data for all approved submissions to the database.

**Table 12.2  The Hotlist Table**

| Column | Type | Length | Not Null | Key |
|---|---|---|---|---|
| UID | longint | 4 | Y | Y |
| URL | char | 100 | Y | N |
| SHORTDESC | char | 50 | N | N |
| DESCRIPTION | char | 200 | N | N |

New submissions are stored in the Submissions table until they have been approved by the database administrator, as shown in Table 12.3. The Hotlist table and the Submissions table are otherwise identical.

**Table 12.3   The Submissions Table**

| Column | Type | Length | Not Null | Key |
|---|---|---|---|---|
| UID | longint | 4 | Y | Y |
| URL | char | 100 | Y | N |
| SHORTDESC | char | 50 | N | N |
| DESCRIPTION | char | 200 | N | N |

**Directory Layout**   The data tables are stored by the database server (mSQL was used for this example). Although any database server almost certainly stores the actual data as disk files, the database server manages those files internally; indeed, that's the fundamental reason for using a database server. In addition to the database tables described in the preceding section, my sample application consists of three HTML documents and three Perl scripts placed in three directories, as follows:

```
~hhealy/public_html: (documents)
    DemoHome.html
    Search.html
    Submission.html
```

The three files are the top-level main screen and the two forms for searching and submitting data. Because the files reside in my public HTML directory, they can be viewed by any user on the Web.

The following two programs reside in an unprotected directory within the CGI-BIN hierarchy on this Web server, so they can be run as CGI scripts by anyone on the Web:

```
.../cgi-bin/healy/public: (public CGI programs)
    SearchHotlist.p
    ShowDetails.p
```

The following directory is password-protected by means of the .HTPASSWD and .HTACCESS files, so you must type a name and password to run the program in this directory as a CGI script:

```
.../cgi-bin/healy/private: (private program)
    .htpasswd
    .htaccess
    ListSubmissions.p
```

## Searching the Hotlist

The user of this application typically begins with a simple opening screen that lists the available options. I've intentionally kept the screen in figure 12.4 as simple as possible. Most of the hot links in this opening screen point to scripts that perform the actual work of providing database access.

**FIG. 12.4**

The opening screen for the Hotlist database has hot links to the available programs for database access.

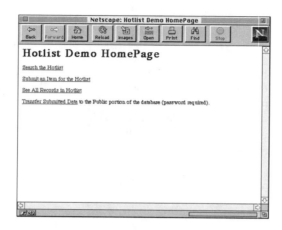

Listing 12.5 shows the HTML for the opening screen.

### Listing 12.5   The Opening Screen

```
<HTML>
<HEAD><TITLE>Hotlist Demo HomePage</TITLE></HEAD><BODY>
<H1>Hotlist Demo HomePage</H1>

<A HREF="Search.html">Search the Hotlist</A><p>

<A HREF="Submission.html">Submit an Item for the Hotlist</A><p>

<a HREF="/cgi-bin/healy/SearchHotlist.p">See All Records in Hotlist</a><p>

<a HREF="/cgi-bin/healy/ListSubmissions.p">Transfer Submitted Data</a>
to the Public portion of the database (password required).<p>
</PRE></BODY>
</HTML>
```

Clicking Search the Hotlist calls up the search form, which I've likewise kept as simple as possible (see fig. 12.5).

**FIG. 12.5**

The user enters search criteria in this form, which then posts the criteria to the searching script.

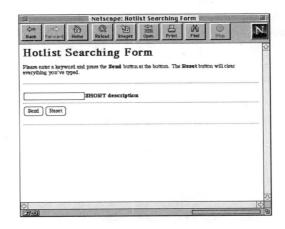

Listing 12.6 shows the HTML for the search form shown in figure 12.5.

## Listing 12.6 The Search Form

```
<HTML>
<HEAD>
<TITLE>Hotlist Searching Form</TITLE>
</HEAD>
<BODY>
<H1>Hotlist Searching Form</h1>
Please enter a keyword and click the <b>Send</b> button at the bottom.
The <b>Reset</b> button will clear everything you've typed.<P>
<FORM ACTION="http://server.wherever/cgi-bin/healy/SearchHotlist.p"
METHOD="POST"><hr>
<p>
<INPUT name="SHORTDESC" size=20 value=""><b>SHORT description</b><BR>
<hr>
<INPUT TYPE="submit" VALUE="Send"> <INPUT TYPE="reset" VALUE="Reset"><P>
<hr>
</FORM>
</BODY>
</HTML>
```

Part
IV

Ch
12

Submitting a search request (by entering a key to search and clicking the submit button) POSTs the search key to a simple searching script. This script generates a SQL query and submits it to the server. The script works just like the three sample database query scripts shown in listings 12.2 through 12.4, except that the SQL string is built up from the form data. SQL that has been generated on the fly is known as *dynamic SQL*.

**N O T E** I do no error checking on input; I just wrap it in an SQL like clause in the program, which is shown in Listing 12.7 later in this section. ▪

To keep this example as simple as possible, I provided only one search field, and I converted that field to all uppercase in the database. If your search form provides multiple lookup fields, you must generate a complex where clause based on which fields contain search strings. The WDB package (discussed in "WDB" later in this chapter) can build up such a where clause based on form contents.

In the program shown in Listing 12.7 (and in all my other form-handling CGI programs), to avoid all the messy details of reading and parsing the form information, I call Steven Brenner's cgi-lib.pl routines. You can find this library at many FTP sites or on the CD-ROM that is included with this book. One particular advantage of using cgi-lib.pl for database work is the fact that it handles GET or POST identically. Name–value pairs can be appended to the URL as ?name1=value1&name2=value2… or sent as a POST data block.

### Listing 12.7   Perl Code to Perform the Search

```perl
#!/usr/local/bin/perl
#
#This program tested with Msql 1.0.6 under SunOS 4.1.4 and
#NCSA httpd 1.5 with Perl 5.001m

#do this as soon as possible!
print "Content-type:text/html\n\n";

#Define two little subroutines for urlencode/decode
#
#replace funny characters with %xx hex for urls
sub escape
{
    ($_)=@_;
    s/([^a-zA-Z0-9_\-.])/uc sprintf("%%%02x",ord($1))/eg;
    $_;
}

#replace + with space and %xx with that ASCII character
sub unescape {
    ($_)=@_;
    tr/+/ /;
    s/%(..)/pack("c",hex($1))/ge;
    $_;
}

#load the cgi library
require "cgi-lib.pl";
#load the Msql database interface library
require 'msql_dbi.pl';

# Start output
```

```
#read in the form contents:

&ReadParse(); #handles GET or POST forms w/identical results
#now @in has key=value pairs, and %in{key} = value
#Main Program Begins Here

$SHORTDESC = $in{'SHORTDESC'};
$SHORTDESC =~ tr/a-z/A-Z/;  #convert to uppercase
$SCRIPT_NAME = $ENV{'SCRIPT_NAME'};

#connect to database server
$user = "healy";
$server = "server.wherever";
$passwd = "dummy";  #not used, for msql goes by Unix UID;
$database = "test";
&dbi_connect( $user, $pswd, $server, $database );

$Query = "select UID,URL,SHORTDESC from HOTLIST";
$Query = $Query . " where SHORTDESC like '%";
$Query = $Query . $SHORTDESC . "%'";

&dbi_dosql($Query);
#the next line is msql-specific; comment-out for other ver
&dbi_fieldnames('UID','URL','SHORTDESC','DESCRIPTION');

print "<h1>Search Results</h1>\n";

while( %row = &dbi_nextrow  )
    {
      print '<a href="';
      print "$row{'URL'}";
      print '">';
      print &unescape($row{'SHORTDESC'});
      print "</a> ";
      print '<a href="';
      print '/cgi-bin/healy/ShowDetails.p?';
      print 'UID=';
      print $row{'UID'};
      print '">';
      print "Details</a><p>\n";
    }

  print "Click on a link to go there, or click on
  <b>details</b> for a more-detailed description of the link\n";
```

After a search is performed, the output looks something like the sample screen shown in figure 12.6.

**FIG. 12.6**

After searching the hotlist database, the user sees a list of hot links like this one. Each hot link calls a Perl script that shows the details of that record.

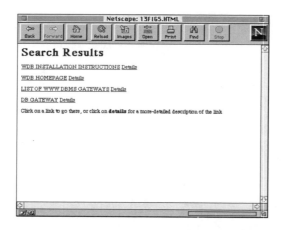

Listing 12.8 is the HTML generated for the search results shown in figure 12.6.

**Listing 12.8  Typical Output from Search of Hotlist Database, With URLs to Detailed Views**

```
<h1>Search Results</h1>

<a href="http://arch-http.hq.eso.org/bfrasmus/wdb/install.html">
WDB INSTALLATION INSTRUCTIONS</a>
<a href="/cgi-bin/healy/public/ShowDetails.p?UID=2">Details</a><p>
<a href="http://arch-http.hq.eso.org/bfrasmus/wdb/">WDB HOMEPAGE</a>
<a href="/cgi-bin/healy/public/ShowDetails.p?UID=3">Details</a><p>
<a href="http://cscsun1.larc.nasa.gov/~bbeowulf/db/
existing_products.html">LIST OF WWW DBMS GATEWAYS</a>
<a href="/cgi-bin/healy/public/ShowDetails.p?UID=7">Details</a><p>
<a href="http://server.wherever/~hhealy/Submission.html">DB GATEWAY</a>
<a href="/cgi-bin/healy/public/ShowDetails.p?UID=13">Details</a><p>
Click on a link to go there, or click on <b>details</b>
for a more-detailed description of the link
```

## Viewing the Detail Record

Notice that the Details links in the search-results screen shown in figure 12.6 (with the HTML given in Listing 12.8) point to a second CGI script and that each URL has ?UID=nn appended. This simple example shows how state is maintained on the client browser side; no history is maintained on the stateless server. Listing 12.9 shows the code for ShowDetails.p, the CGI program that generates the detail record. This program is similar to the preceding example.

## Listing 12.9  Perl Code to Return the Detail View

```perl
#Up to here code is identical with SearchHotlist.p above
#
#now @in has key=value pairs, and %in{key} = value
#Main Program Begins Here
#
$UID = $in{'UID'};

#connect to database server
$user = "healy";
$server = "server.wherever";
$passwd = "dummy";  #not used, for msql goes by Unix UID;
$database = "test";
&dbi_connect( $user, $pswd, $server, $database );

$Query = "select UID,URL,SHORTDESC,DESCRIPTION from HOTLIST where UID = $UID";

&dbi_dosql($Query);
#the next line is msql-specific; comment-out for other ver
&dbi_fieldnames('UID','URL','SHORTDESC','DESCRIPTION');

print "<h1>Detail View</h1>\n";

while( %row = &dbi_nextrow  )
    {
    print "Hot link to this item: ";
    print '<a href="';
    print "$row{'URL'}";
    print '">';
    print &unescape($row{'SHORTDESC'});
    print "</a><br>";
    print "Detailed description: ";
    print &unescape($row{'DESCRIPTION'});
    print "<p>\n";
    }
```

Part
IV

Ch
12

Figure 12.7 shows an example of the detail screen, and Listing 12.10 shows the HTML generated for this screen.

## Listing 12.10   The Detail View of Figure 12.7

```html
<h1>Detail View</h1>
Hot link to this item:
<a href="http://cscsun1.larc.nasa.gov/~bbeowulf/db/existing_products.html">
LIST OF WWW DBMS GATEWAYS</a><br>
Detailed description: Comprehensive List of Tools for Building RDBMS CGI
Gateways<p>
```

**FIG. 12.7**

Clicking an URL in the search-results screen of figure 12.6 generates a detail view such as this one.

This simple example has only one hot link—to the URL that is being described. In a real application, you can (and should) have multiple hot links in your detail screens—hot links that perform lookups on this database or other databases. The HTML snippet in Listing 12.11, taken from a hypothetical Employee Detail screen, shows what I mean.

**Listing 12.11  A Hypothetical Employee Detail Screen**

```
<h1>Tom Anderson</h1>
Department:
<a href="http://server.wherever/cgi-bin/DeptSrch?Deptid=17">Engineering</a><p>
Location:
<a href="http://server.wherever/cgi-bin/LocSrch?Locid=29">Podunk</a><p>
Position:
<a href="http://server.wherever/cgi-bin/PosSrch?Posid=17">CAD Technician</a><p>
Mail Stop:
<a href="http://server.wherever/cgi-bin/EmpSrch?Mailid=97">POD-43</a><p>
```

Clicking any field in the detail record performs a lookup of related records in that category. The list would contain the names of employees, and the URL behind each name would perform a lookup on the employee ID. This use of URLs to generate further searches effectively converts a relational database to a giant hypertext document.

Such hyperlinks can just as easily link one database with another. Several large international databases that are widely used in molecular biology, for example, have Web interfaces. A local database used by one research group for its own internal data can include hot links to related information from one or more of the international databases.

### Some Major Scientific Databases on the WWW

If you want to check out some major biological and chemical databases, use the following URLs:

- **http://expasy.hcuge.ch/**—the molecular-biology server of Geneva University Hospital
- **http://dot.imgen.bcm.tmc.edu:9331/seq-annot/home.html**—the Sequence Annotation server
- **http://www.ncbi.nlm.nih.gov/**—the National Center for Biotechnology Information home page
- **http://www3.ncbi.nlm.nih.gov/Omim/**—the Online Mendelian Inheritance in Man Genetic Database
- **http://www.pdb.bnl.gov/**—the Brookhaven Protein Data Bank
- **http://www.unige.ch/crystal/w3vlc/data.index.html**—a list of crystallography databases

Most of these URLs have links to other sites that have related information.

Consider a hypothetical business-related example. The marketing people in your company have created a Web-accessible database of product information, including which company locations build given parts of each product. Now suppose that you're a programmer in the personnel department and that you've been given the job of putting your company directory on the Web.

You could use hyperlinks in your directory database to link product information with directory information. The location field in a directory detail screen could show the list of products made at that location, for example.

With the cooperation of the people who maintain the product-information database, you could also work the other way. When you see a record that lists the various locations that make each part of the product, you could click links that locate people who work at each location.

The possibilities for using the Web to integrate multiple databases in different locations are limited only by the programmer's imagination—and by the quality of available databases. The task may also require a much higher degree of connection among the parts of your MIS organization than was the case before. After all, Internet and intranet applications are basically *about* pulling scattered information together.

Part
IV

Ch
12

# Submitting Data to the Hotlist

A database is scarcely complete without providing a means for entering data. For some databases, the Web front end allows only searching. For this example, however, I also include a simple data-submission form, so that any user can submit proposed records for possible inclusion in the publicly searchable database. Figure 12.8 shows the submission screen.

**FIG. 12.8**

This form is used for the remote submission, via the Web, of records to be added to the database.

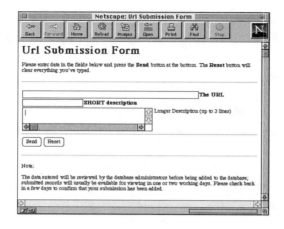

Listing 12.12 shows the HTML for the submission screen.

---

**Listing 12.12   A Simple HTML Form to Submit New Data via the Web**

```
<HTML>
<HEAD>
<TITLE>Url Submission Form</TITLE>
</HEAD>
<BODY>
<H1>Url Submission Form</h1>
Please enter data in the fields below and click the <b>Send</b> button
at the bottom. The <b>Reset</b> button will clear everything you've
typed.<P>
<FORM ACTION="http://server.wherever/cgi-bin/healy/public/Submit.p"
METHOD="POST">
<hr>
<p>
<INPUT name="URL" size=60 value="" ><b>The URL</b><BR>
<INPUT name="SHORTDESC" size=20 value=""><b>SHORT description</b><BR>
<TEXTAREA name="DESCRIPTION" ROWS=2 COLS=40></TEXTAREA>
Longer Description (up to 3 lines)<BR>
<hr>
<INPUT TYPE="submit" VALUE="Send"> <INPUT TYPE="reset" VALUE="Reset"><P>
<hr>
</FORM>
Note:<p>
The data entered will be reviewed by the database administrators before being
added to the database; submitted records will usually be available for viewing
in one or two working days. Please check back in a few days to confirm that your
submission has been added.<p>
</BODY>
</HTML>
```

Submitted data is posted to the script shown in Listing 12.13.

### Listing 12.13    Perl Script to Handle Data-Submission Form

```
#Up to here code is identical with SearchHotlist.p above
#
#now @in has key=value pairs, and %in{key} = value
#Main Program Begins Here
#connect to database server
$user = "healy";
$server = "server.wherever";
$passwd = "dummy";  #not used, for msql goes by Unix UID;
$database = "test";
&dbi_connect( $user, $pswd, $server, $database );

$UID = $in{'UID'};
$URL = $in{'URL'};
$SHORTDESC = &escape($in{'SHORTDESC'});
$SHORTDESC =~ tr/a-z/A-Z/;   #convert to uppercase
$DESCRIPTION = &escape($in{'DESCRIPTION'});
$Query = "select MaxUID from UIDs where TableName = 'SUBMISSIONS'";
&dbi_dosql($Query);
#the next line is msql-specific; comment-out for other ver
&dbi_fieldnames('MaxUID');
%row = &dbi_nextrow;
$MaxUID = $row{'MaxUID'} + 1;
$Query = "Update UIDs Set MaxUID = $MaxUID where TableName =
   Â'SUBMISSIONS'";

&dbi_dosql($Query);
$Query = "Insert into SUBMISSIONS values(";

$Query = $Query . $MaxUID . ",'";

$Query = $Query . $URL . "','";
$Query = $Query . $SHORTDESC . "','";
$Query = $Query . $DESCRIPTION . "')";

&dbi_dosql($Query);

print "<h1>Submission Accepted</h1>\n";
print "Thank you for your submission. \n";
print "It will be reviewed by the database administrator \n";
print "for possible inclusion in our hotlist \n";
```

Part
IV

Ch

12

A couple of interesting wrinkles to this script don't appear in the other programs:

■ All data is inserted—in URL-encoded form—into the Submissions table, not into the publicly searchable Hotlist table. This feature gives the administrator a chance to review all submissions.

■ The UIDs table is used to generate a unique ID for each submitted record.

The possibility exists that two people might submit new data at precisely the same moment, so between the instant of getting the current value of MaxUID and the instant of updating UIDs, another user could get the same UID value. Although that scenario is not very likely for a simple application such as this one, it's a real concern for active databases. Most high-end database engines have a feature called *transactions* (which mSQL doesn't support). The programmer declares the actions of getting the UID and updating the UID to be one transaction that must be run as a unit or not at all.

> **N O T E**   For simplicity, the script shown in Listing 12.13 doesn't validate user input—it simply sticks whatever the user entered into a table. Your real applications should perform appropriate validation on the input data. Your script also could try to GET the URL entered by the user, to verify that it's a valid URL. ■

## Generating SQL Code to Transfer Submitted Data

The last piece of this package is a mechanism by which an administrator can transfer data from the Submissions table to the Hotlist table. To sidestep the complexities of updating via the stateless Web server, I use a different approach: a CGI script that doesn't perform any updating itself but that generates a SQL script to perform the required actions. Listing 12.14 shows the Perl code.

**Listing 12.14   Generating Transfer SQL to Move Data to Public Table**

```
#Up to here code is identical with SearchHotlist.p above
#
#now @in has key=value pairs, and %in{key} = value
#Main Program Begins Here
#connect to database server
$user = "healy";
$server = "server.wherever";
$passwd = "dummy";   #not used, for msql goes by Unix UID;
$database = "test";
&dbi_connect( $user, $pswd, $server, $database );

$Query = "select UID,URL,SHORTDESC,DESCRIPTION from SUBMISSIONS";
    print "#SQL Query: $Query\n\n";
    print "#\n#\n#\n";
    print "#Review this SQL script with care, then ";
    print "pipe it through msql\n#\n#\n";

&dbi_dosql($Query);
#the next line is msql-specific; comment-out for other ver
&dbi_fieldnames('UID','URL','SHORTDESC','DESCRIPTION');

print "#Inserting into HOTLIST\n\n";
while( %row = &dbi_nextrow  )
     {
       print "Insert into HOTLIST values(\n";

       print "$row{'UID'}'\n,";
```

```
      print "$row{'URL'}'\n,'";
      print "$row{'SHORTDESC'}'\n,'";
      print "$row{'DESCRIPTION'}'";
      print ')\g';
      print "\n";
      }

$Query = "select MaxUID from UIDs where TableName = 'SUBMISSIONS'";
&dbi_dosql($Query);
#the next line is msql-specific; comment-out for other ver
&dbi_fieldnames('MaxUID');
$MaxUID=0;
$Query = "select MaxUID from UIDs where TableName = 'SUBMISSIONS'";
&dbi_dosql($Query);
#the next line is msql-specific; comment-out for other ver
&dbi_fieldnames('MaxUID');
$MaxUID=0;
%row = &dbi_nextrow;
$MaxUID = $row{'MaxUID'};
print "\n\n#Updating UIDs\n\n";
print "Update UIDs Set MaxUID = $MaxUID where"
print " TableName = 'HOTLIST'" . '\g' . "\n\n";

print "\n\n#Deleting from SUBMISSIONS\n\n";
print 'delete from SUBMISSIONS where UID <= ' . $MaxUID . '\g';
```

Running this script via the Web generates SQL similar to that shown in Listing 12.15.

## Listing 12.15  Typical Transfer SQL Generated by the Program in Listing 12.14

```
#SQL Query: select UID,URL,SHORTDESC,DESCRIPTION from SUBMISSIONS
#
#
#Review this SQL script with care, then pipe it through msql
#
#
#Inserting into HOTLIST

Insert into HOTLIST values(
18
,'http://gasnet.med.yale.edu/'
,'GASNET'
,'The%20Gasnet%20server%20has%20various%20resources%0D%0Afor
➥%20Anesthesiology...')\g
Insert into HOTLIST values(
17
,'http://www.ncbi.nlm.nih.gov/BLAST/'
,'BLAST'
,'BLAST%20Homepage%20at%20the%20National%20Center%0D%0Afor
➥%20Biotechnology%20Information')\g
```

*continues*

**Listing 12.15   Continued**

```
Insert into HOTLIST values(
16
,'http://www.eol.ists.ca/~ddunlop/wdb-p95/'
,'WDB%20POSTGRES'
,'WDB%20Port%20to%20Postgres')\g
Insert into HOTLIST values(
15
,'http://www.comvista.com/net/www/cgidata.html'
,'MAC%2FWWW%2FDB'
,'List%20of%20URLs%20with%20info%20on%20Mac%20WWW%2FDBMS%0D
➥%0Ascripting')\g

#Deleting from SUBMISSIONS

delete from SUBMISSIONS where UID <= 18\g
#Updating UIDs

Update UIDs Set MaxUID = 18 where TableName = 'HOTLIST'\g
```

The database administrator edits the SQL that is generated to delete records that shouldn't be added to the Hotlist table and then feeds the script through the mSQL command line. Alternatively, if you want a purely Web solution, you can modify this script to generate a form that contains all the SQL in a scrollable text area. That form would submit the edited SQL to another script that pipes the SQL through the mSQL command line.

Probably the cleanest approach is to generate updating forms that contain database fields instead of SQL code. You then would need to address the issue of conflicting updates, however, probably by using time stamps. The sequence would be something like the following:

1. Generate an updating form with all data in editable fields and the time stamp included in the form as a hidden field.

2. On submission of the edited form, first check the time stamp in the database record against the time stamp in the form. If the time stamps vary, generate an error message and quit without updating the record.

3. When you update the record, also update the time-stamp value.

With mSQL, you need to update the time stamps in the CGI script and in every program that updates the database. With many higher-end servers, you can define a time stamp that the database engine maintains automatically, eliminating the possibility that a programmer will forget to change time stamps whenever data changes.

**N O T E**   In Sybase, the term *time stamp* is a misnomer; the time-stamp value has no relationship to clock time at all. Sybase simply takes responsibility for guaranteeing that the value of this field will change every time that any other field in that record changes. Thus, the sole value of Sybase time-stamp fields is to check for conflicting updates. ■

# Perl Tools for Web/DBMS Work

Database access via the Web is such a hot area that listing every available or promised product would be impossible. Every major database vendor either has a Web-related product available now or promises to have one soon, and many programmers are working on their own database gateways, running with a wide range of database engines. You can safely assume that a mechanism exists for linking any reasonable combination of database server and HTTP server, but the quality of the implementations varies wildly.

If you're thinking about putting a database on the Web, I suggest that you start by reading Usenet postings in newsgroups that are related to your favorite database packages. You also should look at the Web site of your database vendor.

The following sections list a few tools that are available on the Web and some Web sites that contain pointers to information about Web/database tools.

---

### Installing Web/Database Tools

Some of the tools mentioned in the following sections are commercial programs, which generally come with installation instructions; others are shareware or freeware. With all shareware and freeware programs, part of the price that you pay for low-cost software is less hand-holding when it comes to installation. Generally, you install these programs in the same manner that you would install any shareware program for your OS.

Many of the tools are for UNIX servers and typically come as source code in `tar` form. If you've never installed such a package, you should seek out your local UNIX guru for assistance. UNIX comes in many flavors, and every system that I've used has had local customizations added to the standard system, so giving detailed directions here is impossible. Most of the UNIX packages mentioned in this chapter come with makefiles or other installation scripts, but you probably need to check and edit these scripts as required by your local configuration. Pay particular attention to where various directories are located on your system.

Installation and configuration information for most of these tools is available on their authors' Web sites, so visit those sites for details. The directions for many database interfaces assume that you have the database and its API library already installed, so you should do that part first.

Most tools for microcomputer operating systems (such as Windows and the Macintosh System software) are distributed as executable binaries, rather than source code, so installation typically is somewhat simpler than for UNIX.

---

## WDB

On the CD

WDB is a freeware package, written entirely in Perl, that greatly simplifies the task of building a Web front end to a relational database under UNIX. (Source code and installation directions for WDB, in UNIX `tar` format, are included on the CD-ROM that comes with this book.) Because all the database-specific aspects of WDB are confined to one module of the program, and because the entire package is written in Perl, porting WDB to various databases has proved to be relatively easy. WDB has been successfully ported to several database servers and to many versions of UNIX, including Linux. If you're UNIX- and Perl-oriented, WDB should be high on your short list of preferred free solutions, especially because the excellent shareware database mSQL is one of the supported SQL engines.

The heart of WDB is what its author, Bo Frese Rasmussen, calls a *form definition file* (FDF). For each searching form, you write a description in a relatively high-level form definition language to list the tables and fields to be used for this form, the search constraints, how you want the output to be formatted, and so on. WDB comes with a utility that generates an FDF template from a database table or view by querying the metadata provided; you then edit its output. Although the program can't do your thinking for you, many details that otherwise would require tedious hand-hacking are filled in by the FDF-making utility.

Given an FDF, WDB generates an HTML search form on the fly. As with the program-generated FDFs, you may want to edit the output. When the user submits a completed search form, WDB generates the SQL query; performs the search; and returns a list of matching records, each item of which has a hot link to the full screen view of that record.

The upshot is that WDB does much of the donkey work (especially for ad hoc searches) for you. WDB's feature set is somewhat limited, but if you know Perl, you probably can modify it to your heart's content; the code is well structured and well commented. You can handle simpler customizations by adding snippets of Perl code to the FDF, because several "hooks" enable you to call your own code at various stages in the query process.

A particularly nice feature is the capability to define input- and output-conversion functions that apply to specified fields. WDB automatically invokes these functions at the correct time in its query-generation and formatting cycle. WDB also has several features that help you generate URLs from database lookups, which can perform other lookups of related data when they are clicked. Clever use of this elegant feature of WDB can effectively turn your relational database into a gigantic hypertext document.

**ON THE WEB**

You can find information about WDB, installation instructions, and the downloadable source code at **http://venus.dtv.dk/~bfr/**.

# Web/Genera

Web/Genera (by Stanley Letovsky, Mary B. Berlyn, and others) is another public-domain software tool set that simplifies the integration of Sybase databases into the Web. You can use the tool to retrofit a Web front end to an existing Sybase database or to create a new database. Like WDB, Web/Genera requires you to use a high-level schema notation to write a specification of the Sybase database (and of the desired appearance of its contents on the Web). The Web/Genera programs process this description to generate SQL commands and formatting instructions that together extract objects from a database and format them in HTML.

Web/Genera also supports form-based relational querying and whole-database formatting into text and HTML formats. The notation of Web/Genera seems to be richer than that of WDB, because the former includes notions (such as set and group) for field values, enabling you to build pick lists on the fly. Unlike WDB, however, Web/Genera doesn't provide hooks that allow users to write customized extensions. To make any extensions to Web/Genera, a user must change its source code, which is written mainly in C and Perl.

**ON THE WEB**

You can find information about Web/Genera, installation instructions, and the downloadable source code at **http://gdbdoc.gdb.org/letovsky/genera/genera.html**.

## MiniSQL (mSQL) and W3-mSQL

mSQL is a shareware SQL engine (free to academic users) that has been ported to most versions of UNIX. In combination with WDB, mSQL provides an excellent, low-cost way to build a simple relational database with a Web front end. An excellent Perl interface for mSQL is available, and the combination of WDB with mSQL is known to work well under Linux.

mSQL's author, David Hughes, has also written a new program called W3-mSQL, which was in alpha at the time when this chapter was written. Although both mSQL and W3-mSQL are included on the CD-ROM that comes with this book, I haven't yet tried W3-mSQL, so I don't know how well it works. According to Hughes, W3-mSQL works via HTML documents with embedded tags that perform database lookups, so you don't need to write any CGI scripts to use it.

mSQL supports only a relatively small subset of SQL, but what it does support is in strict conformance to ANSI standards. According to the mSQL WWW site, David Hughes is working on a major upgrade of mSQL that will support a much larger set of features, but he doesn't yet know when this upgrade will be released.

**ON THE WEB**

You can find information about mSQL and W3-mSQL, installation instructions, and the downloadable source code at **http://Hughes.com.au/**.

## DBI

The long-term future of Perl-database interfaces in many applications, including Web interfaces, may well lie with the new DBI project. The long-term goal of this project is to create a generic Perl interface with versions for every SQL database, in the hope of providing greater portability for Perl database applications. DBI also takes advantage of the Perl 5.0 object-oriented extensions.

**ON THE WEB**

You can find information about the evolving DBI standard at **http://www.hermetica.com/technologia/DBI/index.html**.

Part
IV

Ch
12

---

**Why I Chose the WDB Library Instead of This One**

The DBI (uppercase) interface defined by this project isn't the same as the dbi (lowercase) interface used in WDB. I used the WDB version in my examples for three reasons:

- The WDB interface is simpler.

- The DBI version for mSQL was released recently; all my existing code for both Sybase and mSQL uses the WDB interface.

- At the time when this chapter was written, the new DBI standard was something of a moving target. DBI's authors recently performed a complete rewrite based on ODBC standards.

---

# ODBC Tools

In the Windows/Windows NT environment, ODBC has long been one of the most popular ways to access databases from other programs. As a result, most popular Windows databases, and most programming languages targeted for the Windows environment, have ODBC drivers included or available. If you come from a UNIX-oriented background, you may want to use one of the ODBC drivers for NTPerl, which you can find in various places on the Net. If you come from a Windows background, you'll probably be happier using Visual Basic or Visual C with any of the numerous ODBC drivers that are available for those languages.

**N O T E** If you use ODBC under Windows or Windows NT for your database CGI programs, you have a choice of query languages: the SQL interface to ODBC, or such ODBC-specific features as dynasets. On one hand, dynasets can improve performance significantly, because the SQL parsers in many ODBC drivers are rather slow; and dynasets can be easier to code than SQL for simple lookups. On the other hand, the use of SQL is more portable to non-ODBC environments. ■

**ON THE WEB**

You can find information about ODBC access from Perl under NT at the following URLs:

**http://info.hip.com/ntperl/PerlFaq.htm**

**http://www.bhs.com/**

**ftp://ftp.digex.net/pub/access/psii/public_html/home.html**

# Some Useful Hotlists

Many sites on the Web have pointers to various Web/database tools and projects. The following URLs are the most comprehensive listings of Web/database resources that I have found in an extensive search for such information:

**ON THE WEB**

**http://cscsun1.larc.nasa.gov/~beowulf/db/**[em]is the most comprehensive list of Web/database resources that I have found. The hotlist includes freeware, shareware, and commercial products, as well as a wealth of Perl-database tutorial materials.

**http://cuiwww.unige.ch/~scg/FreeDB/FreeDB.list.html**   is an extensive list of free or low-cost database tools, not all of which are specifically Web-oriented.

# Problem-Solving

Because a Web/database gateway involves multiple programs, possibly running on multiple machines, various things can go wrong. Your application may not work at all, or it may run far too slowly. For database-specific debugging and performance tuning, consult the documentation for your database package. The following  sections provide a few general hints on debugging and tuning a Web/database gateway—hints that should apply to any platform.

> **N O T E**   Bear in mind that no amount of after-the-fact tweaking can replace careful planning at the outset of your project. ■

## Debugging

Debugging a Web/database gateway isn't simple, because problems can occur at multiple levels. I suggest that the first version of any database CGI script not try to access the database, but instead display the generated SQL code in a document that begins with the header `Content-type: text/plain`, followed by a blank line. When you think that the generated SQL looks correct, pipe it through the command-line interface of your database. After this step confirms that you can generate correct SQL, the next step is to write your own client program to send the SQL to the server and execute it from the command line.

If you can't get your CGI script to generate any SQL, try sending your form input to a CGI script that does nothing more than list all the information that it got from the Web server. Given that list, add hard-coded assignment statements to your code, so that you can run it from the command line and watch how it behaves in a simulated CGI environment. Only then should you try to combine the CGI and database interfaces in one program and run that program as a CGI script.

If that procedure doesn't work, look at the error log of your server for any messages that your program may have sent to standard error. If that log tells you little or nothing, you need to think about the differences between a command-line environment and the CGI environment. Are you assuming something about the PATH environment variable, which has far fewer directories in a CGI context? Do you need other environment variables for database work? Most Sybase installations, for example, define an environment variable (DSQUERY) that tells Sybase clients which server to use if none is specified. In the CGI environment, this variable isn't defined, so your script will fail unless you specify the server in your script.

If you have installed cgiwrap (mentioned in "Security Issues" earlier in this chapter), it includes a very handy debugging flag; see the documentation that comes with the cgiwrap distribution. This feature can be a tremendous time saver, and it alone can repay the modest effort of installing cgiwrap.

Finally, remember that CGI scripts usually run at a lower-privilege user ID than regular programs do. If your database server uses OS-level user IDs for authentication, you may have client programs that work from the command line but not as CGI scripts.

The general strategy is to divide and conquer, so that you can isolate the problem to a particular part of your system. Start simply, and build up to the full functionality that you want one step at a time.

# Tuning Performance

From the hardware perspective, database and HTTP servers tend to be I/O-bound, not CPU-intensive, which means that the performance of your Web/database application depends mainly on disk access and process-launching overhead. A fast hard drive and ample memory are more important than a fast processor. A badly designed Web/database application, however, can bring even the most powerful server platform to its knees.

Remember that your application is a client/client/server application in which your CGI script connects as a client to the database engine, sending SQL to the engine and accepting data returned from the engine. Considerable overhead is associated with setting up and tearing down the connection between the CGI script and the database server. Even a well-designed CGI application has to incur this overhead every time a request comes to the HTTP server; from the viewpoint of the remote user, a single session involves multiple database logons. This situation is unavoidable, but a badly designed CGI program can make matters worse if it opens and closes multiple connections to the database engine in a single HTTP request.

Even if you avoid opening an excessive number of connections to the database server, you can still hurt performance by sending too much data back and forth between the CGI script and the database server. It's a nearly universal rule in client/server database programming to do as much work as possible inside the database server, to minimize the overhead associated with transferring data between the database client and the database server. In CGI work, in which you're already incurring some extra overhead because each HTTP request requires a new connection to the database, this principle applies with particular force.

For server efficiency, observe the following rules:

■ Do as much work as possible per connection to the database server.
■ Do as much work as possible per SQL statement.
■ Filter the results inside the database server as much as possible.

These rules apply *especially* if your database engine and your HTTP server reside on different machines, because all data transfer between your CGI program and the database server incurs network overhead, as well as the overhead inherent in any connection to the database server.

Recently, a colleague asked me for help with a CGI interface to an Illustra database that was taking more than three minutes to respond to some queries. By applying these principles and taking advantage of Illustra's unusually powerful version of SQL, he could get the response time to less than 10 seconds. Most database servers can perform only internal manipulation of fixed-size data types; large text fields can be copied in or out but must be manipulated outside the database program. Illustra's string-manipulation commands can be applied to any amount of text. We used this feature of Illustra to build complex SQL queries that would perform extensive string manipulation inside Illustra and return the results. Most Web queries can now be handled by one or two monster SQL statements instead of by many small SQL statements.

# The Future of Web/Database Interfaces

This chapter presented the fundamentals of building a Web gateway to a relational database engine, explaining the unique capabilities that this combination makes possible and pointing out some of the limitations inherent in doing this kind of thing over the Web.

As you've seen, current Web technology has some serious limitations for database work: no client-side validation, no facility for extending the user interface toolkit provided by HTML, and no mechanism for the graceful handling of concurrent updates. Equally serious for multimedia database work—something for which the Web, by its nature, seems to be so well-suited—are the limitations of conventional database technology, which supports a limited set of data types. All other types of data must be stored as text or binary fields that can't be manipulated within the database itself.

On the other hand, object-oriented databases are extensible, but they lack the data integrity and flexible querying features of relational databases. The new object-relational paradigm exemplified by Illustra has enormous promise, because it addresses the limitations of both relational and object-oriented databases. On the one hand, like most relational databases but unlike most object-oriented databases, Illustra has a full SQL implementation and facilities for defining database integrity constraints. On the other hand, unlike standard relational databases, Illustra provides the capability to define new data types and associated operations. And the recent merger of Illustra with Informix means that the object-relational technology of Illustra should have a very bright future indeed—joining the powerful new technology of Illustra with the industrial-strength server technology for which Informix is known.

Object-oriented database technology—and especially object-relational database technology—may also be an excellent server-side counterpart to such client-side extensions as Java and JavaScript. For database work, client-side scripting promises three major advantages:

- An active form written in a client-side scripting language can provide field-level validation of entered data.
- Because Java applets can talk to the network, an active form that's used to edit an existing record could log on to the server and maintain an active connection, thereby averting the problems caused by the stateless nature of the Web.

Part
IV

Ch
12

■ Client-side scripting promises to make Web browsers extensible. Just as you can define a new type of data in a object-oriented database, you can define a new type of data object for use on the Web and write active forms to display it. This method averts the difficulties of the current helper-application approach. With a conventional Web browser, each new type needs a new helper application. Versions of this helper application must be written for every platform that your users have, and you must help users obtain and install your helper application. With a platform-independent language for creating scripts that a browser automatically—and transparently—downloads and executes, creating and using new data types should be much easier.

In my view, these two new technologies have the potential to revolutionize the Web—after the bugs are worked out and robust implementations are made available for every common platform. And I don't say this because of all the media hype about Java; I say it because I'm all too familiar with the limitations of the current Web and database technologies and with the various kludges that developers use to circumvent them. Some real substance exists behind the media excitement; in the fullness of time, we'll all find out whether the implementations of these new ideas live up to their promise. Database-specific Java and JavaScript tools are beginning to appear, but they have yet to be integrated with the database-oriented CGI tools discussed in this chapter. So if you combine client-side scripting with CGI/DBMS programming right now, you truly are on the bleeding edge.

This work was supported in part by the Human Brain Project (NIMH, NASA, and NIDCD) grant R01 DC02307 and by NIH Grant G08LM05583 from the National Library of Medicine's IAIMS Program. The section on Web/GENERA was written by Kei Cheung, one of the authors of that program.

# From Here...

In a single chapter, I have only scratched the surface of what you can do with a relational database engine and some CGI scripts. A whole world of possibilities awaits you; the field is exploding at a truly amazing pace. Above all, remember that the Internet itself is your single most useful resource. I've tried to get you started by listing URLs to every tool that I mention in this chapter, but new things appear every day.

The rest of this book is full of information that you will need as you build your WWW/database application. You especially may want to read the following chapters:

■ Chapter 3, "Advanced Form Processing and Data Storage." This chapter really is about one specific aspect of what Chapter 3 discusses in more general terms.

■ Chapter 7, "Dynamic and Interactive HTML Content in Perl and CGI." The section on using persistent cookies mentions a technique that can be very useful in database work.

■ Chapter 9, "Understanding CGI Security." The CGI security issues discussed in this chapter are especially important if you are hooking a production database to your WWW site.

■ Chapter 11, "Database Interaction." Whether or not you will be working with Oracle, you should at least take a quick look at the Oracle example in this chapter.

# Reference

# Special Variables

*by Mícheál Ó Foghlú*

This chapter looks in detail at the special variables used in Perl. Understanding these variables is crucial to programming effectively in Perl. Some of the variables are essential for nearly all Perl programs. Other variables are merely useful shortcuts that eliminate the need to run external programs that extract information from the system.

Each variable might have three possible names:

- Long name (or English name)
- Intermediate name
- Short name

Most existing Perl programs use only the short name form. This fact is unfortunate, because the short name usually is a cryptic symbol. The use of these symbols in Perl programs may be daunting at first, especially in complex expressions that comprise multiple variables. With the aid of this chapter, however, you soon will be able to identify their meanings, and thus understand the programs.

**Understanding special variables**

Detailed descriptions of the special variables in Perl, ordered alphabetically by their full English names.

**Using special variables**

Examples of the use of each variable.

The long name was introduced in Perl 5. This chapter lists all the special variables of this English name in alphabetical order. In Perl 4, you must use the short name. In Perl 5, you can use any of the name forms, but if you want to use the long English name, you must include the following command:

```
Use English;
```

This command enables the long names in the Perl 5 program.

This chapter categorizes special variables in several ways to make it easier for you to use the list as a reference source. The most important of these categories is Scope, which can have the following values:

- *always global*. These variables are global but have an unambiguous context (they need not be made local in a subroutine).
- *localize*. These variables are global and may need to be made local in subroutines if the value is being changed (especially to prevent unplanned subroutine side effects).
- *local*. These variables are always local and do not need to be made local explicitly.

**N O T E** You should pay special attention to variables that can be localized. A well-known principle of programming is that any subroutine or function should not produce unexpected side effects. A subroutine to print a line on a printer, for example, should not alter the $; ($SUBSCRIPT_SEPARATOR) variable for the rest of the program. If, for some reason, the subroutine does need to change the value, it should do so merely locally within the subroutine itself by localizing the variable. If global changes are required in the global variables, they should be made very explicit so that anyone who reads the program can see clearly what is going on. ■

The other important special-variable category used in this chapter is File Handle Call. Special variables that implicitly refer to the current active file handle can be explicitly bound to any existing file handle. This facility must be activated by the following call:

```
use FileHandle;
```

This call enables calls of these forms:

```
FILEHANDLE->method(EXPR)
method FILEHANDLE EXPR
```

The relevant method name usually is the full long name of the special variable. The optional EXPR is an expression for changing the current value of the file handle, as well as referring to another file handle for purposes of the special-variable reference. This syntax might be confusing at first, but when used consistently, it can make Perl programs with formatting much more readable.

Both the English long names and the use of file handles in references to formats are new features in Perl 5. If you are using Perl 4, you must use the short names and allow format operations to take place in relation to the current active file handle (which you can change by using the select() function). ■

# $<I<digit>>

| | |
|---|---|
| **Short Name:** | $1, $2, ... $<N> |
| **Scope:** | local *(read-only)* |

These variables are used to refer back to pattern matches. In any pattern to be matched, sets of parentheses are used to mark subpatterns. These subpatterns are numbered from left to right. After a match has been made, each subpattern match is referenced by these variables, up to and including the number of subpatterns that are actually specified. $1 is the first subpattern; $2 is the second; and so on, up to and including $<N>, the Nth subpattern specified.

Example:

```
$_ = "AlphaBetaGamma";
/^(Alpha)(.*)(Gamma)$/;
print "$1 then $2 then $3\n";
```

 **TIP** If you have alternative patterns and do not know which one may have matched, try using $LAST_PAREN_MATCH instead.

# $[

| | |
|---|---|
| **Short Name:** | $[ |
| **Scope:** | localize |

This variable, which is usually set to a value of zero, represents the index of the first element in any array. Programmers who are used to using 1 as the index of the first element of an array could change the value of this variable to suit their preference.

Example:

```
$[ = 1;
$_ = "AlphaBetaGamma";
$tmp = index($_,"Beta");
print "Beta located at: $tmp\n";
$[ = 0;
$_ = "AlphaBetaGamma";
$tmp = index($_,"Beta");
print "Beta located at: $tmp\n";
```

# $ACCUMULATOR

| | |
|---|---|
| **Short Name:** | $^A |
| **Scope:** | always global |

This variable allows direct access to the line of output built up with the Perl formatting commands. Normally, this access is not necessary, but it is possible.

Example:

```
$tmp = formline<<'FINISH', Alpha, Beta, Gamma;
@<<<<<<<<<   @|||||||||||||  @<<<<<<<<<
FINISH
print "Accumulator now contains:\n $^A\n";
$^A = "";
```

This variable is not available in Perl 4.

# $ARG

**Short Name:**              $_
**Scope:**                   localize

This variable is the default pattern space. When reading a file, $ARG usually takes on the value of each line in turn. You can assign a value to $ARG directly. Many functions and operators take this variable as the default upon which to operate, so you can make the code more concise by using $ARG.

Example:

```
$_ = "\$\_ is the default for many operations including print().\n";
print;
```

# $ARGV

**Short Name:**              $ARGV
**Scope:**                   always global

When processing an input file, this variable provides access to the name of this file.

Example:

```
print("Assuming this script has been called with an argument as an i/p file:_
  while (<>){
      print "$ARGV\n";
      };
```

# $BASETIME

**Short Name:**              $^T
**Scope:**                   localize

This variable is the time when the Perl program was started, as measured in the basic time units (seconds since the start of 1970).

Example:

```
$nicetime = localtime($^T);
print "This program started at $^T (i.e. $nicetime).\n";
```

# *$CHILD_ERROR*

**Short Name:**           $?
**Scope:**                localize

If a Perl script spawns child processes, you can examine their error codes by using this variable.

Example:

```
'ls -lgd /vir';
print "Child Process error was: $?\n";
```

See the section on the $OS_ERROR variable for system error messages.

# *$DEBUGGING*

**Short Name:**           $^D
**Scope:**                localize

Perl can be run in debugging mode. This variable allows the value of this flag to be accessed and altered.

Example:

```
print "The debug flags are: $^D\n";
```

# *$EFFECTIVE_GROUP_ID*

**Short Name:**           $)
**Intermediate Name:**    $EGID
**Scope:**                localize

In systems that support users and groups, as well as setting new users and groups within a process, Perl can access both the original and the effective user and group information. The effective group variable provides access to a list of numbers that represents the effective group identifiers (*GIDs*).

Example:

```
print("Effective Group ID is a list of GIDs: $)\n");
```

Part

V

Ch

13

# *$EFFECTIVE_USER_ID*

**Short Name:**           $>
**Intermediate Name:**    $EUID
**Scope:**                localize

In systems that support users and groups, as well as setting new users and groups within a process, Perl can access both the original and the effective user and group information. The effective user variable provides access to a single number that represents the effective user identifier (*UID*).

Example:

```
print("Effective User ID is one UID: $>\n");
```

# $EVAL_ERROR

**Short Name:**      $@
**Scope:**              localize

Perl allows explicit calls to the eval() function to evaluate Perl syntax with a Perl script. This variable allows access to the returned error after such an operation. The error is a string that contains the relevant error message.

Example:

```
print "Passing eval a malformed Perl expression:\n";
eval 'print "Hello';
print "Error: $@\n";
```

# $EXECUTABLE_NAME

**Short Name:**      $^X
**Scope:**              localize

This variable provides access to the name of the Perl executable used by the script.

Example:

```
print "Executable name of Perl is: $^X\n";
```

# $FORMAT_FORMFEED

**Short Name:**          $^L
**Scope:**                  global to a global file handle
**File Handle Call:**    format_formfeed FILEHANDLE EXPR

When you use the Perl formatting commands, you can specify formats to manipulate centering and other formatting of the text. One additional option is to specify the exact code to be inserted between pages of output in the file. The default value is a form-feed character (\f), but this value can be changed.

Example:

```
if ($^L = '\f')
{
  print "The formfeed character is the default break between pages.\n";
}
```

The $^L variable is not available in Perl 4.

# $FORMAT_LINES_LEFT

**Short Name:**        $-
**Scope:**        local
**File Handle Call:**    format_lines_left FILEHANDLE EXPR

When you use the Perl formatting commands, this counter (which exists for each file handle with an associated format) is decremented every time a line is output until it reaches zero, when a new page is generated. You can manually set this variable to zero to force a page break in the output.

Example:

```
format EG_FORMAT =
@<<<<<<<<<<  @|||||||||||| @>>>>>>>>> ^|||||||||||
$one,        $two,        $three     $fitme
.
open(EG_FORMAT,">-");
select(EG_FORMAT);
$one = 'Left';
$two = 'Center';
$three = 'Right';
$fitme= "";
write;
$one = $-;
$two = $-;
$three = $-;
write;
$one = $-;
$two = $-;
$three = $-;
write;
select(STDOUT);
```

# $FORMAT_LINES_PER_PAGE

**Short Name:**        $=
**Scope:**        local
**File Handle Call:**    format_lines_per_page FILEHANDLE EXPR

Each format file handle has an associated number of lines per page, which you can access and change by using this variable.

Example:

```
select(EG_FORMAT);
$one = 'Left';
$two = 'Center';
$three = 'Right';
$fitme= "";
write;
$one = $=;
$two = $=;
$three = $=;
write;
select(STDOUT);
```

Part
**V**

Ch
**13**

# $FORMAT_LINE_BREAK_CHARACTERS

| | |
|---|---|
| **Short Name:** | $: |
| **Scope:** | localize |
| **File Handle Call:** | format_line_break_characters FILEHANDLE EXPR |

When you are outputting a value to a formatted area by using the format code

```
^|||||||||||||||
 |||||||||||||||
```

(or the other multiple-line formats), the line-break character determines how strings are split into lines to fit into the formatted space. By default, the legal break characters are space, hyphen, and new line.

Example:

```
select(EG_FORMAT);
$: = ' \n-';
$one = 1;
$two = 2;
$three = 3;
$fitme= "One-One-One-One-One-One";
write;
write;
write;
select(STDOUT);
```

# $FORMAT_NAME

| | |
|---|---|
| **Short Name:** | $~ |
| **Scope:** | local |
| **File Handle Call:** | format_name FILEHANDLE EXPR |

Each format has a name, which may also be the name of the file handle. You can access the name directly through this variable.

Example:

```
select(EG_FORMAT);
$one = $~;
$two = $~;
$three = $~;
write;
select(STDOUT);
```

# $FORMAT_PAGE_NUMBER

| | |
|---|---|
| **Short Name:** | $% |
| **Scope:** | always global |
| **File Handle Call:** | format_page_number FILEHANDLE EXPR |

Because each format can produce multiple pages of output, this counter simply counts them.

Example:

```
select(EG_FORMAT);
$one = $%;
$two = $%;
$three = $%;
write;
select(STDOUT);
```

# $FORMAT_TOP_NAME

**Short Name:**       $^
**Scope:**            always global
**File Handle Call:** format_top_name FILEHANDLE EXPR

Each format can have an associated format that is reproduced every time a new page is generated. (No equivalent automatic page footer exists.) By default, these are given the same name as the base format with a _TOP suffix, although any name can be set.

Example:

```
format EG_TOP =
           [Sample Page Header]
To the left  In the center To the right
-----------  ------------- ------------
.
open(EG_FORMAT,">-");
select(EG_FORMAT);
$- = 0;
$^ = EG_TOP;
$one = '111';
$two = '222';
$three = '333';
$fitme= "";
write;
write;
write;
select(STDOUT);
```

# $INPLACE_EDIT

**Short Name:**   $^I
**Scope:**        localize

Perl often is used to edit files and sometimes, the input file is also the output file (the result replaces the original). In this case, you can specify (with command-line options) the suffix to be used for the temporary file created while the edits are in progress. You can set or simply access this value from within the script itself by using this variable.

Example:

```
$^I=bak;
print "Tmp file extension when editing in place... $^I\n";
```

# $INPUT_LINE_NUMBER

```
Short Name:            $.
Intermediate Name:     $NR
Scope:                 localize (read-only)
File Handle Call:      input_line_number FILEHANDLE EXPR
```

This variable counts the number of lines of input from a file and is reset when the file is closed. The variable counts lines cumulatively across all input files read with the <> construct (because these are not closed explicitly).

Example:

```
print "The last file read had $. lines\n";
```

# $INPUT_RECORD_SEPARATOR

```
Short Name:            $/
Intermediate Name:     $RS
Scope:                 localize
File Handle Call:      input_record_separator FILEHANDLE EXPR
```

By default, an input file is split into records, each of which comprises one line. The input-record separator is a new-line character. This variable can be set to have no value (in which case entire input files are read in at the same time) or to have other values, as required.

Example:

```
undef $/;
 open(INFILE,"infile.tst");
 $buffer = <INFILE>;
 print "$buffer\n";
```

# $LAST_PAREN_MATCH

```
Short Name:            $+
Scope:                 local
```

This variable returns the value of the last pattern marked with parentheses. In most contexts, you could simply use $1, $2, and so on rather than $+. When the pattern has a series of sets of parentheses as alternatives to be matched, using $+ is useful.

Example:

```
$_ = "AlphaBetaDeltaGamma";
/Alpha(.*)Delta(.*)/;
print "The last match was $+\n";
```

# $LIST_SEPARATOR

**Short Name:**           $"
**Scope:**                localize

When arrays are converted to strings, the elements are separated by spaces by default (which is what happens when arrays are printed, for example). This variable allows you to specify any string as the list separator, which may be useful for output formatting or for other reasons.

Example:

```
$" = ' ! ';
@thisarray = (Alpha, Beta, Gamma);
print "@thisarray.\n";
$" = ' ';
```

# $MATCH

**Short Name:**           $&
**Scope:**                local *(read-only)*

This variable references the entire pattern that matched the most recent pattern-matching operation.

Example:

```
$_ = "AlphaBetaGamma";
/B[aet]*/;
print "Matched: $&\n";
```

# $MULTILINE_MATCHING

**Short Name:**           $*
**Scope:**                localize

By default, Perl optimizes pattern matching on the assumption that each pattern does not contain embedded new lines—that is, it is optimized for single-line matching. If you are using a pattern that has embedded new lines, you should set this variable to a value of 1 so that this optimization is disabled and the correct result is obtained.

Example:

```
print("\nTest 26 Perl Version ($])\n");
$_ = "Alpha\nBeta\nGamma\n";
$* = 0; # Assume string comprises a single line
/^.*$/;
print "a) Assuming single line: $& (which is wrong - the assumption was
wrong).\n";
$* = 1; # Do not assume string comprises a single line
/^.*$/;
print "a) Not assuming single line: $& (which is correct).\n";
$* = 0;
```

Part
**V**

Ch

**13**

# $OFMT

**Short Name:**          $#
**Scope:**               localize

This variable mimics the UNIX awk utility variable of the same name, which permits numeric formatting. The default value is:

```
%.2g
```

See the UNIX awk documentation for information about the possible values.

Example:

```
$# = "%.6g";
print 5467.4567, "\n";
$# = "%.8g";
print 5467.4567, "\n";
```

 **TIP**   Use of the $OFMT variable is discouraged. You can format values by using the print() function directly.

# $OS_ERROR

**Short Name:**          $!
**Intermediate Name:**   $ERRNO
**Scope:**               localize

If an operating-system-error condition exists, this variable is set to the error number (and, if it is evaluated in a string context, to the equivalent error message). You can manually set the error number and then access the relevant error message in a string context.

Example:

```
ls -lgd /vir';
print "OS Error was $!\n";
```

See the section on the $CHILD_ERROR variable for subprocess errors, which are not necessarily system errors.

# $OUTPUT_AUTOFLUSH

**Short Name:**          $|
**Scope:**               always global
**File Handle Call:**    autoflush FILEHANDLE EXPR

If this Boolean variable (which is associated with a file handle) has a nonzero value, that file is autoflushed (the output is written after each print or write operation) rather than being buffered.

 **TIP**   When the output file is a pipe, it is best to set autoflush on so that other programs can access the pipe immediately after each write or print operation.

Example:

```
select(STDERR);
$¦ = 1;
select(STDOUT);
print "Autoflush setting for STDOUT is $¦\n";
```

# $OUTPUT_FIELD_SEPARATOR

| | |
|---|---|
| **Short Name:** | $, |
| **Intermediate Name:** | $OFS |
| **Scope:** | localize |
| **File Handle Call:** | output_field_separator FILEHANDLE EXPR |

This variable can alter the behavior of the print() function. The default behavior of print(), when it is given a comma-separated list of arguments, is to print each argument with no output separator. You can use this variable to specify any string as a separator.

Example:

```
$, = "=";
print STDOUT a, b, c, "\n";
$, = "";
```

# $OUTPUT_RECORD_SEPARATOR

| | |
|---|---|
| **Short Name:** | $\ |
| **Intermediate Name:** | $ORS |
| **Scope:** | localize |
| **File Handle Call:** | output_record_separator FILEHANDLE EXPR |

This variable can alter the behavior of the print() function. The default behavior of print(), when it is given a comma-separated list of arguments, is to print each argument. If a new line is required at the end, you must add it explicitly. You can use this record-separator variable to specify any string as the end-of-record string, and you most commonly would set it to the new-line character to avert the need for explicit new lines.

Example:

```
$\ = "\n";
print "No need for an explicit newline now.";
$\ = "";
```

# $PERLDB

| | |
|---|---|
| **Short Name:** | $^P |
| **Scope:** | localize |

This flag represents the debug level of the Perl script. Normally, $PERLDB is used internally by the debugger to disable debugging of the debugger script itself.

Example:

```
print "Value of internal Boolean debug flag: $^P\n";
```

# $PERL_VERSION

**Short Name:**      $]
**Scope:**           localize

This variable represents the version string that identifies the Perl version that is being run. You can assign a value to the variable, if necessary. In a numeric context, the variable evaluates to a number made up of the version plus the (patch level/1000).

Example:

```
$ver = $]+0;
print "So every test has tested the version $] (numeric $ver).\n";
```

# $POSTMATCH

**Short Name:**      $'
**Scope:**           local *(read-only)*

When a string is matched by pattern, the pattern is actually split into three parts: the part of the string before the match, the part of the string that matched, and the part of the string after the match. Any of these parts could be empty, of course. This variable refers to the part of the string after the match.

Example:

```
$_ = "AlphaBetaGamma";
/Beta/;
print "Postmatch = $'\n";
```

# $PREMATCH

**Short Name:**      $'
**Scope:**           local *(read-only)*

When a string is matched by pattern, the pattern is actually split into three parts: the part of the string before the match, the part of the string that matched, and the part of the string after the match. Any of these parts could be empty, of course. This variable refers to the part of the string before the match.

Example:

```
$_ = "AlphaBetaGamma";
/Beta/;
print "Prematch = $`\n";
```

# $PROCESS_ID

Short Name:            $$
Intermediate Name:     $PID
Scope:                 localize

In systems that support multiple processes, Perl can identify the process number of the Perl script process itself via this variable.

Example:

```
print "The process ID (PID) is: $$\n";
```

# $PROGRAM_NAME

Short Name:            $0
Scope:                 localize

This variable contains the name of the Perl script that is being executed. You can alter this variable if you want the script to identify itself to the operating system as having a particular name.

Example:

```
print "The program name is: $0\n";
```

# $REAL_GROUP_ID

Short Name:            $(
Intermediate Name:     $GID
Scope:                 localize

In systems that support users and groups, as well as setting new users and groups within a process, Perl can access both the original and the effective user and group information. The real group variable provides access to a list of numbers that represents the real group identifiers (GIDs). Effective group identifiers may be set using flags in the script or explicit calls to functions. This will not alter the real GIDs.

Example:

```
print("The Real Group ID is a list of GIDs: $(\n");
```

Part

V

Ch

13

# $REAL_USER_ID

Short Name:            $<
Intermediate Name:     $UID
Scope:                 localize

In systems that support users and groups, as well as setting new users and groups within a process, Perl can access both the original and the effective user and group information. The real user variable provides access to a list of numbers that represents the real user identifiers

(UID). Effective user ID may be set by flags on the script or explicit calls to functions. This does not alter the real user ID.

Example:

```
print("The Real User ID is a list of UID: $<\n");
```

# $SUBSCRIPT_SEPARATOR

| | |
|---|---|
| **Short Name:** | `$;` |
| **Intermediate Name:** | `$SUBSEP` |
| **Scope:** | `localize` |

This variable is used in emulating multidimensional arrays. The value must be one that is not used by any element in the array. The default value is \034.

Perl 5 supports multidimensional arrays directly, so the use of `$SUBSCRIPT_SEPARATOR` (`$;`) should not be necessary.

# $SYSTEM_FD_MAX

| | |
|---|---|
| **Short Name:** | `$^F` |
| **Scope:** | `localize` |

By default, Perl treats three files as system files 0, 1, and 2—normally, STDIN, STDOUT, and STDERR. The value of `$^F` is 2 by default. System files are treated specially; in particular, the file descriptors are passed to exec() processes.

Example:

```
print "The default maximum file descriptors is $^F\n";
```

# $WARNING

| | |
|---|---|
| **Short Name:** | `$^W` |
| **Scope:** | `localize` |

This variable is a Boolean warning flag that you normally set to true by using the command-line -w switch, although you can set it within the script, if necessary. When this variable is on, the Perl program reports more verbose warnings.

Example:

```
print "Boolean warning flag is set to: $^W\n";
```

# %ENV<variable_name>,<variable_value>

| | |
|---|---|
| **Short Name:** | `%ENV{<variable_name>,<variable_value>}` |
| **Scope:** | `always global` |

This variable is an associative array that links the names of the environment variables to their values. This variable makes it easy to look up a value with the appropriate name.

Example:

```
$tmp = $ENV{SHELL};
 print "The current SHELL is set to $tmp\n";
```

# %INC<file-name>,<file-load-status>

**Short Name:**     %INC{<file-name>,<file-load-status>}
**Scope:**          always global

This variable is an associate array that links the names of the required files to a status (whether they were successfully loaded). Normally, the Perl script itself uses this array to determine whether files have already been loaded so as to minimize the number of file loads that are carried out.

Example:

```
require 'another.pl';
 $tmp = $INC{'another.pl'};
 print "The required file did exist: $tmp\n";
```

# %SIG<signal-name>,<signal-value>

**Short Name:**     %SIG{<signal-name>,<signal-value>}
**Scope:**          always global

This variable is an associative array that links the standard signals to values. These values dictate the way that the script processes those signals. You can assign signal-handling subroutines to certain signals or set the script to ignore certain signals.

Example:

```
$SIG{'HUP'} = 'IGNORE';
print "This process now ignores hangup signals.\n";
```

# @ARGV

**Short Name:**     @ARGV
**Scope:**          always global

This variable is an array of the arguments passed to the script. Unlike the situation in the C language, the first element of this array is the first argument (not the program name). As the arguments are processed, the value of this variable can alter.

Example:

```
$Example46String = "There were $#ARGV arguments, first argument was @ARGV[0]\n";
print $Example46String;
```

# @INC

| | |
|---|---|
| **Short Name:** | @INC |
| **Scope:** | always global |

This variable is an array of the directories to search for included files. These directories are normally specified either on the command line of the Perl invocation or in an environment variable.

Example:

```
print "The possible include script directories are: @INC\n";
```

# From Here...

This chapter lists only Perl special variables; you should consult other reference chapters for Perl functions and Perl operators. (You may easily confuse some variables with some operators, so check the list of operators if the symbol that you require is not covered in this chapter.)

For details on the other elements in the Perl reference, see the following chapters:

- Chapter 14, "Operators," provides detailed descriptions of the Perl operators.
- Chapter 15, "Function List," provides detailed descriptions of the Perl functions.

# Operators

*by Mícheál Ó Foghlú*

**P**erl has a range of operators, many of which are similar to the operators used in C. Also, many Perl functions can be used either as a unary operator or as a function. The difference in the syntax is that the function call has parentheses enclosing the parameters. The difference in semantics is that the function form has a higher precedence. All such operators are listed as functions rather than as operators in this book.

This chapter categorizes each operator in several ways:

- **Name.** Unlike the special variables, no standard agreed long form exists for the name of each operator. You must use the symbolic name itself.

- **Precedence.** Each operator is categorized with a precedence number, the lowest number being the highest precedence. Higher-precedence operations are evaluated before lower-precedence operations.

- **Associativity.** Each operator may be left, right, or nonassociative. This associativity determines the order in which operands are evaluated.

- **Type of operands.** This category indicates whether the operator operates on numeric or string arguments, lists, or files.

- **Number of operands.** Each operator can operate on one (*unary*), two (*binary*), or three (*ternary*) operands.

**Understanding operators**

Detailed descriptions of the operators in Perl, ordered by the symbols used

**Using operators**

Examples of the use of each operator

■ **Context.** Each operator can expect an array or a scalar context. Some operators have separate behaviors for each context.

The following list shows the precedence of the operators:

1. TERMS, LIST operators (leftward)
2. `->`
3. `++ --`
4. `**`
5. `! ~ - (unary) + (unary)`
6. `=~ !~`
7. `* / % x`
8. `+ (binary) - (binary)`
9. `<< >>`
10. NAMED unary operators
11. `< > <= >= lt gt le ge`
12. `== != <=> eq ne cmp`
13. `&`
14. `| ^`
15. `&&`
16. `||`
17. `..`
18. `?:`
19. `= += -= *= /= %= |= &= ^= <<= >>= **= ||= &&=`
20. `, =>`
21. LIST operators (rightward)
22. `not`
23. `and`
24. `or xor`

This chapter contains detailed descriptions of these operators. ■

**!**

| | |
|---|---|
| **Name:** | logical negation |
| **Precedence:** | 5 |
| **Associativity:** | right |
| **Type of operands:** | numeric, string |

| | |
|---|---|
| **Number of operands:** | one (unary) |
| **Context:** | scalar |

The return value of this operation is 1 (true) if the operand has a false value that is defined as 0 in a numeric operand, a null string, or an undefined value. Otherwise, the return value is ' ' (false)—that is, a null string that evaluates to 0 in a numeric context.

Example:

```
$one = !1;
$two = !22;
$three = !0;
$four = !'hello';
$five = !'';
print "1=$one, 2=$two, 3=$three, 4=$four, 5=$five, \n";
```

# !=

| | |
|---|---|
| **Name:** | relational not equal to |
| **Precedence:** | 12 |
| **Associativity:** | nonassociative |
| **Type of operands:** | string |
| **Number of operands:** | two (binary) |
| **Context:** | scalar |

The return value of this operation is 1 (true) if the string operands are not equal. The return value is ' ' (false) if the string operands are equal. Every character in the strings is compared based on the character codes.

Example:

```
$tmp = "aaa ";
$ans = "aaa" != $tmp;
if ($ans)
     { print "true\n"; }
else
     { print "false\n"; }
```

# !~

| | |
|---|---|
| **Name:** | bind pattern (with negation of return value) |
| **Precedence:** | 6 |
| **Associativity:** | left |
| **Type of operands:** | string |
| **Number of operands:** | two (binary) |
| **Context:** | scalar |
| **See also:** | =~ |

Part
**V**

Ch
**14**

This operator binds a pattern-matching operation to a string variable other than $_. If the pattern match is successful, the return value is ' ' (false); if the pattern match is not successful, the return value is 1 (true).

Example:

```
$tmp = "superduper";
if ($tmp !~ s/duper/dooper/)
    {print "Did not do a substitute, tmp still is: $tmp\n";}
else
    {print "Did a substitute, tmp now is: $tmp\n";}
```

# %

| | |
|---|---|
| **Name:** | modulus |
| **Precedence:** | 7 |
| **Associativity:** | left |
| **Type of operands:** | numeric |
| **Number of operands:** | two (binary) |
| **Context:** | scalar |

The operands are converted to integers, if necessary. The left side is divided by the right side, and the integer remainder is returned.

Example:

```
$ans = 48 % 5;
print "48 mod 4 is: $ans\n";
```

# %=

| | |
|---|---|
| **Name:** | modulus assignment |
| **Precedence:** | 18 |
| **Associativity:** | right |
| **Type of operands:** | numeric |
| **Number of operands:** | two (binary) |
| **Context:** | scalar |

This operation, like all the extra assignment operations, is a way to make the evaluation of the arguments more efficient.

Example:

```
$ans = 48;
$ans %= 5;
print "48 mod 4 is: $ans\n";
```

# &

| | |
|---|---|
| **Name:** | bitwise and |
| **Precedence:** | 13 |
| **Associativity:** | left |
| **Type of operands:** | numeric (integer) |
| **Number of operands:** | two (binary) |
| **Context:** | scalar |

This operator performs a bitwise and on the binary representation of the two numeric operands.

Example:

```
$ans = 456 & 111;
print "Bitwise and 456 & 111 is: $ans\n";
```

# &&

| | |
|---|---|
| **Name:** | symbolic logical and |
| **Precedence:** | 15 |
| **Associativity:** | left |
| **Type of operands:** | numeric, string |
| **Number of operands:** | two (binary) |
| **Context:** | scalar |

As in all logical operations, a null string and zero are false. This operator returns 1 (true) if both of the operands are true or null (false) if either operand is false or both operands are false.

Example:

```
$ans = 1 && print("This will print.\n") && 0 && print("This won't print!\n");
if ($ans)
    {print("So it's all true!\n");}
else
    {print("So it's not all true. (expected)\n");}
```

# &&=

| | |
|---|---|
| **Name:** | assignment logical and |
| **Precedence:** | 19 |
| **Associativity:** | right |
| **Type of operands:** | numeric, string |

Part
V

Ch
14

| | |
|---|---|
| **Number of operands:** | two (binary) |
| **Context:** | scalar |

This operator is a combination of the logical and assignment operators. This operator is more efficient when a new value is being reassigned to the same variable, because the reference needs to be computed only one time.

Example:

```
$ans = 1;
$ans &&= "eggs" eq "eggs";
if ($ans)
     {print("It's as true as eggs is eggs. (expected)\n");}
else
     {print("Not true, I'm afraid.");}
```

## &=

| | |
|---|---|
| **Name:** | assignment bitwise and |
| **Precedence:** | 19 |
| **Associativity:** | right |
| **Type of operands:** | numeric (integer) |
| **Number of operands:** | two (binary) |
| **Context:** | scalar |

This operator is a combination of the bitwise and assignment operators. This operator is more efficient when a new value is being reassigned to the same variable, because the reference needs to be computed only one time.

Example:

```
$ans = 456;
$ans &= 111;
print("Bitwise and 456 & 111 is $ans\n");
```

## *

| | |
|---|---|
| **Name:** | multiplication |
| **Precedence:** | 7 |
| **Associativity:** | left |
| **Type of operands:** | numeric |
| **Number of operands:** | two (binary) |
| **Context:** | scalar |

This operator returns the numeric result of multiplying the two numeric operands.

Example:

```
$ans = 7 * 10;
print("$ans (expected 70)\n");
```

## **

| | |
|---|---|
| **Name:** | exponentiation |
| **Precedence:** | 4 |
| **Associativity:** | right |
| **Type of operands:** | numeric |
| **Number of operands:** | two (binary) |
| **Context:** | scalar |

The operation $x**y$ returns the value of $x$ raised to the power of $y$.

Example:

```
$ans = 2 ** 3;
print ("$ans (expected 8)\n");
```

## **=

| | |
|---|---|
| **Name:** | assignment exponentiation |
| **Precedence:** | 19 |
| **Associativity:** | right |
| **Type of operands:** | numeric |
| **Number of operands:** | two (binary) |
| **Context:** | scalar |

This operator is a combination of the exponentiation and assignment operators. This operator is more efficient when a new value is being reassigned to the same variable, because the reference needs to be computed only one time.

Example:

```
$ans = 2;
$ans **= 3;
print ("$ans (expected 8)\n");
```

## *=

| | |
|---|---|
| **Name:** | assignment multiplication |
| **Precedence:** | 19 |
| **Associativity:** | right |

Part

V

Ch

14

| | |
|---|---|
| **Type of operands:** | numeric |
| **Number of operands:** | two (binary) |
| **Context:** | scalar |

This operator is a combination of the multiplication and assignment operators. This operator is more efficient when a new value is being reassigned to the same variable, because the reference needs to be computed only one time.

Example:

```
$ans = 7;
$ans *= 10;
print ("$ans (expected 70)\n");
```

# + (Unary)

| | |
|---|---|
| **Name:** | unary plus |
| **Precedence:** | 5 |
| **Associativity:** | right |
| **Type of operands:** | numeric, string |
| **Number of operands:** | one (unary) |
| **Context:** | scalar |

This operator does not actually have any operation on a numeric or a string operand. In certain circumstances, the operator can disambiguate an expression. When a parenthesis follows a function name, it is taken to indicate a complete list of the arguments to the function, unless the parenthesis is preceded by + to make the parenthesized expression just one of the list arguments for that function.

Example:

```
@ans = sort +(5 + 5) * 10, -4;
print("@ans (expected 100, -4)\n");
```

# + (Binary)

| | |
|---|---|
| **Name:** | addition |
| **Precedence:** | 8 |
| **Associativity:** | left |
| **Type of operands:** | numeric |
| **Number of operands:** | two (binary) |
| **Context:** | scalar |

This operator returns the sum of the two operands.

Example:

```
$ans = 15 + 5;
print("$ans (expected 20)\n");
```

## ++

| | |
|---|---|
| **Name:** | autoincrement |
| **Precedence:** | 3 |
| **Associativity:** | nonassociative |
| **Type of operands:** | numeric, string |
| **Number of operands:** | one (unary) |
| **Context:** | scalar |

In a numeric context, the autoincrement adds 1 to the operand. If the syntax is prefix, the value before the increment is returned. If the syntax is postfix, the value after the increment is returned.

With a string operand (that has never been used in a numeric context), the autoincrement has a "magic" behavior. If the string is an alphanumeric expression, such as /^[a-zA-Z]*[0-9]*$/, the increment is carried out on the string, including a carry.

Example:

```
$ans = 45;
print $ans,   " (expected 45) ";
print $ans++, " (expected 45) ";
print ++$ans, " (expected 47)\n";
```

## +=

| | |
|---|---|
| **Name:** | assignment addition |
| **Precedence:** | 19 |
| **Associativity:** | right |
| **Type of operands:** | numeric |
| **Number of operands:** | two (binary) |
| **Context:** | scalar |

This operator is a combination of the summation and assignment operators. This operator is more efficient when a new value is being reassigned to the same variable, because the reference needs to be computed only one time.

Example:

```
$ans = 15;
$ans += 5;
print("$ans (expected 20)\n");
```

Part
**V**

Ch
**14**

**,**

| | |
|---|---|
| **Name:** | comma |
| **Precedence:** | 20 |
| **Associativity:** | left |
| **Type of operands:** | numeric, string |
| **Number of operands:** | two (binary) |
| **Context:** | scalar, list |

In a scalar context, the comma operator evaluates the operand to the left, discards the result, evaluates the operand to the right, and returns that value as the result.

In an array context, the comma operator separates items in the list. The operator behaves as though it returns both operands as part of the list.

Example:

```
$ans = ('one', 'two', 'three');
print("$ans (expected three)\n");
```

# – (Unary)

| | |
|---|---|
| **Name:** | negation |
| **Precedence:** | 5 |
| **Associativity:** | right |
| **Type of operands:** | numeric, string, identifier |
| **Number of operands:** | one (unary) |
| **Context:** | scalar |

This operator returns the negated value of a numeric operand. If the operand is a string that begins with a plus (+) or minus (–) sign, the operator returns a string that has the opposite sign. If the argument is an identifier, the operator returns a string that comprises the identifier prefixed with a minus sign.

Example:

```
$ans = 45;
$ans = -$ans;
print("$ans (expected -45)\n");
```

# – (Binary)

| | |
|---|---|
| **Name:** | subtraction |
| **Precedence:** | 8 |
| **Associativity:** | left |

| Type of operands: | numeric |
| Number of operands: | two (binary) |
| Context: | scalar |

This operator returns the first operand minus the second operand.

Example:

```
$ans = 50 - 10;
print("$ans (expected 40)\n");
```

**– –**

| Name: | autodecrement |
| Precedence: | 3 |
| Associativity: | nonassociative |
| Type of operands: | numeric |
| Number of operands: | one (unary) |
| Context: | scalar |

This operator decrements its operand. The value returned is before the decrement takes place if the operator is in prefix notation (--56 returns 56), and the value returned is with the decrement having taken place if the operator is in postfix notation (56--returns 55).

Unlike the autoincrement operator, ++, this operator does not operate on strings.

Example:

```
$ans = 45;
print $ans,   " (expected 45) ";
print $ans--, " (expected 45) ";
print --$ans, " (expected 43)\n";
```

**–=**

| Name: | assignment subtraction |
| Precedence: | 19 |
| Associativity: | right |
| Type of operands: | numeric |
| Number of operands: | two (binary) |
| Context: | scalar |

This operator is a combination of the subtraction and assignment operators. This operator is more efficient when a new value is being reassigned to the same variable, because the reference needs to be computed only one time.

Part
V

Ch

14

Example:

```
$ans = 50;
$ans -= 10;
print("$ans (expected 40)\n");
```

**->**

| | |
|---|---|
| **Name:** | dereference |
| **Precedence:** | 2 |
| **Associativity:** | left |
| **Type of operands:** | special |
| **Number of operands:** | two (binary) |
| **Context:** | scalar, array |

This operator is new to Perl 5. The capability to create and manipulate complex data types with references provides flexibility in Perl 5 that was not present in Perl 4. This operator is just one of the aspects of this functionality.

The operands for this operator can be:

- A right side comprising array braces [] or {} and a left side comprising a reference to an array (or hash)

- A right side comprising a method name (or a variable with a method name) and a left side of either an object or a class name

The operator allows you to access the elements in the data structure referenced by the left side (an array name, a hash name, an object, or a class name). Because there is no automatic dereferencing, you must use this syntax to dereference such a reference.

Example:

```
@ans = (100, 200, 300);
$ansref = \@ans;
$ansref->[2] = 400;
print $ans[2], " (expected 400)\n";
```

| | |
|---|---|
| **Name:** | string concatenation |
| **Precedence:** | 8 |
| **Associativity:** | left |
| **Type of operands:** | string |
| **Number of operands:** | two (binary) |
| **Context:** | scalar |

This operator joins the two string operands, returning a longer string.

Example:

```
$ans = "jordy" . " jordy";
print $ans, " (expected jordy jordy)\n";
```

**..**

| Name: | range operator |
|---|---|
| Precedence: | 17 |
| Associativity: | nonassociative |
| Type of operands: | numeric, string |
| Number of operands: | two (binary) |
| Context: | scalar, list |

In a list context, the range operator returns an array of values, starting from the left operand up to the right operand in steps of 1. In this context, the range operator can use "magic" increments to increment strings, as with the autoincrement operator (++).

In a scalar context, the range operator returns a Boolean value. In effect, the return value remains false as long as the left operand is false. When the left operand becomes true, it becomes true until the right operand is true, after which it becomes false again.

The range operator can be used in a scalar context to set conditions for certain ranges of line numbers of an input file. This works because the default behavior when either operand is numeric is to compare that operand with the current line number (the $INPUT_LINE_NUMBER or $. special variable). Thus it is easy, using this construct, to treat certain lines in an input file differently. In the following example, the first five lines of the input file are suppressed from being output.

Example:

```
@ans = 1..5;
print("@ans (expected 12345)\n");
open(INFILE,"<infile.tst");
while(<INFILE>) {
    print unless (1..5);
}
```

**.=**

| Name: | assignment concatenation |
|---|---|
| Precedence: | 19 |
| Associativity: | right |
| Type of operands: | string |

| | |
|---|---|
| **Number of operands:** | two (binary) |
| **Context:** | scalar |

This operator is a combination of the concatenation and assignment operators. This operator is more efficient when a new value is being reassigned to the same variable, because the reference needs to be computed only one time.

Example:

```
$ans = "jordy";
$ans .= " jordy";
print $ans, " (expected jordy jordy)\n";
```

# /

| | |
|---|---|
| **Name:** | division |
| **Precedence:** | 7 |
| **Associativity:** | left |
| **Type of operands:** | numeric |
| **Number of operands:** | two (binary) |
| **Context:** | scalar |

This operator returns the product of the operands.

Example:

```
$ans = 10/2;
print("$ans (expected 5)\n");
```

# /=

| | |
|---|---|
| **Name:** | assignment division |
| **Precedence:** | 19 |
| **Associativity:** | right |
| **Type of operands:** | numeric |
| **Number of operands:** | two (binary) |
| **Context:** | scalar |

This operator is a combination of the division and assignment operators. This operator is more efficient when a new value is being reassigned to the same variable, because the reference needs to be computed only one time.

Example:

```
$ans = 10;
$ans /= 2;
print("$ans (expected 5)\n");
```

# <

| | |
|---|---|
| **Name:** | numeric less then |
| **Precedence:** | 11 |
| **Associativity:** | nonassociative |
| **Type of operands:** | numeric |
| **Number of operands:** | two (binary) |
| **Context:** | scalar |

This operator returns 1 if the left operand is numerically less than the right operand; otherwise, it returns null.

Example:

```
$ans = 45 < 36;
if ($ans)
     { print("True.\n");}
else
     { print("False. (expected)\n");}
```

# <<

| | |
|---|---|
| **Name:** | bitwise shift left |
| **Precedence:** | 9 |
| **Associativity:** | left |
| **Type of operands:** | numeric (integer) |
| **Number of operands:** | two (binary) |
| **Context:** | scalar |

This operator shifts the operand left 1 bit in binary representation and returns the result.

Example:

```
$ans = 1024<<1;
print("$ans (Bitwise left shift of 1024 by 1 place)\n");
```

# <<=

| | |
|---|---|
| **Name:** | assignment bitwise shift left |
| **Precedence:** | 19 |
| **Associativity:** | right |
| **Type of operands:** | numeric (integer) |
| **Number of operands:** | two (binary) |
| **Context:** | scalar |

Part
V

Ch
14

This operator is a combination of the bitwise shift left and assignment operators. This operator is more efficient when a new value is being reassigned to the same variable, because the reference needs to be computed only one time.

Example:

```
$ans = 1024;
$ans <<= 1;
print("$ans (Bitwise left shift of 1024 by 1 place)\n");
```

# <=

| | |
|---|---|
| **Name:** | numeric less than or equal to |
| **Precedence:** | 11 |
| **Associativity:** | nonassociative |
| **Type of operands:** | numeric |
| **Number of operands:** | two (binary) |
| **Context:** | scalar |

This operator returns 1 (true) if the left operand is numerically less than or equal to the right operand.

Example:

```
$ans = 345 <= 345;
print("Comparing 345 <= 345 yields $ans. (expected 1 for true).\n");
```

# <=>

| | |
|---|---|
| **Name:** | numeric comparison |
| **Precedence:** | 12 |
| **Associativity:** | nonassociative |
| **Type of operands:** | numeric |
| **Number of operands:** | two (binary) |
| **Context:** | scalar |

This operator returns 0 if the two numeric operands are equal. The operator returns -1 if the left operand is less than the right operand and +1 if the left operand is greater than the right operand.

Example:

```
$ans = 345 <=> 347;
print("Comparing 345 with 437 yields $ans. (expected -1 for less than).\n");
```

# =

| | |
|---|---|
| **Name:** | assignment |
| **Precedence:** | 19 |
| **Associativity:** | right |
| **Type of operands:** | numeric, string |
| **Number of operands:** | two (binary) |
| **Context:** | scalar, list |

In a scalar context, the assignment assigns the value of the right side to the variable on the left side. The assignment returns the variable on the left side.

In an array context, the assignment can assign multiple values to an array as the left operand if the right side results in a list.

Example:

```
$ans = 43;
print("Assignment to \$ans: $ans (expected 43)\n");
```

# ==

| | |
|---|---|
| **Name:** | numeric equality |
| **Precedence:** | 12 |
| **Associativity:** | nonassociative |
| **Type of operands:** | numeric |
| **Number of operands:** | two (binary) |
| **Context:** | scalar |

This operator returns 1 (true) if the left and right numeric operands are numerically equal; otherwise, it returns null (false).

Example:

```
$ans = 345 == 347;
print("Comparing 345 with 347 yields +$ans+. (expected null not equal).\n");
```

# =>

| | |
|---|---|
| **Name:** | comma |
| **Precedence:** | 20 |
| **Associativity:** | left |
| **Type of operands:** | numeric, string |
| **Number of operands:** | two (binary) |
| **Context:** | scalar, list |

This operator is an alternative to the comma operator.

Example:

```
$ans = (1 => 2 => 3);
print("$ans (expected 3)\n");
```

## =~

| | |
|---|---|
| **Name:** | pattern binding |
| **Precedence:** | 6 |
| **Associativity:** | left |
| **Type of operands:** | special |
| **Number of operands:** | two (binary) |
| **Context:** | scalar |

The default string matched by pattern-match operations is $_. Any other string can be bound to a pattern-matching operation using the pattern-binding operator. The left operand is a string to be searched. The right operand is a pattern-match operation (search, substitution, translation). The return value is true or false, depending on the success of the operation.

Example:

```
$tmp = "superduper";
if ($tmp =~ s/duper/dooper/)
    {print "Did do a substitute, tmp now is: $tmp\n";}
else
    {print "Did not a substitute, tmp still is: $tmp\n";}
```

## >

| | |
|---|---|
| **Name:** | numeric greater than |
| **Precedence:** | 11 |
| **Associativity:** | nonassociative |
| **Type of operands:** | numeric |
| **Number of operands:** | two (binary) |
| **Context:** | scalar |

This operator returns 1 (true) if the left numeric operand is greater than the right numeric operand; otherwise, it returns null (false).

Example:

```
$ans = 45 > 36;
if ($ans)
    { print("True.\n");}
else
    { print("False. (expected)\n");}
```

# >=

| | |
|---|---|
| **Name:** | numeric greater than or equal to |
| **Precedence:** | 11 |
| **Associativity:** | nonassociative |
| **Type of operands:** | numeric |
| **Number of operands:** | two (binary) |
| **Context:** | scalar |

This operator returns 1 (true) if the left numeric operand is greater than or equal to the right numeric operand; otherwise, it returns null (false).

Example:

```
$ans = 345 >= 345;
print("Comparing 345 >= 345 yields $ans. (expected 1 for true).\n");
```

# >>

| | |
|---|---|
| **Name:** | bitwise shift right |
| **Precedence:** | 9 |
| **Associativity:** | left |
| **Type of operands:** | numeric (integer) |
| **Number of operands:** | two (binary) |
| **Context:** | scalar |

This operator shifts the operand right 1 bit in binary representation and returns the result.

Example:

```
$ans = 1024>>1;
print("$ans (Bitwise right shift of 1024 by 1 place)\n");
```

# >>=

| | |
|---|---|
| **Name:** | assignment bitwise shift right |
| **Precedence:** | 19 |
| **Associativity:** | left |
| **Type of operands:** | numeric (integer) |
| **Number of operands:** | two (binary) |
| **Context:** | scalar |

This operator is a combination of the bitwise shift right and assignment operators. This operator is more efficient when a new value is being reassigned to the same variable, because the reference needs to be computed only one time.

Part
V

Ch
14

Example:

```
$ans = 1024;
$ans >>= 1;
print("$ans (Bitwise right shift of 1024 by 1 place)\n");
```

# ?

| | |
|---|---|
| **Name:** | conditional operator |
| **Precedence:** | 18 |
| **Associativity:** | right |
| **Type of operands:** | numeric, string |
| **Number of operands:** | three (ternary) |
| **Context:** | scalar, list |

This operator is like a symbolic if/then/else clause. If the leftmost operand is true, the center operand is returned; otherwise, the rightmost operand is returned. Either of the operands can return scalar or list values, and these values will be returned if the context allows.

Example:

```
$ans = (45 == 45) ? "Equal (expected).\n" : "Not equal.\n";
print $ans;
```

# *LIST* Operators (Leftward)

| | |
|---|---|
| **Name:** | all named list operators |
| **Precedence:** | 1 |
| **Associativity:** | left |
| **Type of operands:** | special |
| **Number of operands:** | list |
| **Context:** | list |

Several functions require a list as a parameter. The list can be written with or without the function parentheses. These list functions are in fact operators that behave like functions when their arguments are in parentheses. If they are written with parentheses, everything within the parentheses is taken as the list argument to the function, and they behave as a TERM.

**See** Chapter 15, "Function List," **p. 423**

When the function call is written without parentheses, the precedence is slightly more complex. The list operator has a different precedence, depending on whether the comparison is to the left of the list operator (*leftward*) or to the right of the list operator (*rightward*). The list operator has higher (or equal) precedence compared with all operators to its left. Thus, in the following example, join is evaluated before print, because print is to the left of join.

Example:

```
print 'Ones ', 'Twos ', join 'hoho ', 'Threes ', 'Fours ', "\n";
```

# *LIST* Operators (Rightward)

| | |
|---|---|
| **Name:** | all named list operators |
| **Precedence:** | 21 |
| **Associativity:** | nonassociative |
| **Type of operands:** | special |
| **Number of operands:** | list |
| **Context:** | list |

Several functions require a list as a parameter. The list can be written with or without the function parentheses. These functions are in fact operators that behave like functions when their arguments are in parentheses. If they are written with parentheses, everything within the parentheses is taken as the list argument to the function, and they behave as a TERM.

**See** Chapter 15, "Function List," **p. 423**

When the function is written without parentheses, the precedence is slightly more complex. The list operator has a different precedence, depending on whether the comparison is to the left of the list operator (leftward) or to the right of the list operator (rightward). The list operator has lower (or equal) precedence compared with all operators to its right. Thus, in the following example, print is evaluated after join, because join is to the right of print.

Example:

```
print 'Ones ', 'Twos ', join 'hoho ', 'Threes ', 'Fours ', "\n";
```

# *NAMED* Unary Operators

| | |
|---|---|
| **Name:** | all named unary operators |
| **Precedence:** | 10 |
| **Associativity:** | nonassociative |
| **Type of operands:** | special |
| **Number of operands:** | one (unary) |
| **Context:** | scalar |

In a similar way to list operators, NAMED unary operators can behave as a TERM by being expressed with a function syntax, with the argument placed in parentheses.

**See** Chapter 15, "Function List," **p. 423**

When the function is written without parentheses, the precedence of these operators is lower than arithmetic types of operators, but greater than the symbolic string and numeric comparisons. Thus, in the following example, the first int takes the result of the arithmetic division 7/2 as its argument, so 3 is printed. The second int is a term bound to 7, which returns 7 and then is divided by 2 to yield 3.5.

Example:

```
print 'Ones ', 'Twos ', int 7/2, (int 7)/2, ' Fours', "\n";
```

# TERMs

| Name: | TERMS |
|---|---|
| Precedence: | 1 |
| Associativity: | left |
| Type of operands: | special |
| Number of operands: | N/A |
| Context: | N/A |

A TERM can be any variable, any expression enclosed in parentheses, any function with its arguments in parentheses, and also a quoted expression (using the so-called quote and quotelike operators). TERMs have the highest possible precedence—in other words, they are replaced by their return value when the entire expression is being evaluated before any other operator of lower precedence is evaluated. TERMs appear in this chapter on operators to show where they fall in the order of precedence.

Example:

```
print 'One ', (1, 2, 3), "(expect One 3)\n";
```

**"**

| Name: | reference |
|---|---|
| Precedence: | 5 |
| Associativity: | right |
| Type of operands: | one (unary) |
| Number of operands: | special |
| Context: | scalar |

This operator permits the creation of references and the use of complex data types. One example is the capability to create another reference to an existing array variable.

```
@ans = (100, 200, 300);
$ansref = \@ans;
$ansref->[2] = 400;
print $ans[2], " (expected 400)\n";
```

The capability to create a reference to a variable is new to Perl 5.

# ^

| | |
|---|---|
| **Name:** | bitwise exclusive or |
| **Precedence:** | 14 |
| **Associativity:** | left |
| **Type of operands:** | two (binary) |
| **Number of operands:** | numeric (integer) |
| **Context:** | scalar |

This operator returns the result of a bitwise exclusive or on the two operands.

Example:

```
$ans = 456 ^ 111;
print "Bitwise xor 456 & 111 is: $ans\n";
```

# ^=

| | |
|---|---|
| **Name:** | assignment bitwise exclusive or |
| **Precedence:** | 19 |
| **Associativity:** | right |
| **Type of operands:** | numeric (integer) |
| **Number of operands:** | two (binary) |
| **Context:** | scalar |

This operator is a combination of the bitwise exclusive or and assignment operators. This operator is more efficient when a new value is being reassigned to the same variable, because the reference needs to be computed only one time.

Example:

```
$ans = 456;
$ans ^= 111;
print "Bitwise xor 456 & 111 is: $ans\n";
```

# and

| | |
|---|---|
| **Name:** | and |
| **Precedence:** | 23 |
| **Associativity:** | left |
| **Type of operands:** | numeric, string |
| **Number of operands:** | two (binary) |
| **Context:** | scalar |

Part
V

Ch
14

This operator is the lower-precedence version of symbolic and &&.

Example:

```
$ans = (1 and 3 || 0);
if ($ans)
    { print "true (expected)\n"; }
else
    { print "false\n"; }
```

 This alternative to the symbolic form is new to Perl 5.

# cmp

| | |
|---|---|
| **Name:** | string comparison |
| **Precedence:** | 12 |
| **Associativity:** | nonassociative |
| **Type of operands:** | string |
| **Number of operands:** | two (binary) |
| **Context:** | scalar |

This operator compares two string operands and returns –1 if the first is less than the second, 0 if the operands are equal, and 1 if the first operand is greater than the second.

Example:

```
$ans = "abc" cmp "aba";
print("Comparing (cmp) abc with aba yields $ans (expected +1 aba > abc).\n");
```

# eq

| | |
|---|---|
| **Name:** | string equality |
| **Precedence:** | 12 |
| **Associativity:** | nonassociative |
| **Type of operands:** | string |
| **Number of operands:** | two (binary) |
| **Context:** | scalar |

This operator tests whether two strings are equal, returning 1 (true) if they are and null (false) if they are not.

Example:

```
$ans = "abc" eq "abc";
print("Comparing (eq) abc with abc yields $ans (expected 1 true).\n");
```

# ge

| | |
|---|---|
| **Name:** | string greater than or equal to |
| **Precedence:** | 11 |
| **Associativity:** | nonassociative |
| **Type of operands:** | string |
| **Number of operands:** | two (binary) |
| **Context:** | scalar |

This operator compares two strings and returns 1 (true) if the first string is greater than or equal to the second; otherwise, it returns null (false).

Example:

```
$ans = "abc" ge "abc";
print("Comparing (ge) abc with abc yields $ans (expected 1 true).\n");
```

# gt

| | |
|---|---|
| **Name:** | string greater than |
| **Precedence:** | 11 |
| **Associativity:** | nonassociative |
| **Type of operands:** | string |
| **Number of operands:** | two (binary) |
| **Context:** | scalar |

This operator compares two strings and returns 1 (true) if the first is greater than the second; otherwise, it returns null (false).

Example:

```
$ans = "abc" gt "aba";
print("Comparing (gt) abc with aba yields $ans (expected 1 true).\n");
```

# le

| | |
|---|---|
| **Name:** | string less than or equal to |
| **Precedence:** | 11 |
| **Associativity:** | nonassociative |
| **Type of operands:** | string |
| **Number of operands:** | two (binary) |
| **Context:** | scalar |

This operator compares two strings and returns 1 (true) if the first is less than or equal to the second; otherwise, it returns null (false).

Example:

```
$ans = "abc" le "aba";
print("Comparing (le) abc with aba yields +$ans+ (expected null false).\n");
```

# lt

| | |
|---|---|
| **Name:** | string less than |
| **Precedence:** | 11 |
| **Associativity:** | nonassociative |
| **Type of operands:** | string |
| **Number of operands:** | two (binary) |
| **Context:** | scalar |

This operator compares two strings and returns 1 (true) if the first is less than the second; otherwise, it returns null (false).

Example:

```
$ans = "abc" lt "aba";
print("Comparing (lt) abc with aba yields +$ans+ (expected null false).\n");
```

# ne

| | |
|---|---|
| **Name:** | string not equal to |
| **Precedence:** | 12 |
| **Associativity:** | nonassociative |
| **Type of operands:** | string |
| **Number of operands:** | two (binary) |
| **Context:** | scalar |

This operator compares two strings and returns 1 (true) if they are not equal; otherwise, it returns null (false).

Example:

```
$ans = "abc" ne "aba";
print("Comparing (ne) abc with aba yields $ans (expected 1 true).\n");
```

# not

| | |
|---|---|
| **Name:** | not |
| **Precedence:** | 22 |
| **Associativity:** | right |

| | |
|---|---|
| **Type of operands:** | numeric, string |
| **Number of operands:** | one (unary) |
| **Context:** | scalar |

This operator is the lower-precedence version of symbolic not !.

Example:

```
$ans = not 1;
print("Not 1 is +$ans+ (expected null)\n");
```

This alternative to the symbolic form is new to Perl 5.

# or

| | |
|---|---|
| **Name:** | or |
| **Precedence:** | 24 |
| **Associativity:** | left |
| **Type of operands:** | numeric, string |
| **Number of operands:** | two (binary) |
| **Context:** | scalar |

This operator is the lower-precedence version of symbolic or ¦¦.

Example:

```
open TSTFILE, "<nofile.txt" or print "The file doesn't exist\n";
```

This alternative to the symbolic form is new to Perl 5.

# x

| | |
|---|---|
| **Name:** | repetition |
| **Precedence:** | 6 |
| **Associativity:** | left |
| **Type of operands:** | string and numeric (integer) |
| **Number of operands:** | two (binary) |
| **Context:** | scalar |

The first operand must be a string, and the second operand must be an integer. The operator returns a string comprising the string operand repeated the specified number of times.

Example:

```
print "Hello " x 5, "\n";
```

# x=

| | |
|---|---|
| **Name:** | assignment repetition |
| **Precedence:** | 19 |
| **Associativity:** | right |
| **Type of operands:** | string and numeric (integer) |
| **Number of operands:** | two (binary) |
| **Context:** | scalar |

This operator is a combination of the repetition and assignment operators. This operator is more efficient when a new value is being reassigned to the same variable, because the reference needs to be computed only one time.

Example:

```
$ans = 'Hello ';
$ans x= 5;
print("$ans\n");
```

# xor

| | |
|---|---|
| **Name:** | exclusive or |
| **Precedence:** | 24 |
| **Associativity:** | left |
| **Type of operands:** | numeric, string |
| **Number of operands:** | two (binary) |
| **Context:** | scalar |

This operator returns 1 (true) or null (false) as an exclusive or of the two operands: the result is true if either, but not both, of the operands is true.

Example:

```
for (0..1) {
    $a = $_;
    for (0..1) {
        $b = $_;
        print $a, ,' ', $b, ' ', ($a xor $b) ? 1 : 0, "\n";
        }
    }
```

The xor operator is new to Perl 5.

|

| Name: | bitwise or |
|---|---|
| Precedence: | 14 |
| Associativity: | left |
| Type of operands: | numeric (integer) |
| Number of operands: | two (binary) |
| Context: | scalar |

This operator returns an integer that is the result of a bitwise or between the two integer operands.

Example:

```
$ans = 2 ¦ 1024;
print("2 OR 1204 is $ans\n");
```

|=

| Name: | assignment bitwise or |
|---|---|
| Precedence: | 19 |
| Associativity: | right |
| Type of operands: | numeric (integer) |
| Number of operands: | two (binary) |
| Context: | scalar |

This operator is a combination of the bitwise or and assignment operators. This operator is more efficient when a new value is being reassigned to the same variable, because the reference needs to be computed only one time.

Example:

```
$ans = 2;
$ans ¦= 1024;
print("2 OR 1204 is $ans\n");
```

||

| Name: | symbolic or |
|---|---|
| Precedence: | 11 |
| Associativity: | left |
| Type of operands: | numeric, string |
| Number of operands: | two (binary) |
| Context: | scalar |

Part
V

Ch
14

This operator returns 1 (true) if either of the two operands is true and null (false) otherwise.

Example:

```
$ans = '' || 'okay';
print("null || okay is $ans (expected okay true)\n");
```

# ||=

| | |
|---|---|
| **Name:** | assignment symbolic or |
| **Precedence:** | 19 |
| **Associativity:** | right |
| **Type of operands:** | numeric, string |
| **Number of operands:** | two (binary) |
| **Context:** | scalar |

This operator is a combination of the symbolic or and assignment operators. This operator is more efficient when a new value is being reassigned to the same variable, because the reference needs to be computed only one time.

Example:

```
$ans = '';
$ans ||= 'okay';
print("null || okay is $ans (expected okay true)\n");
```

# ~

| | |
|---|---|
| **Name:** | bitwise not |
| **Precedence:** | 5 |
| **Associativity:** | right |
| **Type of operands:** | numeric (integer) |
| **Number of operands:** | one (unary) |
| **Context:** | scalar |

This operator returns the bitwise negation of an integer operand. The result of this operation is sometimes known as the *one's complement*.

Example:

```
$ans = ~1000000000;
print("Bitwise negation of 1000000000 is $ans\n");
```

# From Here...

This chapter lists only Perl operators; you should consult other reference sections for Perl special variables and Perl functions. (You may easily confuse some variables with some operators, so check the list of operators if the symbol that you require is not covered in this chapter.)

Be aware that all Perl functions can behave as operators and as functions. The difference is in the syntax; functions have parentheses—as in `example()`. Any named LIST operators/functions and NAMED unary operators/functions, including the file-test operators, are covered in the functions chapter.

For details on the other elements in the Perl reference, see the following chapters:

- Chapter 13, "Special Variables," provides detailed descriptions of the Perl special variables.
- Chapter 15, "Function List," provides detailed descriptions of the Perl functions.

# Function List

▬ A detailed description of each Perl function, ordered alphabetically.

▬ An example of the function's usage, where applicable.

**P**erl has a large number of functions that come as standard with most implementations, and an even wider range of additional modules, each with its own additional functions. This chapter lists all the standard functions alphabetically for reference.

Each function is assigned a category. There are two main categories; list operators, which can take more than one argument, and named unary operators, which can only take one argument. A secondary category is noted in parentheses so you can see, at a glance, the type of operation the function performs. This is a very rough categorization, as many functions might overlap in any category scheme.

For each function the form of the arguments is listed. If there are multiple forms of calling the function, there will be multiple lines describing each form. The meanings of the arguments are described in the text.

The type of value returned by the function is listed. This is usually specified in more detail in the function description.

Two categories of functions, those dealing with sockets and those dealing with System V inter-process communications, are not dealt with in great detail. Both of these categories of functions are direct counterparts of UNIX system functions. ▬

# -A

## Compliance

## Syntax

```
Category  named unary operator (file test)
Arguments  handle
Arguments  filename
Arguments  none
Return Value  integer (age of file in days since last
              access relative to $BASETIME)
```

## Definition

The file test operator takes one file handle or filename as an argument. It returns age of file in days since last access relative to $BASETIME. All file test operators can take a special argument underscore, which means that the test is carried out on the same file handle as the last file test, stat(), or lstat() call. If no argument is supplied, $_ is used.

## Example

```
print "-A ", -A "/etc/fstab", "\n";
```

# -B

## Compliance

## Syntax

```
Category  named unary operator (file test)
Arguments  handle
Arguments  filename
Arguments  none
Return Value  1 (true) '' (false)
```

## Definition

The file test operator takes one file handle or filename as an argument. It returns 1 (true) if the file is binary. It returns '' (false) if the file is not binary. The first characters of the file are checked to see if the high bit is set and if a suitable number do have the high bit set the file is assumed to be binary. If the file is empty it is returned as binary. Because this test involves reading the file itself, it is best to test to learn if the file exists as a plain file (-f), first. All file test operators can take a special argument underscore, which means that the test is carried out on the same file handle as the last file test, stat(), or lstat() call. If no argument is supplied, $_ is used.

## Example

```
(-B "/etc/fstab") ? print("-B fstab is binary\n") :

        print("-B fstab is not binary\n");
```

# -b

## Compliance

## Syntax

```
Category  named unary operator (file test)
Arguments  handle
Arguments  filename
Arguments  none
Return Value  1 (true) '' (false)
```

## Definition

The file test operator takes one file handle or filename as an argument. It returns 1 (true) if the file is a block special file (that is, a UNIX /dev device file). It returns '' (false) if the file is not a block special file. All file test operators can take a special argument underscore, which means that the test is carried out on the same file handle as the last file test, stat(), or lstat() call. If no argument is supplied, $_ is used.

## Example

```
(-b "/dev/hda1") ? print("-b hda1 is block\n") :

        print("-b hda1 is not block\n");
```

# -C

## Compliance

## Syntax

```
Category  named unary operator (file test)
Arguments  handle
Arguments  filename
Arguments  none
Return Value  integer (age of file in days since last
              inode change relative to $BASETIME)
```

## Definition

The file test operator takes one file handle or filename as an argument. It returns age of file in days since last inode change relative to $BASETIME. All file test operators can take a special argument underscore, which means that the test is carried out on the same file handle as the last file test, stat(), or lstat() call. If no argument is supplied, $_ is used.

## Example

```
print "-C ", -C "/etc/fstab", "\n";
```

# -c

## Compliance

## Syntax

```
Category  named unary operator (file test)
Arguments  handle
Arguments  filename
Arguments  none
Return Value  1 (true) '' (false)
```

## Definition

The file test operator takes one file handle or filename as an argument. It returns 1 (true) if the file is a character special file. It returns '' (false) if the file is not a character special file. All file test operators can take a special argument underscore, which means that the test is carried out on the same file handle as the last file test, stat(), or lstat() call. If no argument is supplig™, $_ is used.

## Example

```
(-c "/dev/tty0") ? print("-c tty0 is char\n") :
        print("-c tty0 is not char\n");
```

# -d

## Compliance

## Syntax

```
Category  named unary operator (file test)
Arguments  handle
Arguments  filename
Arguments  none
Return Value  1 (true) '' (false)
```

## Definition

The file test operator takes one file handle or filename as an argument. It returns 1 (true) if the file is a directory. It returns '' (false) if the file is not a directory. All file test operators can take a special argument underscore, which means that the test is carried out on the same file `handle` as the last `file test`, `stat()`, or `lstat()` call. If no argument is supplied, `$_` is used.

## Example

```
(-d "/") ? print("-d / is dir\n") : print("-d / is not dir\n");
```

# -e

## Compliance

## Syntax

```
Category    named unary operator (file test)
Arguments   handle
Arguments   filename
Arguments   none
Arguments   none
Return Value  1 (true) '' (false)
```

## Definition

The `file test` operator takes one file `handle` or `filename` as an argument. It returns 1 (true) if file exists. It returns `''` (false) if the file does not exist. All `file test` operators can take a special argument underscore, which means that the test is carried out on the same file `handle` as the last `file test`, `stat()`, or `lstat()` call. If no argument is supplied, `$_` is used.

## Example

```
(-e "/") ? print("-e / exists\n") : print("-e / exists\n");
```

# -f

## Compliance

## Syntax

```
Category    named unary operator (file test)
Arguments   handle
Arguments   filename
Arguments   none
Return Value  1 (true) '' (false)
```

## Definition

The `file test` operator takes one file `handle` or `filename` as an argument. It returns 1 (true) if the file is a plain file. It returns `''` (false) if the file is not a plain file. A plain file is any file that is not a special block device (`-b`), a special character device (`-c`), a directory (`-d`), a symbolic link (`-l`), a pipe (`-p`), a named socket (`-s`), or a direct link to an I/O terminal (`-t`). All `file test` operators can take a special argument underscore, which means that the test is carried out on the same file `handle` as the last `file test`, `stat()`, or `lstat()` call. If no argument is supplied, `$_` is used.

## Example

```
(-f "/") ? print("-f / is plain\n") : print("-f / is not plain\n");
```

# -g

## Compliance

## Syntax

```
Category   named unary operator (file test)
Arguments  handle
Arguments  filename
Arguments  none
Return Value 1 (true) '' (false)
```

## Definition

The `file test` operator takes one file `handle` or `filename` as an argument. It returns 1 (true) if the file has the `setgid` bit set. It returns `''` (false) if the file does not have the `setgid` bit set. In UNIX, `setgid` allows an executable to run as if it was being run by the group, which owns the executable itself while executing (for example, if a binary is owned by the group wwwstat, and the binary has the `getgid` bit set, then that binary has access to all files that the wwwstat group can access while the binary is running, even when the binary is run by someone who is not actually a member of the wwwstat group). All `file test` operators can take a special argument underscore, which means that the test is carried out on the same file `handle` as the last `file test`, `stat()`, or `lstat()` call. If no argument is supplied, `$_` is used.

## Example

```
(-g "/vmlinuz") ? print("-g /vmlinuz has setgid\n") :
        print("-g /vmlinuz has not setgid\n");
```

# -k

## Compliance

## Syntax

```
Category   named unary operator (file test)
Arguments  handle
Arguments  filename
Arguments  none
Return Value 1 (true) '' (false)
```

## Definition

The `file test` operator takes one file `handle` or `filename` as an argument. It returns 1 (true) if the sticky bit is set. It returns `' '` (false) if the sticky bit is not set. In UNIX, the sticky bit can mark an executable file to be held in memory when exited (for example, if the binary `ls` is marked as sticky, when the first person runs it, it is loaded from disk to memory and executed, but when the execution finishes, the binary stays in memory so that when the next person runs `ls` it does not need to be loaded into memory again because it is already there). This is normally set for frequently used commands to optimize execution speed. All `file test` operators can take a special argument underscore, which means that the test is carried out on the same file `handle` as the last `file test`, `stat()`, or `lstat()` call. If no argument is supplied, `$_` is used.

## Example

```
(-k "/vmlinuz") ? print("-k /vmlinuz is sticky\n") :
        print("-k /vmlinuz is not sticky\n");
```

# -l

## Compliance

## Syntax

```
Category   named unary operator (file test)
Arguments  handle
Arguments  filename
Arguments  none
Return Value  1 (true) '' (false)
```

## Definition

The `file test` operator takes one file `handle` or `filename` as an argument. It returns 1 (true) if the file is a symbolic link. It returns `' '` (false) if the file is not a symbolic link. All `file test` operators can take a special argument underscore, which means that the test is carried out on the same file `handle` as the last `file test`, `stat()`, or `lstat()` call. If no argument is supplied, `$_` is used.

## Example

```
(-l "/vmlinuz") ? print("-l /vmlinuz is symlink\n") :
        print("-l /vmlinuz is not symlink\n");
```

# -M

## Compliance

## Syntax

```
Category    named unary operator (file test)
Arguments   handle
Arguments   filename
Arguments   none
Return Value  integer (age of file in days relative to $BASETIME)
```

## Definition

The file test operator takes one file handle or filename as an argument. It returns the age of the file in days relative to $BASETIME. All file test operators can take a special argument underscore, which means that the test is carried out on the same file handle as the last file test, stat(), or lstat() call. If no argument is supplied, $_ is used.

## Example

```
print "-M ", -M "/etc/fstab", "\n";
```

# -O

## Compliance

## Syntax

```
Category    named unary operator (file test)
Arguments   handle
Arguments   filename
Arguments   none
Return Value  1 (true) '' (false)
```

## Definition

The file test operator takes one file handle or filename as an argument. It returns 1 (true) if the file is owned by the real UID/GID and it returns '' (false) otherwise. For the superuser it always returns true. All file test operators can take a special argument underscore, which means that the test is carried out on the same file handle as the last file test, stat(), or lstat() call. If no argument is supplied, $_ is used.

## Example

```
(-o "/vmlinuz") ? print("-o /vmlinuz is owned by real uid/gid\n") :
        print("-o /vmlinuz is not owned by real uid/gid\n");
```

# -o

## Compliance

## Syntax

```
Category    named unary operator (file test)
Arguments   handle
Arguments   filename
Arguments   none
Return Value 1 (true) '' (false)
```

## Definition

The `file test` operator takes one file `handle` or `filename` as an argument. This function returns 1 (true) if the file is owned by the effective UID/GID and it returns `''` (false) otherwise. For the superuser it always returns true. All `file test` operators can take a special argument underscore, which means that the test is carried out on the same file `handle` as the last `file test`, `stat()`, or `lstat()` call. If no argument is supplied, `$_` is used.

## Example

```
(-O "/vmlinuz") ? print("-O /vmlinuz is owned by effective uid/gid\n") :
      print("-o /vmlinuz is not owned by effective uid/gid\n");
```

# -p

## Compliance

## Syntax

```
Category    named unary operator (file test)
Arguments   handle
Arguments   filename
Arguments   none
Return Value 1 (true) '' (false)
```

## Definition

The `file test` operator takes one file `handle` or `filename` as an argument. It returns 1 (true) if the file is a named pipe. It returns `''` (false) if the file is not a named pipe. All `file test` operators can take a special argument underscore, which means that the test is carried out on the same file `handle` as the last `file test`, `stat()`, or `lstat()` call. If no argument is supplied, `$_` is used.

## Example

```
(-p "/vmlinuz") ? print("-p /vmlinuz is named pipe\n") :
      print("-p /vmlinuz is not named pipe\n");
```

# -R

## Compliance

## Syntax

```
Category  named unary operator (file test)
Arguments  handle
Arguments  filename
Arguments  none
Return Value  1 (true) '' (false)
```

## Definition

The `file test` operator takes one file `handle` or `filename` as an argument. It returns 1 (true) if the file is readable by the effective UID/GID and it returns `''` (false) otherwise. For the superuser it always returns true. All `file test` operators can take a special argument underscore, which means that the test is carried out on the same file `handle` as the last `file test`, `stat()`, or `lstat()` call. If no argument is supplied, `$_` is used.

## Example

```
(-R "/vmlinuz") ? print("-R /vmlinuz is readable by effective uid/gid\n") :
     print("-R /vmlinuz is not readable by effective uid/gid\n");
```

# -r

## Compliance

## Syntax

```
Category  named unary operator (file test)
Arguments  handle
Arguments  filename
Arguments  none
Return Value  1 (true) '' (false)
```

## Definition

The `file test` operator takes one file `handle` or `filename` as an argument. It returns 1 (true) if the file is readable by the real UID/GID and it returns `''` (false) otherwise. For the superuser it always returns true. All `file test` operators can take a special argument underscore, which means that the test is carried out on the same file `handle` as the last `file test`, `stat()`, or `lstat()` call. If no argument is supplied, `$_` is used.

## Example

```
(-r "/vmlinuz") ? print("-r /vmlinuz is readable by real uid/gid\n") :
     print("-r /vmlinuz is not readable by real uid/gid\n");
```

# -S

## Compliance

## Syntax

```
Category   named unary operator (file test)
Arguments  handle
Arguments  filename
Arguments  none
Return Value  1 (true) '' (false)
```

## Definition

The file test operator takes one file handle or filename as an argument. It returns 1 (true) if the file is a symbolic link. It returns '' (false) if the file is not a symbolic link. All file test operators can take a special argument underscore, which means that the test is carried out on the same file handle as the last file test, stat(), or lstat() call. If no argument is supplied, $_ is used.

## Example

```
(-S "/vmlinuz") ? print("-S /vmlinuz is socket\n") :
      print("-S /vmlinuz is not socket\n");
```

# -s

## Compliance

## Syntax

```
Category   named unary operator (file test)
Arguments  handle
Arguments  filename
Arguments  none
Return Value  integer (size) '' (false)
```

## Definition

The file test operator takes one file handle or filename as an argument. It returns size in bytes as an integer if the file has a non-zero size. It returns '' (false) if the file has zero size. All file test operators can take a special argument underscore, which means that the test is carried out on the same file handle as the last file test, stat(), or lstat() call. If no argument is supplied, $_ is used.

## Example

```
(-s "/vmlinuz") ? print("-s /vmlinuz has non-zero size\n") :
      print("-s /vmlinuz does not have non-zero size\n");
```

# -T

## Compliance

## Syntax

```
Category  named unary operator (file test)
Arguments  handle
Arguments  filename
Arguments  none
Return Value  1 (true) '' (false)
```

## Definition

The `file test` operator takes one file `handle` or `filename` as an argument. It returns 1 (true) if the file is a text file. It returns `''` (false) if the file is not a text file. The first characters of the file are checked to see if the high bit is set, and if a suitable number is not set the file is assumed to be text. If the file is empty, true is returned. Because this test involves reading the file itself, it is best to test to learn if the file exists as a plain file (`-f`) first. All `file test` operators can take a special argument underscore, which means that the test is carried out on the same file `handle` as the last `file test`, `stat()`, or `lstat()` call. If no argument is supplied, `$_` is used.

## Example

```
(-T "/vmlinuz") ? print("-T /vmlinuz is text file\n") :
        print("-T /vmlinuz is not text file\n");
```

# -t

## Compliance

## Syntax

```
Category  named unary operator (file test)
Arguments  handle
Arguments  filename
Arguments  none
Return Value  1 (true) '' (false)
```

## Definition

The `file test` operator takes one file `handle` or `filename` as an argument. It returns 1 (true) if the file is a terminal tty device. It returns `''` (false) if the file is not. All `file test` operators can take a special argument underscore, which means that the test is carried out on the same file `handle` as the last `file test`, `stat()`, or `lstat()` call. If no argument is supplied, `STDIN` is used.

## Example

```
(-t "/vmlinuz") ? print("-t /vmlinuz is tty\n") :
        print("-t /vmlinuz is not tty\n");
```

# -u

## Compliance

## Syntax

```
Category  named unary operator (file test)
Arguments  handle
Arguments  filename
Arguments  none
Return Value  1 (true) '' (false)
```

## Definition

The file test operator takes one file handle or filename as an argument. It returns 1 (true) if the file has the setuid bit set. It returns '' (false) if the files does not have the setuid bit set. In UNIX, setuid allows an executable to take on the uid of the user ownership of the executable itself while executing. All file test operators can take a special argument underscore, which means that the test is carried out on the same file handle as the last file test, stat(), or lstat() call. If no argument is supplied, $_ is used.

## Example

```
(-u "/vmlinuz") ? print("-u /vmlinuz has suid set\n") :
        print("-u /vmlinuz does not have suid set\n");
```

# -W

## Compliance

## Syntax

```
Category  named unary operator (file test)
Arguments  handle
Arguments  filename
Arguments  none
Return Value  1 (true) '' (false)
```

## Definition

The file test operator takes one file handle or filename as an argument. It returns 1 (true) if the file is writable by the real UID/GID. It returns '' (false) otherwise. For the superuser it always returns true. All file test operators can take a special argument underscore, which means that the test is carried out on the same file handle as the last file test, stat(), or lstat() call. If no argument is supplied, $_ is used.

# Example

```
(-W "/vmlinuz") ? print("-W /vmlinuz is writable by real uid/gid\n") :
      print("-W /vmlinuz is not writable by real UID/GID\n");
```

# -W

## Compliance

## Syntax

```
Category  named unary operator (file test)
Arguments  handle
Arguments  filename
Arguments  none
Return Value  1 (true) '' (false)
```

## Definition

The file test operator takes one file handle or filename as an argument. It returns 1 (true) if the file is writable by the effective UID/GID. It returns '' (false) otherwise. For the superuser it always returns true. All file test operators can take a special argument underscore, which means that the test is carried out on the same file handle as the last file test, stat(), or lstat() call. If no argument is supplied, $_ is used.

# Example

```
(-w "/vmlinuz") ? print("-w /vmlinuz is writable by effective uid/gid\n") :
      print("-l /vmlinuz is not writable by effective uid/gid\n");
```

# -X

## Compliance

## Syntax

```
Category  named unary operator (file test)
Arguments  handle
Arguments  filename
Arguments  none
Return Value  1 (true) '' (false)
```

## Definition

The file test operator takes one file handle or filename as an argument. It returns 1 (true) if the file is executable by the real UID/GID. It returns '' (false) otherwise. For the superuser it always returns true. All file test operators can take a special argument underscore, which means that the test is carried out on the same file handle as the last file test, stat(), or lstat() call. If no argument is supplied, $_ is used.

# Example

```
(-X _) ? print("-X /bin/ls is executable by real uid/gid\n") :
        print("-X /bin/ls is not executable by real uid/gid\n");
```

# -X

# Compliance

# Syntax

**Category** named unary operator (file test)
**Arguments** handle
**Arguments** filename
**Arguments** none
**Return Value** 1 (true) '' (false)

# Definition

The file test operator takes one file handle or filename as an argument. It returns 1 (true) if the file is executable by the effective UID/GID. It returns '' (false) otherwise. For the superuser it always returns true. All file test operators can take a special argument underscore, which means that the test is carried out on the same file handle as the last file test, stat(), or lstat() call. If no argument is supplied, $_ is used.

# Example

```
(-x "/bin/ls") ? print("-x /bin/ls is executable by effective uid/gid\n") :
        print("-x /bin/ls is not executable by effective uid/gid\n");
```

# -Z

# Compliance

# Syntax

**Category** named unary operator (file test)
**Arguments** handle
**Arguments** filename
**Arguments** none
**Return Value** 1 (true) '' (false)

# Definition

The file test operator takes one file handle or filename as an argument. It returns 1 (true) if the file has zero size. It returns '' (false) otherwise. All file test operators can take a special argument underscore, which means that the test is carried out on the same file handle as the last file test, stat() or lstat() call. If no argument is supplied, $_ is used.

## Example

```
(-z "/vmlinuz") ? print("-z /vmlinuz has zero size\n") :
        print("-z /vmlinuz does not have zero size\n");
```

# abs

## Compliance

## Syntax

```
Category   named unary operator (numeric)
Arguments  numeric value
Return Value  numeric
```

## Definition

This function returns the absolute value of its argument (it ignores any sign).

## Example

```
print("abs(-10) = ",abs(-10),"\n");
```

# accept

## Compliance

## Syntax

```
Category   list operator (socket)
Arguments  newsocket, genericsocket
Return Value  integer (address of socket), '' (false)
```

## Definition

This function performs the low-level UNIX socket call accept().

# alarm

## Compliance

## Syntax

```
Category   named unary operator (process)
Arguments  integer (seconds)
Return Value  integer (seconds to previous alarm)
```

Part
V

Ch
15

## Definition

This function sets up a UNIX SIGALRM signal to be generated in the number of seconds specified. It is possible for Perl to trap such signals by calling specific signal handling subroutines, such as trap(). Subseqent calls reset the alarm() time, retaining the number of seconds which were needed before the previous SIGALRM would have been generated. A call with zero seconds as an argument cancels the current alarm().

## Example

```
print("alarm(10) ",alarm(10),
" (to illustrate it needs to trapped c.f. trap)\n");
```

# atan2

## Compliance

## Syntax

```
Category  list operator (numeric)
Arguments  numeric, numeric
Return Value  numeric
```

## Definition

The atan2 function returns the arctangent of the arguments.

## Example

```
print("atan2(60,2) = ",atan2(60,2),"\n");
```

# bind

## Compliance

## Syntax

```
Category  list operator (socket)
Arguments  sockethandle, numeric (network address)
Return Value  1 (true)  '' (false)
```

## Definition

This function binds a network address to the socket handle, see the UNIX bind() call.

# binmode

## Compliance

## Syntax

```
Category  named unary operator (i/o)
Arguments  handle
Return Value  1 (success) or undefined (error)
```

## Definition

On systems that distinguish between text and binary files, this function forces binary mode treatment of the given file handle. In systems which do make the distinction, text files have the end of line characters (Carriage Return, Linefeed) automatically translated to the UNIX end of line character (Linefeed) when reading from the file (and vice versa when writing to the file); binary mode files do not have this automatic transformation.

## Example

```
open(FIL,"file.dat");
binmode(FIL);
```

# bless

## Compliance

## Syntax

```
Category  list operator (class)
Arguments  variable
Arguments  variable, classname
Return Value  reference
```

## Definition

This function assigns a class to the referenced object. This class is either explicitly stated in the call, or the name of the current package is used if a second argument is not used in the call. The reference is returned.

 **TIP** Explictly state the class (use the two-argument version of the call) if the code can be inherited by other classes, because the class in the single-argument call would not return the required value.

## Example

```
$tmp = {};
bless $tmp, ATMPCLASS;
print "bless() \$tmp is now in class ",ref($tmp),"\n";
```

# caller

## Compliance

## Syntax

```
Category    named unary operator (scope)
Arguments   expression
Arguments   none
Return Value  1 (true) '' (false)
Return Value  (package, filename, line)
```

## Definition

This function is used to test the current scope of a subroutine call. If evaluated in a scalar context, it returns 1 or '' depending on if the current code has been called as a subroutine (this includes code which is included using a require() or an eval() call). In an array context it supplies details of the calling context in a list comprising the package name, filename, and line of the call.

## Example

```
sub testcaller {
    ($package, $file, $line) = caller;
}
&testcaller;
print "caller() Package=$package File=$file Line=$line \n";
```

# chdir

## Compliance

## Syntax

```
Category    named unary operator (files)
Arguments   expression
Arguments   none
Return Value  1 (true) '' (false)
```

## Definition

This function changes the current directory to the directory specified. If no argument is given this call changes the current directory to be the home directory of the current user. It returns 1 upon success and '' otherwise.

## Example

```
chdir("/") ? print("It worked.\n") : print("It didn't work.\n");
```

# chmod

## Compliance

## Syntax

```
Category  list operator (files)
Arguments  list
Return Value  numeric
```

## Definition

The first element in the list is the UNIX octal number representing the file permission. This function applies the mode specified by the octal number to all the files in the list that follows. It returns the number of files successfully modified.

## Example

```
print "chmod() changed ",
chmod(0744,"/tmp/test1.txt","/tmp/test2.txt")," files.\n";
```

# chomp

## Compliance

## Syntax

```
Category  list operator (string)
Arguments  list
Arguments  variable
Arguments  none
Return Value  numeric
```

## Definition

This is an alternative to the chop() function. It removes characters at the end of strings corresponding to the $INPUT_LINE_SEPARATOR ($/). It returns the number of characters removed. It can be given a list of strings upon which to perform this operation. When given no arguments, the operation is performed on $_.

## Example

```
$tmp="Aaagh!\n";
$ret = chomp $tmp;
print("chomp() ", $tmp, " returned ", $ret, "\n");
```

# chop

## Compliance

## Syntax

```
Category list operator (string)
Arguments list
Arguments variable
Arguments none
Return Value character
```

## Definition

This function removes the last character of a string and returns that character. If given a list of arguments, the operation is performed on each one and the last character chopped is returned.

## Example

```
$tmp = "1234";
$ret = chop $tmp;
print("chop() ", $tmp, " returned ", $ret, "\n");
```

 **TIP** Use chomp() (with $/ set to "\n") rather than chop() if you are unsure that the string has a trailing newline because chop() will remove the last character regardless, but chomp() only removes it if it is a newline.

# chown

## Compliance

## Syntax

```
Category list operator (files)
Arguments list
Return Value numeric
```

## Definition

This function changes the ownership of the specified files. The first two elements of the list define the user ID and the group ID to set this ownership; the subsequent items in the list are the file names that are changed. The return value is the number of files successfully changed.

## Example

```
print("chown() ");
chown(1,1,"/tmp/test1.txt") ? print("Worked\n") : print("Didn't work\n");
```

Part
V

Ch
15

# chr

## Compliance

## Syntax

**Category** named unary operator (string)
**Arguments** numeric
**Return Value** character

## Definition

This function returns the character indicated by the numeric argument.

## Example

```
$E = chr(69);
print("chr() $E \n");
```

# chroot

## Compliance

## Syntax

**Category** named unary operator (files)
**Arguments** directoryname
**Arguments** none
**Return Value** 1 (true) '' (false)

## Definition

This function is equivalent to the UNIX chroot() function. Given a directory name, this directory is treated as the root directory by all subseqent file system references, thus effectively hiding the rest of the file system outside the specified directory. This restriction applies to all subprocesses of the current process as well.

 Normal UNIX security limits this function to the superuser, and it is normally used to make processes safer by only allowing them access to the subdirectory tree relevant to their purpose.

## Example

```
print("chroot() ");
chroot("/") ? print("Worked.\n") : print("Didn't work.\n");
```

# close

## Compliance

## Syntax

```
Category  named unary operator (files)
Arguments  handle
Return Value  1 (true) '' (false)
```

## Definition

This function closes the file opened with the file `handle`. This operation flushes all buffered output. If the file `handle` refers to a pipe, the Perl program waits until the process being piped has finished.

## Example

```
open(INF,"/tmp/test1.txt");
$ret = close(INF);
print("close() Returned ",$ret," on success\n");
```

# closedir

## Compliance

## Syntax

```
Category  named unary operator (file)
Arguments  handle
Return Value  1 (true) '' (false)
```

## Definition

This function closes the directory opened by `opendir()` by specifying the relevant directory `handle`.

## Example

```
opendir(IND,"/tmp");
$ret = closedir(IND);
print("closedir() Returned ",$ret," on success\n");
```

# connect

## Compliance

## Syntax

```
Category  list operator (socket)
Arguments  socket, name
Return Value  1 (true) '' (false)
```

## Definition

This function is equivalent to the UNIX function call, which initiates a connection with a process, assuming that the process that is connected is waiting to accept.

# continue

## Compliance

## Syntax

```
Category  flow control
Arguments  block
Return Value  n/a
```

## Definition

A continue block is a syntax structure that allows a condition to be attached to another block (normally a while block). Any statements in the continue block are evaluated before the attached block is repeated.

## Example

```
$i=0;
print "continue() ";
while ($i<10) {
      if ($i % 2)
          { print "${i}o "; next; }
      else
          {print "${i}e ";}
} continue {$i++}
print "\n";
```

# cos

## Compliance

## Syntax

```
Category  named unary operator (numeric)
Arguments  expression
Return Value  numeric
```

## Definition

This function returns the cosine value of the numeric expression supplied as an argument.

## Example

```
print "cos() ",cos(60),"\n";
```

# crypt

## Compliance

## Syntax

```
Category  list operator
Arguments  string, string
Return Value  string
```

## Definition

This function is equivalent to the crypt() UNIX call (where available). It encrypts a string (the first argument) using a key (usually the first two letters of the first string itself) and returns the encrypted string.

## Example

```
print "crypt() Password PA: ",crypt("Password","PA"),"\n";
```

# dbmclose

## Compliance

## Syntax

```
Category  named unary operator (i/o)
Arguments  arrayname
Return Value  1 (true) '' (false)
```

## Definition

This function undoes the linking of an associative array to a dbm file (see `dbmopen()`).

> **N O T E**   This is depreciated in Perl 5; use `untie()` instead. ■

# dbmopen

## Compliance

## Syntax

```
Category  list operator (i/o)
Arguments  arrayname, dbname, mode
Return Value  fatal error if dbm not supported (Perl 4)
```

## Definition

This function links the associative array referred to by `arrayname`, to the dbm database (or equivalent) referred to by `dbname` (this name should not include the suffix). If the database does not exist, a new one with the specified mode will be opened (the mode being an octal `chmod()` style file protection).

> **N O T E**   This is depreciated in Perl 5; use `tie()` instead. ■

# defined

## Compliance

## Syntax

```
Category  named unary operator (misc)
Arguments  expression
Return Value  1 (true) '' (false)
```

## Definition

This function returns a Boolean value depending on whether the argument is defined or not. There is a subtle distinction between an undefined and a defined null value. Some functions return an undefined null to indicate errors, while others return a defined null to indicate a particular result (use a comparison with the null string to test for this, rather than using `defined()`)

## Example

```
@iexist = (1,2,3);
print("defined() The array \@iexist ");
defined @iexist ? print("exists.\n") : print("does not exist.\n");
```

# delete

## Compliance

## Syntax

**Category** named unary operator (hash)
**Arguments** expression
**Return Value** value

## Definition

Use this function to delete an element from a hash array, given the key for the element to delete, returning the value of the deleted element.

## Example

```
%Hash = (1, One, 2, Two, 3, Three);
print("delete() Deleted ",delete($Hash{1}),"\n");
```

# die

## Compliance

## Syntax

**Category** list operator (i/o)
**Arguments** list
**Return Value** errorlevel

## Definition

This function terminates execution of the Perl script when called printing the value of the list argument to STDERR (as if called with print(STDERR, list)). The exit value is the current value of $OS_ERROR ($!), which may have been set by a previous function. If this has a value of zero it returns $CHILD_ERROR ($?). If this is zero, it exits with errorlevel 255. If the error message string specified by the list does not end in a newline, the text "at $PROGRAM_NAME at line *line*, where *line* is the line number of the Perl script.

## Example

```
die("die() Now we can give an example of die()...exiting");
```

# do

## Compliance

## Syntax

```
Category   (flow)
Arguments  block
Arguments  subroutine(list)
Arguments  expression
Return Value  special
```

## Definition

This is a syntax structure that allows repeated execution of a block of statements. The value returned is the result of the last statement in the block. Normally an exit condition is supplied after the block. The second form where the argument is subroutine() is a depreciated form. The third form executes the contents of the file name specified by the expression (but it is better to use use() or require() instead, because this has better error checking).

## Example

```
$i=1;
print("do ");
$return = do {
  print $i, " ";
  $i++;
} until $i==3;
print("Returned $return\n");
```

# dump

## Compliance

## Syntax

```
Category   named unary operator (misc)
Arguments  label
Return Value  N/A
```

## Definition

This function causes the program to create a binary image core dump. This then allows the dumped image to be reloaded using the undump() function (if supported) which can effectively allow the use of precompiled Perl images. When reloaded, the program begins execution from the `label` specified. It is possible to set up a program which initializes data structures to `dump()` after the initialization so that execution is faster when reloading the dumped image.

# each

## Compliance

## Syntax

```
Category  named unary operator (hash)
Arguments  variable
Return Value  key, value
```

## Definition

This function allows iteration over the elements in an associative array. Each time it is evaluated, it returns another list of two elements (a key, value pair from the associative array). When all the elements have been returned, it returns a null list.

## Example

```
%NumberWord = (1, One, 2, Two, 3, Three);
print("each() ");
while (($number,$wordform)=each(%NumberWord)) {
  print("$number:$wordform ");
}
print("\n");
```

# endgrent

## Compliance

## Syntax

```
Category  (system files)
Arguments  none
Return Value  1 (true) '' (false)
```

## Definition

This function closes the `/etc/group` file used by `getgrent()` and other group-related functions. It is equivalent to the UNIX system call.

## Example

```
($name,$pw,$gid,@members)=getgrent();
$returned = endgrent();
print("endgrent() Closes /etc/group [$name,$gid]",
      " file returning $returned.\n");
```

# endhostent

## Compliance

## Syntax

```
Category  (system files)
Arguments  none
Return Value  1 (true) '' (false)
```

## Definition

This function closes the TCP socket used by name server queries `gethostbyname()` and host-related functions. It is equivalent to the UNIX system call.

## Example

```
$host = gethostbyname("lynch");
$returned = endhostent();
print("endhostent() Closes /etc/hosts [$host]",
       " returning $returned.\n");
```

# endnetent

## Compliance

## Syntax

```
Category  (system files)
Arguments  none
Return Value  1 (true) '' (false)
```

## Definition

This function closes the `/etc/networks` file used by `getnetent()` and network-related functions. This function is equivalent to the UNIX system call.

## Example

```
($name,$alias,$net,$net) = getnetent();
$returned = endnetent();
print("endnetent() Closes /etc/networks [$name]",
       " returning $returned.\n");
```

# endprotoent

## Compliance

## Syntax

```
Category  (system files)
Arguments  none
Return Value  1 (true) '' (false)
```

## Definition

This function closes the /etc/protocols file used by getprotoent() and protocol-related functions. It is equivalent to the UNIX system call.

## Example

```
($name, $alias, $protocol) = getprotoent();
$returned = endprotoent();
print("endprotoent() Closes /etc/protocols ",
        "[$name,$alias,$protocol] file returning $returned.\n");
```

# endpwent

## Compliance

## Syntax

```
Category  (system files)
Arguments  none
Return Value  1 (true) '' (false)
```

## Definition

This function closes the /etc/passwd file used by getpwent() and password-related functions. It is equivalent to the UNIX system call.

## Example

```
($name,$pass,$uid,$gid,$quota,$name,$gcos,$logindir,$shell) = getpwent();
$returned = endpwent();
print("endpwent() Closes /etc/passwd [$logindir,$shell] ",
        "file returning $returned.\n");
```

# endservent

## Compliance

## Syntax

```
Category  (system files)
Arguments  none
Return Value  1 (true) '' (false)
```

## Definition

This function closes the /etc/servers file used by getservent() and related functions. It is equivalent to the UNIX system call.

## Example

```
($name,$aliases,$port,$protocol) = getservent();
$returned = endservent();
print("endservent() Closes /etc/servers [$name]",
        " file returning $returned.\n");
```

# eof

## Compliance

## Syntax

```
Category  named unary operator (i/o)
Arguments  handle
Arguments  ()
Arguments  none
Return Value  1 (true) '' (false)
```

## Definition

This function tests if the file pointer to file specified by the file handle is at the end of the file. This is done by reading the next character and then undoing this operation (so is only suitable on files where this can be done safely). If no argument is supplied the file tested is the last file that was read. If the empty list is supplied then this tests if all the last files that supplied an argument to the Perl script are eof() (that is, it can be used as a termination condition in a while loop).

## Example

```
open INF, "/tmp/test1.txt";
if (eof INF)
  {print "eof() TRUE\n";}
else
  {print "eof() FALSE\n";}
close INF;
```

# eval

## Compliance

## Syntax

```
Category  named unary operator (flow)
Arguments  expression
Arguments  block
Arguments  none
Return Value  special
```

## Definition

This function treats the expression like a Perl program and executes it by returning the return value of the last statement executed. As the context of this execution is the same as that of the script itself, variable definitions and subroutine definitions persist. Syntax errors and runtime errors (including die()) are trapped and an undefined result is returned. If such an error does occur, $EVAL_ERROR ($@) is set. If no errors are found, $@ is equal to a defined null string. If no expression is supplied, $_ is the default argument. If the block syntax is used, the expressions in the block are evaluated only once within the script, which may be more efficient for certain situations.

 **TIP** eval() traps possible error conditions that would otherwise crash a program. Therefore, it can be used to test if certain features are available that would cause runtime errors if used when not available.

## Example

```
$ans = 3;
eval "$ans = ;";
if ($@ eq "")
    {print "eval() returned success.\n";}
else
    {print "eval() error: $@";}
```

# exec

## Compliance

## Syntax

```
Category  list operator (process)
Arguments  list
Return Value  N/A
```

## Definition

This function passes control from the script to an external system command. There is no retain from this call so there is no return value. Note that `system()` calls external commands and does return to the next line in the calling Perl program.

This is equivalent to the UNIX system call `execvp()`.

## Example

```
exec("cat /etc/motd");
```

# exists

## Compliance

## Syntax

```
Category  named unary operator (hash)
Arguments  expression
Return Value  1 (true) '' (false)
```

## Definition

This function tests if a given key value exists in an associative array, returning a Boolean value.

## Example

```
%test = ( One, 1, Two, 2);
if (exists $test{One})
   {print "exists() returned success.\n";}
else
   {print "exists() returned an error.\n";}
```

# exit

## Compliance

## Syntax

```
Category  named unary operator (flow)
Arguments  expression
Arguments  none
Return Value  value
```

## Definition

This function evaluates the expression given as an argument and exits the program with that error. The default value for the error is 0 if no argument is supplied. Note that `die()` allows an error message.

## Example

```
exit(16);
```

# exp

## Compliance

## Syntax

```
Category  named unary operator (numeric)
Arguments  expression
Arguments  none
Return Value  numeric
```

## Definition

This function returns the natural log base (e) to the power of expression (or of $_ if none specified).

## Example

```
print "exp() e**1 is ",exp(1),"\n";
```

# fcntl

## Compliance

## Syntax

```
Category  list operator (i/o)
Arguments  handle, function, packed_parameters
```

## Definition

This function is equivalent to the UNIX fnctl() call. In Perl 5, use the fntcl module. In Perl 4, there should be some mechanism for linking the Perl functions to the system functions. This is usually executed when Perl is installed.

# fileno

## Compliance

## Syntax

```
Category  named unary operator (i/o)
Arguments  handle
Return Value  descriptor
```

## Definition

This function returns the file descriptor given a file `handle`.

## Example

```
print("fileno() ",fileno(INF),"\n");
```

# flock

## Compliance

## Syntax

```
Category  list operator (i/o)
Arguments  handle, operation
Return Value  1 (true) '' (false)
```

## Definition

This calls the UNIX `flock()` function to access file locks. The `handle` is a Perl file `handle`. The operation is any valid `flock()` operation: place exclusive lock, place shared lock, unlock. These operations are represented by numeric values.

# fork

## Compliance

## Syntax

```
Category  (process)
Arguments  none
Return Value  pid
```

## Definition

The `fork` function calls the UNIX `fork()` function or equivalent to fork a subprocess at this point. Returns the process ID (pid) of the child process to the calling process; returns 0 to the child process itself. The calling program should `wait()` on any child process it `forks` to avoid creating zombie processes.

## Example

```
$pid = fork;
# Child only prints this
if ($pid != 0) {
  print("fork() Forking a process duplicates o/p: $pid \n");
}
```

```
waitpid($pid,0);
# Child exits here
if ($$ != $origpid) { die; }
```

# format

## Compliance

## Syntax

```
Category:  list operator (i/o)
Arguments:  format
```

## Definition

This function declares an output `format` specification. These formats are used in conjunction with the `write()` function to control the output of variables and text to conform to a standard layout structure. Normally, the specification includes some variables, specifying how many characters to output and whether to justify these left, right, or centered. When `write()` is called, the actual values of the variables are used. This is useful for printing simple text reports and tables. The `format` specification itself is terminated by a period on a line by itself. The specification itself is in pairs of lines, the first describing the layout, and the second describing the variables to use in this layout.

## Example

```
format STDOUT =
format()  @>>>>>>> @>>>>>>> @>>>>>>>
          $t1,     $t2,       $t3
.
$t1 = One;
$t2 = Two;
$t3 = 3;
write;
```

# formline

## Compliance

## Syntax

```
Category:  list operator (i/o)
Arguments:  picture, list
```

## Definition

This function is not usually called explictly (it is an implicit part of the `format` mechanism). It allows direct manipulation of the `format` process by adding values to the `format` accumulator (`$^A`).

## Example

```
$tmp = formline <<'FINISH', Alpha, Beta, Gamma;
formline()  @>>>>>> @>>>>>> @>>>>>>
FINISH
print $^A;
```

# getc

## Compliance

## Syntax

**Category** named unary operator (i/o)
**Arguments** handle
**Arguments** none
**Return Value** character

## Definition

This function returns the next character in specified file `handle`. The file defaults to `STDIN` if none is specified. If there are no more characters, null is returned.

## Example

```
open INF, "/etc/motd";
print "getc() ",getc(INF),"\n";
close INF;
```

# getgrent

## Compliance

## Syntax

**Category** list operator (system files)
**Arguments** none
**Return Value** name

## Definition

This returns the next group name (or undefined) in the `/etc/group` system file. In a list context, it returns extra information taken from this file (or null list). This function is equivalent to the UNIX system call `getgrent()`.

## Example

```
($name,$pw,$gid,@members)=getgrent();
print("getgrent() Examines /etc/group [$name,$gid] file.\n");
```

# getgrgid

## Compliance

## Syntax

**Category** named unary operator (system files)
**Arguments** gid
**Return Value** name

## Definition

This function returns the next group name (or undefined) in the /etc/group system file with the supplied group ID (gid). In a list context it returns extra information taken from this file (or null list). Equivalent to the UNIX system call getgrgid().

## Example

```
($grname,$grpw,$gid,@members) = getgrgid(0);
print("getgrgid() Returns group name given GID [$grname]\n");
```

# getgrname

## Compliance

## Syntax

**Category** named unary operator (system files)
**Arguments** name
**Return Value** gid

## Definition

This function returns the next group ID, gid, (or undefined) in the /etc/group system file with the supplied group name. In a list context, it returns extra information taken from this file (or null list). It is equivalent to the UNIX system call getgrname().

## Example

```
($grname,$grpw,$gid,@members) = getgrnam("root");
print("getgrnam() Returns group GID given name [$gid]\n");
```

# gethostbyaddr

## Compliance

## Syntax

```
Category  named unary operator (system files)
Arguments  address
Return Value  name
```

## Definition

It returns the host name, (or undefined) in the /etc/hosts system file (or via a Domain Name Server lookup) with the supplied host address. In a list context, The function returns extra information taken from this file (or null list). It is equivalent to the UNIX system call gethostbyaddr().

## Example (Perl 5 only)

```
use Socket;
@a=(140,203,7,103);
$addr=pack('C4',@a);
($name,$alias,$adrtype,$length,@address)=gethostbyaddr($addr,AF_INET);
print("gethostbyaddr() [$alias].\n");
```

# gethostbyname

## Compliance

## Syntax

```
Category  named unary operator (system files)
Arguments  name
Return Value  address
```

## Definition

This function returns the host address, (or undefined) in the /etc/hosts system file (or via a Domain Name Server lookup) with the supplied host name. In a list context, it returns extra information taken from this file (or null list). This function is equivalent to the UNIX system call gethostbyname().

## Example

```
($name,$alias,$adrtype,$length,@address)=gethostbyname("lynch");
print("gethostbyname() [$alias].\n");
```

# gethostent

## Compliance

## Syntax

    Category  (system files)
    Arguments  none
    Return Value  name

## Definition

gethostent returns the next host name, (or undefined) in the /etc/hosts system file (or via a Domain Name Server lookup). In a list context, it returns extra information taken from this file (or null list). This function is equivalent to the UNIX system call gethostent().

## Example

    ($name,$alias,$adrtype,$length,@address)=gethostbyname("lynch");
    print("gethostent() [$alias].\n");

# getlogin

## Compliance

## Syntax

    Category  (system files)
    Arguments  none
    Return Value  name

## Definition

This function returns the current login name from the /etc/utmp system file. It is better to than the getpwuid() function for more information on the login because the information stored in /etc/utmp is limited.

## Example

    print ("getlogin() ",getlogin(),"\n");

# getnetbyaddr

## Compliance

## Syntax

**Category** (system files)
**Arguments** address
**Return Value** name

## Definition

getnetbyaddr returns the network name from the /etc/networks system file given a network address. In a list context, it returns extra information from this file. This function is equivalent to UNIX's getnetbyaddr() call.

## Example

```
($name,$alias,$addrtype,$net) = getnetent();
($name,$alias,$addrtype,$net) = getnetbyaddr($net,$addrtype);
print("getnetbyaddr() Reads /etc/networks [$name]\n");
```

# getnetbyname

## Compliance

## Syntax

**Category** named unary operator (system files)
**Arguments** name
**Return Value** address

## Definition

Returns the network address from the /etc/networks system file, given a network name. In a list, context returns extra information from this file. Equivalent to the UNIX getnetbyname() call.

## Example

```
($name,$alias,$addrtype,$net) = getnetbyname("localnet");
print("getnetbyname() Reads /etc/networks [$name]\n");
```

# getnetent

## Compliance

## Syntax

    Category  (system files)
    Arguments  none
    Return Value  name

## Definition

This function returns the next network name from the /etc/networks system file. In a list context, it returns extra information from this file. getnetent is equivalent to the UNIX getnetent() call.

## Example

```
($name,$alias,$addrtype,$net) = getnetent();
print("getnetent() Reads /etc/networks [$name,$addrtype]\n");
```

# getpeername

## Compliance

## Syntax

    Category  named unary operator (socket)
    Arguments  socket
    Return Value  name

## Definition

getpeername is equivalent to the UNIX system getpeername() system call.

# getpgrp

## Compliance

## Syntax

    Category  named unary operator (process)
    Arguments  pid
    Return Value  gid

## Definition

This function returns the group ID (`gid`) of the process with the process ID (`pid`).

## Example

```
print("getpgrp() ",getpgrp(0),"\n");
```

# getppid

## Compliance

## Syntax

```
Category  (process)
Arguments  none
Return Value  pid
```

## Definition

`getppid` returns the process ID (`pid`) of the parent process of the current process.

## Example

```
print("getppid() ",getppid(),"\n");
```

# getpriority

## Compliance

## Syntax

```
Category  list operator (process)
Arguments  type, id
Return Value  priority
```

## Definition

This function calls the UNIX `getpriority()` function. The type is one of `PRIO_PROCESS`, `PRIO_PGGRP`, and `PRIO_USER`. The `id` is the relevent ID for this (`pid` for `PRIO_PROCESS`, `pid` for `PRIO_PGGRP`, `uid` for `PRIO_USER`). If zero is used as the `id`, the current process, process group, or user is used.

## Example

```
print("getpriority() ",getpriority(0,0),"\n");
```

# getprotobyname

## Compliance

## Syntax

```
Category  named unary operator (system files)
Arguments  name
Return Value  protocol
```

## Definition

This function returns the protocol number from the /etc/protocols system file, given the
protocol name. In a list context, it returns extra information from this file. getprotobyname is
equivalent to the UNIX getprotobyname() call.

## Example

```
($name, $alias, $protocol) = getprotobyname("IP");
print("getprotobyname() /etc/protocols [$name,$alias,$protocol].\n");
```

# getprotobynumber

## Compliance

## Syntax

```
Category  named unary operator (system files)
Arguments  protocol
Return Value  name
```

## Definition

This function returns the protocol name from the /etc/protocols system file, given the protocol number. In a list context, it returns extra information from this file. getprotobynumber is
equivalent to the UNIX getprotobynumber() call.

## Example

```
($name, $alias, $protocol) = getprotobynumber(0);
print("getprotobynumber() /etc/protocols [$name,$alias,$protocol].\n");
```

# getprotoent

## Compliance

## Syntax

    Category  (system files)
    Arguments  none
    Return Value  name

## Definition

This returns the next protocol name from the /etc/protocols system file. In a list context, it returns extra information from this file. This function is equivalent to UNIX's getprotoent() call.

## Example

```
($name, $alias, $protocol) = getprotoent();
print("getprotoent() Closes /etc/protocols [$name,$alias,$protocol].\n");
```

# getpwent

## Compliance

## Syntax

    Category  (system files)
    Arguments  none
    Return Value  name

## Definition

getpwent returns the user name from the next entry in the /etc/passwd system file. In a list context, it returns extra information from this file. This function is equivalent to the UNIX getpwent() call.

## Example

```
($name,$pass,$uid,$gid,$quota,$name,$gcos,$logindir,$shell) = getpwent();
print("getpwent() /etc/passwd [$logindir,$shell].\n");
```

# getpwnam

## Compliance

## Syntax

**Category** named unary operator (system files)
**Arguments** name
**Return Value** uid

## Definition

This function returns the user ID (uid) from the /etc/passwd system file given the user name. In a list context, it returns extra information from this file. It is equivalent to the UNIX getpwnam() call.

## Example

```
($name,$pass,$uid,$gid,$quota,$name,$gcos,$logindir,$shell)
        = getpwnam("root");
print("getpwnam() /etc/passwd [$logindir,$shell].\n");
```

# getpwuid

## Compliance

## Syntax

**Category** named unary operator (system files)
**Arguments** uid
**Return Value** name

## Definition

getpwiud returns the user name from the /etc/passwd system file given the user ID (uid). In a list context, getpwuid returns extra information from this file. This function is equivalent to the UNIX getpwnam() call.

## Example

```
($name,$pass,$uid,$gid,$quota,$name,$gcos,$logindir,$shell)
        = getpwuid(0);
print("getpwuid() /etc/passwd [$logindir,$shell].\n");
```

# getservbyname

## Compliance

## Syntax

```
Category  list operator (system files)
Arguments  name, protocol
Return Value  port
```

## Definition

getservbyname returns the port number of the service from the /etc/services system file given the service name and the protocol name. In a list context, it returns extra information from this file. This function is equivalent to UNIX's getservbyname() call.

## Example

```
($name,$aliases,$port,$protocol) = getservbyname("tcpmux","tcp");
print("getservbyname() /etc/servers [$name].\n");
```

# getservbyport

## Compliance

## Syntax

```
Category  list operator (system files)
Arguments  port, protocol
Return Value  name
```

## Definition

getservbyport returns the service name of the service from the /etc/services system file given the port number and the protocol name. In a list context, it returns extra information from this file. It is equivalent to the UNIX getservbyport() call.

## Example

```
($name,$aliases,$port,$protocol) = getservbyport(512,"tcp");
print("getservbyport() Problem with this! [$name]\n");
```

# getservent

## Compliance

## Syntax

```
Category  (system files)
Arguments  none
Return Value  name
```

## Definition

This function returns the next service name of the service from the /etc/services system file. In a list context, it returns extra information from this file. It is equivalent to the UNIX getservet() call.

## Example

```
($name,$aliases,$port,$protocol) = getservent();
print("getservent() /etc/servers [$name].\n");
```

# getsockname

## Compliance

## Syntax

```
Category  named unary operator (socket)
Arguments  socket
Return Value  address
```

## Definition

This function is equivalent to the UNIX getsockname() system call and returns the address of the socket.

# getsockopt

## Compliance

## Syntax

```
Category  list operator (socket)
Arguments  socket, level, optionname
Return Value  option
```

## Definition

This function is equivalent to the UNIX `getsockopt()` system call and returns the socket option requested. However, if an error has happened, the function's return is undefined.

# glob

## Compliance

## Syntax

```
Category  named unary operator (files)
Arguments  expression
Return Value  list
```

## Definition

This function returns the `list` of files resulting from expanding the expression with any wildcards. This is equivalent to `<*.*>`.

## Example

```
@files = glob("/tmp/*.txt");
print "glob() ",$files[1],"\n";
```

# gmtime

## Compliance

## Syntax

```
Category  named unary operator (time)
Arguments  expression
Arguments  none
Return Value  list
```

## Definition

Given a time as an argument (measured in seconds since 1 Jan 1970), `gmtime` returns a `list` of nine elements with that time broken down into seconds, minutes, hours, day of month, month, year, day of week, day of year, and daylight saving-enabled (daylight saving-enabled is either 1 for on or 0 for off). If no argument is used, the current time is reported. If the system supports POSIX time zones, the time returned is localized for the Greenwich Mean Time.

In a scalar context, the `ctime()` style output (a string describing the time in readable form) is returned.

## Example

```
($sec,$min,$hour,$mday,$mon,$year,$wday,$ydat,$isdst) = gmtime();
print "gmtime() 19$year-$mon-$mday\n";
```

# goto

## Compliance

## Syntax

```
Category   (flow)
Arguments  label
Arguments  expression
Arguments  &name
Return Value  N/A
```

## Definition

The first form transfers control flow in the program to the specified label. The second allows the evaluation of an expression to supply the label name to transfer control to. The third form is a way of passing control from one subroutine to another subroutine so that, to the original caller, it appears that the second subroutine was called directly.

## Example

```
print "goto ";
$count = 1;
TESTGOTO: {
    print $count, " ";
    $label = "TESTGOTO";
    if ($count < 2) {
        $count++;
        goto $label;
    }
    else {
        goto FINISH;}
}
FINISH: print "\n";
```

# grep

## Compliance

## Syntax

```
Category   list operator (lists)
Arguments  expression, list
Arguments  block, list
Return Value  list
```

## Definition

This function evaluates the `expression` or `block` for each of the elements in the supplied list, returning a list of the elements that were evaulated as TRUE. The most common use for this is with a pattern match operation as the expression, and a list of strings to be processed.

## Example

```
@a = ("One","Two","Three","Four","Five");
print("grep(), ",grep(/^T.*/,@a), "\n");
```

# hex

## Compliance

## Syntax

```
Category  named unary operator (numeric)
Arguments  expression
Return Value  numeric
```

## Definition

This function evaluates the expression as a hexadecimal string and returns the decimal equivalent.

## Example

```
print("hex() ",hex("ff"), "\n");
```

# import

## Compliance

## Syntax

```
Category  list operator (scope)
Arguments  list
Return Value  1 (true) '' (false)
```

## Definition

In the Perl 5 module system, each module has a local `import()` method. This is called when `use()` includes modules.

# index

## Compliance

## Syntax

```
Category  list operator (string)
Arguments  string substring
Arguments  string substring position
Return Value  position
```

## Definition

index returns the position in the supplied string where the substring first occurs. If a position is supplied as an argument, the search begins at this element (thus repeated calls can find all occurrences if the found position is passed back as the argument to the subsequent calls). If the substring is not found, the return value is -1. All array element numbers are based on $[, which is normally set to zero. If this value is altered it will change the way index() works. This is because index will start its search from $[ if no position argument is supplied, and it will return $[ -1 when there is no match found.

## Example

```
$ans1 = index("abcdefghijiklmdef:-)","def");
$ans2 = index("abcdefghijiklmdef","def",$ans1+3);
print("index() def is at $ans1 and next at $ans2\n");
```

# int

## Compliance

## Syntax

```
Category  named unary operator (numeric)
Arguments  expression
Arguments  none
Return Value  integer
```

## Definition

This function returns the integer part of the expression. It uses $_ as the argument if none is specified.

## Example

```
print("int() ",int(345.678), "\n");
```

# ioctl

## Compliance

## Syntax

**Category**  list operator (files)
**Arguments**  handle, function, parameter
**Return Value**  numeric

## Definition

This function calls the UNIX ioctl() function with the specified packed parameter. It returns undefined if the operating system returns -1. It returns the string 0 but true if the operating system returns 0. Otherwise, it returns the value returned by the operating system.

# join

## Compliance

## Syntax

**Category**  list operator (lists)
**Arguments**  expression, list
**Return Value**  string

## Definition

This function returns the string comprising each element in the list joined with the string expression.

## Example ·

```
@listone = (0, 1, 2, 3);
print("join() ",join("-",@listone),"\n");
```

# keys

## Compliance

## Syntax

**Category**  named unary operator (hash)
**Arguments**  array
**Return Value**  list

## Definition

This function returns a list comprising each key in the associative array passed as a parameter. In a scalar context, the number of keys is returned. The returned list is ordered by the internal storage requirements, so it is often useful to sort this array before processing.

## Example

```
%assocone = (
        One, 1,
        Two, 2,
        Three, 3,
        Four, 4
        );
print("keys() ",join("-",keys(%assocone)),"\n");
```

# kill

## Compliance

## Syntax

```
Category  list operator (process)
Arguments signal, list
Return Value 1 (true) '' (false)
```

## Definition

This function kills the processes with the pids in the supplied list by sending the signal level specified. If the signal level is negative, the process groups are killed.

# last

## Compliance

## Syntax

```
Category  (flow)
Arguments label
Arguments none
Return Value N/A
```

## Definition

This causes control to exit the loop specified by label (or the innermost loop if none is specified).

## Example

```
i=1;
print("last() ");
loop: while (I<10) {
        last loop if i=3;
        print(i);
}
print("\n");
```

# lc

## Compliance

## Syntax

**Category** named unary operator (string)
**Arguments** expression
**Return Value** string

## Definition

This function returns the lowercase version of any supplied expression.

## Example

```
print"lc() ",lc("ABCDef"), "\n";
```

# lcfirst

## Compliance

## Syntax

**Category** named unary operator (string)
**Arguments** expression
**Return Value** string

## Definition

This function returns the string with the first character of the expression lowercased.

## Example

```
print"lcfirst() ",lcfisrt("ABCDef"), "\n";
```

# length

## Compliance

## Syntax

```
Category  named unary operator (string)
Arguments  expression
Arguments  none
Return Value  numeric
```

## Definition

length returns the length of the string specified by expression. If no expression is supplied, $_ is evaluated.

## Example

```
print("length() ",length("01234"),"\n");
```

# link

## Compliance

## Syntax

```
Category  list operator (files)
Arguments  filename, linkname
Return Value  numeric
```

## Definition

This function creates a new link named after the second argument linking to the filename specified in the first argument; returns 1 or 0 for success or failure.

## Example

```
$result = link("/usr/local",:"/tmp/link");
print("link() $result\n");
```

# listen

## Compliance

## Syntax

```
Category  list operator (socket)
Arguments  socket, queuesize
Return Value  1 (true) '' (false)
```

## Definition

This is equivalent to the UNIX `listen()` system call. If you are using `accepts` on a socket, `listen` tells the system that it is available.

# local

## Compliance

## Syntax

```
Category  named unary operator (scope)
Arguments  expression
Return Value  N/A
```

## Definition

Modifies all the variables listed to be local to the current block. If there is more than one element, the list must be enclosed in parentheses. Any errors would be syntax errors. Although `local()` does prevent pollution of the global namespace with variables in subroutines, `my()` is safer than `local()` because it also creates new copies of the variables for each recursive call of a subroutine.

# localtime

## Compliance

## Syntax

```
Category  named unary operator (time)
Arguments  expression
Arguments  none
Return Value  list
```

## Definition

Given a time as an argument (measured in seconds since 1 Jan 1970), this function returns a list of nine elements with that time broken down into seconds, minutes, hours, day of month, month, year, day of week, day of year, and daylight saving-enabled (daylight saving-enabled is either 1 for on or 0 for off). If no argument is used, the current time is reported. If the system supports POSIX time zones, the time returned is localized for the current time zone.

In a scalar context, the `ctime()` style output is returned (a string describing the time in readable form).

## Example

```
($sec,$min,$hour,$mday,$mon,$year,$wday,$ydat,$isdst) = localtime();
print "localtime() 19$year-$mon-$mday\n";
```

# log

## Compliance

## Syntax

```
Category  named unary operator (numeric)
Arguments  expression
Arguments  none
Return Value  numeric
```

## Definition

This returns the logarithm (using the natural logarithm base e) of the expression (or of $_ if none specified).

## Example

```
print("log() ",log(2.5),"\n");
```

# lstat

## Compliance

## Syntax

```
Category  named unary operator (files)
Arguments  handle
Arguments  expression
Return Value  list
```

## Definition

The lstat function returns the file statstics of the file pointed to by the file handle (or a file handle produced by evaluating the expression). This is equivalent to stat(), but if the file is a symbolic link, the statistics are generated for the symbolic link itself rather than the file being linked to. Note that, like the file test operators, lstat() can take a special argument underscore, which means that the test is carried out on the same file handle as the last file test, stat(), or lstat() call.

## Example

```
($device,$inode,$mode,$nlink,$uid,$gid,$rdev,$size,
$atime,$mtime,$ctime,$blksize,$blocks) = lstat("/tmp/link");
print("lstat() $device, $inode, $ctime \n");
```

# m//

## Compliance

## Syntax

```
Category  named unary operator (pattern)
Arguments  m/<pattern>/<optionlist>
Arguments  /<pattern>/<optionlist>
Return Value  1 (true) '' (false)
```

## Definition

This function searches the default string for the pattern using regular expression pattern matching. It returns 1 if a match is found. Otherwise, ' ' is returned. The default string can be assigned to the match using either the =~ or !~ operators; otherwise, it is $_.

## Example

```
$_ = "Happy MaN";
print "m// ",/n$/i,"\n";
```

# map

## Compliance

## Syntax

```
Category  list operator (list)
Arguments  block list
Arguments  expression, list
Return Value  list
```

## Definition

This function evaluates the specified expression (or block) for each individual member of the specified list. This is done by assigning $_ to each member of the list and evaluating the expression (or block). The value returned is the list of all these results (not necessarily one Perl element of the list).

## Example

```
@result = map($_+1,(0,1,2));
print("map() ",@result,."\n");
```

# mkdir

## Compliance

## Syntax

```
Category  list operator (files)
Arguments  filename, mode
Return Value  1 or 0
```

## Definition

The mkdir function creates a directory with a name specified by the filename, with the mode specified by the octal mode. If it fails, $OS_ERROR ($!) is set to operating system error.

## Example

```
print("mkdir() ",mkdir("/tmp/testdir",0777), "\n");
```

# msgctl

## Compliance

## Syntax

```
Category  list operator (System V)
Arguments  id, cmd, arg
Return Value  special
```

## Definition

This function is equivalent to the UNIX system call msgctl(), if supported, and provides a variety of message control operations as specified by CMD.

# msgget

## Compliance

## Syntax

```
Category  list operator (System V)
Arguments  key, flags
Return Value  special
```

## Definition

This function is equivalent to the UNIX system call msgget(), if supported, and returns the message queue identifier associated with key.

# msgrcv

## Compliance

## Syntax

```
Category  list operator (System V)
Arguments  id, var.size, type, flags
Return Value  special
```

## Definition

This is equivalent to the UNIX system call msgrcv(), if supported. This function reads a message from the queue associated with the message queue identifier, specified by msqid, and places it in the structure pointed to by msgp.

# msgsnd

## Compliance

## Syntax

```
Category  list operator (System V)
Arguments  id, msg, flags
Return Value  special
```

## Definition

The msgsnd function is equivalent to the UNIX system call msgsnd(), if supported, and sends a message to the queue associated with the message queue identifier.

# my

## Compliance

## Syntax

```
Category  named unary operator (scope)
Arguments  expression
Return Value  N/A
```

## Definition

This function declares each of the variables listed to be local() to the block. If more than one variable is specified, parentheses are required. The my() specification is stronger than the the local() specification because it not only stops pollution of the global namespace but also creates a stack frame for subroutine calls so that recursive calls will behave as one would expect with local variables.

# next

## Compliance

## Syntax

```
Category  named unary operator (flow)
Arguments label
Arguments none
Return Value N/A
```

## Definition

This operator allows branching within a loop so that the execution skips onto the next instance of the loop.

## Example

```
print("next ");
@array = ("a","b","c");
loop: foreach $elem (@array) {
        next if $elem =~ /^a/;
        print $elem;
}
print "\n";
```

# no

## Compliance

## Syntax

```
Category  list operator (module)
Arguments module, list
Return Value N/A
```

## Definition

Using this function, particularly useful when using pragmas, is the reverse of use().

## Example

```
use integer;
# code using integer arithmetic here
no integer;
# back to floating point arithmetic
```

# oct

## Compliance

## Syntax

```
Category  named unary operator (numeric)
Arguments  expression
Return Value  numeric
```

## Definition

This function evaluates the expression as an octal string and returns the decimal value.

## Example

```
print("oct() ",oct("88"), "\n");
```

# open

## Compliance

## Syntax

```
Category:  list operator (files)
Arguments:  handle, filename
Arguments:  handle
Return Value  TRUE (non zero) or FALSE (undefined)
```

## Definition

This function opens a file using the specified file `handle`. The file `handle` may be an expression; the resulting value is used as the `handle`. If no `filename` is specified, a variable with the same name as the file `handle` is used (this should be a scalar variable with a string value referring to the `filename`).

The `filename` string may be prefixed with the following values to indicate the mode:

- ◼ < Read, this is the default.
- ◼ > Write.
- ◼ +> Read/write—starting with new file.
- ◼ +< Read/write using existing file.
- ◼ >> Append.
- ◼ \<command\> ¦ Input pipe; the file name is actually a subshell command from which the file handle is piped.
- ◼ ¦ \<command\> Output pipe; the file name is actually a subshell command to which the output of the file handle is piped.

The special file name - can refer to either STDIN (-) when reading, or STDOUT (>-), when writing.

## Example

```
open(FIL,"/tmp/notexist") ||
        print("open() failed as file did not exist.\n");
```

# opendir

## Compliance

## Syntax

```
Category  list operator (files)
Arguments  handle, dirname
Return Value  1 (true) '' (false)
```

## Definition

Opens a directory handle for the directory name specified. If the dirname is an expression this can be evaluated to return a name.

## Example

```
opendir (DIR, "/tmp/notexist") ||
        print("opendir() dialed as directory does not exist.\n");
```

# ord

## Compliance

## Syntax

```
Category  named unary operator (string)
Arguments  expression
Arguments  none
Return Value  numeric
```

## Definition

This function returns the numeric ASCII code of the first character in the expression (or $_ if none specified).

## Example

```
print("ord() ",ord("A"), "\n");
```

# pack

## Compliance

## Syntax

```
Category list operator (records)
Arguments template, list
Return Value string
```

## Definition

This function returns a packed version of the data in the list using the template to determine how it is coded. The template comprises a sequence of characters, each specifying the data type of the matching data item in the list.

| Character | Description |
| --- | --- |
| @ | Null fill to absolute position |
| A | ASCII string with spaces to pad |
| a | ASCII string with nulls to pad |
| b | Bit string (ascending bit order) |
| B | Bit string (descending bit order) |
| c | Signed char value |
| C | Unsigned char value |
| d | Double-precision float in the native format |
| f | Single-precision float in the native format |
| h | Hex string (low nybble first) |
| H | Hex string (high nybble first) |
| i | Signed integer value |
| I | Unsigned integer value |
| l | Signed long integer value |
| L | Unsigned long integer value |
| n | Short integer "network" order |
| N | Long integer "network" order |
| p | Pointer to a null-terminated string |
| P | Pointer to a structure (fixed-length string) |
| s | Signed short integer value |
| S | Unsigned short integer value |
| u | UUencoded string |
| v | Short integer "VAX" (little-endian) order |

| v | Long integer "VAX" (little-endian) order |
| x | Null byte |
| X | Back up a byte |

A concise form of template can be used by appending a number after any letter to repeat that format specifier. For aA, the number uses one value and pads the rest. For bB, the number indicates the number of bits. For hH, the number indicates the number of nybbles. For P, the number indicates the size of the pointer structure. Using an asterisk in place of a number means to repeat the format specifier as necessary to use up all list values. Note that some packed structures may not be portable across machines (in particular, network and floating point formats). It should be possible to unpack the data using the same format specification with an unpack() call.

## Example

```
Use Socketl
@a=(140,203,7,103);
$addr=pack('C4',@a);
($name,$alias,$adrtype,$length,@address)=gethostbyaddr($addr,AF_INET);
print("pack() ",@a, "packed as: $addr".\n");
```

# package

## Compliance

## Syntax

**Category** named unary operator (class)
**Arguments** name
**Return Value** N/A

## Definition

Calling this function declares that all unqualified dynamic variables in the current block are in the scope of the specified package name. This is normally done in the header of a file to be included as a package or a module in other programs that require() or use(). Note that this does apply to variables declared as local() but not to variables declared as my().

# pipe

## Compliance

## Syntax

**Category** list operator (process)
**Arguments** readhandle, writehandle
**Return Value** 1 (true) '' (false)

## Definition

Links named pipes like the UNIX function `pipe()`.

# pop

## Compliance

## Syntax

**Category**  name unary operator (array)
**Arguments**  variable
**Return Value**  value

## Definition

This function removes the top item from the array specified and returns that element.

## Example

```
@a = (1,2,3,4);
print("pop() ",pop(@a), "leaves ",@a,"\n");
```

# pos

## Compliance

## Syntax

**Category**  named unary operator (pattern)
**Arguments**  variable
**Return Value**  numeric

## Definition

Returns the offset that the last pattern match (`m//g`) reached when searching the scalar variable specified as an argument. It can be assigned to alter the bahavior of the next match.

## Example

```
$name = "alpha1 alpha2 alpha3 alpha4";
$name =~ m/alpha/g;
print("pos() ", pos($name), "\n");
```

# print

## Compliance

## Syntax

```
Category  list operator (i/o)
Arguments  handle, list
Arguments  list
Arguments  none
Return Value  1 (true) '' (false)
```

## Definition

Prints the list to the file represented by the file handle. If no file handle is specified the default file handle is STDOUT. This default file handle may be altered using the select() operator. If no list argument is specified, $_ is printed.

## Example

```
$return = print "print() ";
print "returns $return on success.\n");
```

# printf

## Compliance

## Syntax

```
Category  list operator (i/o)
Arguments  filehandle list
Arguments  list
Return Value  1 (true) '' (false)
```

## Definition

This function uses the C printf format specifiers to control the printed output. It is equivalent to

```
print filehandle, sprintf(list);
```

As with print() the default file handle is STDOUT.

## Example

```
printf("printf() An integer printed with leading zeroes %05d.\n",9);
```

# push

## Compliance

## Syntax

```
Category  list operator (array)
Arguments  array, list
Return Value  numeric
```

## Definition

This appends the elements in the specified list on the end of the specified array and returns the new number of elements in the list.

## Example

```
@a = (1);
$num = push(@a,2,3,4,5);
print("push() Added ",$num-1," elements to array: ",@a,"\n");
```

# q/STRING/

## Compliance

## Syntax

```
Category  (string)
Arguments  q/string/
Return Value  value
```

## Definition

This is a standard quote used to surpress special interpretation of characters giving a literal string. You can use single quotes 'string' or the letter q with delimiters. Any delimiter will do as long as it is not used in the string. The backslash character can be used to escape any reference to the delimiting character itself in the string.

## Example

```
print(q!q// The only special character is the delimiter itself \!!, "\n");
```

# qq/STRING/

## Compliance

## Syntax

```
Category  (string)
Arguments  qq/string/
Return Value  value
```

## Definition

This is a double quote, used to allow interpolation of special characters within the string as required. You can use double quote "string" or the double qq with delimiters. The backslash character can be used to disable the special meaning of interpolated characters, including the delimiter itself.

## Example

```
$newline = "\n";
print(qq!qq// double quoted with interpolation! $newline!);
```

# quotemeta

## Compliance

## Syntax

```
Category  named unary operator (pattern)
Arguments  expression
Return Value  string
```

## Definition

quotemeta returns the value of the expression with all the metacharacters backslashed.

## Example

```
print(quotemeta("quotameta() I can use any metcharacter $ \ "),"\n");
```

# qw/STRING/

## Compliance

## Syntax

```
Category  (list)
Arguments  qw/string/
Return Value  list
```

## Definition

This function returns a list of words in string. Spaces are used as delimiters in the string to produce this list.

## Example

```
print("qw// ",qw("1 2 3 4 5"),"\n");
```

# qx/STRING/

## Compliance

## Syntax

```
Category  (process)
Arguments  qx/string/
Return Value  special
```

## Definition

This is a back quote, used to allow interpolation of special characters within the string as required and then execute the resulting command as a system command. You can use back quotes 'string' or the letters qx with delimiters. The backslash character can be used to disable the special meaning of interpolated characters, including the delimiter itself. The return value is the return value of the system() call.

## Example

```
print("qx// ",qx!du -s /tmp!);
```

# rand

## Compliance

## Syntax

```
Category  named unary operator (numeric)
Arguments  expression
Arguments  none
Return Value  numeric
```

## Definition

This function returns a real number between 0 and the number evaluated as expression (the upper limit is 1 if no expression is specified). The upper limit must be positive. As the function calls a pseudorandom generator, it should be possible to generate the same sequence of numbers repeatedly unless the initial seed value is altered with srand().

## Example

```
print("rand(), ",rand,"\n");
```

# read

## Compliance

## Syntax

```
Category  list operator (i/o)
Arguments  handle, variable, length, offset
Arguments  handle, variable, length
Return Value  1 (true) '' (false)
```

## Definition

Reads length bytes from file handle into variable (starting at offset if specified). It returns the number of bytes actually read.

## Example

```
open(INF,"/etc/services") ¦¦ die "Error reading file, stopped";
read(INF,$result,10);
print("read() $result \n");
close(INF)
```

# readdir

## Compliance

## Syntax

```
Category  list operator (i/o)
Arguments  dirhandle
Return Value  lname
```

## Definition

In a list context, this function returns a list of the files in the directory specified by the directory handle. In a scalar context, it returns the next file name in the directory.

## Example

```
opendir(DIR,"/tmp");
@file = readdir(DIR);
print("readdir() ",@files, "\n");
```

# readlink

## Compliance

## Syntax

```
Category  named unary operator (files)
Arguments  expression
Arguments  none
Return Value  value
```

## Definition

This function returns the value of the symbolic link specified by expression (or $_ if none specified). If symbolic links are not implemented, it gives a fatal error. If symbolic links are supported, but there is some system error, the error is returned in $OS_ERROR ($!).

# recv

## Compliance

## Syntax

```
Category  list operator (socket)
Arguments  socket, variale, length, flags
Return Value  address
```

## Definition

The recv function is equivalent to UNIX system call recv() and receives a message on a socket.

# redo

## Compliance

## Syntax

```
Category  (flow)
Arguments  label
Arguments  none
Return Value  N/A
```

## Definition

This function passes control directly to the label without executing any contine block. If no label is specified, the innermost loop is used.

# ref

## Compliance

## Syntax

```
Category  named unary operator (class)
Arguments  expression
Return Value  package
```

## Definition

This function returns the package of a bless()ed variable, TRUE if the variable is a reference, or FALSE. The return value for TRUE is actually the type of the variable (for example ARRAY, HASH, REF, SCALAR).

## Example

```
$tmp = {};
bless $tmp, ATMPCLASS;
print "ref() \$tmp is now in class ",ref($tmp),"\n";
```

# rename

## Compliance

## Syntax

```
Category  list operator (files)
Arguments  oldname, newname
Return Value  1 (true) 0 (false)
```

## Definition

This function renames files on the same file system from oldname to newname.

## Example

```
$returned = rename("/tmp/test","/tmp/test2");
print("rename() returned $returned \n");
```

# require

## Compliance

## Syntax

```
Category  named unary operator (module)
Arguments  expression
Arguments  none
Return Value  1 (true) '' (false)
```

## Definition

If the expression is a scalar, the library specified by the `filename` is included (if it has not already been).

In Perl 5, if the expression is numeric this requires that the version of Perl being used (in `$PERL_VERSION` or `$[`) is greater than or equal to the version specified.

Note that Perl 5 also has the `use()` mechanism for including modules; `use()` is more robust than `require`.

## Example

```
require "cgilib.pl";
```

# reset

## Compliance

## Syntax

```
Category  named unary operator (misc)
Arguments  expression
Arguments  none
Return Value  1
```

## Definition

This function provides a way of resetting variables in the current package (especially pattern match variables). The expression is interpreted as a list of single characters. All variables starting with those characters are reset. The letters are case sensitive (as Perl variables are). Hyphens may be used to specify ranges of variables to reset. If called without any argument, `reset` simply resets all search matches.

> **CAUTION**
> Use of this operator can reset system variables you may not want to alter. For example, be very careful with the following:
>
>     reset A-Z;

# return

## Compliance

## Syntax

    Category  list operator (flow)
    Arguments  list
    Return Value  list

## Definition

This function returns from a subroutine (or an eval()) with the value specified.

## Example

```
sub test {
        return 1;
}
$test = &test;
print("return() Returned $test \n");
```

# reverse

## Compliance

## Syntax

    Category  list operator (list)
    Arguments  list
    Return Value  list

## Definition

The reverse function returns the list given as an argument in reverse order. In a scalar context it reverses the letters of its first argument.

## Example

```
@a = (1,2,3);
print("reverse() ",reverse(@a),"\n");
```

# rewinddir

## Compliance

## Syntax

```
Category  named unary operator (i/o)
Arguments  dirhandle
Return Value  1 (true) '' (false)
```

## Definition

When reading a directory using readdir(), it is possible to reset the directory to the first file name.

## Example

```
opendir(DIR,"/tmp");
print("rewinddir() (a): "
file: while ($file=readdir(DIR) {
        print $file, " ";
}
rewinddir();
print(" (b): "
file: while ($file=readdir(DIR) {
        print $file, " ";
}
print("\n");
closedir(DIR);
```

# rindex

## Compliance

## Syntax

```
Category  list operator (string)
Arguments  string, substring, position
Arguments  string, substring
Return Value  position
```

## Definition

This function is very similar to index() except that, instead of scanning for the substring from the first character in the string, it scans backwards from the last character. So it returns the starting position of the last occurrence of substring in string (scanning backwards from the specified position or from the end if no position is specified).

## Example

```
$ans1 = rindex("abcdefghijiklmdef:-)","def");
$ans2 = rindex("abcdefghijiklmdef","def",$ans1+3);
print("rindex() def is at $ans1 and next at $ans2\n");
```

# rmdir

## Compliance

## Syntax

**Category**  named unary operator (files)
**Arguments**  filename
**Return Value**  1 or 0

## Definition

This function deletes the directory specified (or $_) if it is empty and sets $OS_ERROR ($!) to the error value if there is a system error.

# s///

## Compliance

## Syntax

**Category**  (pattern)
**Arguments**  s/pattern/replacement/options
**Return Value**  numeric

## Definition

This function searches the default string for pattern (a regular expression) and replaces this with the replacement string (the actual replacemnt behavior depends on the options). It returns the number of replacements made. The default string is set using either of the pattern binding operators (=~ or ¬~ ) or $_ is used if none have been bound. The valid options are

| Option | Description |
| --- | --- |
| e | Evaluate the right side as an expression |
| g | Global (replace all occurrences) |
| i | Case-insensitive pattern matching |

*continues*

*continued*

| Option | Description |
|---|---|
| m | Ignore \n in string (multiple lines) |
| o | Optimize (compile pattern once) |
| s | Treat string as single line |
| x | Extended regular expressions |

## Example

```
$oldstr = "abcdefABCDEFabcdefABCDEF";
$newstr= $oldstr;
$str =~ s/abc/zzz/ig;
print("s/// $oldstr became $newstr \n");
```

# scalar

## Compliance

## Syntax

```
Category  named unary operator (misc)
Arguments  expression
Return Value  value
```

## Definition

This operator forces the argument to be interpreted in a scalar context, rather than as a list, so that it can override the default context if necessary.

# seek

## Compliance

## Syntax

```
Category  list operator (i/o)
Arguments  handle, position, start
Return Value  1 (true) '' (false)
```

## Definition

This function sets the file pointer to a specified offset position in a file. The offset is relative to the start that can have three values: 0 (start of file), 1 (current position), 2 (end of file). This allows the use of random access files, and the implentation of fast-read algorithms (for example binary search techniques) on file handles, especially with fixed-length data where the offsets are easier to calculate.

# seekdir

## Compliance

## Syntax

```
Category  list operator (i/o)
Arguments  dirhandle. position
Return Value  1 (true) '' (false)
```

## Definition

This function allows the position in a directory to be reset to a position saved with telldir(). This is useful when processing directories with readdir().

# select

## Compliance

## Syntax

```
Category  named unary operator (i/o)
Arguments  handle
Arguments  rbits, wbits, ebits, timeout
Return Value  handle
```

## Definition

This operator selects the default file handle used for I/O operations such as print() and write(). By default STDOUT is selected, but this function can select any other file handle to be the default instead. The return value is the currently selected file handle (before any change) so it is useful to assign this to a variable in order to be able to restore the original handle as the default at a later stage.

The second form calls the UNIX system select() function.

## Example

```
open(OUT,"/tmp/t.out");
$return = select(OUT);
print("This goes in /tmp/t.out.\n");
select($return);
print("select() restored to STDOUT.\n");
```

# semctl

## Compliance

## Syntax

```
Category  list operator (System V)
Arguments  id, semnum, command, arg
Return Value  value
```

## Definition

This function is equivalent to the UNIX `semctl()` function. This is a semaphore control operation with several variables.

# semget

## Compliance

## Syntax

```
Category  list operator (System V)
Arguments  key, nsems, flags
Return Value  value
```

## Definition

This function is equivalent to the UNIX `semget()` function and returns the semaphore ID.

# semop

## Compliance

## Syntax

```
Category  list operator (System V)
Arguments  key, opstring
Return Value  1 (true) '' (false)
```

## Definition

The `semop` function is equivalent to the UNIX `semop()` function call and performs semaphore signalling and waiting functions.

# send

## Compliance

## Syntax

```
Category    list operator (socket)
Arguments   socket, message, flags, to
Arguments   socket, message, flags
Return Value  numeric
```

## Definition

This function is equivalent to the UNIX system send() function and sends a message socket.

# setgrent

## Compliance

## Syntax

```
Category    (system files)
Arguments   none
Return Value  n/a
```

## Definition

This function rewinds the /etc/group file to the start of the file for subsequent accesses using getgrent().

## Example

```
print("setgrent() ",setgrent(), "\n");
```

# sethostent

## Compliance

## Syntax

```
Category    named unary operator (system files)
Arguments   flag
Return Value  N/A
```

## Definition

If called with an argument of 1, this function tells the system to keep a TCP socket open for name server queries such as gethostbyname(). If this is not, then the name server queries use UDP datagrams.

## Example

```
print("sethostent() ",sethostent(1), "\n");
```

# setnetent

## Compliance

## Syntax

**Category** named unary operator (system files)
**Arguments** flag
**Return Value** N/A

## Definition

This function rewinds the /etc/networks file used by getnetent() and other network-related functions. If the flag has a value of 1, then the file is kept open between calls to getnetbyname() and getnetbyaddr().

## Example

```
print("setnetent() ",setnetent(1), "\n");
```

# setpgrp

## Compliance

## Syntax

**Category** list operator (process)
**Arguments** pid, pgrp
**Return Value** 1 (true) '' (false)

## Definition

This function sets the current process group for the specified process (pid); if this is zero, the current process is set.

# setpriority

## Compliance

## Syntax

**Category** list operator (proxess)
**Arguments** type, id, priority
**Return Value** 1 (true) '' (false)

## Definition

This function calls the UNIX `setprority()` function. The `type` is one of `PRIO_PROCESS`, `PRIO_PGGRP`, or `PRIO_USER`. The `id` is the relevent ID for this (`pid`, a `pid` for a group of processes, or `uid`). If `0` is used as the `id`, the current process, process group, or user is used. The `priority` is a number representing the level of priority (normally in the range `120` to `20`) where the lower the priority, the more favorable the scheduling of the process by the operating system.

## Example

```
print("setpriority() ",setpriority(0,0,-20),"\n");
```

# setprotoent

## Compliance

## Syntax

```
Category  named unary operator (system files)
Arguments  flag
Return Value  1 (true) '' (false)
```

## Definition

This function rewinds the `/etc/protocols` file used by `getprotoent()` and other protocol-related functions. If the `flag` has a value of `1`, then the file is kept open between calls to `getprotobyname()` and `getnetbynumber()`.

## Example

```
print("setprotoent() ",setprotoent(1), "\n");
```

# setpwent

## Compliance

## Syntax

```
Category  (system files)
Arguments  none
Return Value  1 (true) '' (false)
```

## Definition

This function rewinds the `/etc/passwd` file used by `getpwent()` and other password-related functions.

## Example

```
print("setpwent() ",setpwent(), "\n");
```

# setservent

## Compliance

## Syntax

```
Category  named uanry operator (system files)
Arguments  flag
Return Value  1 (true) '' (false)
```

## Definition

This function rewinds the /etc/services file used by getservent() and other service related functions. If the flag has a value of 1, then the file is kept open between calls to getservbyname() and getnetbyport().

## Example

```
print("setservent() ",setservent(1), "\n");
```

# setsockopt

## Compliance

## Syntax

```
Category  list operator (socket)
Arguments  socket, level, optname, optval
Return Value  1 (true) '' (false)
```

## Definition

This function is equivalent to UNIX system call setsockopt() and sets the socket options.

# shift

## Compliance

## Syntax

```
Category  named unary operator (array)
Arguments  array
Arguments  none
Return Value  value
```

## Definition

This function takes the leftmost element from the array specified and returns it, reducing the array by one element. When no array is specified, the array of arguments passed to the Perl script, $ARGV, is used if the context is not in a subroutine; otherwise, the array of arguments passed to the subroutine, @_, is used.

The return value is undefined if the array is empty.

## Example

```
print("shift() ");
while ($arg = shift) {
        print($arg,' ');
}
print("\n");
```

# shmctl

## Compliance

## Syntax

```
Category  list operator (System V)
Arguments  id, cmd, arg
Return Value  value
```

## Definition

This function is equivalent to the UNIX shmctl() function, and performs shared memory control operations.

# shmget

## Compliance

## Syntax

```
Category  list operator (System V)
Arguments  key.size, flags
Return Value  value
```

## Definition

This function is equivalent to the UNIX shmget() function and returns shared memory segment ID.

# shmread

## Compliance

## Syntax

```
Category  list operator (System V)
Arguments  id, var. pos, size
Return Value  value
```

## Definition

This function is equivalent to the UNIX shmread() function and reads from the shared memory segment ID.

# shmwrite

## Compliance

## Syntax

```
Category  list operator (System V)
Arguments  id, string, pos, size
Return Value  value
```

## Definition

This function is equivalent to the UNIX shmwrite() function and writes to the shared memory segment ID.

# shutdown

## Compliance

## Syntax

```
Category  list operator (socket)
Arguments  socket, how
Return Value  1 (true) '' (false)
```

## Definition

This function is equivalent to the UNIX shutdown() function and shuts down a socket.

# sin

## Compliance

## Syntax

```
Category   named unary operator (numeric)
Arguments  expression
Arguments  none
Return Value  numeric
```

## Definition

This function returns the sine of the expression in radians. If there is no explicit argument, $_
is used.

## Example

```
print("sin() ",sin(4), "\n");
```

# sleep

## Compliance

## Syntax

```
Category   named unary operator (process)
Arguments  expression
Arguments  none
Return Value  numeric
```

## Definition

This function causes the current process to sleep for the number of seconds specified in
expression (if none is specified, it sleeps forever, but may be woken up by a signal if this has
been programmed).

## Example

```
print("sleep() ",sleep(5),"\n");
```

# socket

## Compliance

## Syntax

```
Category  list operator (socket)
Arguments  socket, domain, type, protocol
Return Value  value
```

## Definition

This function is equivalent to the UNIX socket( ) system call and opens a specified type of socket and attaches it to a file handle.

# socketpair

## Compliance

## Syntax

```
Category  list operator (socket)
Arguments  socket1, socket2, domain, type, protocol
Return Value  value
```

## Definition

This function is equivalent to the UNIX socketpair() system call and creates a pair of sockets, which are unnamed, in the specified domain.

# sort

## Compliance

## Syntax

```
Category  list operator (list)
Arguments  subname list
Arguments  block list
Arguments  list
Return Value  list
```

## Definition

This function sorts the list specified and returns the sorted list. The sort method can be specified with the optional subroutine or block argument. A subroutine may be specified that takes two arguments (passed as global package variables, $a  $b) and returns TRUE if the first is less than or equal to the second by any criteria used. Similarly, a block can be specified (effectively an anonymous subroutine) to perform this function. The default sort order is based on the standard string comparison order.

## Example

```
@a = ("z","w","r","i","b","a");
print("sort() ",sort(@a),"\n");
```

# splice

## Compliance

## Syntax

```
Category  list operator (array)
Arguments  array, offset, length, list
Arguments  array, offset, length
Arguments  array, offset
Return Value  list
```

## Definition

This function removes the elements specified by offset and length from the array and re-places them with the elements in the list supplied as the last argument. A list of those elements removed is returned. If no length is specified, all the items from offset to the end of the array are removed.

## Example

```
@a = ("a","e","i","o","u");
print("splice() ",splice(@a,0,3,"A","E","I"),"\n");
```

# split

## Compliance

## Syntax

```
Category  list operator (pattern)
Arguments  /pattern/,expression,limit
Arguments  /pattern/,expression
Arguments  /pattern/
Arguments  none
Return Value  list
```

## Definition

This function manipulates a string, splitting the string denoted by the expression (or the $_ if none is specified) into an array of strings based on some separator string specified by the pattern (if the pattern has no specified whitespace as the default). An optional limit restricts the number of elements returned. A negative limit has no effect.

If not in a list context, the number of elements found is returned. In an scalar context, it returns the number of elements and puts the resulting array into the @_ array (the use of the @_ as the result is depreciated).

## Examples

```
print("spilt() ",split(/:/,"1:2:3:4:5"),"\n");
```

# sprintf

## Compliance

## Syntax

```
Category  list operator (string)
Arguments  format, list
Return Value  string
```

## Definition

This is equivalent to the C sprintf() call. The format is a string with special metacharacters to specify how may values/variables follow and how to represent each of these in the resulting string. This enables the explicit formatting of floating point and integer numbers (also enabling binary, hexidecimal, and octal formats).

## Example

```
print("strintf() ",sprintf("%0d \n",9),"\n");
```

# sqrt

## Compliance

## Syntax

```
Category  named unary operator (numeric)
Arguments  expression
Return Value  numeric
```

## Definition

This function returns the result of evaluating the expression and finding its square root.

## Example

```
print("sqrt() ",sqrt(4),"\n");
```

# srand

## Compliance

## Syntax

```
Category  named unary operator (numeric)
Arguments expression
Arguments none
Return Value 1 (true) '' (false)
```

## Definition

This function sets the seed used by the pseudorandom number generation algorithm when generating rand() numbers. In order to randomize the possible sequences, the seed should be set to a different value each time the script is called. The default behavior, when no expression is supplied, is to use the result of a call to time(). This is not a secure method of randomizing for scripts that need to be secure because it is possible to predict what sequence the script will return.

Note that, when using a set of pseudorandom data generated using rand(), it is possible to generate exactly the same data repeatedly (without having to save the entire sequence) simply by stetting and saving the seed. Restoring the seed and calling rand() will then produce the same sequence again.

## Example

```
srand(26);
print("rand() ",rand(),", ");
srand(26);
print(rand()," (should produce the same \"random\" number twice) \n");
```

# stat

## Compliance

## Syntax

```
Category  list operator (files)
Arguments handle
Arguments expression
Arguments none
Return Value list
```

## Definition

This function returns the file statistics of the file pointed to by the file `handle` (or a file `handle` produced by evaluating the expression). Note that, like the file test operators, `stat()` can take a special argument underscore; this means that the test is carried out on the same file `handle` as the last `file test, stat()`, or `lstat()` call.

## Example

```
($device,$inode,$mode,$nlink,$uid,$gid,$rdev,$size,$atime,
       $mtime,$ctime,$blksize,$blocks) = stat("/etc/passwd");
print("stat() $device, $inode, $ctime \n");
```

# study

## Compliance

## Syntax

```
Category  named unary operator (pattern)
Arguments  scalar
Arguments  none
Return Value  1 (true) '' (false)
```

## Definition

When many pattern match operations are being performed on the same string, the efficiency of these patterns can be improved with the `study()` function. If no string is sepcified, the `$_` is studied by default. The call sets up internal lookup tables based on the string studied so that pattern-matching operations can use this information to processs the pattern match more quickly. Only one string at a time can be studied (subsequent calls effectively "unstudy" any previous `study()` removing the lookup tables). The function `study()` is often used in a loop processing lines of a text file where each line is studied before being processed with various pattern matches.

# sub

## Compliance

## Syntax

```
Category  (flow)
Arguments  name block
Arguments  name
Arguments  name
Return Value  value
```

## Definition

This is the syntax for a subroutine declaration. The full form defines a subroutine with the `name` and associates this with the statements in block. When evoked, it will return the result of the last statement executed in the block (often a `return()` statement). If no name is supplied, it is an anonymous subroutine (certain functions such as `sort()` allow anonymous subroutines as arguments). With only a name as an argument, the statement is a forward reference to a subroutine which is fully declared later in the script.

# substr

## Compliance

## Syntax

```
Category list operator (string)
Arguments expression, offset, length
Arguments expression, offset
Return Value string
```

## Definition

This function returns a substring of a string specified by expression. The substring starts at the specified `offset` and has the specified `length`. If the offset is negative, it starts from the right-hand side of the string instead of the left-hand side. If the length is negative, it means to trim the string by that number of characters.

## Example

```
print("substr() ",substring("okay",0,2),"\n");
```

# symlink

## Compliance

## Syntax

```
Category list operator ((files)
Arguments oldfile, newfile
Return Value 1 or 0
```

## Definition

This function creates a symbolic link from the existing file specified by `oldfile` to the specified `newfile` and returns 1 on success and 0 on failure. If symbolic links are not supported by the operating system, this will return a fatal error.

## Example

```
print("symlink() ",symlink("/usr/local","/tmp/symlinktousrlocal"),"\n");
```

# syscall

## Compliance

## Syntax

```
Category list operator (i/o)
Arguments list
Return Value varies
```

## Definition

This mechanism allows Perl to call corresponding UNIX C system calls directly. It relies on the existence of the set of Perl header files Syscall.ph which declares all of these calls. The script h2ph that is normally executed when Perl is installed, sets up the Syscall.ph files. Each call has the same name as the equivalent UNIX system call with the SYS_ prefix. As these calls actually pass control to the relevant C system function, care must be taken with passing parameters.

The first element in the list used as an argument to syscall() itself, is the name corresponding to the UNIX system call (that is, with the SYS_ prefix). The next elements in the list are interpreted as parameters to this call. Numeric values are passed as the C type int. String values are passed as pointers to arrays. The length of these strings must be able to cope with any value assigned to that parameter in the call.

## Example

```
require "syscall.ph";

print("syscall() ",syscall(&SYS_getpid)," equivalent to $PID\n");
```

# sysopen

## Compliance

## Syntax

```
Category list operator (i/o)
Arguments handle, name, mode, permissions
Arguments handle, name, mode
Return Value 1 (true) '' (false)
```

## Definition

This function calls the UNIX C open() function directly from the Perl script, which opens a file for reading or writing.

# sysread

## Compliance

## Syntax

```
Category list operator (i/o)
Arguments handle, scalar, length, offset
Arguments handle, scalar, length
Return Value 1 (true) '' (false)
```

## Definition

This function calls the UNIX C read() function directly from the Perl script, which reads a line from the standard input source.

# system

## Compliance

## Syntax

```
Category list operator (process)
Arguments list
Return Value status
```

## Definition

This call is executes the specified list as an operating system call. The process to execute this command is forked and the script waits for the child process to return. The return value is the exit status of the child process.

 **TIP** To capture the output from a system call, use the qx// (back quote mechanism) rather than system().

## Example

```
print("system() ",system("ls -F /var > /tmp/t.tmp"),"\n");
```

# syswrite

## Compliance

## Syntax

```
Category  list operator (i/o)
Arguments  handle, scalar, length, offset
Arguments  handle, scalar, length
Return Value  1 (true) '' (false)
```

## Definition

This function calls the UNIX C write() function directly from the Perl script, which is an interactive write to another user process.

# tell

## Compliance

## Syntax

```
Category  named unary operator (i/o)
Arguments  expression
Arguments  none
Return Value  position
```

## Definition

This function returns the current position in the file specified by the expression (which should evaluate to a file handle). If no handle is specified, the last file accessed is used. This value can be used by seek() to return to this position if appropriate.

## Example

```
print("tell() ",tell(STDOUT),"\n");
```

# telldir

## Compliance

## Syntax

```
Category  named unary operator (i/o)
Arguments  dirhandle
Return Value  position
```

## Definition

This function returns the current position in the directory `handle` specified. This value can be used by `seekdir()` to return to this position if appropriate.

## Example

```
opendir(DIR,"/tmp");
readdir(DIR);
print("telldir() ",telldir(DIR),"\n");
```

# tie

## Compliance

## Syntax

```
Category  list operator (class)
Arguments  variable, classname, list
Return Value  object
```

## Definition

This function binds a variable to a package class. It creates an instance of this class by running the `new()` method associated with that class. Any parameters for the `new()` method may be specified in the list.

The behavior depends on the way the package class is written, and on the type of variable. Most common are package classes written to support associative arrays. In particular, package classes exist to bind associative arrays to various databases.

The `tie()` mechanism hides all the complexities of implemention behind a simple interface so that, for example, the records in a database can be accessed by looking at the associative array bound to the database though an appropriate package class.

The example here uses the Configure.pm module. This module gives access to information about the machine on which Perl was installed. It is possible to bind an associative array to this class and examine it to find out the value of any of the configuration parameters.

## Example

```
use Configure;
$return = tie %c, Configure;
print("tie() returned \"$return\" and ",
      "a sample value is $c{installbin}\n");
```

# tied

## Compliance

## Syntax

```
Category  named unary operator
Arguments  variable
Return Value  object
```

## Definition

This function was first implemented in Perl 5.002 and returns a reference to the object that the variable is an instance of. This is same as is returned by the original call to `tie()` when it is bound.

# time

## Compliance

## Syntax

```
Category  (time)
Arguments  none
Return Value  time
```

## Definition

This function returns the time, in seconds, since 1 January 1970. The format can be converted into more useful parts using `gmtime()` or `localtime()`.

# times

## Compliance

## Syntax

```
Category  (process)
Arguments  none
Return Value  list
```

## Definition

This function returns a list of four elements representing the time, in seconds, used. The four elements represent the system time and the user time used by the current process and child processes.

## Example

```
($usertime,$systemtime,$childsystem,$childuser) = times();
print("times() $usertime $systemtime $childsystem $childuser\n");
```

# tr///

## Compliance

## Syntax

```
Category  (string)
Arguments  tr/searchlist/replacelist/<options>
Return Value  numeric
```

## Definition

This function translates all occurrences of items in the search list with the equivalent items in the replacement list. The string searched is the default search string bound by =~ or !=, or if no string is bound to the pattern match, the $_ string is used. The return value is the number of characters translated or deleted.

The valid options are

| Option | Description |
|--------|-------------|
| c | Complement (non-matching characters in search list are used) |
| d | Delete (delete any characters not in search list, as well as translating) |
| s | Squash (if the trasnslation results in a sequence of repeated characters from the replace list, then reduce this to one occurance of the character) |

The searchlist and the replacelist may contain the character to indicate a range of characters.

## Examples

```
tr/AEIOU/aeiou/        # Make all vowels lowercase
tr/[A-M]/[a-m]/        # Make first half of alphabet lowercase
tr/aeiou/ /c           # Replace all non-vowles with space
tr/aeiou/AEIOU/d       # Make all vowels uppercase and remove
                       # all other characters
tr/aeiou/-/s           # Replace all vowels with -,
                       # but only one - for adjacent vowels
```

# truncate

## Compliance

## Syntax

```
Category  list operator (i/o)
Arguments  handle, length
Arguments  expression, length
Return Value  1 (true) '' (false)
```

## Definition

This function truncates the file referenced by the file `handle` to `length`. An expression can be used that evaluates to the file `handle`, if the operating system does not implement this feature.

# uc

## Compliance

## Syntax

```
Category  named unary operator (string)
Arguments  expression
Return Value  string
```

## Definition

This function returns an uppercase version of the specified `expression`.

## Example

```
print("uc() ",uc("This is All Caps"), "\n");
```

# ucfirst

## Compliance

## Syntax

```
Category  named unary operator (string)
Arguments  expression
Return Value  string
```

## Definition

This function returns a `string` with the first character of the `expression` in uppercase.

## Example

```
print("ucfirst() ",ucfirst("this is Capitalized"), "\n");
```

# umask

## Compliance

## Syntax

```
Category  named unary operator (files)
Arguments newumask
Arguments none
Return Value oldumask
```

## Definition

This function sets the file mask using the specified newumask. It returns the oldumask so that it can be stored and restored later if required. If called without any arguments, it returns the current umask. This is the mechanism UNIX uses to modify the permissions of any files created.

## Example

```
print("umask() The current umask is: ",umask,"\n");
```

# undef

## Compliance

## Syntax

```
Category  named unary operator (misc)
Arguments expression
Arguments none
Return Value value
```

## Definition

This function undefines the value of the expression. The expression may be a scalar value, and array, or a subroutine (specified with a & prefix). When called without an expression, this function returns an undefined value.

# unlink

## Compliance

## Syntax

```
Category  list operator (files)
Arguments  list
Return Value  numeric
```

## Definition

This function deletes the files in the list and returns the number of files deleted.

## Example

```
system("touch /tmp/t.tst");
print("unlink() ",unlink("/tmp/t.tst"),"\n");
```

# unpack

## Compliance

## Syntax

```
Category  list operator (data)
Arguments  template, expression
Return Value  list
```

## Definition

This function unpacks data that are packed with pack(). It uses the same template mechanism to specify the format of the data in the packed string. In a scalar context, the first value in the list is returned.

# unshift

## Compliance

## Syntax

```
Category  list operator (array)
Arguments  array, list
Return Value  numeric
```

## Definition

This function prepends the list to the front of the specified array and returns the new number of elements in array.

## Example

```
@a = (a, b, c);
$ret = unshift(@a, 1, 2, 3);
print("unshift() Array has $ret elements:",@a,"\n");
```

# untie

## Compliance

## Syntax

**Category** named unary operator (class)
**Arguments** variable
**Return Value** 1 (true) '' (false)

## Definition

This function undoes the bining between a variable and a package class that was created using tie().

# use

## Compliance

## Syntax

**Category** list operator (module)
**Arguments** module, list
**Return Value** N/A

## Definition

This function imports the specified module into the current block. The import() method defined for the package class represented by the module is evaluated. The specified list is passed as optional arguments to this import() method. If you do not specify a list argument, then the default methods for that module will be those imported. You can specify the empty list() in order to avoid adding any items to the local namespace.

## Example

```
use English;
```

Note that this is the mechanism for implementing compiler directives known as pragmas. You can for example force all arithmetic to be integer-based by

```
use integer;
```

And then this can be turned off again with

```
no integer;
```

# utime

## Compliance

## Syntax

```
Category  list operator (files)
Arguments  list
Return Value  numeric
```

## Definition

This function sets the access and modification time of all the files in the `list` to the time specified in the first two items in the list. The time must be in the numeric format (that is, seconds since 1 Januray 1970) as returned by the `time()` function.

## Example

```
$time = now;
print("utime() ",utime($time,$time,"/tmp/t.tst"),"\n");
```

# values

## Compliance

## Syntax

```
Category  named unary operator (hash)
Arguments  variable
Return Value  list
```

## Definition

This function returns the array comprising all the values in the associate array specified. In a scalar context, it returns the number of values in the array.

## Example

```
%a = (1, "one", 2, "two", 3, "three");
print("vaules() ",values(%a),"\n");
```

# vec

## Compliance

## Syntax

```
Category  list operator (fixed)
Arguments  expression, offset, bits
Return Value  value
```

## Definition

This function uses the string specified by expression as a vector of unsigned integers. The return value is the value of the bitfield specified by offset. The specified bits are the number of bits that are reserved for each entry in the bit vector. This must be a power of 2 from 1 to 32. Note that the offset is the marker for the end of the vector, and it counts back the number of bits specified to find the start.

Vectors can be manipulated with the logical bitwise operators ¦, &, and ^.

## Example

```
$vec = '';
vec($vec,3,4) = 1;       # bits 0 to 3
vec($vec,7,4) = 10;      # bits 4 to 7
vec($vec,11,4) = 3;      # bits 8 to 11
vec($vec,15,4) = 15;     # bits 12 to 15
# As there are 4 bits per number this can be decoded by
# unpack() as a hex number
print("vec() Has created a string of nybbles, in hex: ",
        unpack("h*",$vec),"\n");
```

# wait

## Compliance

## Syntax

```
Category  (process)
Arguments  none
Return Value  pid
```

## Definition

This function waits for a child process to exit. It returns the process ID (pid) of the terminated process and -1 if there are no child processes.

# waitpid

## Compliance

## Syntax

```
Category  list operator (process)
Arguments  pid, flags
Return Value  pid
```

## Definition

This function waits for a specified child process to exit and returns `pid` of the terminated process and `-1` if there is no child process matching the `pid` specified. The `flags` can be set to various values that are equivalent to the `waitpid()` UNIX system call (if the operating system supports this), a `flags` value of `0` should work on all operating systems supporting processes.

# wantarray

## Compliance

## Syntax

```
Category  (flow)
Arguments  none
Return Value  1 (true) '' (false)
```

## Definition

This function returns `1` if the current context is an array context; otherwise, it returns `''`. This construct is most often used to return two alternatives from a subroutine, depending on the calling context.

## Example

```
return wantarray ? (8, 4, 33) : 3;
```

# warn

## Compliance

## Syntax

```
Category  list operator (i/o)
Arguments  list
Return Value  1 (true) '' (false)
```

## Definition

This function prints the supplied list to STDERR, like die(). If there is no newline in the list, warn() appends the text at line <line number>\n to the message. However, the script will continue after a warn().

# write

## Compliance

## Syntax

```
Category  list operator (i/o)
Arguments expression
Arguments handle
Arguments none
```

## Definition

This function writes a formatted record to the file handle (or the file handle that the expression evaluates to). If no file handle is specified, the default is STDOUT; this can be altered using select() if necessary.

A format for use by that file handle must have been declared using the format() function. This defaults to the name of the file handle being used, but other format names can be associated with the current write() operation using the $FORMAT_NAME ($~) special variable.

# y///

## Compliance

## Syntax

```
Category  (string)
Arguments y/searchlist/replacelist/<options>
Return Value numeric
```

## Definition

The y/// operator is a synonym for the translation operator tr///.

# CHAPTER 16

# Subroutine Definition

*by Mícheál Ó Foghlú*

One important factor in developing Perl programs is understanding the different ways of sectioning Perl code into functional units. This sectioning is important, both as a method of segmenting your own code so that such segments can be reused in various ways and as a method of using code developed by other people rather than having to reinvent the wheel.

There are three basic levels of segmentation. Within a package, Perl provides for the creation and use of subroutines. As in many structured programming languages, segmentation allows frequently used code, or code designed for a particular subtask, to be grouped logically. This concept also enables the use of recursive subroutines, which is a powerful mechanism for solving certain problems.

When you want to use subroutines that were originally developed in one program in another program, you can do so in two ways in Perl. The first way is to create a library, which you can subsequently include in other programs, giving them access to the suite of subroutines.

In Perl 5.0, this mechanism was expanded and generalized with the introduction of the concept of modules. Although they are more complex to create, modules are a more flexible method of developing and distributing suites of subroutines relating to specific tasks. ■

**The creation and use of subroutines**

This section describes how to declare a subroutine and the various methods of calling a subroutine.

**The creation and use of libraries**

This section describes how to set up a library and how to include subroutines, which are part of a library, in a Perl script.

**The creation and use of modules**

This section describes how to include subroutines (and objects), which are part of a module, in a Perl script. Some details on how to create modules are also included.

# Subroutines

The basic subunit of code in Perl is a subroutine. A *subroutine* is similar to a function in C and to a procedure or a function in Pascal. A subroutine can be called with various parameters and returns a value. Effectively, the subroutine groups a sequence of statements so that they can be reused.

## The Simplest Form of Subroutine

Subroutines can be declared anywhere in a program. If more than one subroutine with the same name is declared, each new version replaces the older ones, so that only the last one is effective. You can declare subroutines within an `eval()` expression. These subroutines will not actually be declared until the run-time execution reaches the `eval()` statement.

Subroutines are declared in the following syntax:

```
sub <subroutine-name> {
<statements>
}
```

The simplest form of subroutine is one that does not return any value and does not access any external values. The subroutine is called by prefixing the name with the & character. (Other ways of calling subroutines are explained in more detail later in this chapter, in the section "How to Pass Values to Subroutines.")  Following is an example of a program that uses the simplest form of subroutine:

```
#!/usr/bin/perl -w
# Example of subroutine which does not use external values and does not return a
  value
&egsub1; # Call the subroutine once
&egsub1; # Call the subroutine a second time
sub egsub1 {
    print "This subroutine simply prints this line.\n";
}
```

 Although you can refer from a subroutine to any global variable directly, this method normally is considered to be bad programming practice. Referring to global variables from subroutines makes reusing the subroutine code more difficult. (Will the same global variables always exist and have relevant values?) It is best to make any such references to external values explicit by passing explicit parameters to the subroutine, as described later in this chapter, in "How to Pass Values to Subroutines."

Similarly, it is best to avoid programming subroutines that directly change the values of global variables. This practice could lead to unpredictable side effects if the subroutine is reused in a different program. Use explicit return values or explicit parameters passed by reference, as described in "How to Pass Values to Subroutines" later in this chapter.

# How to Return Values from Subroutines

Subroutines can also return values, thus acting as functions. The return value is the value of the last statement executed; it can be a scalar or an array value. You can test whether the calling context requires an array or a scalar value by using the wantarray construct, thus returning different values depending on the required context. The following example, as the last line of a subroutine, would return the array (a,b,c) in an array context and the scalar value 0 in a scalar context:

```
wantarray ? (a, b, c) : 0;
```

The following example subroutine returns a value but is not passed any values:

```
#!/usr/bin/perl -w
# Example of subroutine which does not use external values but does return a
    value
$scalar-return = &egsub2; # Call the subroutine once, returning a scalar value
print "Scalar return value: $scalar-return.\n";
@array-return = &egsub2; # Call the subroutine a second time, returning an array
    value
print "Array return value:", @array-return, ".\n";
sub egsub2 {
    print "This subroutine prints this line and returns a value.\n";
    wantarray ? (a, b, c) : 0;
}
```

You can return from a subroutine before the last statement by using the return() function. The argument to the return function is the returned value, in this case. The use of return() is illustrated in the following example (which is not a very efficient way to do the test but illustrates the point):

```
#!/usr/bin/perl -w
# Example of subroutine which does not use external values but does return a
    value using "return"
$returnval = &egsub3; # Call the subroutine once
print "The current time is $returnval.\n";
sub egsub3 {
    print "This subroutine prints this line and returns a value.\n";
    local($sec, $min, $hour, @rest) =
        gmtime(time);
    ($min == 0) && ($hour == 12) && (return "noon");
if ($hour > 12) {
        return "after noon";
    }
    else {
        return "before noon";
    }
```

Notice that any variables used within a subroutine usually are made local() to the enclosing block, so that they do not interfere with any variables in the calling program that have the same name. In Perl 5.0, you can make these variables lexically local rather than dynamically local by using my() instead of local(). (This procedure is discussed in more detail later in this chapter, in "Issues of Scope with my() and local().")

When multiple arrays are returned, the result is flattened into one list so that effectively, only one array is returned. In the following example, all the return values are in @return-a1, and the send array, @return-a2, is empty.

```
#!/usr/bin/perl -w
# Example of subroutine which does not use external values returning an array
(@return-a1, @return-a2) = &egsub4; # Call the subroutine once
print "Return array a1",@return-a1," Return array a2 ",@return-a2, ".\n";
sub egsub4 {
    print "This subroutine returns a1 and a2.\n";
    local(@a1) = (a, b, c);
    local(@a2) = (d, e, f);
    return(@a1,@a2);
}
```

In Perl 4.0, you can avert this problem by passing the arrays by reference, using a typeglob (see the following section). In Perl 5.0, you can do the same thing and also manipulate any variable by direct reference (see the following section).

# How to Pass Values to Subroutines

The next important aspect of subroutines is the fact that the call can pass values to the subroutine. The call simply lists the variables to be passed, which are passed in the list @_ to the subroutine. These variables are known as the parameters or the arguments. It is customary to assign a name to each value at the start of the subroutine, so that it is clear what is going on. Manipulating these copies of the arguments is equivalent to passing arguments by value (for example, their values may be altered, but this alteration does not alter the value of the variable in the calling program).

The following example illustrates how to pass parameters to a subroutine by value:

```
#!/usr/bin/perl -w
# Example of subroutine is passed external values by value
$returnval = &egsub5(45,3); # Call the subroutine once
print "The (45+1) * (3+1) is $returnval.\n";
$x = 45;
$y = 3;
$returnval = &egsub5($x,$y);
print "The ($x+1) * ($y+1) is $returnval.\n";
print "Note that \$x still is $x, and \$y still is $y.\n";
sub egsub5 { # Access $x and $y by value
    local($x, $y) = @_;
    return (++$x * ++$y);
}
```

To pass scalar values by reference rather than by value, you can access the elements in @_ directly, which will change their values in the calling program. In such a case, the argument must be a variable rather than a literal value, because literal values cannot be altered.

The following example illustrates passing parameters by reference to a subroutine:

```
#!/usr/bin/perl -w
# Example of subroutine is passed external values by reference
```

```
$x = 45;
$y = 3;
print "The ($x+1) * ($y+1) ";
$returnval = &egsub6($x,$y);
print "is $returnval.\n";
print "Note that \$x now is $x, and \$y now is $y.\n";
sub egsub6 { # Access $x and $y by reference
     return (++$_[0] * ++$_[1]);
}
```

You can pass array values by reference in the same way; however, several restrictions apply. First, as is true of returned array values, the @_ list is one single flat array, so passing multiple arrays in this way is tricky. Also, you can use this method to alter individual elements of the subroutine; you cannot alter the size of the array within the subroutine, so you cannot use push() and pop().

Therefore, another method has been provided to facilitate the passing of arrays by reference. This method, known as *typeglobbing*, works with Perl 4.0 or Perl 5.0. The principle is that the subroutine declares that one or more of its parameters are typeglobbed, which means that all the references to that identifier in the scope of the subroutine are taken to refer to the equivalent identifier in the namespace of the calling program.

The syntax for this declaration prefixes the identifier with an asterisk (*) rather than an at sign (@), as in *array1 typeglobs @array1. In fact, typeglobbing links all forms of the identifier, so the *array1 typeglobs @array1, %array1, and $array1. (Any reference to any of these variables in the local subroutine actually refers to the equivalent variable in the calling program's namespace.) Using this construct within a local() list makes sense, because it effectively creates a local alias for a set of global variables. The following example illustrates the use of typeglobbing:

```
#!/usr/bin/perl -w
# Example of subroutine using arrays passed by reference (type globbing)
&egsub7(@a1,@a2); # Call the subroutine once
print "Modified array a1",@a1," Modified array a2 ",@a2, ".\n";
sub egsub7 {
     local(*arr1,*arr2) = @_;
     print "This subroutine modifies arr1 and arr2";
     print " and thus a1 and a2 via typeglobbing.\n";
     @arr1 = (a, b, c);
     @arr2 = (d, e, f);
}
```

In Perl 4.0, this method is the only way to use references to variables rather than variables themselves. Perl 5.0 also has a generalized method for dealing with references. Although this method looks more awkward in its syntax (because of the abundance of underscores), it actually is more precise in its meaning. Typeglobbing automatically aliases the scalar, the array, and the hashed array form of an identifier, even if only the array name is required. With Perl 5.0 references, you can make this distinction explicit; only the array form of the identifier is referenced.

The following example illustrates how to pass arrays by reference in Perl 5.0:

```
#!/usr/bin/perl -w
# Example of subroutine using arrays passed by reference (Perl 5 references)
&egsub7(\@a1,\@a2); # Call the subroutine once
print "Modified array a1",@a1," Modified array a2 ",@a2, ".\n";
sub egsub7 {
      local($a1ref,$a2ref) = @_;
      print "This subroutine modifies a1 and a2.\n";
      @$a1ref = (a, b, c);
      @$a2ref = (d, e, f);
}
```

## Subroutine Recursion

One the most powerful features of subroutines is their capability to call themselves. Many problems can be solved by repeated application of the same procedure. You must take care to set up a termination condition wherein the recursion stops and the execution can unravel itself. Typical examples of this approach occur in list processing: Process the head item and then process the tail; if the tail is empty, do not recurse. Another neat example is the calculation of a factorial value, as follows:

```
#!/usr/bin/perl -w
#
# Example factorial using recursion

for ($x=1; $x<100; $x++) {
      print "Factorial $x is ",&factorial($x), "\n";
}

sub factorial {
      local($x) = @_;
      if ($x == 1) {
            return 1;
      }
      else {
            return ($x*($x-1) + &factorial($x-1));
      }
}
```

## Subroutine Prototypes

Perl 5.002 introduces the capability to declare limited forms of subroutine prototypes. This capability allows early detection of errors in the number and type of parameters and generation of suitable warnings. This is primarily to allow the declaration of replacement subroutines for built-in commands. To use the stricter parameter checking, however, you must make the subroutine call by using only the subroutine name (without the & prefix). The prototype declaration syntax is concise and not as strict as the named formal parameters mechanism is in languages such as Pascal.

The main use for these prototypes at present is in writing modules for wider use, allowing the modules to specify their parameter types so as to trap errors and print diagnostic messages. Therefore, this chapter does not discuss this mechanism in detail.

## Issues of Scope with *my()* and *local()*

Chapter 1, "Perl Overview," alluded to some issues related to scope. These issues are very important with relation to subroutines. In particular, all variables inside subroutines should be made lexical local variables (via `my()`) or dynamic local variables (via `local()`). In Perl 4.0, the only choice is `local()`, because `my()` was introduced in Perl 5.0.

Variables declared with the `my()` construct are considered to be lexical local variables. These variables are not entered in the symbol table for the current package; therefore, they are totally hidden from all contexts other than the local block within which they are declared. Even subroutines called from the current block cannot access lexical local variables in that block. Lexical local variables must begin with an alphanumeric character (or an underscore).

Variables declared by means of the `local()` construct are considered to be dynamic local variables. The value is local to the current block and any calls from that block. You can localize special variables as dynamic local variables, but you cannot make them into lexical local variables. These two differences from lexical local variables show the two cases in Perl 5.0 in which it is still advisable to use `local()` rather than `my()`:

- Use `local()` if you want the value of the local variables to be visible to subroutines.
- Use `local()` if you are localizing special variables.

In general, you should be using `my` instead of `local`, because it's faster and safer. Exceptions to this rule include the global punctuation variables, file handles and formats, and direct manipulation of the Perl symbol table itself. Format variables often use `local`, though, as do other variables whose current value must be visible to called subroutines.

# Perl Libraries

The Perl 4.036 standard library has 31 files. These files have been replaced in Perl 5.0 by a set of standard modules (see the following section). This section describes the older system of libraries based on `require()`. The package mechanism by itself merely provides a way of segmenting the namespace into units. When this mechanism is combined with suites of subroutines stored in a file that can be included by means of `require()`, a library is created.

## Creation of Libraries

A *library* is effectively a collection of subroutines in a package. Setting up a file as a library file is a fairly straightforward process. Place the subroutines in a separate file, and add a package declaration to the top of the file. The file name of the library file and the package name should be the same. Then add the line

```
1;
```

to the end of the file (so that it returns TRUE when included by the `require()` function). If you want any of the subroutines to be in the global namespace automatically, change the name of the subroutine to explicitly name the main package (for example, `main'mysub`).

The following example illustrates how to declare a Perl 4.0 library with a single subroutine, `filtest`:

```
 # Sample library file (Perl 4)
package filtest;
sub main'filtest {
     local($fil) = @_;
     -f $fil && print "File $fil is a normal file.\n";
     -d _ && print "File $fil is a directory.\n";
}
1;
```

In Perl 5.0, the new form `main::mysub` is preferred to `main'mysub` for specifying the package name explicitly, but in Perl 5.0 you should consider making a module rather than a library.

## Invocation of Libraries

To use a library, you simply use `require()` to refer to the library name. Perl searches for all directories specified in the `@INC` special variable when it tries to locate this file. To include the sample library file specified in the preceding section, use the following code:

```
#!/usr/bin/perl -w
#
require "filtest";
&filtest("/usr/bin");
&filtest("/usr/etc/passwd");
```

## Standard Perl 4.0 Library

Following are the files in the standard Perl 4.036 library, which have been superseded by Perl 5.0 modules:

| | |
|---|---|
| abbrev.pl | getcwd.pl |
| assert.pl | getopt.pl |
| bigfloat.pl | getopts.pl |
| bigint.pl | importenv.pl |
| bigrat.pl | look.pl |
| cacheout.pl | newgetopt.pl |
| chat2.pl | open2.pl |
| complete.pl | perldb.pl |
| ctime.pl | pwd.pl |
| dumpvar.pl | shellwords.pl |
| exceptions.pl | stat.pl |
| fastcwd.pl | syslog.pl |
| find.pl | termcap.pl |
| finddepth.pl | timelocal.pl |
| flush.pl | validate.pl |

# Modules (Perl 5.0)

Perl 5.0 has a new structure for managing code that is designed for reuse. Modules have many more features than the package-based library in Perl 4.0, which simply provides a means of segmenting the namespace into packages.

You can create a Perl 5.0 module in two main conceptual ways. One way is to use the basic concept of a collection of subroutines, with added features that help control which subroutines are compulsory and which are optional. The other way is to use the new object-oriented facilities of Perl 5.0 to make a module become a definition of class, so that instances of that class implicitly call subroutines (methods) in the library. You can mix these two basic approaches to produce hybrid modules.

The object-oriented features expand the idea of a package to incorporate the idea of a class. Special subroutines act as constructors and destructors, creating objects that are members of the class and deleting the objects when the last reference to the object is gone. Other subroutines provide other ways of manipulating objects of that class. So a package can be simply a package, or it can be a class if it provides the associated subroutines to act as methods for the class objects. When you use the special @ISA array, one package class can inherit methods from another package class. The methods are simply subroutines written to deal with objects in the class.

Explaining the conceptual background of object-oriented programming is beyond the scope of this book, but these concepts need to be mentioned so as to put the descriptions of the standard modules in context, because many of them use these features.

## Standard Module List

This section lists the standard modules and pragmatic modules (*Pragmas*) in Perl 5.002. All these modules should be located in the Perl library path (@INC), should have the extension .PM, and should include their own documentation. Pragmas do not contain subroutines or classes, but act as compile-time directives through side effects that occur when they are referenced.

> **N O T E**  Many other modules exist. See Appendix B, "Perl Web Reference," for information on other nonstandard Perl modules.  ▦

Some Perl modules are developed in C rather than in Perl. These modules are called *extension modules*. Because of the problems involved in ensuring that these modules work under all operating systems, they are not as well standardized as the standard modules listed in the following table.

| Module Name | Description |
| --- | --- |
| AnyDBM_File | Provides access to external databases |
| AutoLoader | Special way of loading subroutines on demand |

*continues*

Part V
Ch
16

*continued*

| Module Name | Description |
|---|---|
| AutoSplit | Special way to set up modules for the use of AutoLoader |
| Benchmark | Time code for benchmarking |
| Carp | Reports errors across modules |
| Config | Reports compiler options used when Perl was installed |
| Cwd | Functions to manipulate current directory |
| DB_File | Provides access to Berkeley DB files |
| Devel::SelfStubber | Allows correct inheritance of autoloaded methods |
| diagnostics | Pragma enables diagnostic warnings |
| DynaLoader | Used by modules that link to C libraries |
| English | Pragma allows the use of long special variable names |
| Env | Allows access to environment variables |
| Exporter | Standard way for modules to export subroutines |
| ExtUtils::Liblist | Examines C libraries |
| ExtUtils::MakeMaker | Creates makefiles for extension modules |
| ExtUtils::Manifest | Helps maintain a MANIFEST file |
| ExtUtils::Miniperl | Used by makefiles generated by ExtUtils::MakeMaker |
| ExtUtils::Mkbootstrap | Used by makefiles generated by ExtUtils::MakeMaker |
| Fcntl | Provides access to C fcntl.h |
| File::Basename | Parses file names according to various operating systems' rules |
| File::CheckTree | Performs multiple file tests |
| File::Find | Finds files according to criteria |
| File::Path | Creates/deletes directories |
| FileHandle | Allows object syntax for file handles |
| Getopt::Long | Allows POSIX-style command-line options |
| Getopt::Std | Allows single-letter command-line options |
| I18N::Collate | Allows POSIX locale rules for sorting 8-bit strings |
| integer | Pragma uses integer arithmetic |
| IPC::Open2 | Inter Process Communications (process with read/write) |

| Module Name | Description |
|---|---|
| IPC::Open3 | Inter Process Communications (process with read /write/error) |
| less | Pragma unimplemented |
| Net::Ping | Tests network node |
| overload | Allows overloading of operators (for example, special behavior, depending on object type) |
| POSIX | Allows POSIX standard identifiers |
| Safe | Can evaluate Perl code in safe memory compartments |
| SelfLoader | Allows specification of code to be autoloaded in module (alternative to the AutoLoader procedure) |
| sigtrap | Pragma initializes some signal handlers |
| Socket | Provides access to C socket.h |
| strict | Pragma forces safe code |
| subs | Pragma predeclares specified subroutine names |
| Text::Abbrev | Creates abbreviation table |
| Test::Harness | Runs the standard Perl tests |

# How to Create a Simple Module

Creating a module that is made up of a series of subroutines, in place of an old-style Perl library, is relatively simple. It is slightly more complicated to create the other style of module— which is made up completely of methods associated with an object class—if only because you need to understand the object-oriented approach better. Even the simpler style of modules use one of the object-oriented features. Every module should use an import() method inherited from the Exporter class or define its own import() method.

The following example converts the example library used earlier in this chapter (in "Creation of Libraries") to a module:

```
package FilTest;

=head1 NAME

FilTest - test a file printing status

=head1 SYNOPSYS

    use FilTest;
    filtest1("/tmp/file");

    use FilTest qw(filtest2);
    filtest2("/tmp/file");

=head1 DESCRIPTION
```

```
This is an example module which provides one subroutine which tests a file.
filtest1() is exported by default, filtest2() must be explicitly imported.

=cut

# Sample module

require Exporter;
@ISA = qw(Exporter);

@EXPORT = (filtest1);
@EXPORT_OK = qw(filtest2);

sub filtest1 {
    my($fil) = @_;
    -f $fil && print "File $fil is a normal file.\n";
    -d _ && print "File $fil is a directory.\n";
}
sub filtest2 {
    my($fil) = @_;
    -f $fil && print "File $fil is a normal file.\n";
    -d _ && print "File $fil is a directory.\n";
}
1;
```

The documentation for modules normally is built into the .PM file in POD format (as illustrated by the bare-bones documentation in the preceding example, from the first =head1 to the =cut) but is not necessary for the module to work.

The module specifies that it is prepared to have the filtest2() subroutine imported by those who use the module, but because it is in the @EXPORT_OK list rather than the @EXPORT list, it will not be exported by default, but must be explicitly included. However, filtest1() is exported by default.

# Module Use and Invocation

The standard way to include a module is with the use() function. Later, you can disable the effect of pragmatic functions (Pragmas) that act as compiler directives by using the no() syntax. The following example enables the use of the integer pragma and then disables it:

```
use integer;
....
no integer;
```

Normal modules import symbols into the current package or provide access to symbols in the module. If you do not specify any arguments after the module name, the default behavior is to import all symbols specified in the module as EXPORT. If you specify the null list as an argument, no symbols are imported. The following paragraphs describe the various ways to import from the sample module.

The following defines filtest1() in the global namespace:

```
use FilTest;
filtest1("/etc/passwd");
```

The following explicitly asks to use `filtest2()` as well:

```
use FilTest qw(filtest2);
filtest1("/etc/passwd");
filtest2("/etc/passwd");
```

The following imports neither subroutine name to the current namespace:

```
use FilTest ();
```

Even when the null list is used to avoid importing any names, the subroutines in the module are still accessible via an explicit reference to the `FilTest` package in the subroutine name. The following example illustrates how to access the subroutines directly:

```
use FilTest ();
FilTest::filtest1("/etc/passwd");
FilTest::filtest2("/etc/passwd");
```

Part

V

Ch

16

# From Here...

This chapter forms one part of the reference section of this book. The chapter attempts to describe all the features of the language in a way that can serve as an easy reference. You can see the other reference chapters as forming one unit with this chapter. You also may want to refer to the portion of Appendix B, "Perl Web Reference," that deals with other nonstandard Perl modules—in particular, the CGI module.

The other chapters that comprise the reference section are:

- Chapter 13, "Special Variables," provides detailed descriptions of the Perl special variables.
- Chapter 14, "Operators," provides detailed descriptions of the Perl operators.
- Chapter 15, "Function List," provides detailed descriptions of the Perl functions.

# Appendixes

# Perl Acquisition and Installation

Perl is easily and readily available on the Internet. Best of all, it's free. As mentioned in Chapter 1, "Perl Overview," Perl is protected under the GNU General Public License, which maintains copyright protection for the author but allows other people to freely use and modify the software. The only costs that you can be charged are transferring costs, warranty protection, or support; you cannot be charged for Perl itself. If the software is modified, the modification must carry notices to this effect, and the modified Perl itself must be licensed under the GNU General Public License. One method of highlighting extensive modifications is renaming Perl to fit the new functionality; this policy accounts for the versions or extensions of Perl called MacPerl or oraperl.

After you access Perl and install it, you have several sources of help on the Internet. Appendix B, "Perl Web Reference," lists several sites that have Perl-related libraries, modules, or documentation. Also included in Appendix B is a list of several Usenet groups that you can visit to find the latest information on Perl or to post a question.

In addition, a couple of books on Perl 5.0 can provide help:

- *Teach Yourself Perl 5 in 21 Days, 2nd Edition* (SAMS Publishing, 1996)
- *Perl 5 How-To* (Waite Group Press, 1996)

# History and Version Information

**ON THE WEB**

Perl has been around for several years. Usenets on Perl (such as **comp.lang.perl.misc**) existed in the late 1980s, and the defining book on Perl, *Programming Perl*, was published in 1991 by O'Reilly & Associates, Inc. Since that time, the numbers of users—and uses—of this language have grown considerably, aided in part by the considerable interest in applications on the Internet and by the ease with which this language can be used with CGI programming.

The popularity of Perl can be attributed to several factors, the first of which is, of course, its price. Most people would much rather use a tool that works and does not cost anything than one that works and does have a cost. A second factor is that you get a considerable amount of functionality with a minimum amount of code, yet the code is not so cryptic that it's almost painful to work with, as awk can be. A third factor must be that you can get a small program up and running within minutes, without having to set up makefiles, compile the program (in the traditional sense), or perform any of the other processes that you have to follow when you work with a compiled language such as C.

A fourth factor that has to be included among the advantages of using Perl is the availability of so many libraries, modules, and sample code and scripts on the Internet. Appendix B, "Perl Web Reference," lists the URLs of many locations that have these resources. When reading through these URLs, you might wonder (as many people probably do) whether anything related to CGI programming has not already been created. The really great thing about all this is that, like Perl, the vast majority of these tools, libraries, and scripts are free. Really, this Perl-and-CGI thing sounds better all the time.

A last factor in the strength of using Perl, particularly for Web application development, is the fact that it is available for many platforms. You might have to make some modifications to the Perl script, based on the operating system that you are working on, but the basic components, concepts, and capabilities are the same, providing that the platform supports the release of Perl for which you are coding.

**N O T E**   My first exposure to Perl was at the request of a customer for a contract that I was working on. The customer requested that I use Perl to complete the job. I was reluctant to use a scripting language, because I had recently completed a fairly massive job by using shell scripts and "fun" tools such as awk. By the time I was done with the job, however, I was impressed with Perl, and I have become even more so with Perl 5.0. After working with CGI, I knew that I had found a perfect partnership: CGI and Perl. ▪

# Perl Version 5.0

In 1993, Larry Wall, the creator of Perl, began to issue alpha releases of a new version of Perl. On October 19, 1994, Perl 5.0 was officially released. This new version of Perl was a basic rewrite of the Perl language that included new and improved features, of which the following are only a small subset:

- Improved configuration and a faster interpreter
- POSIX compliance
- Object-oriented features
- The capability to import the Perl library as modules
- Extensibility with C or C++
- Enhancements to the grammar and regular expressions, scoping, and data structures

The original version of Perl 5.0 could be compiled primarily on UNIX and VMS systems. Since that time, the original version of Perl 5.0 has been migrated to most systems. In addition, there have been two major releases of Perl 5.0: Perl 5.001 and Perl 5.002. Ports to Perl 5.002 are still occurring, but Perl 5.001 should be readily available for most operating systems.

If the original Perl can be considered to be a perfect blend of the best of C and shell scripting, Perl 5.0 can be extended to include C++. This version allows you to work with objects, which you can instantiate and use as easily as this:

```
use FOO;
$somevar = new FOO;
```

After you create an instance of the object, you can reference its methods as easily as this:

```
$somevar->method;
```

Another excellent enhancement of Perl 5.0 is its integration with OLE on Windows 95 and Windows NT. Using OLE automation techniques with Perl 5.0 is now very similar to accessing them with Visual Basic and other applications, such as PowerBuilder 5.0. With this main-streaming of the technique, a developer can transfer his or her knowledge between the tools, rather than learn a new technique to use what should be an open technology.

These features, and those listed earlier in this section and discussed on the Internet, have definitely opened intriguing new possibilities for this language.

# Availability by OS

You can obtain Perl from any of the CPAN (Comprehensive Perl Archive Network) mirror sites listed in Table A.1. You also can find some of these sites through Yahoo, at **http://www.yahoo.com/Computers_and_Internet/Programming_Languages/Perl/CPAN_Comprehensive_Perl_Archive_Network/**.

**Table A.1   CPAN Mirror Sites**

| Site | URL |
| --- | --- |
| North America: Canada | **ftp://enterprise.ic.gc.ca/pub/perl/CPAN/** |
| North America: California | **ftp://ftp.digital.com/pub/plan/perl/CPAN/** |
| North America: California | **ftp://ftp.cdrom.com/pub/perl/CPAN/** |

*continues*

### Table A.1  Continued

| Site | URL |
|------|-----|
| North America: Colorado | ftp://ftp.cs.colorado.edu/pub/perl/CPAN/ |
| North America: Florida | ftp://ftp.cis.ufl.edu/pub/perl/CPAN/ |
| North America: Illinois | ftp://uiarchive.cso.uiuc.edu/pub/lang/perl/CPAN/ |
| North America: New York | ftp://ftp.rge.com/pub/languages/perl/CPAN/ |
| North America: Oklahoma | ftp://ftp.uoknor.edu/mirrors/CPAN/ |
| North America: Texas | ftp://ftp.sterling.com/programming/languages/perl/ |
| North America: Texas | ftp://ftp.sedl.org/pub/mirrors/CPAN/ |
| North America: Texas | ftp://ftp.metronet.com/pub/perl/ |
| Africa | ftp://ftp.is.co.za/programming/perl/CPAN/ |
| Australia | ftp://coombs.anu.edu.au/pub/perl/ |
| Australia | ftp://ftp.mame.mu.oz.au/pub/perl/CPAN/ |
| New Zealand | ftp://ftp.tekotago.ac.nz/pub/perl/CPAN/ |
| Europe: Austria | ftp://ftp.tuwien.ac.at/pub/languages/perl/CPAN/ |
| Europe: Belgium | ftp://ftp.kulnet.kuleuven.ac.be/pub/mirror/CPAN/ |
| Europe: Czech Republic | ftp://sunsite.mff.cuni.cz/Languages/Perl/CPAN/ |
| Europe: Denmark | ftp://sunsite.auc.dk/pub/languages/perl/CPAN/ |
| Europe: Finland | ftp://ftp.funet.fi/pub/languages/perl/CPAN/ |
| Europe: France | ftp://ftp.ibp.fr/pub/perl/CPAN/ |
| Europe: France | ftp://ftp.pasteur.fr/pub/computing/unix/perl/CPAN/ |
| Europe: Germany | ftp://ftp.leo.org/pub/comp/programming/languages/perl/CPAN/ |
| Europe: Germany | ftp://ftp.rz.ruhr-unibochum.de/pub/CPAN/ |
| Europe: Greece | ftp://ftp.ntua.gr/pub/lang/perl/ |
| Europe: Hungary | ftp://ftp.kfki.hu/pub/packages/perl/CPAN/ |
| Europe: Italy | ftp://cis.utovrm.it/CPAN/ |
| Europe: The Netherlands | ftp://ftp.cs.ruu.nl/pub/PERL/CPAN/ |
| Europe: Poland | ftp://ftp.pk.edu.pl/pub/lang/perl/CPAN/ |
| Europe: Poland | ftp://sunsite.icm.edu.pl/pub/CPAN/ |
| Europe: Portugal | ftp://ftp.ci.uminho.pt/pub/lang/perl/ |

| Site | URL |
| --- | --- |
| Europe: Spain | ftp://ftp.etse.urv.es/pub/mirror/perl/ |
| Europe: Spain | ftp://ftp.rediris.es/mirror/CPAN/ |
| Europe: Sweden | ftp://ftp.sunet.se/pub/lang/perl/CPAN/ |
| Europe: Switzerland | ftp://ftp.switch.ch/mirror/CPAN/ |
| Europe: United Kingdom | ftp://ftp.demon.co.uk/pub/mirrors/perl/CPAN/ |
| Europe: United Kingdom | ftp://sunsite.doc.ic.ac.uk/packages/CPAN/ |
| Europe: United Kingdom | ftp://unix.hensa.ac.uk/mirrors/perl-CPAN/ |
| Japan | ftp://ftp.lab.kdd.co.jp/lang/perl/CPAN/ |
| Taiwan | ftp://dongpo.math.ncu.edu.tw/perl/CPAN/ |
| South America: Chile | ftp://sunsite.dcc.uchile.cl/pub/Lang/perl/CPAN/ |

If you access these sites by using a Web browser, you will see a listing of subdirectories and files similar to that shown in figure A.1. In addition, you can enter **http://www.perl.com/CPAN/** into your browser, and you will automatically be routed to the CPAN site nearest to your location.

**FIG. A.1**
This figure shows a typical CPAN site in a WWW browser.

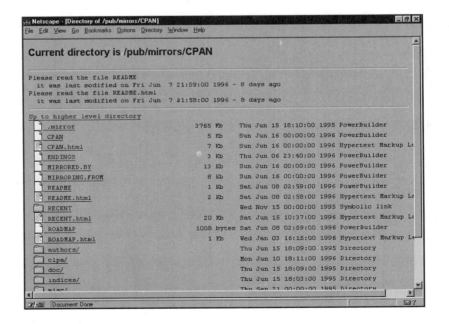

The Perl ports and their locations relative to the CPAN location are listed in the following sections. For all operating systems, the most recent version and release are given as they were known at the time when this book was written.

**N O T E**    For most operating systems, Perl has been ported to version 5.0, but some operating
systems are still in version 4.0. ■

## UNIX

Perl was originally created for UNIX, and new releases of Perl make it to this operating system
before any other. You can access the most current release by opening the URL **http://
www.perl.com/CPAN/src/5.0/** with your WWW browser. At this location, you are in the
source directory of Perl 5.0. Access the most recent stable build by downloading the file named
LATEST.TAR.GZ. In the summer of 1996, the latest stable build for UNIX was Perl
version 5.002.

    You may be tempted to try some of the code in the /PATCHES and /UNSUPPORTED subdirectories.
These subdirectories contain work in progress and unstable code releases. Unless you like to work with
buggy code, you probably will want to avoid these subdirectories and access only the "official"
releases.

## Amiga

You can access Perl for Amiga by referencing the /PORTS/AMIGA subdirectory of the nearest CPAN location. To access the subdirectory directly, enter **http://www.perl.com/ports/
amiga** into your browser. The most recent version of Amiga is version 5.002.

## AOS

You can access Perl for AOS by referencing the /PORTS/AOS subdirectory of the nearest
CPAN location. The most recent version of AOS is version 5.002.

## Atari

Access the Atari Perl installation by accessing /PORTS/ATARI from CPAN. The most recent
version of Atari appears to be version 4.035.

## LynxOS

The most recent version of Perl ported to LynxOS is version 4.036, and you can access it by
going to the /PORTS/LYNXOS subdirectory from CPAN.

## Mac

The MacPerl home page lists the current version of MacPerl as version 5.0.7. Based on the
date of this home page and on our access of this page during the summer of 1996, I estimate
that this version is equivalent to UNIX version 5.001. The best place to access this installation is
**ftp://ftp.switch.ch/software/mac/perl/**.

# MS-DOS

The most recent port to MS-DOS of Perl, made in November 1994, is a preliminary port of version 5.0. You can locate this version of Perl at /PORTS/MSDOS/PERL5 from a CPAN site. The author of the product has issued a disclaimer about the product; you can access this disclaimer as the PERL5A.README file.

# MVS

Version 4.036 of Perl is the most recent release for MVS. You can access this release at any CPAN site by accessing the /PORTS/MVS subdirectory.

# NetWare

NetWare's newest version of Perl, 4.036, is available at the /PORTS/NETWARE CPAN subdirectory.

# Windows 95 and Windows NT

These two operating systems have been combined, and the same version of Perl can be used for both. The current version of Perl that has been implemented for the Win32 port is version 5.001; you can access it directly at **ftp://ftp.perl.hip.com/ntperl/**. The most current release of Win32 Perl probably will be in the CURRENTBUILD subdirectory, and the file will be called 107-i86.ZIP. The source code is located in the file 107-SRC.ZIP. Information about the port is available at **http://www.perl.hip.com/PerlFaq.htm**.

# OS/2

The 5.001 version of Perl has been ported to OS/2; you can find it at any of the CPAN sites under /PORTS/OS2.

# QNX

You can find a port of version 5.0 of Perl for QNX at /PORTS/QNX of any of the CPAN sites.

# VMS

VMS has been ported to version 5.0, but unfortunately, the port was not working at this time when this chapter was written (summer 1996). You can access the 4.036 port from any CPAN site in the /PORTS/VMS SUBDIRECTORY.

# Xenix

Version 4.036 of Perl has been ported for the Xenix operating system; you can find it at /PORTS/XENIX on any CPAN site.

# Linux

Version 5.001 for Linux is available at **http://www.onshore.com/software/perl-linux.html**.

# Installation

This section contains the installation instructions for the most recent and stable port for the most common operating systems. For the most up-to-date information about a release of Perl for a specific operating system, check the CPAN site for that operating system.

## UNIX Installation

You need to download the Perl installation file from the UNIX site listed in the preceding section of this appendix. The file will most likely be named LATEST.TAR.GZ. When you have the file, extract the files into a subdirectory.

In the new subdirectory that contains the Perl files, open the text file called INSTALL. This file contains detailed instructions about installing the version of Perl that you downloaded. Following is a synopsis of these instructions:

```
mv config.sh config.sh.old
```

This code renames the existing CONFIG.SH file.

```
sh Configure [options]
```

This code runs the Configure shell script, which attempts to find information about your system, run make on the Perl source, and install Perl in your system's binary subdirectory (usually, /USR/LOCAL/BIN). When you run Configure, you can specify options, such as specifying a different location for Perl or a different compiler.

Perl 5.0 can interface with a database through extensions. If you have these extensions installed on your system, `Configure` includes the extension if it can find the header files and libraries. Again, you have the option to inform `Configure` of the subdirectory in which the files are installed, if they are not in the standard directory that the C compiler searches for.

Table A.2 lists some of the `Configure` options and their impact. To see the full list of options, check the INSTALL file of the version of Perl that you downloaded.

### Table A.2   UNIX Installation *Configure* Options

| Option | Result |
| --- | --- |
| -Dcc | Specifies an alternative compiler |
| -h | Lists options |
| -O | Uses existing CONFIG.SH file but overrides some of the items |
| -des | Accepts defaults and provides terse output |

| Option | Result |
|--------|--------|
| -Dprefix | Specifies the directory in which Perl will be installed |
| -Uusedl | Forces static compile of Perl |

**ON THE WEB**

To find more information about Perl and UNIX, you should access the Perl FAQ at **http://www.perl.com/perl/faq/index.html**. Documentation from Larry Wall is available at **http://www.atmos.washington.edu/perl/perl.html**.

## Windows 95 and Windows NT

Installing Perl 5.0 for Windows NT or Windows 95 is relatively easy. After downloading the zipped file 107-i86, use WinZip to extract the files to the subdirectory that is included as part of the zipped file information. If you want to install Perl on your C drive, just specify that drive; the files will be installed in a subdirectory called PERL5.

After extracting the files, look for a README file called INSTALL.TXT. This file includes the most current information regarding the installation of Perl 5.0. Another file, README.TXT, includes other information, such as the GNU General Public License, the system requirements, and the differences between Perl for UNIX and Perl for Win32.

In addition to these text files, you might find one called WIN95.TXT, which details any problems with running Perl for Win32 on Windows 95. At the time when this book was written, some of the problems with running Perl for Win32 on Windows 95 had to do with some problems with the 16-bit shell, COMMAND.COM.

To install Perl for Win32, run INSTALL.BAT from a command prompt. This file adds Perl to the Registry, creates the \PERL5\BIN subdirectory (if it does not already exist), and adds this subdirectory to the path. In addition, if this version is an upgrade to an existing installation, the application renames the file that contains the existing version of PERL.EXE to include the version number (PERL.4.36.EXE, for example).

If you have any existing Perl scripts or libraries, you can copy them to the \PERL5\BIN subdirectory after the installation process.

You can compile PERL.EXE by using the source in the zipped file 107-SRC.ZIP. After downloading this file, extract the files into the same \PERL5 subdirectory that you used to extract the binary files. Perl 5.0 was compiled with Microsoft Visual C++, and you can compile the source code by accessing the makefile called PERL.MAK in \PERL5\EXE-SRC.

You also can use nmake to compile the PERL.EXE and PERLGLOB.EXE files.

**ON THE WEB**

You can find a FAQ on Perl for Win32 at **http://www.perl.hip.com/PerlFaq.htm**.

## MacPerl

The instructions for installing MacPerl are available at **ftp://ftp.switch.ch/software/mac/ perl/**. Look for a file called MAC_PERL.INFO. Currently, the installation consists of four files: MAC_PERL_507R1M_APPL.BIN, MAC_PERL_507R1M_APPL.DISK1.BIN, MAC_PERL_507RLM_APPL.DISK2.BIN, and MAC_PERL_507RLM_TOOL.BIN.

You must be running System 7 to install MacPerl. In addition, you need the Metrowerks CodeWarrier C/C++ compiler (see **http://www.metrowerks.com**), the CWGUSI_164.SIT.BIN Socket Library, and the DB_185b.SIT.BIN Berkeley db library.

Follow the instructions given with Metrowerks CodeWarrier to compile.

The MacPerl home page is located at **http://err.ethz.ch/~neeri/macintosh/perl.html**, and an FAQ is available at **http://www.unimelb.edu.au/~ssilcot/macperl-primer/home.html**. A MacPerl primer is available at **http://www.unimelb.edu.au/~ssilcot/macperl-primer/ home.html**.

## OS/2

Download the zipped file that contains the Perl executable and associated files. At this time, the version of Perl for OS/2 is Perl 5.001 and Patchlevel "m." After you download the file, extract the files to your hard drive. Then open the README file to review installation instructions and last-minute information.

The current version of the file specifies that the Perl user needs to format his or her system for HPFS and then copy PERL5X.EXE AND PERLGLOB.EXE to a PATH subdirectory. PERL5.DLL is copied to a LIBPATH subdirectory, and a variable called PERL5LIB is set to any existing and new Perl library subdirectories.

Check the README file for additional information, and to see what other files and applications you might need to install and run Perl.

## Linux

If you are using Slackware's Linux installation, a copy of Perl 5.001 is included with version 3.0. When you are installing Linux or using the package install tool, make sure that you install disk set D. This disk set includes the C libraries and GNU compilers, as well as Perl.

## Other OSes

Each version of Perl for whatever operating system usually includes instructions with the installation files. If the installation files are compressed, you need to have the appropriate software to extract the files. You also want to look for any files named README, INSTALL, or SETUP. ●

# Perl Web Reference

**P**erl has become very popular, both because of its ease of use in proportion to its capability and because it is freely and easily available for many different operating systems. Appendix A, "Perl Acquisition and Installation," describes where you can access Perl for your operating system and provides some installation instructions for some of the most popular operating systems. This appendix lists some of the Internet sites where you can get Perl-related libraries, scripts, documents, and other goodies.

The first section describes usenets that you can browse through and pick up useful information. Additionally, any time you have a question on Perl or on CGI programming, you can post to one of these groups and usually get at least one response within eight hours.

The second section describes sites that have useful Web-, CGI-, and Perl-related libraries, samples, code, and documentation that can be extremely helpful. The sites might also include libraries for database access and for other important Internet and intranet activities.

The last section describes sites that have useful Perl libraries, samples, code, and documentation that are not necessarily Web-related. ■

**TIP** If you are new to CGI programming with Perl, you will want to visit each of the sites listed in this appendix. Doing so will give you a good understanding of what scripts, libraries, modules, and documentation are available (in addition to this book) to help you become a great CGI programmer. As you visit the sites, jot down the downloadable files that interest you, including their versions and the date. When you finish visiting the sites, you will know where to access the most recent tools, and you can begin to download and build your own CGI development library.

# Perl, Web, and CGI-Related Usenets

One of the most useful Perl-related sites is **comp.lang.perl**. This site is the one that you will most likely post to when you have a perl-language problem or general perl-language question. Now that I've said that, I want to recommend yet another extremely useful site, which is **comp.lang.perl.misc**. If **comp.lang.perl** does not have what you need, **comp.lang. perl.misc** probably will, especially in regard to Perl on various operating systems and Perl in comparison with other tools, such as Tcl. Both of these sites are useful and should be on your subscribe-to list. Before you post at either of these usenets, you might want to read the Perl FAQ at **http://www.perl.com/perl/faq/**. In addition, this site points you to other FAQs.

To see the latest Perl-related announcements, check out **comp.lang.perl.announce**. You should also check out the CPAN sites (listed in Appendix A and repeated later in this appendix) for announcements of new releases. In addition, you can find archives of this usenet at any of the CPAN sites, in the /CLPA subdirectory.

The usenet **comp.lang.perl.modules** is very helpful if you want to check out what modules are available and how they are being used, if you have questions about or problems with existing Perl modules, or if you want to ask about the existence of modules to support a particular need.

The last perl-specific usenet is **comp.lang.perl.tk**. Tk is an interface tool (developed by Sun) primarily for use with Tcl, an embeddable scripting language. Tk extensions to Perl 5.0 have been made to allow integration. If you are interested in using both tools, you definitely want to check out this usenet. You also can find a FAQ for this usenet at **http://w4.lns.cornell.edu/ ~pvhp/ptk/ptkFAQ.html**.

Another useful usenet is **comp.infosystems.www.authoring.cgi**. This group contains many references to CGI programming with Perl, which is still one of the most popular approaches. You will want to glance through all the usenets that begin with **comp.infosystems.www** to find those that best meet your needs.

Table B.1 recaps the usenets discussed in this section.

**Table B.1 Web Programming with Perl Usenets**

| Usenet Name | Subject |
|---|---|
| comp.lang.perl | General perl language discussions |
| comp.lang.perl.misc | General perl language and tool discussions |
| comp.lang.perl.announce | Perl-related announcements |
| comp.lang.perl.tk | Perl/Tk integration discussions |
| comp.infosystems.www.authoring.cgi | CGI issues in Web authoring |

# Web-Related Perl and CGI Sites

The following sites are terrific places to visit to build up your CGI script library. In addition, the sites give you an idea of what you can use or modify for your own use. You will be amazed by the amount of freeware and shareware that is available.

## Yahoo

One of the best places to begin a search for information or files is Yahoo (see fig. B.1), which is one of the best organized and most comprehensive search sites on the Web. You can access Yahoo at **http://www.yahoo.com**.

**FIG. B.1**
This figure shows the Yahoo WWW site.

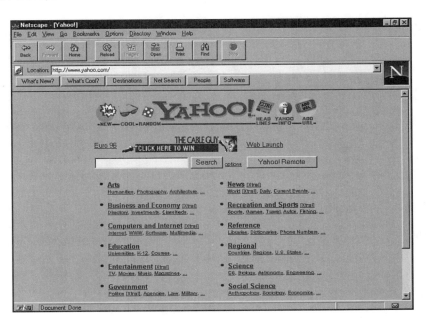

To find several sources that have Perl-related information, access Yahoo's site on Perl programming at **http://www.yahoo.com/Computers_and_Internet/Programming_Languages/ Perl/**. You can access information on CGI programming in general by starting at **http:// www.yahoo.com/Computers_and_Internet/Internet/World_Wide_Web/ CGI_Common_Gateway_Interface/**. In addition, you can access **http://www.yahoo.com/ Computers_and_Internet/Internet/World_Wide_Web/Programming/** to find information that is specific to programming on the Web, including a section on Perl scripts.

## The *cgi-lib.pl* Home Page

One of the most important libraries for CGI development with Perl is `cgi-lib.pl`, created by Steven Brenner. You can find this simple, easy-to-use library—as well as instructions on its use and examples of using it—at **http://www.bio.cam.ac.uk/cgi-lib/**. The library includes functions such as `ReadParse` (which parses the data passed to the script from the form) and `HtmlTop/HtmlBot`, which print specific `<HEAD>` and end-of `<BODY>` sections of an HTML document. This library, which works with Perl 4.0 and Perl 5.0, is a must to review and use.

## *cgi.pm*

`cgi.pm` is another CGI perl library that provides powerful functions for performing CGI programming with perl. This library, which requires Perl 5.001m, uses Perl 5.0 objects for Web-related activity. This library is another must for your perl-library list. Access the documentation, source code, and samples at **http://www-genome.wi.mit.edu/ftp/pub/software/ WWW/cgi_docs.html**.

## The CGI Collection

This site has a set of scripts, some of which were created with perl and some of which were created with C. Table B.2 lists some of the scripts that you can find at this site. In particular, check out the simple script `Logger.cgi`, which performs a very useful function. You can reach the site at **http://www.selah.net/cgi.html**.

**Table B.2   The CGI Collection Scripts**

| Script/Module | Covers |
| --- | --- |
| MailForm.cgi | Customizable mail-form CGI script |
| Guestbook.cgi | Guestbook CGI script |
| Logger.cgi | Simple script that logs visitors |
| FrameChat | Odd little application that implements a frames-based chat service (requires Perl 5.0) |

# HFPM Home Page

Sites such as this one mean that CGI/Perl programmers will have an easier time. The modules provided at this site take form contents; perform some processing; and output the result to e-mail, a file, or communication with the Web page reader, or return a new URL. You need Perl 5.0 and a UNIX-based system to use the modules listed at this site. You also need a copy of `cgi.pm` (discussed earlier in this chapter), as well as `pipeline.pl` (which is available with the HFPM distribution).

You can reach the site at **http://seclab.cs.ucdavis.edu/~hoagland/hfpm/**.

# Selina Sol's CGI Script Archive

This attractive and very useful site contains links to many fairly sophisticated CGI scripts, such as Web Chat 1.0, a slide-show script, a guestbook script, and a complete shopping-cart example. This site not only provides the sample scripts, but also allows you to see them in action. In addition, you can view the HTML and other documents that the examples use. The examples are fully documented and easy to understand.

This site is a must-visit site; you can reach it at **http://www2.eff.org/~erict/Scripts/**. Table B.3 lists some of the samples and describes what they do.

**Table B.3   Selina Sol's CGI Script Examples**

| Example | Description |
| --- | --- |
| Selena Sol's Electronic Outlet 2.0 (database) | Complete set of files to implement a databaselike shopping-cart system |
| Selena Sol's Electronic Outlet 2.0 (HTML) | Same as preceding example, but HTML-based |
| Cool Runnings Music Catalog | Shopping-cart concept for catalogs |
| The Form Processor | Processes form input, using hidden variables |
| Database Manager 2.0 | Flat-file database management tool |
| Database Search Engine 1.0 | Search engine for Database Manager 2.0 |
| Groupware Calendar | Calendar that can be read/modified by group |
| Keyword Search Engine 3.0 | Traverses HTML documents, searches for keyword, and returns output |
| `authentication-lib.pl` | Authentication perl module |
| `date.pl` | Date-based perl module |

## Reach for the Stars at www.stars.com

This site is a very comprehensive resource, self-described as a "Web developer's encyclopedia." The site is located at **http://www.stars.com**. Useful documents include tutorials on HTML, CGI, HTTP, databases, and style guidelines.

When you access the Library of Web Development at **http://WWW.Stars.com/Vlib/**, you will think that you have died and gone to some version of a pleasant afterlife. Accessing the encyclopedia only confirms this thought. This site is an incredibly rich source of links to virtually any Web development topic that you can think of. The CGI page has 69 links, the HTML has 55 links, and so on.

This site is a definite must to visit, especially when you have time to do a little link-hopping and exploring or when you need to find a Web development resource.

# CGI Scripts to Go

Another excellent resource for CGI scripts, this site has several CGI script examples, listed by category. The site uses HTML tables to provide the name of the script's author, a description of the script, the type of script, the language, and a link to the file(s). You can reach the site at **http://www.virtualville.com/library/scripts.html**. The site also contains an introduction to CGI at **http://www.virtualville.com/library/cgi.html**.

The categories listed at the site are:

- Animators
- Automated WWW Page Generators
- Bulletin Boards
- Chat Scripts
- Comments Pages Scripts
- Counters
- Dynamic Links (Add Links)
- Environment Variable Scripts
- File Upload
- Form Mail
- Guestbooks
- Height/Width Tag Inserters
- Phone Directory
- Random Number Generators
- Shopping Carts
- Web-Based E-Mail
- WWW Page Editors

## PureAmiga

Lest you think that all CGI scripting with Perl is done only in UNIX or Windows NT, this site has many excellent examples of CGI scripting, including animation, bulletin boards, calendars, counters, and mail. You can reach the site at **http://www.netlink.co.uk/users/PureAmiga/ pcgi/index.html**.

## MacPerl

Some helpful MacPerl scripts are available at Adam's Perl Page, located at **http:// www.marketspace.com.au/~adam/**. You can find the MacPerl home page at **http:// err.ethz.ch/~neeri/macintosh/perl.html**, a MacPerl primer at **http://www. unimelb.edu.au/~ssilcot/macperl-primer/home.html**, and the MacPerl FAQ at **ftp:// ftp.netcom.com/pub/ha/hal/MacPerl/faq.html**.

## Perl for Win32

A helpful site for information on the Perl for Win32 port is **http://www.perl.hip.com/ PerlFaq.htm**. The company that maintains this site also provides what is considered to be the most stable port for Windows NT and Windows 95.

In addition, a Dynamic Link Library (DLL) called PERLS.DLL is available at **http:// www.perl.hip.com/perlis.htm**, This library works with the Microsoft Internet Information Server to improve the efficiency of CGI access with Perl. Notice that the release of this DLL might still be a beta release.

## An Instantaneous Introduction to CGI Scripts and HTML Forms

This site, which contains a nice little introduction to CGI and forms, can be reached at **http:// kufacts.cc.ukans.edu/info/forms/forms-intro.html**. The site not only describes the process, but also provides graphics that demonstrate how HTML forms and CGI interact.

## CGI Documentation by NCSA

If you want to learn something, sometimes you have to go back to the source. This site, at **http://hoohoo.ncsa.uiuc.edu/docs/cgi/**, provides a CGI overview. The site also includes tips on writing secure CGI scripts—an activity that must always concern CGI programmers.

# Server-Side Includes

Yahoo maintains a site that covers server-side includes (SSI). You can reach the site at **http:// www.yahoo.com/Computers_and_Internet/Internet/World_Wide_Web/HTTP/Serv- ers/Server_Side_Scripting/Server_Side_Includes_SSI_/**. (Access probably will be faster if you access Yahoo at **www.yahoo.com** and then follow the links until you access this site, rather than try to type the entire URL.)

From this site, you can access a helpful tutorial on SSI, located at **http://www.carleton.ca/ ~dmcfet/html/ssi1.html**. Additionally, although SSI works with a Web server such as NCSA

HTTPd (**http://hoohoo.ncsa.uiuc.edu/docs/tutorials/includes.html**), it does not work with the CERN server. You can, however, access a Perl module, `fakessi.pl`, at **http://sw.cse.bris.ac.uk/WebTools/fakessi.html**. This module provides SSI-like functionality.

# Sites Containing General Perl Information

This section lists sites that contain references to standard Perl material that may not be Web- or CGI-related but that can be used regardless of application type.

## Basic Perl Documentation

When you are working with Perl, you will want to review some of the basic Perl documentation. Check out the following sites:

- The basic Perl manual, provided by Larry Wall (**http://www.atmos.washington.edu/perl/perl.html**)
- The Perl Language Home Page, maintained by Tom Christiansen (**http://www.perl.com/perl/**)
- A brief overview of the Perl 5.0 extensions (**http://www.perl.com/perl/info/perl5-brief.html**)
- The Perl FAQ (**http://www.perl.com/perl/faq/index.html**)
- General Perl information (**http://www.perl.com/perl/everything_to_know/index.html**)
- The University Perl Archive (**http://www0.cise.ufl.edu/perl/**)
- The Perl Data Structures Cookbook, provided by Tom Christiansen (**http://www.perl.com/perl/pdsc/**)

## CPAN Sites

*CPAN* stands for *Comprehensive Perl Archive Network*. Table B.4 lists the CPAN sites.

**Table B.4 CPAN Mirror Sites**

| Site | URL |
| --- | --- |
| North America: Canada | **ftp://enterprise.ic.gc.ca/pub/perl/CPAN/** |
| North America: California | **ftp://ftp.digital.com/pub/plan/perl/CPAN/** |
| North America: California | **ftp://ftp.cdrom.com/pub/perl/CPAN/** |
| North America: Colorado | **ftp://ftp.cs.colorado.edu/pub/perl/CPAN/** |
| North America: Florida | **ftp://ftp.cis.ufl.edu/pub/perl/CPAN/** |
| North America: Illinois | **ftp://uiarchive.cso.uiuc.edu/pub/lang/perl/CPAN/** |
| North America: New York | **ftp://ftp.rge.com/pub/languages/perl/CPAN/** |

| Site | URL |
|------|-----|
| North America: Oklahoma | **ftp://ftp.uoknor.edu/mirrors/CPAN/** |
| North America: Texas | **ftp://ftp.sterling.com/programming/languages/perl/** |
| North America: Texas | **ftp://ftp.sedl.org/pub/mirrors/CPAN/** |
| North America: Texas | **ftp://ftp.metronet.com/pub/perl/** |
| Africa | **ftp://ftp.is.co.za/programming/perl/CPAN/** |
| Australia | **ftp://coombs.anu.edu.au/pub/perl/** |
| Australia | **ftp://ftp.mame.mu.oz.au/pub/perl/CPAN/** |
| New Zealand | **ftp://ftp.tekotago.ac.nz/pub/perl/CPAN/** |
| Europe: Austria | **ftp://ftp.tuwien.ac.at/pub/languages/perl/CPAN/** |
| Europe: Belgium | **ftp://ftp.kulnet.kuleuven.ac.be/pub/mirror/CPAN/** |
| Europe: Czech Republic | **ftp://sunsite.mff.cuni.cz/Languages/Perl/CPAN/** |
| Europe: Denmark | **ftp://sunsite.auc.dk/pub/languages/perl/CPAN/** |
| Europe: Finland | **ftp://ftp.funet.fi/pub/languages/perl/CPAN/** |
| Europe: France | **ftp://ftp.ibp.fr/pub/perl/CPAN/** |
| Europe: France | **ftp://ftp.pasteur.fr/pub/computing/unix/perl/CPAN/** |
| Europe: Germany | **ftp://ftp.leo.org/pub/comp/ programming/languages/perl/CPAN/** |
| Europe: Germany | **ftp://ftp.rz.ruhr-uni-bochum.de/pub/CPAN/** |
| Europe: Greece | **ftp://ftp.ntua.gr/pub/lang/perl/** |
| Europe: Hungary | **ftp://ftp.kfki.hu/pub/packages/perl/CPAN/** |
| Europe: Italy | **ftp://cis.utovrm.it/CPAN/** |
| Europe: The Netherlands | **ftp://ftp.cs.ruu.nl/pub/PERL/CPAN/** |
| Europe: Poland | **ftp://ftp.pk.edu.pl/pub/lang/perl/CPAN/** |
| Europe: Poland | **ftp://sunsite.icm.edu.pl/pub/CPAN/** |
| Europe: Portugal | **ftp://ftp.ci.uminho.pt/pub/lang/perl/** |
| Europe: Spain | **ftp://ftp.etse.urv.es/pub/mirror/perl/** |
| Europe: Spain | **ftp://ftp.rediris.es/mirror/CPAN/** |
| Europe: Sweden | **ftp://ftp.sunet.se/pub/lang/perl/CPAN/** |
| Europe: Switzerland | **ftp://ftp.switch.ch/mirror/CPAN/** |
| Europe: United Kingdom | **ftp://ftp.demon.co.uk/pub/mirrors/perl/CPAN/** |

App

B

*continues*

**Table B.4   Continued**

| Site | URL |
| --- | --- |
| Europe: United Kingdom | **ftp://sunsite.doc.ic.ac.uk/packages/CPAN/** |
| Europe: United Kingdom | **ftp://unix.hensa.ac.uk/mirrors/perl-CPAN/** |
| Japan | **ftp://ftp.lab.kdd.co.jp/lang/perl/CPAN/** |
| Taiwan | **ftp://dongpo.math.ncu.edu.tw/perl/CPAN/** |
| South America: Chile | **ftp://sunsite.dcc.uchile.cl/pub/Lang/perl/CPAN/** |

The CPAN sites have a subdirectory labeled /MODULES, which contains references to various Perl modules that are stored at each of the CPAN sites. To access a list of the modules, access the subdirectory at **/modules/01modules.index.html**. You can find a description of a standard for development for the modules at **/modules/00modlist.long.html**. The modules are listed by author, category, and by module.

An additional subdirectory to check out is the /SCRIPTS subdirectory at each CPAN site. This subdirectory is itself divided into subdirectories, each of which represents a different category. Each category can have one to many Perl scripts that you can examine, use, and reuse.

# DBI

DBI, which is the Perl Database Interface, is a database API for Perl. The best place to access information about this interface is **http://www.hermetica.com/technologia/DBI/index.html**. You can download the most recent copy at **http://www.hermetica.com/technologia/DBI/DBI/index.html**. In addition, you can access any of the existing drivers from this site. Some of the available drivers are for the Oracle, Sybase, mSQL, Informix, and Quickbase databases. Plans are currently under way to implement an interface for ODBC.

An additional site for information on DBI is located at **http://www.fugue.com/dbi/**. You can also subscribe to three DBI mailing lists at this location.

# The *gd.pm* Graphics Library

gd is a graphics library that was originally written (and still is written) in C, but a version of gd has been ported to Perl. You can access this library at **http://www-genome.wi.mit.edu/ftp/pub/software/WWW/GD.html**. This library allows you to create three classes: Image, Font, and Polygon.

# *sgmls.pm*

This Perl library parses the output of the sgmls and nsgmls parsers, which you can find at **http://www.jclark.com/sp/index.htm**. The Perl library is located at **http://www.uottawa.ca/~dmeggins/SGMLSpm/definition.html**. A sample application, sgmlspl, is documented; you can reference it at **http://www.uottawa.ca/~dmeggins/sgmlspl/definition.html**. ●

# What's On the CD?

**T**he CD-ROM included with this book contains the source code and reference materials that have been developed throughout the book. The goal of this approach is to allow you to cut and paste any applicable code examples so that you can reuse them quickly, as well as provide the scripts, applications, and sample Web pages in complete form.

Another (and perhaps more exciting) goal of the CD-ROM is to provide new, unique, and helpful software, shareware, and evaluation software for you to use. To that end, you'll find an array of software, including the add-ins, utilities, and other software packages that we've been able to arrange for you.

Following is an overview of what you can expect:

- All the sample code and applications from the book
- A collection of demonstration applications, scaled-down software, and shareware
- An electronic version of this book in HTML format, which you can read in any World Wide Web browser on any platform
- An electronic version of this book in Windows Help File format, which allows you to quickly search for and annotate any topic covered in the book

The CD contains several subdirectories located off the root directory. Table C.1 lists the directories that you'll find on the CD, along with application, code, or chapter-specific subdirectories. ■

**Table C.1  Directory Structure on the CD**

| Subdirectory | Description |
| --- | --- |
| \EBOOKS | HTML and Windows Help File versions of the electronic books included on the CD. |
| \CODE | The source code from the book. Each chapter that contains sample files, source code, and so on is contained in a subdirectory named for the chapter that it references. |
| \SOFTWARE | The software provided for your use and evaluation. |

**NOTE**  The products on the CD are demos and shareware. You might have some difficulty running these programs on your machine; if you do, feel free to contact the vendor. (Vendors would rather have you evaluate their products than ignore them.) ■

# Using the Electronic Book

*Special Edition Using Perl for Web Programming* is available as an HTML document that you can read in any World Wide Web browser installed on your machine (such as Internet Explorer or Netscape Navigator). If you don't have a Web browser, you'll find Microsoft Internet Explorer on the CD-ROM. You also can read the book on-screen as a Windows Help File.

## Reading the Electronic Book as an HTML Document

To read the electronic book, start your Web browser and open the document file TOC.HTML, located in the \HTMLVER subdirectory of the CD. Alternatively, you can browse the CD directory by using File Manager and double-clicking TOC.HTML.

After you open the TOC.HTML page, you can access the book's contents by clicking a highlighted chapter number or topic name. The electronic book works like any other Web page; when you click a hot link, a new page opens or the browser takes you to the new location in the document.

As you read the electronic book, you will notice other highlighted words or phrases. Clicking one of these cross-references also takes you to a new location in the electronic book. You can always use your browser's forward or backward button to return to your original location.

## Installing the Internet Explorer

If you don't have a Web browser installed on your machine, you can use Microsoft Internet Explorer 2.0, which is included on the CD-ROM.

The Microsoft Internet Explorer can be installed from the self-extracting file in the \EXPLORER directory. Double-click MSIE20.EXE, or use the Control Panel's Add/Remove Programs option and follow the instructions in the installation routine.

> **N O T E** You must have Windows 95 or Windows NT installed on your machine to use this version of Internet Explorer. You can download other versions of this software from Microsoft's Web site at **http://www.microsoft.com/ie**. ■

## Reading the Electronic Book as a Windows Help File Document

To read the electronic book as a Windows Help File document, open the file named PERLWP.HLP in the \EBOOKS subdirectory of the CD-ROM. Clicking the forward or backward arrow moves you forward or backward through the text of the book, chapter by chapter. To view the book's table of contents, select the Contents tab; then click the number of the chapter that you want to view.

App
C

# Finding Sample Code

As you read this book, you will notice sample applications and program segments set apart from the main text by a *code listing header*, like this one:

```
Listing 10.1  (10_01.HTM) Creating the new snarfle page...
```

This listing indicates that this particular code snippet (or example) is included on the CD. To find the code, browse to the \CODE subdirectory on the CD, and select the file name that matches the one referenced in the listing header from the chapter indicated. For this example, you would look in the Chapter 10 subdirectory and open the 10_01.HTM file. ●

# Index

## Symbols

# Check out Que® Books on the World Wide Web
## http://www.mcp.com/que

As the biggest software release in computer history, Windows 95 continues to redefine the computer industry. Click here for the latest info on our Windows 95 books

Make computing quick and easy with these products designed exclusively for new and casual users

Examine the latest releases in word processing, spreadsheets, operating systems, and suites

The Internet, The World Wide Web, CompuServe®, America Online®, Prodigy® —it's a world of ever-changing information. Don't get left behind!

Find out about new additions to our site, new bestsellers and hot topics

In-depth information on high-end topics: find the best reference books for databases, programming, networking, and client/server technologies

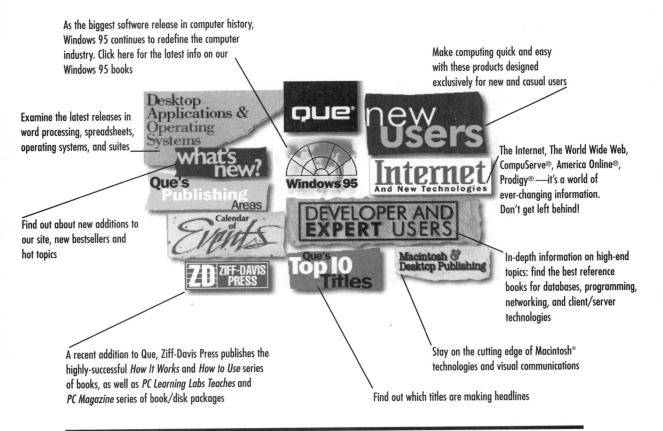

A recent addition to Que, Ziff-Davis Press publishes the highly-successful *How It Works* and *How to Use* series of books, as well as *PC Learning Labs Teaches* and *PC Magazine* series of book/disk packages

Stay on the cutting edge of Macintosh® technologies and visual communications

Find out which titles are making headlines

---

With 6 separate publishing groups, Que develops products for many specific market segments and areas of computer technology. Explore our Web Site and you'll find information on best-selling titles, newly published titles, upcoming products, authors, and much more.

- Stay informed on the latest industry trends and products available
- Visit our online bookstore for the latest information and editions
- Download software from Que's library of the best shareware and freeware

# Complete and Return this Card
# for a *FREE* Computer Book Catalog

Thank you for purchasing this book! You have purchased a superior computer book written expressly for your needs. To continue to provide the kind of up-to-date, pertinent coverage you've come to expect from us, we need to hear from you. Please take a minute to complete and return this self-addressed, postage-paid form. In return, we'll send you a free catalog of all our computer books on topics ranging from word processing to programming and the internet.

Mr. ☐     Mrs. ☐     Ms. ☐     Dr. ☐

Name (first) ☐☐☐☐☐☐☐☐☐☐☐☐  (M.I.) ☐  (last) ☐☐☐☐☐☐☐☐☐☐☐☐☐☐

Address ☐☐☐☐☐☐☐☐☐☐☐☐☐☐☐☐☐☐☐☐☐☐☐☐☐☐☐☐

☐☐☐☐☐☐☐☐☐☐☐☐☐☐☐☐☐☐☐☐☐☐☐☐☐☐☐☐

City ☐☐☐☐☐☐☐☐☐☐☐☐☐☐☐☐☐☐  State ☐☐  Zip ☐☐☐☐☐  ☐☐☐☐

Phone ☐☐☐  ☐☐☐  ☐☐☐☐    Fax ☐☐☐  ☐☐☐  ☐☐☐☐

Company Name ☐☐☐☐☐☐☐☐☐☐☐☐☐☐☐☐☐☐☐☐☐☐☐☐☐☐☐

E-mail address ☐☐☐☐☐☐☐☐☐☐☐☐☐☐☐☐☐☐☐☐☐☐☐☐☐☐☐

## 1. Please check at least (3) influencing factors for purchasing this book.

Front or back cover information on book ....................... ☐
Special approach to the content ................................... ☐
Completeness of content............................................. ☐
Author's reputation ................................................... ☐
Publisher's reputation ............................................... ☐
Book cover design or layout ....................................... ☐
Index or table of contents of book ............................. ☐
Price of book............................................................. ☐
Special effects, graphics, illustrations ......................... ☐
Other (Please specify): _____ ☐

## 2. How did you first learn about this book?

Saw in Macmillan Computer Publishing catalog ........... ☐
Recommended by store personnel ................................... ☐
Saw the book on bookshelf at store ............................... ☐
Recommended by a friend .............................................. ☐
Received advertisement in the mail ............................... ☐
Saw an advertisement in: _____. ☐
Read book review in: _____ ☐
Other (Please specify): _____ ☐

## 3. How many computer books have you purchased in the last six months?

This book only ....... ☐     3 to 5 books...................... ☐
2 books .................. ☐     More than 5 ...................... ☐

## 4. Where did you purchase this book?

Bookstore ................................................................. ☐
Computer Store ......................................................... ☐
Consumer Electronics Store ....................................... ☐
Department Store ...................................................... ☐
Office Club .............................................................. ☐
Warehouse Club ....................................................... ☐
Mail Order ............................................................... ☐
Direct from Publisher ................................................ ☐
Internet site ............................................................. ☐
Other (Please specify): _____ ☐

## 5. How long have you been using a computer?

☐ Less than 6 months          ☐ 6 months to a year
☐ 1 to 3 years                     ☐ More than 3 years

## 6. What is your level of experience with personal computers and with the subject of this book?

|  | With PCs | With subject of book |
| --- | --- | --- |
| New | ☐ | ☐ |
| Casual | ☐ | ☐ |
| Accomplished | ☐ | ☐ |
| Expert | ☐ | ☐ |

Source Code ISBN: 0-7897-0659-8

## 7. Which of the following best describes your job title?

Administrative Assistant ....................................... ☐
Coordinator ....................................................... ☐
Manager/Supervisor ........................................... ☐
Director ........................................................... ☐
Vice President ................................................... ☐
President/CEO/COO ........................................... ☐
Lawyer/Doctor/Medical Professional ..................... ☐
Teacher/Educator/Trainer .................................... ☐
Engineer/Technician ........................................... ☐
Consultant ........................................................ ☐
Not employed/Student/Retired .............................. ☐
Other (Please specify): _____ ☐

## 8. Which of the following best describes the area of the company your job title falls under?

Accounting ....................................................... ☐
Engineering ...................................................... ☐
Manufacturing .................................................. ☐
Operations ....................................................... ☐
Marketing ........................................................ ☐
Sales .............................................................. ☐
Other (Please specify): _____ ☐

## 9. What is your age?

Under 20 ......................................................... ☐
21-29 .............................................................. ☐
30-39 .............................................................. ☐
40-49 .............................................................. ☐
50-59 .............................................................. ☐
60-over ........................................................... ☐

## 10. Are you:

Male ............................................................... ☐
Female ............................................................ ☐

## 11. Which computer publications do you read regularly? (Please list)

_____
_____
_____
_____
_____
_____
_____
_____
_____

*Comments*: _____

Fold here and scotch-tape to mail.

# QUE® has the right choice for every computer user

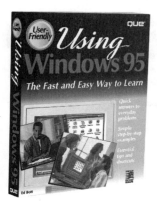

From the new computer user to the advanced programmer, we've got the right computer book for you. Our user-friendly *Using* series offers just the information you need to perform specific tasks quickly and move onto other things. And, for computer users ready to advance to new levels, QUE *Special Edition Using* books, the perfect all-in-one resource—and recognized authority on detailed reference information.

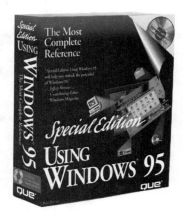

## The *Using* series for casual users

### Who should use this book?

Everyday users who:

- Work with computers in the office or at home
- Are familiar with computers but not in love with technology
- Just want to "get the job done"
- Don't want to read a lot of material

### The user-friendly reference

- The fastest access to the one best way to get things done
- Bite-sized information for quick and easy reference
- Nontechnical approach in plain English
- Real-world analogies to explain new concepts
- Troubleshooting tips to help solve problems
- Visual elements and screen pictures that reinforce topics
- Expert authors who are experienced in training and instruction

## *Special Edition Using* for accomplished users

### Who should use this book?

Proficient computer users who:

- Have a more technical understanding of computers
- Are interested in technological trends
- Want in-depth reference information
- Prefer more detailed explanations and examples

### The most complete reference

- Thorough explanations of various ways to perform tasks
- In-depth coverage of all topics
- Technical information cross-referenced for easy access
- Professional tips, tricks, and shortcuts for experienced users
- Advanced troubleshooting information with alternative approaches
- Visual elements and screen pictures that reinforce topics
- Technically qualified authors who are experts in their fields
- "Techniques from the Pros" sections with advice from well-known computer professionals

# Licensing Agreement

By opening this package, you are agreeing to be bound by the following:

This software product is copyrighted, and all rights are reserved by the publisher and author. You are licensed to use this software on a single computer. You may copy and/or modify the software as needed to facilitate your use of it on a single computer. Making copies of the software for any other purpose is a violation of the United States copyright laws.

This software is sold *as is* without warranty of any kind, either expressed or implied, including but not limited to the implied warranties of merchantability and fitness for a particular purpose. Neither the publisher nor its dealers or distributors assumes any liability for any alleged or actual damages arising from the use of this program. (Some states do not allow for the exclusion of implied warranties, so the exclusion may not apply to you.)